AF560221

PUNJAB POLITICS, 1936-1939: THE START OF PROVINCIAL AUTONOMY

Governors' Fortnightly Reports and other Key Documents

Punjab Politics, 1936-1939: The Start of Provincial Autonomy

Governors' Fortnightly Reports and other Key Documents

compiled and edited by
LIONEL CARTER
Former Librarian, Centre of South Asian Studies, University of Cambridge

MANOHAR
2004

First published 2004

ISBN 81-7304-568-2

Published by
Ajay Kumar Jain for
Manohar Publishers & Distributors
4753/23 Ansari Road, Daryaganj
New Delhi 110 002

Printed at
Lordson Publishers Pvt Ltd
Delhi 110 007

Contents

Editor's Introduction

The object of this volume is to reproduce in full the Fortnightly Reports of the Governor of the Punjab to the Viceroy (with copies to the Secretary of State for India) from their start until the end of 1939. Considerations of space do not allow the inclusion of the Viceroy's replies. Enclosures to the Governors' Reports are only reproduced when they are of significance. In addition to the Reports, other key documents sent by the Governor or his Secretary to the Viceroy have been included. These additional documents (which were not necessarily sent on to London) are normally letters but other documentary forms are not excluded.

For many years prior to the introduction of Provincial autonomy in 1937 there had been systematic and regular reporting of developments in the Punjab. For example, throughout the first world war there had been Fortnightly Provincial Reports which are now in the Deposit Home Political Proceedings in the National Archives of India. By 1936 there had grown up a procedure whereby the Government of the Punjab sent the Government of India twice monthly a printed report of four pages or more. These reports were known by various names such as the 'Chief Secretary's Report', or the 'Provincial Report'. They give much valuable and detailed information but are rather dry and sometimes a little unfocussed. Although they are not printed in this volume, they are often referred to and copies of them were filed in London with the Governors' Fortnightly Reports once that series had begun.

With the beginning of Provincial autonomy it became obvious in both New Delhi and London that the Chief Secretary's Reports would not meet all the requirements of policy-making and that further regular reports of a shorter and more political nature were going to be needed from the Provinces. The Viceroy was the first to act and on 11 October 1936 his Private Secretary wrote[1] asking the Governors to supply a confidential appreciation of local developments of a more personal character at possibly monthly intervals. This request resulted in Sir Herbert Emerson's lengthy and most valuable survey of the Punjab political scene, dated 19 October 1936, which is the first document printed in this volume.

By the spring of 1937, the Secretary of State for India and his officials were also feeling the need for increased information, a problem which was accentuated by the ending of the annual published series of developments in India entitled *Moral and Material Progress*. In Despatch No. 3 of 25 March 1937, Lord Zetland asked Governors to send him at short intervals, reports 'of the more important events and tendencies, political, administrative and economic, in the Province . . . with an expression of the Governor's personal views upon them'.[2] In response to this request, Emerson had his Report of 24 April 1937 (No. **8**) copied to London. This thus technically forms the first Fortnightly Report printed in this volume.

The Governors' Fortnightly Reports were, therefore, an innovation of the last decade of the Raj and we are fortunate that the information needs of the Viceroy and the Secretary of State allow us to see in detail the working of the late colonial mind and to be privy to some of its most secret thoughts. We are also able to witness at close hand how Governors, Ministers and officials came to cope with a more representative constitution. In the present volume, the calibre of the two Governors who held office, Emerson and Craik, will inevitably be compared.[3] Emerson strikes one as the deeper and more reflective thinker. Craik, on the other hand, is noteworthy for his businesslike approach and his vast knowledge of, and personal contacts with, the more important officials, politicians and families in the Punjab.

If the documents printed here are mainly the work of the British Governors, there can be no doubt that the single person who dominates the volume is the Muslim leader of the Unionist Party, Sir Sikander Hyat Khan, first Premier of the Punjab under the 1937 constitutional arrangements. Indeed in his last report to the Viceroy as Governor in April 1938, Emerson confided that one of his anxieties for the future concerned this very dominance: 'success has depended very largely on the personality and popularity of the Premier. It would be very difficult to replace him, if for any reason he were not able to carry on.' (No. **42**.) The documentation printed here throws considerable light on Sikander's activities during these years. His negotiation of the Sikander-Jinnah Pact at Lucknow in October 1937 was to prove of major importance for the future of the Punjab and, indeed, for the Muslim cause as a whole in the run-up to independence.[4] There has been considerable debate over the years as to just what the Pact amounted to. The accounts given here by Emerson of the Lucknow negotiations will, therefore, be studied with interest. (See particularly Nos. **22-4**.) One consequence of the Pact was that Sikander was admitted to the inner councils of the Muslim League and was able to report to the Governor what had taken place at meetings. One suspects however that Sikander's reports were tinged with more than a hint of wishful thinking (see particularly No. **97** and its note 55). Sikander, too, was sometimes asked by the British to mediate with the League on some aspect of its activities (see, for example, No. **118**.) The complaint has been made that because Sikander was so much involved in bringing together different individuals and groups, there is no clear statement of what his Unionist Government stood for in these pre-war years. I have, therefore, included as Enclosure to No. **10** the text of an important speech which Sikander delivered in May 1937. This provides the nearest thing we have to a manifesto outlining the political programme of the Unionist Ministry.

For Sikander the year 1939 was to prove of great importance in his political career. At the end of May he was approached by an emissary of the new right-wing Congress leadership with an offer for a Congress-League political arrangement (see No. **92** and its note 43). Unfortunately we do not have the full details of this negotiation and regrettably nothing was to come of it despite two long meetings between Sikander and Gandhi (see No. **97**). Then in August, Sikander put his and the Punjab's full weight behind the British Government in the coming war with Germany (see No. **103** and its note 70). But perhaps the most interesting development was the publication during the summer of 1939 of Sikander's 'Outlines' of an alternative scheme of Federation. In order to make some of the documents in this volume intelligible, a key extract from these 'Outlines' is reproduced as the Attachment to Appendix III.

Reading the documents in this volume one has a strong sense that one is witnessing the last self-confident years of the Raj. The impression is strengthened by the fact that under the Unionist Ministry the Punjab was insulated from developments which were occurring in Provinces with Congress governments. Craik on returning to the Punjab after four years was able to report in April 1938 that 'I see singularly little change in the general tone of the administration' (No. **43**). The Governor continued until the close of 1939 to express his view that Congress was not a major force in the Punjab. Yet Congress was making subtle advances by winning the odd by-election and through activity by individual members in the adjacent Princely States. At the start of hostilities, Sikander was even thinking (on the assumption Congress would support the war) of including two Congress leaders in his Ministry (see No. **104**) – an idea which did not commend itself to Craik and Linlithgow.

Sikh politics, as usual, were a matter of considerable complexity with the Akalis (and particularly their main leader Master Tara Singh) being the cause of great concern to both the Governors and the Ministry. The issue which agitated the Sikhs throughout the period of the volume was the dispute with the Muslims over the Shahidganj Mosque (see No. **1** and its note 2). In its way the dispute had remarkable similarities to the Ayodhya dispute of the 1990s except that the parties involved here were Muslims and Sikhs rather than Muslims and Hindus. By the close of the volume we find Craik relieved that the war would probably prevent an immediate hearing of the appeal on the matter by the Privy Council (No. **112**).

I have included, as Appendix II, the text of a note which was put away on one of the 1939 India Office files of Punjab Governor's Reports. The note records a visit to the province by Sir John Ewart, the Director of the Intelligence Bureau. This document is in any event of great interest as giving an assessment by an outside observer of the working of the Punjab administration under the new Constitution. However one cannot help wondering whether the visit in March 1939 was made with a particular purpose in view. Craik had shortly before taken a very strong stand with Lord Zetland over the Unionist's Ministry's land legislation (see No. **76**, and its note 12) and one harbours the suspicion that the D.I.B. was sent to check up on the Governor.

The documents in this volume (with the exception of Appendix I) are British Crown Copyright. Most are reproduced from a series of prints made in the Viceroy's Secretariat in New Delhi.[5] In the India Office Records these prints are given the following references:

R/3/1/1	October 1936-March 1937
R/3/1/2	April-December 1937
R/3/1/59	January-9 August 1938
R/3/1/60	24 August-December 1938
R/3/1/61	January-December 1939

If no reference is given to a document in the present volume, it may be assumed that the document is taken from the above prints. When a document is printed from a different source, that source is indicated in a footnote. All references in this volume (with the exception of Appendix I) are to items in the India Office Records.

In conclusion, I would like once again to express my thanks for help and advice received from Anthony Farrington, formerly head of the India Office Records at the British Library. I would also like to thank Graham Shaw, Director of the Asia, Pacific and Africa Collections at the British

Library, for his interest. I owe a special debt to Ramesh Dogra, M.B.E. and to Urmila Dogra for advice on a wide range of issues. My publisher, Ramesh Jain, has, as ever, extended many kindnesses to me. None of the foregoing bears any responsibility for errors and omissions in the book. The responsibility for these rests solely with me.

Harrow, July 2003 LIONEL CARTER

NOTES

1. Laithwaite's circular letter is on R/3/1/1.
2. Lord Zetland's Despatch is on L/P&J/9/287. This file is on the subject of the 'Supply of Information to the Secretary of State'. Similar papers are on L/P&J/7/989.
3. Sir Herbert Emerson had served as Secretary to the Punjab Finance Department between 1926 and 1930. From 1930 to 1933, he was Secretary of the Home Department of the Government of India. Emerson served as Governor of the Punjab between 1933 and 1938.

   Sir Henry Craik had been Chief Secretary, Punjab between 1927 and 1930. From 1930 to 1934 he was a Member of the Punjab Executive Council. Between 1934 and 1938, Craik served as Home Member of the Governor-General's Executive Council. Craik was Governor of the Punjab between 1938 and 1941.
4. For convenience of reference, the text of the Sikander-Jinnah Pact, as preserved in the Quaid-e-Azam Papers, is reproduced as Appendix I.
5. Identical copies of these prints are held in the Linlithgow papers under the references MSS.EUR.F 125/86-8 and 112-13.

Abbreviations

A. & S.	Argyll and Sutherland.
A.C.	Assistant Commissioner.
A.P.I.	Associated Press of India.
C.-in-C.	Commander-in-Chief.
C.I.D.	Criminal Investigation Department.
C.I.O.	Central Intelligence Officer.
C.O.	Commanding Officer.
C.P.	Central Provinces.
D.C.	Deputy Commissioner.
D.I.B.	Director of the Intelligence Bureau.
D.I.G.	Deputy Inspector General
D.M.	District Magistrate.
D.-O.	Demi-Official.
E.A.C.	Extra Assistant Commissioner.
F.L.	Fortnightly Letter.
G. of I.	Government of India.
G.S.	Governor's Secretary.
H.D.C.	(Sir) Henry Duffield Craik.
H.E.	His Excellency.
H.Q.	Headquarters.
I.A.	Indian Army.
I.C.S.	Indian Civil Service.
I.P.	Indian Police.
I.P.S.	Indian Political Service.
K.L.M.	Koninklijke Luchtvaartmaatschappij NV (Royal Dutch Airlines).
M.L.A.	Member of the Legislative Assembly.
M.L.C.	Member of the Legislative Council.
N.-W.	North-West.
N.-W.F.P.	North-West Frontier Province.
P.C.S.	Punjab Civil Service.
P.S.V.	Private Secretary to the Viceroy.

Rs.	Rupees.
S.G.P.C.	Shiromani Gurdwara Parbandhak Committee.
S. of S.	Secretary of State.
U.P.	United Provinces.
Y.E.	Your Excellency.

Glossary

Akali	Particularly strict devotee of the Sikh faith; in modern usage a member of the extreme Sikh nationalist party.
Anna	One-sixteenth of a rupee.
Ashram	Hermitage; retreat for research and study; home for community living.
Chaudhuri	Headman of village or caste.
Chaukidar	Watchman in town or village.
Crore	One hundred lakhs or ten million.
Dal	Organisation, association.
Durbar	Royal court or levee.
Ghee	Clarified butter.
Giani	One who possesses knowledge; among Sikhs, a person well-versed in the scriptures.
Gurdwara	A Sikh temple, generally also the centre of Sikh social activity.
Hartal	Shopkeepers' strike; strike.
Id	A Muslim holy festival. Bakr-Id commemorates Abraham's sacrifice; Id-ul-fitr the feast on breaking the Ramzan fast.
Jamadar	(1) A native officer in a sepoy regiment holding ranking next below a Subahdar; (2) a junior officer of police, customs and other civil departments.
Jatha	An armed band or procession; a procession of religious or political protest.
Khaksars	*Lit.*: like the earth, humble; semi-military organisation of Muslims armed with spades, under the leadership of Inayatullah Khan.
Khalsa	The Sikh brotherhood instituted by Guru Gobind Singh; used for an individual as well as for the collective body.

Khan	A title borne by Muslim nobles especially when of Persian or Pathan descent.
Kharif	Grain crops sown in summer and reaped by early winter.
Kisan	Peasant, cultivator, tenant.
Lakh	One hundred thousand.
Lathi	Thick stick, usually bamboo, sometimes bound with iron rings.
Madrassa	Islamic education institution, generally of high learning.
Maharaja	A sovereign prince.
Malik	A Muslim title inferior to Khan and Amir.
Mandi	Market (grain-market).
Masjid	Muslim place of worship, Mosque.
Maulana	The title of a person of learning or respectability; teacher, doctor.
Maulvi	Muslim religious teacher.
Maund	A measure of weight. The standard maund is 37.32 kilograms.
Mian	A term of respectful address to an old or respectable person; sir; master.
Morcha	Procession, protest march, generally for political or industrial purposes.
Nawab	Originally a Governor under the Moghul Empire; thence a title or rank conferred on Muslim nobles.
Nawabzada	Son of a Nawab.
Paisa	One-fourth of an anna.
Pir	A Sufi saint or master.
Rabi	Principal grain harvest sown after the rains and reaped in the spring season.
Raja	Chief, king.
Ramzan	The ninth Muslim lunar month observed as a 30 days' fast during daylight hours by all Muslims.
Red shirts	Congress volunteer movement of the North-West Frontier Province started by Khan Abdul Ghaffar Khan.
Sardar	*Lit.*: a chief, leader. Title borne by all Sikhs and also by some Hindus and Muslims.

Sarkar (Sirkar)	District, Government.
Shia	One of the two main branches of Islam (cf. Sunni); followers of Ali, the son-in-law of Muhammad.
Sri	Sanskrit title used by Hindus.
Subahdar	The chief native officer of a company of sepoys.
Sunni	The majority in Indian Islam, who regard Caliphs Abu Bakr, Omar and Osman as spiritual descendants of Muhammad.
Taccavi	Loans given to agriculturists for seed, bullocks or agricultural improvements.
Tahsil	Revenue sub-division of a district.
Ulama	The learned in Muslim law and religion.
Zamindar	Landed proprietor paying land revenue to Government, revenue farmer.

Principal Holders of Office, October 1936-December 1939

UNITED KINGDOM

Secretary of State for India	The Marquess of Zetland

INDIA

Viceroy, Governor-General and Crown Representative	The Marquess of Linlithgow (Lord Brabourne acted 25 June-24 October 1938)
Private Secretary to the Viceroy	Mr Gilbert Laithwaite
Commander-in-Chief, India	General Sir Robert Cassels

THE PUNJAB

Governor	Sir Herbert Emerson Sir Henry Craik (from 8 April 1938)
Secretary to Governor	Lt.-Col. R.T. Lawrence Mr E.P. Moon (from 3 June 1938)
Chief Secretary to Government	Mr F.H. Puckle Mr James Penny (from 4 May 1937) (Mr. F.C. Bourne acted 11 April-30 September 1939)

Appointments under the 1919 Constitution operative until 1 April 1937

MEMBERS OF THE EXECUTIVE COUNCIL OF THE GOVERNOR OF THE PUNJAB

Finance Member	Sir Donald Boyd
Revenue Member	Sir Sikander Hyat Khan (from 20 October 1936)

MINISTERS TO THE GOVERNOR OF THE PUNJAB

Agriculture	Sir Jogendra Singh
Local Self-Government	Sir Gokul Chand Narang
Education	Sir Shahab-ud-Din

Appointments under the 1935 Constitution operative from 1 April 1937

MEMBERS OF THE COUNCIL OF MINISTERS

Premier	Sir Sikander Hyat Khan
Minister of Revenue	Sir Sunder Singh Majithia
Minister of Development	Sir Chhotu Ram
Finance Minister	Mr Manohar Lal
Minister of Public Works	Nawabzada Khizar Hyat Khan
Minister of Education and Medical Relief and Public Health	Mian Abdul Haye

PUNJAB LEGISLATIVE ASSEMBLY

Speaker	Sir Shahab-ud-Din
Deputy Speaker	Sardar Daswandha Singh

Summaries of Documents

CHAPTER 1 – DOCUMENTS FOR 1936

	Name and Number	*Date*	*Main subject or subjects*
		Oct.	
1	Emerson to Linlithgow Letter	19	Account of existing parties in Punjab Legislative Council
		Nov.	
2	Emerson to Linlithgow Letter	16	Legislative Council session; Lahore Municipal Committee superseded; Itihad-i-Millat; Aitchison College
		Dec.	
3	Emerson to Linlithgow Letter	19	Abdication of King Edward VIII; electioneering for new Punjab Assembly; risk of communal incidents in Rawalpindi; re-assessment of Lyallpur District

CHAPTER 2 – DOCUMENTS FOR 1937

	Name and Number	*Date*	*Main subject or subjects*
		Jan.	
4	Emerson to Linlithgow Letter	21	Muslim and Sikh agreement in Rawalpindi; electioneering for new Punjab Assembly; Nehru's visit; Ahmadis – talk with Mirza Bashir Ahmad; difficulties arising from Indianisation of Services
		Feb.	
5	Emerson to Linlithgow Letter	19	Probable trend of events following elections, in particular likely attitude of Congress to Ministries

6	Emerson to Linlithgow Letter	22	Analysis of results of elections to new Punjab Assembly
		Mar.	
7	Emerson to Linlithgow Letter	26	New Ministry; assessment of some of the new MLAs; Congress' attitude to office
		April	
8	Emerson to Linlithgow Report	24	Assembly session; assessment of new Ministry; communal troubles in Panipat and Kot Fateh Khan; reports received that Congress will focus attention on working of new constitution in Punjab
		May	
9	Emerson to Linlithgow Report	8	Coronation celebrations; serious damage from hailstorms and failure of gram crop in places; Akalis losing ground; Congress attempts to capture Muslims
10	Emerson to Linlithgow Report	22	Coronation celebrations; Muslim feeling hardening against Congress; rural reconstruction; committee to examine land revenue system; labour trouble in Lahore; incident at Khalsa College; Enclosure: Sikander's speech to All-India Kshatri Conference
		June	
11	Emerson to Linlithgow Report	1	Incident at Khalsa College and communal trouble in Govt. Engineering School, Rasul; Muslims nationally would prefer Ministerial deadlocks with Congress to continue; irrigation schemes
12	Emerson to Linlithgow Report	19	Communal situation between Sikhs and Muslims has deteriorated particularly in Gujrat district; Assembly session; Conciliation Boards in connection

			with relief for indebtedness; Enclosure (extract) – Note by Chhotu Ram dated 6 June 1937 of tour he made of certain districts in April and May 1937
		July	
13	Emerson to Linlithgow Report	3	Communal rioting in Gujrat; Sikander's attitude to law and order and communal questions; Assembly session; Speaker's actions; question whether Governor should always preside at meetings of Council of Ministers
14	Emerson to Linlithgow Report	18	Sikander's attitude to political offences; Innes' report on Gujrat riots; Assembly session has consolidated Govt.'s position; possible reactions on Punjab of Congress' acceptance of office elsewhere
15	Emerson to Linlithgow Report	31	Govt. obtains sizeable majority in Assembly for its law and order and communal policies; scholarships for boys wishing to train for Army commissions; appointment of junior Ministers; separate regular memoranda to be prepared on Congress activities in Punjab; these memoranda will have only restricted circulation
		Aug.	
16	Emerson to Linlithgow Report	14	Troubles among Ahmadis at Qadian; Sikh civil disobedience in Kot Fateh Khan; hunger strikes in Andamans and elsewhere
17	Emerson to Linlithgow Report	28	Situation in Qadian has little changed; Sikhs abandon civil disobedience in Kot Fateh Khan;

No.	Document	Date	Subject
			agitation against military abattoir at Lahore; six staff dismissed at Khalsa College
		Sept.	
18	Emerson to Linlithgow Report	14	Communal troubles in Sheikhupura, Gujrat and near Panipat; student strike likely at Khalsa College; about ten prisoners to be repatriated from Andamans and Madras; Sikander finding workload heavy; insect damage to cotton crop
19	Emerson to Linlithgow Letter	22	Views on idea of a visit to India by the King and the holding of a royal durbar
20	Emerson to Linlithgow Report F.L.5	28	Attitudes of Services under Sikander Ministry; abandonment of Lahore abattoir project; agitation likely over staff dismissals at Khalsa College; supply of power from Mandi Hydro-Electric Scheme
		Oct.	
21	Emerson to Linlithgow Report F.L.9	8	Strikes at Khalsa College and related fracas at Jallianwala Bagh; action taken against communists and communal mischief-makers; Congress activities in Punjab; hostile attitude of Punjab press
22	Emerson to Linlithgow Report F.L.12	21	Nehru's visit and Congress policy; All-India Muslim League meeting at Lucknow; Sikander's account of meeting and of the negotiation of the so-called Sikander-Jinnah Pact
		Nov.	
23	Emerson to Linlithgow Report F.L.16	12	Viceroy's visit; Shahidganj agitation continues; effects in Punjab of Sikander-Jinnah Pact; Congress demonstrations during tour by Chhotu Ram; campaign against

			Chief Justice; anxiety over low cotton price
		Dec.	
24	Emerson to Linlithgow Report 22-F.L.	3	Shahidganj agitation; Sikander's assertion that Pact with Jinnah does not affect position or policy of Unionist Party; Ministerial tours; effects of U.P. situation on law and order
25	Emerson to Linlithgow Report 28-F.L.	18	Govt. activity and propaganda has fallen off in counrtyside; Govt. not examining legislative proposals sufficiently nor consulting adequately on them; Shahidganj agitation; U.P. situation
26	Emerson to Linlithgow Report 30-F.L.	27	Settlement of U.P. crisis; Governor urges Sikander to improve his party organisation; bold Ministerial programme for next financial year; financial prospects; rural development programme

CHAPTER 3 – DOCUMENTS FOR 1938

		Jan.	
27	Emerson to Linlithgow Report 31(a)-F.L.	11	Ahrar civil disobedience over Shahidganj; Assembly session; conference on rural reconstruction; prospects for spring harvest
28	Emerson to Linlithgow Report 37-F.L.	27	Ahrar civil disobedience continues; Shahidganj judgment; violent protests over 'political' prisoners; Nehru's visit to Lahore and talk with Sikander
29	Emerson to Linlithgow Letter 39-F.L.	30	Explains that no 'State' prisoners are on hunger strike; Shahidganj situation is as favourable as could be expected

No.	Document	Date	Subject
		Feb.	
30	Emerson to Linlithgow Report 41-F.L.	12	Twenty 'political' prisoners are on hunger strike; Shahidganj situation unchanged; Muslim League Council meeting in Delhi; tour by Sikander and Chhotu Ram
31	Emerson to Linlithgow Letter 43	24	Gives information on behaviour of 'political' prisoners released in the Punjab
32	Emerson to Linlithgow Letter 44	24	Appreciation of the situation in the Punjab following the constitutional crisis with Congress in U.P. and Bihar over the release of political prisoners
33	Emerson to Linlithgow Letter 45	24	Views on the release of the prisoner Yashpal
34	Emerson to Linlithgow Letter 46	27	Sends text of two proposed private Bills on Shahidganj; reports discussion of the matter in Council of Ministers; indicates action he is thinking of taking
35	Emerson to Linlithgow Report 47- F.L.	28	U.P. and Bihar crises; Shahidganj; 'political' prisoners abandon hunger strikes; Kiroo alleged torture case; bumper spring harvest expected
		Mar.	
36	Emerson to Linlithgow Letter 48	4	Reports further discussion in Council of Ministers that morning on Shahidganj question; Sikander had said he felt ultimately Ministry would have to resign; Emerson considers ways in which the situation might be handled
37	Emerson to Linlithgow Letter 49	7	Encloses letter from Eustace (D.C., Attock) dated 1 February 1938 asking for guidance as to action he should take with regard to anti-government propaganda
38	Emerson to Linlithgow Letter 50	7	Sends account of conversation with Sikander on 6 March;

			Premier is taking resolute line on Shahidganj Bills
39	Emerson to Linlithgow Letter 51	9	Reports meeting which Sikander had had with Muslim supporters; Ministers will advise Emerson to withhold consent to introduction of Shahidganj Bills; this action will be delayed until after Muharram holidays
40	Emerson to Linlithgow Report 52-F.L.	17	Emerson withholds consent assent to introduction of Shahidganj Bill; Kiroo case; Congress followers run amok after meeting in Fatehwal; budget received favourably; idea of Bill to stop places of worship being converted for other uses; Muharram passes off peacefully
41	Emerson to Linlithgow Letter 54	31	Press reactions to Sikander's statement on Shahidganj; Sikhs show little sign of making conciliatory gesture; Sikander's meeting with Jinnah in Delhi
		April	
42	Emerson to Linlithgow Report 60-F.L.	5	Sikander's talk with Tara Singh on Shahidganj; criminal case started against police involved in Kiroo case; Fatehwal case has gone to court; Emerson's valedictory review of first year of provincial autonomy
43	Craik to Linlithgow Report 62-F.L.	18	Craik takes over as Governor; he finds little change in tone of administration under new Constitution; Services happy working with Ministry; need to check speeches discouraging recruitment to Army; communal tension still acute; concern over situation at Hissar; no further developments relating to Shahidganj

44	Craik to Linlithgow Letter 65	25	Reports talk with Sikander that morning on League meeting at Calcutta; Sikh attitudes to Shahidganj
		May	
45	Craik to Linlithgow Letter 66	3	Gives background to letter which Home Secretary had sent recommending commutation of death sentences on four prisoners
46	Craik to Linlithgow Report 67-F.L.	10	Shahidganj developments; Congress win by-election near Amritsar; Fatehwal and Kiroo cases continue; loss of efficiency in disticts greater than at first supposed; Craik's meetings with landholders and members of Services
47	Craik to Linlithgow Letter 71	20	Reports talk with Sikander that day on matters relating to Jinnah
48	Craik to Linlithgow Report 72-F.L.	26	Unionist Party wins by-election in Amritsar; labour troubles in Amritsar; improvement in communal situation; Shahidganj developments; visit of V.D. Savarkar to Punjab; Kiroo case proceeds
		June	
49	Craik to Linlithgow Letter 74	5	Attitudes in the Punjab towards Federation; elaborates Sikander's views on the subject
50	Craik to Linlithgow Report 75-F.L.	7	Legislative measures for benefit of cultivator; working of Provincial autonomy in Punjab; accused in Kiroo case likely to be discharged; Sikander reluctant to agree to Prithvi Singh's release
51	Craik to Linlithgow Letter 76	10	Reports talk that day with Sikander on League Council meeting in Bombay
52	Craik to Brabourne Report 80-F.L.	24	Agitation at Lyallpur on remodelling of certain canal outlets; Craik's speech at opening of

			Assembly session; new group of disgruntled members formed within Unionist Party; settlement of differences between Congress members in Punjab is unlikely to be permanent
		July	
53	Moon to Puckle Letter G.S.-257	2	Sends note by Craik appraising various Punjab ministers
54	Craik to Brabourne Report 83-F.-L.	8	Agitation about the remodelling of canal outlets; lack of reaction to Kiroo judgment; Assembly session; Sikander shelves Defamatory Statements Bill; agrarian legislation arouses keen controversy; dissenting members return to Unionist Party; Craik feels Assembly has deteriorated compared with previous Council
55	Craik to Brabourne Report 84-F.L.	22	Almost all agrarian legislation passed although mortgage Bill was amended; Narendra Nath asks Craik in last eventuality to withhold consent from mortgage Bill; opposition of many Hindus to Bills; 14 Congress Assembly members reported to be resigning their seats; released Madras prisoners removed from Punjab; canal water agitiation; disturbances at Amritsar
		Aug.	
56	Craik to Brabourne Report 86-F.L.	9	Feels he may have to 'reserve' agricultural Bills for the Governor-General; opposition to Bills from non-agriculturist classes; feeling by its key Punjab supporters that Congress has betrayed them; canal water agitation has ended; Amritsar disturbances continue; conference

			on methods of preventing corruption in public services
57	Craik to Brabourne Report 87-F.L.	24	Kisan demonstrations at Amritsar end abruptly; tours by Sikander and Chhotu Ram; prestige of ministry enhanced by passing of agrarian legislation; Craik's further views as to whether he will have to 'reserve' the Bills for the Governor-General; Craik receives cordial reception in districts; Sikander's considerable part in shaping positive League attitude to Central Legislature's Dissuasion from Enlistment Bill
		Sept.	
58	Craik to Brabourne Letter 89	2	Explains why he has reserved Punjab Alienation of Land (Second Amendment) Bill for Governor-General's consideration
59	Craik to Brabourne Report 90-F.L.	6	Provincial reactions to agrarian legislation; Non-Agriculturists' Association understood to be preparing for civil disobedience; increased agitation on Palestine
60	Craik to Brabourne Report 93-F.L.	23	European affairs occupying everyone's thoughts; is confident Punjab would respond loyally in event of war; Pir of Makhad convicted of conspiring to murder Nawab of Kalabagh
		Oct.	
61	Craik to Brabourne Report 95-F.L.	11	Munich crisis – Punjab will stand by Empire; agitation against agrarian legislation is steadily losing force; rumoured defections from Unionist Party; Palestine; agitation against Kalsia State; On visit to Ludhiana, Craik warned against communistic ideas;

			anxiety on food situation in S.E. Punjab
62	Craik to Brabourne Letter 98	17	Raja of Sangli's note on activities of Congress in States; general questions on the relationship between the Punjab and the Punjab States
63	Craik to Linlithgow Report 100-F.L.	26	Sikander's tour in S.E. Punjab; prestige of Ministry is high; European crisis has widened breach between Punjab Ministry and Congress Ministries elsewhere; Indian States (Protection) Act put into force in certain districts; famine situation in S.E. Punjab; communal riot in Multan and visit there by two Ministers; arrangements for opening of new Assembly Chamber
		Nov.	
64	Craik to Linlithgow Report 101-F.L.	10	Success of League-Unionist candidate in Multan by-election; Jug Lal's tour of Punjab; ceremonial opening of new Assembly Chamber
65	Craik to Linlithgow Report 102-F.L.	22	Disorderly scenes in Assembly; Armistice Day service; difficulties in securing recruits for Irrigation Branch; famine situation in S.E. Punjab; cattle situation in Hissar and nearby districts; Ministry's attitude to implementing Criminal Law Amendment Act; Palestine; agrarian unrest in parts of Sutlej Valley
66	Craik to Linlithgow Letter 103	25	Explains why he would not favour Zafrullah Khan as a successor to Young as Punjab Chief Justice
67	Craik to Linlithgow Letter 104	25	Explains why he is recommending the conferment of title of 'Nawab' on Qizilbash family

		Dec.	
68	Craik to Linlithgow Report 106-F.L.	8	Marketing Bill not yet passed as Assembly session was adjourned; difficulties within Unionist Party – four Scheduled Castes' MLAs announce they are leaving; famine situation in S.E. Punjab is worsening; Craik feels they will hear little more of Non-Agriculturists' Association; Jullundur zamindars boycott anti-recruitment meetings; Subhas Chandra Bose's visit to Punjab; League meeting in Delhi – Sikander's report of its attitude on his stance supporting Empire in event of war
69	Craik to Linlithgow Report 109-F.L.	23/24	Negotiations between three Scheduled Castes' MLAs and Congress; Bose's visit; improvement in Kisan situation in Sutlej Valley; famine measures in S.E. Punjab; little overt activity at present by Congress in Punjab States; Palestine; 1939-40 Budget; retrenchment measures to pay for famine relief; Nowshera tragedy

CHAPTER 4 – DOCUMENTS FOR 1939

		Jan.	
70	Craik to Linlithgow Letter 110	3	Sends note by Ahmed (C.I.D.) on Congress activities within Punjab States
71	Moon to Laithwaite Letter G.S.-677	5	Encloses note by Craik giving further appraisals of Punjab ministers
72	Craik to Hallett Letter	12	Following talk with Sikander, gives Sikander's account of his actions at League's Patna meeting; encloses note of talk on Patna

			meeting with Khurshid Ali Khan
73	Craik to Linlithgow Letter	12	Lack of comment on Nowshera tragedy; Sikander's attitude at League's Patna meeting
74	Craik to Linlithgow Report 113-F.L.	15	Drought and famine situation; Kapurthala's anxiety on Congress agitation against States; disorder during Assembly session; injuries to prisoners in Multan New Central Jail; Nowshera tragedy; Firoz Khan Noon's arrival
75	Craik to Linlithgow Letter	20	Encloses letter from Hallett thanking Craik for No. 72; Hallett accepts that Sikander acted as a moderating influence; Bihar Govt's. treatment of Muslims
76	Craik to Linlithgow Letter	26	Reports attitude Sikander would adopt if Zetland does not assent to Punjab Alienation of Land (Second Amendment) Bill; Craik considers failure to give assent would have most unfortunate consequences
77	Craik to Linlithgow Letter 114	26/27	Sends his impressions of the famine areas he had just visited in Hissar and Gurgaon
78	Craik to Linlithgow Report 116-F.L.	27	Assembly passes Marketing Bill after prolonged and bitter debates; secessions from Unionist Party; strains on Sikander – his request for a British I.C.S. Officer as his private secretary; Sikander complains permanent officials are not respecting Ministry; deaths in Multan New Central Jail; release of eight 'political' prisoners; deterioration in communal feeling; plan for corps of social service volunteers

		Feb.	
79	Craik to Linlithgow Report 123-F.L.	9	Craik's visit to Montgomery and Lyllapur; communal riot in a famine relief works at Hissar; Congress agitation in Hissar; Craik unwilling to proscribe forthcoming States Peoples' Conference meeting at Ludhiana; Patiala's visit and donation to Sikh National College; Patalia's visit to Ludhiana; Sikander's distress at Jinnah's present position; Sikander intends to appoint Police officer as his private secretary; proposed corps of social service volunteers; attempt to wreck train on N.-W. Railway
80	Craik to Linlithgow Report 124-F.L.	26	Coming of rains will help famine situation; acreage of wheat crop down on previous years; Budget session of Assembly about to open; assent for Marketing Bill to be delayed; meeting of States Peoples' Conference at Ludhiana seems to have fallen flat; detonators found on railway bridge over the Attock; entrepreneurs attracted to Punjab; Sikander's talks with Jinnah; he impresses on League Central Assembly Members desirability of supporting Indo-British Trade Agreement
		Mar.	
81	Craik to Linlithgow Letter 127	7	Reactions in Punjab to Gandhi's fast over Rajkot; suggests a possible settlement which could be put to Gandhi
82	Craik to Linlithgow Letter 128	9	Reactions in Punjab to Linlithgow's settlement with Gandhi

83	Craik to Linlithgow Report 129-F.L.	14	Assembly session is adjourned; Muharram disturbances in Amritsar and Kasur; rains last well into March but attendance at relief works has not declined; sabotage and another incident on railway lines; law and order problems in Hoshiarpur; position of Congress in Punjab
84	Craik to Linlithgow Letter 130	20	Sikander's scheme for Federation not yet reduced to black and white; Sikander hopes to persuade League at Meerut not to adopt Haroon's scheme
		April	
85	Craik to Linlithgow Report 133-F.L.	2	Craik's tour of Jhelum and Rawalpindi; he opens Haveli Project and presents new Colours to a Punjab regiment; communal unrest at Rawalpindi; Craik visits Attock Oil Co.; Budget session still in progress; poor showing by Congress in Hoshiarpur elections; many Provincial meetings on Hyderabad; return of Maulvi Obaidullah; acquittal of Pir of Makhad and three others; rains bring little relief to famine areas; Kapurthala's anxieties over agitators; peasant demonstration in Lahore; Sikander furious with Jinnah over latter's attitude to Indo-British Trade Agreement
86	Craik to Linlithgow Letter 138	17	Explains why Sikander and he do not favour agreeing to Gandhi's request for the release of Prithvi Singh
87	Craik to Linlithgow Letter 140	17	Has told Sikander that Linlithgow and Zetland view his scheme for volunteer corps with misgivings;

			encloses note by Robinson on establishment of Akali and Congress Socialist volunteer organisations
88	Craik to Linlithgow Report 141-F.L.	18	Bill for Sergeant-at-Arms passes third reading; three further secessions from Unionist Party; another 17 Unionists reported to have promised Congress they would secede in a vote of no-confidence; Congress reported to be considering moving no-confidence motion; Kisan demonstrations; Muslim opinion stirred by Albanian situation
		May	
89	Craik to Linlithgow Report 146-F.L.	1	Assembly session concludes with motions of confidence in Ministry and of no-confidence in Haye and Chhotu Ram; Govt. secures substantial majorities; Craik's interview with Pir of Makhad; Mushtaq Ahmed Gurmani's criticisms of Unionist Party; Kisan demonstrations; curtailment of service leave; Enclosure: Note by Moon of talk with Mushtaq Ahmed Gurmani on failings of Sikander and Unionist Party
90	Craik to Linlithgow Report 147-F.L.	17	Viceroy's anxiety over Sikander (with an official Punjab team) presiding at League's Sholapur meeting; Sikander insisting that central Muslim League does not interfere in Punjab local matters; Hyderabad agitation – communal incident at Rohtak; Craik assents to Marketing Bill but reserves Sergeant-at-Arms Bill for Viceroy's assent; Kisan demons-

			trations; lower attendances at famine relief works; Press reactions to Subhas Chandra Bose's resignation as Congress President – right-wing control Punjab Congress; League tour of Punjab likely to increase communal tension
		June	
91	Craik to Linlithgow Report 151-F.L.	5	Economies agreed for relief works; Hissar relief attendances down; Sikander warns Press about the agitation against Hyderabad; deaths of two women and a baby arrested during Kisan disturbances; election of a Unionist M.L.A. disallowed; sweepers strike in Lahore; criticisms of Lahore's Administrator
92	Craik to Linlithgow Letter 153	8	Sikander explains the background to Rajendra Prasad's approach for an arrangement between Congress and League; Sikander not prepared to withdraw his opposition to Federation
93	Craik to Linlithgow Letter 153 [?154]	12	Sends him copy (not traced) of a letter which Sikander had sent Rajendra Prasad's intermediary at the end of May 1939; Craik feels Congress will have difficulty over proposed composition of Indian Army; the intermediary feels negotiations should now be put on more formal basis
94	Craik to Linlithgow Letter 156	19	Attitudes of Muslims in the Punjab towards Federation
95	Craik to Linlithgow Report 157-F.L.	21	Early arrival of monsoon allows relief works to be shut down; strike by Amritsar sweepers; Lahore Kisan demonstration

			continues – N.G. Ranga and Swami Sahajanand decide not to join it; visit of Subhas Chandra Bose to Lahore; explosives train overheats twice near Ferozepore; Ahrar Conference in Gurdaspur is banned; serious riot in Attock; Sikander's appeal for moderation in connection with Hyderabad has little effect; parts of Indian States (Protection) Act brought into force throughout Punjab
		July	
96	Craik to Linlithgow Report 161-F.L.	7	Press reactions to enforcement of Indian States (Protection) Act; Craik hopes Kisan *morcha* at Lahore will collapse; another *morcha* at Ferozepore does not last long; participation by Punjabis in Lucknow Sunni-Shia troubles; Subhas Chandra Bose's visit; commemoration of 100th anniversary of Ranjit Singh's death; Gokal Chand Narang resigns as President of Non-Agriculturists' Association; explosives train from Ferozepore was not sabotaged
97	Craik to Linlithgow Letter 162	10	Sikander's account of League Working Committee meeting at Bombay; meeting considered Prasad-Sikander negotiations and attitude League should take in event of a war
98	Craik to Linlithgow Letter	13	Encloses copy of letter he has sent Haig giving account of talk with Sikander on Sunni-Shia situation in Lucknow
99	Craik to Linlithgow Report 163-F.L.	23	Increase in anti-recruitment speeches; Lahore Kisan *morcha* practically at standstill; Sunni-

			Shia agitation at Lucknow; good rainfall over most of famine areas; two further defections from Unionist Party; Ordinance drafted to deal with any sweepers' strikes
		Aug.	
100	Craik to Linlithgow Report 165-F.L.	11	Sikander's visit to Bombay in connection with Punjab loan; Bill to limit working hours of shop assistants and commercial employees; growth of volunteer organisations in larger towns; agitation against Hyderabad is subsiding as is interest in Lucknow Sunni-Shia situation; sweepers' strike in Multan city collapses; unfavourable reactions to Sikander's Federation scheme
101	Craik to Linlithgow Letter 166	25	After talk with Mahdev Desai, Sikander recommends release of Prithvi Singh (subject to conditions); Craik proposes to accept recommendation
102	Craik to Linlithgow Report 167-F.L.	25	Imminence of European war overshadows everything; talks with Sikander and Chhotu Ram on Punjab's position in a war; special war measures; Sikander to warn organisers of volunteer organisations; Provincial loan oversubscribed; grave situation in famine districts following failure of monsoon; conference of Ministers and officials agrees on scaling-down of relief measures; riot in Lahore; Congress decides to stand in Amritsar by-election
103	Craik to Linlithgow Letter 171	28	Sikander feels his statement on the war will have been very unpalatable to Jinnah and League

			executive; he fears Jinnah may manipulate Punjab Muslim Press; Craik asks for subvention
		Sept.	
104	Craik to Linlithgow Report 174-F.L.	13	Wave of loyalty on outbreak of war; Press appreciates Britain's reasons for war; reactions to statements by Gandhi and Jinnah; Craik considering broadcast to thank those who had made loyal offers; he regrets they cannot take immediate advantage of the enthusiasm; Sikander's talks with journalists and others; Sikander proposing to take two Congress members into Ministry if Congress unconditionally supports war; Kisan leaders call off agitation; famine situation not much improved; Thal irrigation project
105	Craik to Linlithgow Letter 178	25	With reference to Viceroy's forthcoming meeting with Jinnah, sends message from Sikander relating to Federation and League's attitude to the war
106	Craik to Linlithgow Report 179-F.L.	26	Reiterates need to take up loyal offers; Congress and League statements on war appear not to have had any marked effect in Punjab; opposition to recruitment by Forward Bloc and Ahrars intensifies; Amritsar by-election; assumes Sikander has abandoned idea of Congress participation in Ministry; Thal irrigation project
		Oct.	
107	Craik to Linlithgow Letter 183	7	Explains why he doubts authenticity of intelligence report that Sikander had placed in Jinnah's hands his signed resignation as Premier of Punjab

No.	From/To	Date	Summary
108	Craik to Linlithgow Letter 185	10	Supplies resumé of Shahidganj dispute; little prospect of parties concerned sinking their differences; wonders whether Privy Council's hearing might be postponed
109	Craik to Linlithgow Letter 186	11	Corrects an inaccuracy in No.108; suggests way hearing might be postponed; will consult Sikander
110	Craik to Linlithgow Letter 187	12	Is pleased with announcement of measures that will allow people of the Punjab to contribute to war effort; attitude of Akali Sikhs to recruitment; Viceroy's forthcoming interview with Tara Singh
111	Craik to Linlithgow Report 188-F.L.	13	Press comments on Viceroy's talks with Indian leaders; war profiteering stopped; League/ Unionist candidates win Amritsar and Multan by-elections; fears of attack by Russia on India; Ministers on tour find wide enthusiasm for war service but district officers report disappointment at delay in starting recruitment; Punjab Muslims indignant at killing of five Khaksars by police in U.P.; Sikh attitudes to the war; Cabinet agrees to retrenchment of expenditure; despite rainfall, outlook for some famine areas is melancholy
112	Craik to Linlithgow Letter 190	24	Sikander reports that solicitors for the Muslim appellants are applying to Privy Council for postponement of hearing of Shahidganj appeal
113	Moon to Laithwaite Letter G.S.-920	26	Sends (1) Note by Bennett (C.I.D.) of reactions in Punjab to political situation; (2) Text of war

			resolution to be moved in Punjab Legislative Assembly
114	Craik to Linlithgow Report 191-F.L.	29	Reactions in the Punjab to Congress resignations; Sikh recruitment to Army; reactions to Commons' debate on India; Muslim views on political situation; feels Congress spokesmen are slaves of rhetorical expressions; Ahrar campaign against Army recruitment; treatment of Khaksars by U.P. authorities; Turkish Pact welcomed by Muslims; Legislative Assembly session; Enclosure: cutting from *Civil and Military Gazette* on sweeper's war contribution
115	Craik to Linlithgow Letter 192	29	Refers to a letter from Woodhead (Bengal); says Punjab will carry on as hitherto should Section 93 situation occur in other Provinces
		Nov.	
116	Craik to Linlithgow Letter 193	15	Desertion of 35 Sikhs from Army does not mean Sikh community is infected with disloyalty; informs him of message received from Tara Singh; is willing to see Tara Singh
117	Craik to Linlithgow Report 195-F.L.	16	Party of Khaksars dissuaded from making 'loyal demonstration' before Governor; Craik's visits to Hissar and Ferozepore; Assembly debate on war resolution; further arrests of Ahrars; some District Congress Committees reported to be preparing for 'impending struggle'; believes Jinnah's stock has risen considerably; feeling of district officers that Govt. should give country a lead

No.	Document	Date	Summary
118	Craik to Linlithgow Letter 197	28	Reports talk between Sikander and Haroon; latter has agreed to consult Govt. of India, Home Dept. before finally selecting League's correspondents in Near East
		Dec.	
119	Craik to Linlithgow Report 198-F.L.	1	Hardly any anti-recruitment speeches now being made; Congress attitude to war has not commanded general approval; Ahrars now quiet and Khaksars trying to improve relations with Govt.; wheat and cotton prices rise sharply; hardening of Press opinion against Germany; Craik's tour of Hoshiarpur and Gurdaspur; Craik hopes Viceroy's appeal for War Purposes Fund will not be long delayed; Sikander opposes loan of Punjab armed police to Sind
120	Craik to Linlithgow Report 201-F.L.	15	Visit of Haroon and Rashdi to Lahore causes anxiety; Jinnah's 'Deliverance Day' message; Assembly session has so far gone well for Unionists; Cripps' visit and his talk with Sikander
121	Craik to Linlithgow Tel. 16-G.	21	Refers to Press statements that Sikander has gone on secret mission to Jinnah; believes this to be entirely imaginary
122	Craik to Linlithgow Letter 203	22	Sikander is interesting himself in the formation of an N.-W.F.P. Ministry but is not very hopeful of success
123	Craik to Linlithgow Report 204-F.L.	28	Ministers away on Christmas holidays; 'Deliverance Day' passes without any disturbance; unsuccessful attempt to induce

		Ahrars to become involved in Sind agitation; increasing unrest at price rises; endorses Gregory's suggestion of a conference of wheat-producing Provinces

APPENDICES

	1937 *Oct.*	
I Sikander-Jinnah Pact	15	Text of Pact as in Quaid-e-Azam Papers
	1939 *Mar.*	
II Note by Ewart	26	Working of the new Constitution in the Punjab; talk with Sikander on action Punjab would take in event of war
	June	
III Sikander Hyat Khan to Laithwaite Letter	29	Sends and comments on his proposals for an alternative Federal scheme; Attachment: Sikander's 'Outlines of a Scheme for Indian Federation' (as published) (extract)

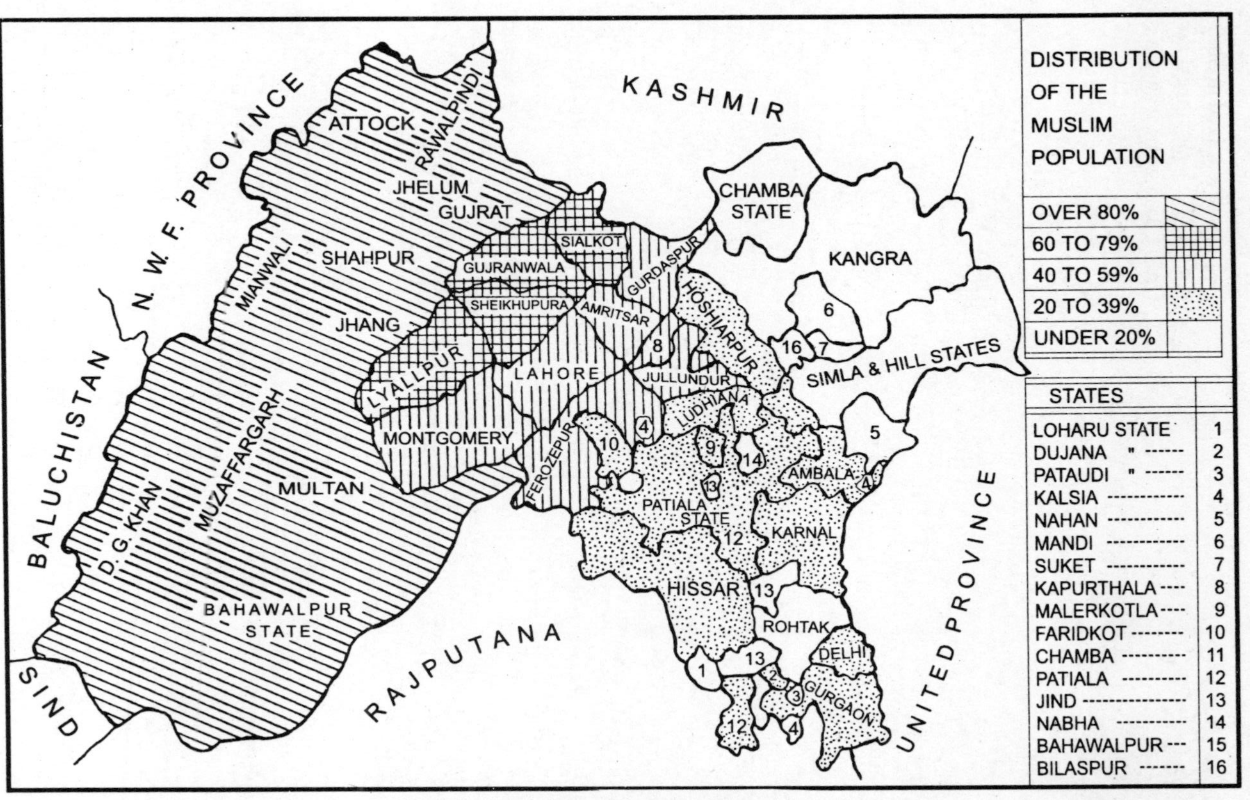

MAP OF PRE-PARTITION PUNJAB

CHAPTER 1

Documents for 1936

1

EMERSON TO LINLITHGOW

Private and Personal

Government House, Lahore,
October 19th, 1936

My dear Lord Linlithgow,

In reply to Your Excellency's private letter of the 11th of October,[1] I write to say that I will try to keep you regularly informed by private monthly letters regarding the evolution of political parties and kindred matters in the Punjab. In my present letter I will attempt to give an account of existing parties in the Legislative Council and incidentally of the formation of future parties as it has so far proceeded.

2. The parties in the present Legislative Council are the following:

(1) The National Unionist Party or the Zamindar Party.
(2) The National Reform Party representing the Party of urban Hindus.
(3) The Sikhs.
(4) The Ahrars.
(5) Oddments.

3. *The Unionist Party* is the largest single party in the present Legislative Council, but is not sufficiently strong to outvote all other non-officials if the latter combine. The party was primarily the creation of the late Sir Fazl-i-Husain. It was intended to be founded on an economic basis and to represent mainly rural interests. With one or two exceptions, however, it is entirely Muslim and, although its policy has been predominantly rural, it includes among its members a number of urban Muslims. It has a party organisation and, on the whole, has kept well together, although splits have been threatened from time to time and its equilibrium is often unstable.

There are two main causes of instability; first, the ambitions and jealousies of younger members regarding office; and second, personal animosities and partisan factions. As Your Excellency knows, a split in the Party was only avoided with difficulty when it became necessary to appoint a Minister on the death of Sir Fazl-i-Husain.

With regard to the second factor, I will deal with this when I come to discuss the position of Muslims.

During his life-time Sir Fazl-i-Husian exercised a very powerful influence over the Party and its organisation, even when he held office outside the Punjab. Had he lived, he would have been the leader of the Party under the New Constitution. His place as leader has been taken by Sir Sikander Hyat Khan, but, while the latter is officiating as a Member of the Executive Council, he cannot be the active leader of the party, although he will no doubt continue to direct its affairs.

For some years the leader of the Party in the Legislative Council has been Rao Bahadur Chaudhuri Chhotu Ram, who has often been the sole Hindu member of the Party, although on particular questions, in which rural interests were involved and communal questions were not outstanding, he has been able to obtain the votes of some rural Hindu members. Chaudhuri Chhotu Ram is a Jat pleader of the Rohtak district, and is accepted as the champion of Jat rights, and in the south-east as the leader of rural Hindus. He was Minister for Education from 22nd September 1924 to 3rd January 1927, and had it not been for strong communal feeling in the Punjab, he would have held office on subsequent occasions. It has, however, become a convention that there should be two Muslims among the four non-official members of the Punjab Government (one non-official Member and three Ministers), and since it has been necessary that urban Hindu interests should be represented, there has been no room for a rural Hindu. Chhotu Ram could thus be a Minister only in place of a Muslim with the consent of the Unionist Party which is practically a Muslim Party. The Muslims have not been able so far to put the interests of the Party above communal considerations, and, as a result, their leader has now for some years not been able to obtain office. Chhotu Ram has been extremely loyal to his Party so far as his personal interests are concerned, but the fact that he has been passed over on many occasions has given urban Hindus, by whom he is bitterly disliked, the opportunity of jeering at him. His position lately has become more difficult in this respect. His rural Hindu followers in the south-east have begun to urge that, if the Unionist Party is keen on their support, they should accommodate their leader. If they come to power under the New Constitution, they will no doubt do so, as Chhotu Ram is the outstanding rural Hindu candidate for a Ministership. In the meantime, however, Chhotu Ram feels that he has to clarify his position and he has, therefore, insisted on standing for the Presidentship of the Legislative Council, which is vacant owing to the appointment of Sir Shahab-ud-Din as Minister in place of Sir Fazl-i-Husain. The election takes place on Tuesday next. The indications are at present that the Unionist Party, with one or two exceptions only, will support Chhotu Ram, but it has required a good deal of manoeuvring by Sir Sikander Hyat Khan to prevent a Muslim revolt, and the situation is still not free from doubt. If by any mischance a considerable section of Unionist Muslims let Chhotu Ram down on this occasion, a great strain will be placed on his loyalty to the Party, and the urban Hindus and Sikhs would, of course, exploit any such event to the utmost. Chhotu Ram is an able and hardworking man, honest in his convictions and a serious politician. He is intensely rural in his views and bitterly opposed to the moneylender. He has always taken a very prominent part in the campaign against them and was responsible for the Debtors Protection Bill which became law a few months ago. He is inclined to be fanatical in this respect, although moderate and reasonable on other subjects. He hopes that in the new elections at least seven rural Hindu seats will be captured by his followers, who will join the Unionist Party. This is a small proportion of the total rural Hindu seats, but some of these seats are certain to he captured by urban Hindus of the Pleader class, while some successful candidates of the rural classes will follow communal lines rather than rural versus urban. The future strength of the Unionist Party depends on two main factors:

First, the ability of Muslims to avoid serious splits; and
Second, the number of rural Hindus willing to join the Party.

It seems unlikely at present that many Sikhs will formally join the Party although some may support a Coalition Ministry even if the Unionist Party is the predominant partner.

4. *The National Reform Party* This primarily consists of urban Hindus, and, whatever the theory of their political programme may be, its aim in practice is to protect Hindu interests, especially of the professional, business and moneyed classes. It is bitterly opposed to the Communal Award, the Alienation of Land Act, and the recent debt legislation. It is apprehensive regarding the future, but its fears regarding Muslim *raj* are less than what they were a few years ago. The more intelligent among them now recognise that even if Muslims succeed in sticking together, their majority will not be sufficient to secure stability, and they are fairly certain that personal

jealousies and intrigues among Muslims will often give them the opportunity to exert their influence and power. They were very afraid and suspicious of Sir Fazl-i-Husain, but are more favourably disposed towards Sir Sikander Hyat Khan, whom they rightly regard as less communal in his views and aims. Sir Gokul Chand Narang, the present Minister for Local Self-Government, is a member of the Party. The leader is Raja Narendra Nath, who before retirement was a statutory member of the Punjab Commission and attained the rank of Commissioner of a Division. He is a man of culture and scholarship, who is generally respected. He is now getting old and his health is indifferent, so it is unlikely that he will play a prominent part in the future. Another member of the Party is Mr. Manohar Lal, who was a Minister some years ago. He is an able and a good speaker, but is not trusted. The Party also contains several prominent members of the Lahore Bar and is strong in debating power. On communal questions it can usually depend on the help of rural Hindus (except Chhotu Ram) and also of most Sikhs. An alliance between Muslims and Sikhs is obviously opposed to its interests, and it is the general complaint of Muslims which has, I think, considerable foundation, that members of this Party and their supporters lose few opportunities of creating strife between the two communities. They certainly used their influence to prevent any reconciliation in the Shahidganj dispute.[2] During the civil disobedience movement many members of the Party, like most urban Hindus, were sympathetic towards Congress, and, if another civil disobedience movement occurred, it is doubtful whether there would be much change in their attitude. For the moment, however, they are actively opposed to Congress mainly because of the latter's attitude towards the Communal Award.

5. *The Sikhs*–There is no definite political party of Sikhs within the Legislative Council. The non-official members consist mostly of Akalis with a few moderate Sikhs of good family. On political issues the Akalis are generally opposed to Government; the moderates often support Government. On rural versus urban issues the Sikhs are divided; on communal issues they generally join hands as a body with Hindus. No Sikh M.L.C. is a member of the Unionist Party, and for the new elections this Party has so far no Sikh candidate. Sardar Sir Jogendra Singh is the Sikh Minister for Agriculture. He has no Party behind him in the Council, but can generally obtain some votes in favour of Government. He is much respected because of his personal qualities, but has no political strength and little influence with his community, when big issues are concerned. He has been quite ineffective in connection with the Shahidganj dispute.

6. *The Ahrars*–The Ahrars came into prominence about 1931 when they took the leading part in the Muslim agitation against the Maharaja of Kashmir. Their special appeal is to Muslims of the lower classes in the towns, and they have considerable following among the riff raff of Lahore, Amritsar, Ludhiana and Sialkot. During the Kashmir agitation they joined hands with the Ahmadis, but a split occurred and the two are now the most bitter enemies. For some years the Ahrars have been carrying on a most virulent campaign against the Ahmadis of Qadian, and especially against the present head of the community. In this campaign they had the sympathy of a large number of orthodox Muslims, and for some time the situation was one of grave potential danger. It looked as if there might be a very widespread Muslim movement against the Ahmadis, and that it would be difficult for Government to protect the latter. The Ahrars had found a popular platform; they were entirely unscrupulous in making the best use of it; and by raising the cry of 'Danger to Islam' they were fast increasing their strength. Then came the Shahidganj incident. The Ahrars, believing that the Ahmadis were at the back of it, refused at a critical time to take the popular Muslim side. They lost a great deal of their influence and have not yet fully recovered the ground that was lost. But they have recovered a great deal of it, and because of their antagonism to the Ahmadia community, they gain more sympathy and support on this account than their merits deserve. They are anti-Government and have flirted with Congress from time to time. They have no outstanding leaders of position, but have several good mob orators and their Party is fairly well organised. For some time they thought of joining Mr. Jinnah's Party, but ultimately refused to do so since they preferred to remain independent and Jinnah would not endorse their programme of opposition to the Ahmadis. The strength of the Party in the Council is only three or four, but they hope to secure more seats in the new Assembly.

7. *Oddments*–Congress is practically unrepresented in the present Council. There are two Ahmadis, one being the brother of Sir Muhammad Zafrullah Khan, and there are a few independent members.

8. For the new elections the main Parties are–

(1) The Unionist Party.

(2) Among Hindus–

(i) The Hindu Sabha Party corresponding to the National Reform Party; and

(ii) Congress party.

(3) Among Sikhs–

(i) The Khalsa Diwan Party; and

(ii) The Akali Party.

(4) Specific Muslim Parties–

(i) Mr. Jinnah's Party; and

(ii) The Ahrars.

(5) Oddments.

9. As already noted, the strength of the Unionist Party will depend primarily on the ability of Muslims to stick together. Some defections are certain to occur, e.g. a few urban members, who belong either to Jinnah's Party or to no party at all. At the moment it seems improbable that the Ahrars will join the Unionists. Apart from casual defections, however, the main question is whether other Muslims, and especially rural Muslim members, can work together. Personal rivalries will always be a danger, but, in addition to these, there is a potential line of cleavage between the Tiwanas and the Noons on the one side and the Wah Party on the other. The Tiwanas and the Noons belong mostly to the Shahpur district, the latter being cousins of the former. In that district they have for long held the position of feudal lords, but in recent years their position has been challenged even there. They are not a political party, but, owing to their family position, they have always been able to exert considerable influence on politics. The recognised head of the tribes is Sir Umar Hyat Khan, whom Your Excellency no doubt knows, and who has lately resigned his seat on the Secretary of State's Council. Sir Umar Hyat Khan himself is now too old to take a leading part in affairs, but his influence is still very great. The most prominent Noons are Nawab Sir Muhammad Hyat Khan, who was a Commissioner in the Punjab and is now a Member of the Council of State, and his son, Sir Firoz Khan Noon, who is now High Commissioner for India. Among prominent Tiwanas are Nawab Allah Bakhsh who was until this session a nominated Member of the Legislative Assembly, and Khizar Hyat Khan, son of Sir Umar Hyat Khan.

The leading members of the Wah family are Sir Sikander Hyat Khan, his brother Sir Liaqat Hyat Khan, Prime Minister, Patiala State, and his cousin Nawab Muzaffar Khan. Their home is at Wah in the Attock district and they belong to a very good family, but the Tiwanas and Noons are apt to look down on them. For some years there has been a division within the Unionist Party itself between these two groups, based on personal and tribal considerations and not on political grounds. It has not extended to the whole of the party. When Sir Sikander Hyat Khan and Sir Firoz Khan Noon, for instance, were in the Punjab Government together, the one as a Member and the other as a Minister, there was considerable rivalry between them. Each had his own group of personal friends and supporters. The ill-feeling between the two groups was increased a couple of years ago when the Wah Party helped a candidate in an Assembly election who had the temerity to stand from the Shahpur district against the Tiwanas. Greatly to the surprise of everybody, the Tiwanas were beaten, and the blow to tribal pride and influence inevitably accentuated feeling against the Wah Party whose assistance had contributed to the result. The Tiwana group were strongly opposed to the appointment of Nawab Muzaffar Khan as Revenue Member, and although the latter and Firoz did their best to work together while they were colleagues, there was no genuine reconciliation, and the situation was one of armed neutrality rather than of peace. The Noon influence was increased by the fact that one of Sir Fazl-i-Husain's daughters was married to one of Firoz's brothers. Sir Fazl-i-Husain found this relationship very embarrassing from the political point of view and greatly deplored the division in the Muslim ranks. Sir Fazli's death has weakened the Noon influence. Each of the two groups has its recognised supporters in certain districts, and sometimes these represent local factions. For instance, the Multan district has for generations been rent by a feud between the leading families of Gilanis and Qureshis. The former belong to the Noon group and the latter to the Wah group. An illustration may be given of the complications which arise from this Wah and Tiwana rivalry among Muslims. In the forthcoming elections the Unionist Party will often not be represented by a single candidate in a particular constituency. In fact the usual position will be two or more Muslim candidates fighting the same constituency, all of whom are prepared to support the Unionist Party if elected. The elections will be fought on personal and tribal lines, and the fact that the candidates subscribe to the same political creed will not mitigate local animosity which will long survive the results. In the Multan district, for example, there are six rural Muslim constituencies. The present position is that there will be a fight in every one between either a Qureshi or Gilani candidate or candidates who will have Gilani or Qureshi support respectively. One of the candidates is the Secretary of the Unionist Party, Khan Bahadur Ahmad Yar Khan Daultana, who is a close personal friend and the chief lieutenant of Sir Sikander Hyat Khan. The Gilanis are putting up a candidate to fight him. The same is happening in the Shahpur district. One of the best members of the present Council is Nawab Muhammad Hyat Qureshi, a big land-owner and a man of good family. He again is one of Sikander's staunchest supporters and a very close personal friend. The Tiwanas are putting up Nawab Allah Bakhsh to oppose him, and intend to use all their influence to defeat him. Situations of this kind obviously give plenty of scope for trouble later on. Whoever wins or loses, there is going to be strong resentment. If the Unionist Party comes actively into the field in support of one of two rival candidates, the fat is in the fire. Probably it will not do so. Or, if Sikander or his relatives use their personal influence in favour of one man against another, then he may have a serious split in his party later on. These matters are at the moment a real cause of anxiety to the Unionist Party and illustrate how unstable it is. I think, however, that Sikander will be wise enough to keep out of local factions, if he and others are not able to reconcile them before the elections take place.

Behind the efforts of the Tiwana group is the natural desire to have sufficient seats in the new Assembly to be able to press their claims for a Ministership. They are, of course, not alone in this desire. Several of the smaller parties know that their only hope of exercising any effective influence in the future is their power of bargaining after the elections are over. The more the votes they can command in the Assembly, the greater will be their bargaining power.

10. The above applies also to some of the larger parties. The Hindu Sabha Party, for instance, have some hope that a split among Muslims might put them with the Sikhs in a predominant position. But the hope is a faint one and they recognise that it is more probable that they will either have to go into opposition against the Unionist Party or bargain with them. They are not committing themselves at present, but there is undoubtedly a good deal of private talk going on between individual urban Hindus and members of the Unionist Party; and a coalition is by no means impossible in which urban Hindus would be given one Ministership. They would, of course, not subscribe to the Unionist Party creed, and, if the Unionists tried to insist on this, there could be no coalition, but there could be a working arrangement by which things would run smoothly unless and until the Ministry put forward measures which the Hindu Sabha Party could not accept. In the meantime the Hindu Sabha Party are trying to capture as many seats as possible. They will get practically all the Hindu urban seats and a considerable proportion of the rural ones, although in the latter the successful candidates may not be urban men.

11. The Hindu Sabha Party is at present strongly opposed to the Congress party especially on the Communal Award issue. Congress is badly organised in the Punjab and is rent by personal dissension. It is unlikely that it will capture more than two or three seats at the most unless Pandit Jawaharlal is called in at the last minute to reinforce local efforts by the personal appeal which he carries.

12. Sikh politics have for years been in a state of confusion, and permutations and combinations are so frequent that it is always difficult

to know what the exact position is at a particular time. The Akalis have exercised a dominating influence for some years largely because Sikhs of good family and moderate views have had neither the courage nor the energy to oppose them. The Akalis have also the great advantage of having control over Gurdwara funds. Akali politics have been controlled to a large extent by non-zamindar Sikhs, especially *Khatris* and *Aroras*, and this has given rise to considerable jealousy. There has also been a serious split among Akalis themselves, the two main parties being led by Master Tara Singh and Giani Sher Singh respectively. The former is a retired schoolmaster of considerable force of character, uncompromising in his views and generally anti-Government. He has obtained control over the various Gurdwara Committees, and Giani Sher Singh's party is now very weak. At the same time Tara Singh has recently been unable fully to control the communist and revolutionary elements among the Sikhs, and his position is to some extent threatened by them. Further, the misappropriation of Gurdwara funds and general mismanagement have lost them a good deal of their former influence. The Akalis are fighting most Sikh constituencies, and it will be surprising if they do not gain a fair number of the Sikh seats. They have not allied themselves with Congress because they are bitterly opposed to the Communal Award, but they profess to follow the Congress creed of non-co-operation and wrecking of the Constitution.

The Khalsa Diwan Party has been formed with the object of getting back the influence which Sikhs of the leading families in the Province have lost. Sir Sunder Singh Majithia is the leader of the party. He was the first Member for Revenue in the Punjab, and controls the Khalsa College, Amritsar. He is a man of strong character, very loyal and generally trusted. Of late years he has devoted most of his time to his private affairs, and he has the biggest sugar factory in India, situated in the United Provinces. He is a very keen and successful businessman. He is now getting old and is probably unable to devote sufficient time and energy to the affairs of the Khalsa Diwan Party. Sir Jogendra Singh is Sir Sundar Singh's chief lieutenant. They are optimistic regarding their chances in the elections, but I am doubtful whether their hopes will be fully realised. Neither of the Sikh parties has committed itself to any coalition with any other Party. Bargaining will take place after the elections. It is probable that the majority party in the Assembly will be able to obtain the support of one or other of the Sikh parties, or at any rate of individual Sikhs attracted by the hope of office.

13. Mr. Jinnah has so far had little success in the Punjab. His adherents are mainly urban Muslims of strong communal views, who think his name

and influence may help them to secure seats. He and Sir Fazli were on very bad terms, and, so far as the Punjab is concerned, one of Jinnah's objects was undoubtedly to make things more difficult for Sir Fazli. He is supposed to have approached Sir Sikander, but the latter has turned him down, and Jinnah in his recent speeches has shown considerable resentment. The only rural Muslim of any importance, who is openly committed to Jinnah, is Khan Bahadur Zaman Mehdi Khan, who formerly belonged to the Noon group. He was a member of the Provincial Civil Service, obtained a 'listed' post and retired about two years ago as a Deputy Commissioner. His reputation was not good. He was a candidate for the Ministership in succession to Sir Fazli, and, when he did not get it, joined Jinnah's Party in a fit of pique. He has not improved his personal repute by doing so. Jinnah's intrusion into Provincial politics is potentially troublesome, because he may be able to take a few seats from the Unionists and because he may be able to cause more serious trouble between existing groups within the Unionist Party itself.

14. There is little to add to what I have already said about the Ahrars. The present prospects are that they will not capture more than four or five seats. They also may bargain when the time comes.

15. Among the small groups are the Ahmadis and a few candidates who are hoping to exploit the Shahidganj affair for electioneering purposes.

16. The general position at the moment is that everyone with political ambitions is thinking in terms of votes. Except among the urban Hindus and the Congress party, the elections wili be fought on personal and tribal lines rather than on party creeds. Between parties, a good deal of private talk is going on, but no definite commitments are being made and none are likely to be made until the elections are over. Everyone is manoeuvring for position. The situation is thus very fluid, but future prospects are probably less unstable than existing circumstances would suggest. Unless the unexpected happens, there is likely to be sufficient combination among parties and groups at least to give initial stability to the first Ministry.

17. This letter is, I am afraid, of inordinate length, but I have thought it advisable to give a fairly full account to begin with, so that in succeeding letters it will be easy to deal briefly with developments as they occur. Might I suggest that if in any of my letters there is any particular matter about which Your Excellency would like further information, Laithwaite should let me know. I can then take it up in the next letter unless Your Excellency wishes to have the information at once.

Yours sincerely,
H.W. EMERSON

2

EMERSON TO LINLITHGOW

Government House, Lahore,
November 16th, 1936

My dear Lord Linlithgow,

In my previous letter I suggested that the election for a new President of the Legislative Council would provide a test as to whether Muslims were ready to put party above communal considerations and support Rao Bahadur Chhotu Ram, a rural Hindu, who has been Leader of the Unionist Party for some time. He was, in fact, elected by a large majority. The Unionist Party voted solidly for him, and every member of the party was present. This was a triumph for Sir Sikander Hyat Khan as Leader of the Party under the New Constitution, and finally destroyed any chance of Chhotu Ram's following of rural Hindus breaking away. It has helped to consolidate the party, and for this reason is much disliked by urban Hindus.

Otherwise there has been little change in the position since I last wrote. It has not been possible to reach any compromise of importance between rival candidates, who are contesting local constituencies on the same ticket. The Unionist Party as such has wisely decided not to interfere, and Sikander is, I believe, keeping aloof so far as possible from local factions. The contests in the Shahpur district are causing considerable bitterness, and, whatever the result may be, will make it more difficult to keep Muslims together later on.

2. The session of the Legislative Council, which finished a week ago, was uneventful apart from the election of the President. The Consolidation of Holdings Bill was passed without opposition, and so also were several measures of minor importance. A Government Bill to increase motor taxation on public vehicles was blocked by a motion for circulation, which meant, of course, that it could not be passed during the life of the present Council. One reason for this was that members, with an eye on the new elections, were unwilling to support new taxation; another was that they suspected that the Bill had something to do with the road and rail controversy and was put forward in the interest of the railways. This, in fact, was not the case.

In my address to the Council I deliberately took an optimistic view regarding the future, with special reference to what had been done in the past. I avoided any lengthy discussion of the New Constitution, and, in particular, of the position of the Governor, thus disappointing anti-Government critics who found little in it on which to dilate.

3. During the month the Municipal Committee of Lahore was superseded and a European I.C.S. officer[3] appointed as Administrator. The Committee has been a hotbed of communal and party factions for some years. Corruption has been rife; the interests of the public have been grossly neglected, and the transaction of business greatly delayed. Four or five years ago an Act, introduced by Government, was passed, providing for the appointment of Executive Officers in those municipalities where Government considered such appointments desirable. The object was to relieve the Committee concerned of ordinary executive work while leaving it the control of policy. This was a very desirable reform, but in practice there is a great deal of friction between the Committee and its Executive Officer, and this was particularly the case in Lahore. Four years ago a Committee was appointed to enquire into the affairs of the Committee, and their report provided ample justification for supersession. It was, however, decided to give the Committee another chance, which they failed to take. As a result they have progressively outraged public opinion, and action, which might have caused considerable agitation a few years ago, has been universally welcomed.

4. The coming Assembly elections in Lahore have been the direct cause of an attempt to revive the Shahidganj agitation. The body immediately responsible is the Ittihad-i-Millat, an association which was formed in July 1935, when the Shahidganj incident occurred. It now has practically no members of any standing or influence outside Lahore, and most respectable Muslims of Lahore have kept aloof from it. The leading members are political agitators, who are out for their own hand and not infrequently quarrel among themselves regarding the division of the loot. The Association has put up several candidates for the new Assembly. In ordinary circumstances they would stand little chance of election, and their influence with the masses has declined as feeling has abated over the Shahidganj affair. In order to improve their election chances they have been engaged for several weeks in an attempt to revive the agitation, and they have talked freely of starting civil disobedience. A conference was held last week at Lahore, which finished yesterday. The leaders were able to persuade Maulana Shaukat Ali to preside, but he made, on the whole, a moderate speech. I have not seen the detailed proceedings as yet, but apparently an influential party was adverse to civil disobedience. It is possible that a few hot heads may take matters into their own hands, but

this seems unlikely. A number of resolutions were passed, the most objectionable of which was to start a movement to boycott British goods, the Coronation Celebrations, and also Muslim recruitment to the Army. Little is likely to come of this, and, provided that irresponsible individuals do not act stupidly, there is a reasonable chance that nothing much will happen in other respects. The attitude of the Ittihad-i-Millat illustrates one danger of the new system, namely, unscrupulous exploitation of religious feeling for party or individual ends.

I may mention that the Ittihad-i-Millat is bitterly opposed to the Ahrars, and there is always the chance of a free fight when the two come into contact.

5. The Aitchison College has at last decided to make some move with the times. It provides for the sons and relatives of Ruling Princes of the Punjab States, and of leading families in the Punjab. The rules of admission have remained practically unchanged since the college was founded more than 50 years ago. They are very exclusive, and, as a result, the college has been unable to compete either in numbers or in education with less aristocratic institutions. It has very fine buildings and excellent grounds, and could easily be made one of the best educational colleges in India. It has at present a keen and progressive Principal,[4] who has already done much for it. We have been trying for the last three years to get the Committee of Management and the Council to liberalise the rules of admission, but, owing largely to the attitude taken by His Highness the Maharaja of Patiala, it was not possible to force the pace too rapidly. I am glad to say, however, that the Council has now unanimously adopted much more liberal rules. Patiala behaved very reasonably and, although the new rules are still restrictive, they are far more liberal than the old ones. I am hoping that the number of boys, which is just over 100, will very considerably increase, and that we shall be able to improve the staff and the educational standards. The question is of considerable importance, since it is largely to the Aitchison College that one must look for men of good families in the Punjab to take a worthy part in the services and public affairs. Undoubtedly a strong influence in favour of change has been an appreciation of the fact that the new Constitution threatens vested interests, and that merit will be a more searching test in the future than in the past. This is all to the good.

6. From the official point of view the conduct of the elections has been simplified by the fact that no primary elections will be necessary for the scheduled caste constituencies. In no case is the number of candidates

more than four. The present programme is to start polling about the 10th January, which will allow the results to be declared early in February. This is, I think, earlier than in some Provinces, but everyone is anxious to get the elections over as soon as possible and to know how parties stand.

Yours sincerely,
H.W. EMERSON

3

EMERSON TO LINLITHGOW

Lahore,
December 19th, 1936

My dear Lord Linlithgow,

I am a few days late in writing my monthly letter, as I wished to give an appreciation of opinion regarding the domestic crisis in England. The material for this is still scanty, since our officers have rightly refrained from canvassing opinion on the subject, and Indians are reluctant to talk about it, but the next fortnightly reports of Deputy Commissioners may contain some opinions of interest. In the meantime one has to rely, so far as Indian views are concerned, mainly on the press, supplemented by a certain amount of comment that one has heard. Practically without exception the Indian press has installed the late King as a hero, who has made the supreme sacrifice for love, and he stands even higher in Indian opinion than he did before his abdication. His sympathy with the under-dog made a great appeal to all. There is an almost complete absence of criticism of the moral issues involved, and there is very wide misunderstanding of the attitude of the British Government and of the Empire generally. To some extent Mr. Baldwin's speech helped Indians to understand the constitutional position, but its chief effect was still further to exalt the late King, and praise has been rightly given to him, because of his refusal to give any encouragement whatever to a King's party, or to make things more difficult than they actually were. So far as King Edward VIII personally is concerned, monarchy has not suffered in prestige. There was genuine and widespread grief on account of the abdication. At first there was an almost general tendency to represent the

King as the victim of conservative and class prejudices, and this persisted among some sections even after Mr. Baldwin's speech and the King's own message. These, however, did a good deal to dispel misunderstanding in some quarters, and I attach an excellent leader[5] that appeared in the *Tribune*. The view there taken is the more surprising, because the *Tribune* is a paper of nationalist views, which rarely loses an opportunity of having a dig at the British and especially the Conservative Party. Its obvious admiration of the success with which the British Constitution surmounted a crisis of unprecedented gravity is shared by many educated Indians, and I think the stock of the British nation as a whole has risen. Although practically nothing of a disloyal character has appeared in the press, some sections of it would not have been displeased, if the crisis had taken a more serious turn, as it might well have done.

So far then little, if any, harm has been done. But there is another aspect of the question about which it is not possible to be so sanguine. It has unquestionably come as a great surprise and shock to very many Indians to learn that even the King of England cannot do as he likes. There has been a hard blow to the conception of the King as all-powerful, and it is impossible to say at present whether this blow will have permanent effect or not. Loyalty to the Crown has always had a very personal side in India. The constitutional side counts for very little. One therefore is apprehensive of anything that shakes the popular belief in the personal prestige of the King. It may, however, be assumed that there will be no immediate effects. Indeed, there has been wide expression of devotion and loyalty towards His Majesty King George VI, and the Proclamation ceremony at Lahore was very well attended. I may add that among Europeans the opinion is unanimous that the facts being what they were, the solution reached was the best. On the whole, it may be said that the crisis has passed off with far less reactions than one would have deemed possible.

2. The internal politics of the Province are pursuing a normal course. Very few candidates have been returned unopposed to the new Assembly, but among them are Sir Sikander Hyat Khan, Sir Shahab-ud-Din, Raja Narendra Nath and Nawab Sir Muhammad Hyat Khan Noon, father of Sir Firoz Khan Noon. Everyone is busy in canvassing, and when I was shooting in a village the other day, the people told me that the motor car of one candidate hardly leaves the village before that of another arrives. There will be very bitter contests in the Multan and Shahpur districts among Muhammadans of the Unionist Party. There will also be strenuous fights in some of the Sikh constituencies, where Akalis and communist Sikhs are opposed to candidates belonging to the moderate Sikh party. Sir Sunder

Singh Majithia, whom I mentioned in my first letter, changed his mind at the last moment, and is standing for election. He would be a very valuable addition to the Assembly, as he is the most experienced, able and reasonable Sikh in the Province. Rumour says that he and Sikander have come to an understanding, and the same is said about Raja Narendra Nath and Sikander. I do not know whether there is any truth in these rumours, as, although Sikander would tell me if I asked him, I am deliberately refraining from acting on the assumption that a particular person is likely to be the Chief Minister, or that there will be any agreement between particular parties or sections. I think that constitutionally I should keep out of the picture, until the elections place the position beyond doubt. Up to the present, however, there is no serious challenge to Sikander's position as the expectant Chief Minister, although some disgruntled Muslims are trying to make capital out of his supposed agreement with non-Muslims. They are not cutting much ice at present. On the whole, election campaigns have been less objectionable than might have been expected, although the critical time has yet to come. Some Communist and Congress candidates are trying to discredit their opponents on the grounds that they voted for special measures in favour of law and order, or that they did something else in support of Government contrary to extremist views. Tactics of this kind are, however, to be expected. We shall have to consider shortly what special police arrangements are necessary during the elections. The indications at present are that there may be a few broken heads here and there, but nothing much in the nature of serious trouble, except perhaps in one or two constituencies. I have seen very few complaints against Government officers, and this suggests that they are obeying orders in not taking sides.

3. The last fortnightly reports mention a number of communal incidents, but none of them is particularly serious. We may, however, have trouble in Rawalpindi. The position there has been delicate for the past year or two, and on several occasions serious clashes between Muslims and Sikhs have been avoided with difficulty. Attempts have recently been made by the local officers to get the two communities to agree on certain matters, and in particular on the conduct of processions. This has always been a serious bone of contention. The Sikh processions pass in front of the main mosque in Rawalpindi, while Muslim processions pass through the main Hindu and Sikh bazaars. On several occasions the Sikhs have been provocative when passing the Jumma Masjid, and have played music during prayers. A few months ago a first class riot was narrowly averted. A Sikh procession was to be held towards the end of November on the occasion of the birthday

of Guru Nanak. A day or two before, negotiations between the communities promised to lead to a satisfactory solution, and a compromise was actually signed by the leaders, under which the Sikhs agreed to change their route, so as not to pass by the Jumma mosque, while the Muslims agreed to change the routes of their processions so as to avoid the main Hindu and Sikh bazaars. Almost at the last moment the Sikhs repudiated their leaders, and the intention was announced of taking out a procession by the old route. Feelings were then such as to have made a serious riot certain, if the procession had been allowed, and the District Magistrate,[6] with the approval of Government, forbade it. We were able to rush up additional police to Rawalpindi, and beyond the mild dispersal of the nucleus of a procession nothing much happened. The Sikh press has since been trying to create excitement, and there is the usual charge of Government depriving them of their rights. They are also bitter against the Superintendent of Police[7] who is a Muslim. Another big Sikh procession is due to come off in a few weeks, and before that a decision will have to be reached as to whether the old route can be allowed or the procession forbidden. Probably the latter course will have to be taken, since, although the normal procedure is to allow no departure from established practice, except by agreement of the communities, the situation is complicated by the fact that the leaders did reach an agreement which one community later repudiated. In any case established practice has sometimes to give way to the clear requirements of law and order.

4. The orders of Government for two tahsils have recently issued regarding the reassessment of the Lyallpur district. Previous to the slump, this was the most prosperous district in the Punjab, and probably the richest area in India for its size. At the prices prevailing during the boom years the assessment was very moderate, and the people had no difficulty in meeting it. Standards of living were high, and as usual, prosperity was accompanied by an abuse of credit. With the fall in prices conditions rapidly changed. Because of the high standards of living, the people were slower in adjusting themselves to adversity than in most districts of the Province. They were also embarrassed by liabilities incurred during the good years. For instance, many had bought land on the instalment system in other canal colonies of the Punjab, in Bahawalpur and in Sind, and they found great difficulty in meeting the instalments. The assessment, which was light when imposed, pressed heavily during the years of very low prices, and it was necessary to give *ad hoc* remissions. During the depression the district became due for re-settlement, and this was taken in hand. The problem before Government was to give sufficient relief when prices were

low, but at the same time not unduly to sacrifice their legitimate share, if and when prices rose. They had not an entirely free hand in this matter, as the revenue law is complicated. A solution was found by what is known as the sliding-scale system. Under the Revenue law Government are entitled to assume commutation prices based on the average of a long period of years, and in this case 20 years were taken. The averages thus obtained were considerably above the level of current prices, and the resulting demand could not equitably be collected until current prices at least approximated to those assumed. The demand resulting from the assumed prices is therefore regarded as the maximum which Government can take, and it will be imposed only if the general level of current prices is at least equal to that of assumed prices. Where this is not the case, the demand each harvest will be reduced accordingly. Thus in the first harvest in which the new assessment comes into force (last autumn harvest), a remission of -/6/- in the rupee is being given on the maximum demand. This corresponds to a remission of -/4/- in the rupee on what would have been the demand for the harvest, had the old rates been in force, and the new system of assessment thus gives very substantial relief even at current prices, which are of course much higher than the lowest experienced during the depression. In addition Government have given a promise that, however high prices may be during the next five years, the actual demand collected during any year will not exceed what would have been assessed had the old rates remained in force. The object of the last concession is to give the people ample time to recover from the slump. Recovery has already gone a long way towards completion, and the concession is certainly on the generous side. At the same time I felt myself that it was important to provide against a sudden and large increase on the old demand, if prices on account of war or other causes suddenly soared, and from the political point of view also the concession has its value. There has been considerable agitation about the settlement during the past two years, largely because of doubt regarding the good faith of Government. I have always considered that the best way of meeting this was to get out orders quickly, and so allow the people themselves to judge of the practical effects of the new system. I have not yet heard how the announcement has been received, but I shall be very surprised, if there is any agitation worth the name. Had the system of *ad hoc* remissions been applied to this harvest, practically nothing would have been remitted, and it is going to be difficult for the most unscrupulous agitators, and there are a good number of them in Lyallpur, to explain away the fact that the ordinary revenue payer has to pay -/12/- only while otherwise he would have had to pay Re. 1/. The relief will of course diminish as prices rise, but for five years at any rate a revenue payer cannot be worse off than he was before, and will almost certainly be better off.

The sliding-scale is already in force in the Lower Bari Doab Colony, having been introduced two years ago, and it will be applied to the Lahore and Amritsar districts, which are now under re-settlement. I hope that it will become general as other districts come under re-assessment. It introduces a new element of flexibility into the revenue system and provides an automatic remedy, so far as Government dues are concerned, to the disturbance resulting from large fluctuations in prices. It is equitable to the revenue payer and subject to a maximum also secures for Government the benefit of high prices.

5. I may mention an interesting feature in Lyallpur. We were considerably perturbed by the increase in the area under mortgage during recent years. Further examination of the position has, however, shown that to a large extent the increase represents the repayment of old debts. Owing to recent legislation and other causes moneylenders have found it extremely difficult to collect their dues. Landowners have taken advantage of this to drive hard bargains, and in many cases moneylenders have been prepared to take a mortgage for a short term of years in full satisfaction of their claims. The mortgagor remains in cultivating possession paying rent to the mortgagee, and at the end of the period, which is often four or five years only, is free from the mortgage and also from the burden of old debt. The increase in mortgages is thus in some measure a sign of recovery and not of increased liability. The guarantee, which Government have given, not to take more during the next five years than what would have been the old demand, will assist this process of liquidation of old debt.

Yours sincerely,
H.W. EMERSON

NOTES

1. A circular letter to all Governors on the subject of the Viceroy's information requirements under the new constitution. Lord Linlithgow suggested that Governors supply him with a confidential appreciation of local developments (of a more personal character) at possibly monthly intervals. R/3/1/1. See also Editor's Introduction.
2. Serious trouble arose in Lahore at the end of June 1935 as a result of a dispute between Muslims and Sikhs about a ruined mosque which lay within the precincts of the Sikh Shahidganj Gurdwara. The mosque had been in Sikh hands for 170 years and a legal decision in 1930 had confirmed the Sikhs'

right of possession. Early in July 1935, the Sikhs re-started the demolition of the mosque. Prompt action by the Punjab authorities limited the immediate extent of Muslim-Sikh clashes. There were, however, serious Muslim riots later in July and tension remained high in Lahore for the rest of 1935. In May 1940, the Judicial Committee of the Privy Council confirmed the Sikhs' ownership of the mosque. India Office papers on this subject are on L/P&J/7/886.

3. Mr A.C. Macnabb.
4. Mr C.H. Barry.
5. This leader is not reprinted in R/3/1/1 (from which the present text is taken).
6. Mr C. King.
7. Mir Qurban Ali Khan.

CHAPTER 2

Documents for 1937

4

EMERSON TO LINLITHGOW

Government House, Lahore,
January 21st, 1937

My dear Lord Linlithgow,

In my last letter of the 19th of December 1936, I mentioned the possibility of communal trouble in Rawalpindi on the occasion of the birthday celebrations of Guru Gobind Singh. In the meantime, the Muslim and Sikh communities got together, and the leaders on both sides signed a new agreement by which the old route of the Sikh procession past the Jumma Masjid was to be observed on this occasion, and thereafter to be abandoned in favour of a new route. Similarly, Muslims are in future to avoid the main Hindu and Sikh bazaars. In accordance with this agreement the procession on the 18th of January followed the old route and the day passed off without any serious trouble. A section of the Muslims were, however, angry with the attitude of their leaders in agreeing to the old route, and according to the press reports, one or two minor incidents occurred. We have not yet received the full official report. The immediate results have thus been fairly satisfactory. Of far greater importance is the fact that Government will now be able to stand on the new agreement and definitely to forbid future Sikh processions past the Jumma Masjid, without laying themselves open to the charge of having gone contrary to established practice without the agreement of the communities concerned.

There was a stupid communal murder in Amritsar a few weeks ago, which almost provoked a general clash. A fanatical Muslim murdered a Sikh for no reason whatsoever, and for several days there was great excitement in the city. Feelings are still strong, but the immediate danger has passed.

2. The elections began three days ago, and so far are pursuing a normal course. There is great keenness, but up to the present there has been no tendency towards disorder, the few incidents that have occurred being checked at once by the police. In Lahore at any rate, impersonation has been dealt with promptly and firmly, and this should have a salutary effect. I doubt whether any village in the Province has not been included in the election campaign by one party or another, and most villages have had a constant succession of visits from canvassers. There has certainly been a great stirring of the political consciousness of the masses. It is too early to say what the effects will be, but I doubt whether they will be more than temporary. In many constituencies the fight has been between local men, who depend on local influences, and general questions have come little into the picture. This is particularly so in Muslim constituencies. On the other hand, where there is a Congress candidate, and also in most Sikh constituencies where the contest is between a moderate and an extremist, there has been a good deal of talk about political questions, using 'political' in the old sense. For instance, capital has been freely made against a candidate who is suspected of being a Government man, or who has been loyal towards Government. This has been specially marked in Sikh constituencies, and I was told the other day that with many of the smaller voters there was a definite prejudice against any one who could be described as pro-Government. The results will show how far this has been an important influence. I think it has been probably confined to a few districts, and within those districts to certain Sikh and Hindu constituencies. The opinion, however, is not infrequently expressed by the bigger men in the Province that this tendency is likely to be much more in evidence five years hence, and they are apprehensive regarding the spreading of communist and socialist ideas.

Pandit Jawaharlal Nehru has just finished a flying visit of three days to the Province. The visit was confined to half a dozen towns, and he was unable to spend much time in any of them. He drew big crowds wherever he went, and there is no doubt about his personal attraction. This, I believe, very largely discounts the unpopularity with some classes of the doctrines he preaches, and it is a mistake to attach undue importance to them as circumscribing his powers of mischief. I have not yet seen official reports of his speeches. From newspaper accounts I have got the impression that he is less concerned with the success of Congress candidates at the polls than with the opportunity which the elections afford of propagating seditious ideas and preaching the programme of independence. While he will no doubt use the new Constitution to stir up as much trouble as he can, he seems to be depending more on external events before attempting action on a serious scale. He is extremely dangerous, especially as he possesses greater qualities of effective leadership than Gandhi. So far as the election results are concerned, his visit to the Punjab may give Congress three or four seats which they might otherwise have lost, but is unlikely to do more.

The election campaign has not been without its humour. In Amritsar, for instance, the rival Sikh candidates decided to carry on a joint campaign, and they organised a tour in the villages of the district. A Stage Secretary was appointed before a meeting was held, and it was his business to see that speakers on either side were allowed the same amount of time. The meetings were attended by the supporters of the two sides, and at several the rival women candidates were also present, who told the audience what they thought of each other. The police reports were amusing, and generally ended with the sentence – 'The meeting then broke up in disorder as the Stage Secretary had allowed too much time to one of the parties.' I imagine every one has got a good deal of fun out of the preamble to the new Constitution, whatever they may get out of its working.

3. Mirza Bashir Ahmad, head of the Ahmadiyya community, came to see me early this month, and I had a long talk with him. For some months he made a habit of abusing myself and the Punjab Government in his Friday sermons, but has been behaving better during the past year. He is, pleased at our having posted Innes as Deputy Commissioner of the Gurdaspur district, in which Qadian, the headquarters of Ahmadis, is situated. Innes is the son of Sir Charles Innes, who was Governor of Burma, and is one of our best men. I posted him to Gurdaspur in the hope that local friction might diminish, and there seems a chance that this will happen. At any rate, the Ahmadis are so far pleased with him, although I told the Mirza Sahib that he would deal with them firmly if they put themselves in the wrong. He said that he had already realised this. Mirza Bashir Ahmad is of middle age, well educated and, in many respects, a man of the world. He has a good grasp of the political situation, and is astute in giving political support to other parties so as to get the best results for his own community. He realises their unpopularity not only with the Ahrars but also with orthodox Muslims, and, although the attack on them is much less violent and dangerous than it was two years ago, he is rightly nervous about its recurrence. I took the opportunity of giving him some advice about the future, and of explaining that a popular Government, dependent on the

votes of orthodox Muslims, would find themselves much embarrassed if they had to defend the Ahmadis against a general campaign of the faithful. I told him that for some time, when the campaign was at its height, I was myself very anxious regarding the strength of feeling among Muslims generally against him and his followers. I advised him therefore to be careful to avoid provocation, and that, so far as it lay within his power, to let the agitation die a natural death. I hope this will happen, but I am a little concerned that the Ahrars, if they do badly in the elections, will try to revive their influence by a renewal of a vigorous campaign against Ahmadis. This would get a good deal of orthodox Muslim support, and might embarrass the new Government. The Governor's position will be a very troublesome one if a situation ever arises in which he has to use his special powers for the protection of the Ahmadis. Fortunately, past experience shows that virulent attacks against them come in cycles, and that between successive campaigns there is comparative peace.

4. Your Excellency will remember the affair last summer at Daska in the Sialkot district, in which a brother of Sir Zafrullah was concerned. The police ran in both parties for rioting, but treated the Ahmadis as the aggressive party and did not prosecute very seriously the other side. A day or two before Your Excellency visited Sialkot, the accused in both cases were acquitted, and the Magistrate described both the prosecuting and defence stories as very exaggerated. I think I told Your Excellency that, after reading the judgement, I was not entirely satisfied that the local police had acted well. Further enquiry has shown that this is almost certainly the case. While there is not sufficient reason to accept the version originally put forward by Sir Zafrullah – and in any case it would be quite impossible at this stage to ascertain the actual facts – there is reason to believe that the Sub-Inspector of Police took an attitude from the beginning hostile to the Ahmadis. We shall probably be able to get at him on the falsification of police diaries, in which case he will be dismissed. The Superintendent of Police[1] has been transferred partly because this case made me feel uneasy about him, but mainly because he and the Hindu Deputy Commissioner[2] are at loggerheads. The Ahmadis themselves have not raised the matter again since the case ended, and the action taken has been on the initiative of Government.

Friction between the Deputy Commissioner and the Superintendent of Police, when both are Indians, is far too common. We have had instances in four or five districts during the past year, and this is going to be a troublesome business for the new Government. We try to avoid it, so far as possible, by making what appear to be suitable appointments to particular districts, but the proportion of Indians in both Services is now so large that it is not possible to arrange in every case that either the Deputy Commissioner or the Superintendent of Police should be a European, and, although there are plenty of cases in which Indians can and do work together in these posts, there is always the danger of their falling out either on some official or social matter of small importance.

Yours sincerely,
H.W. EMERSON

5

EMERSON TO LINLITHGOW

Private and Personal — Government House, Lahore,
February 19th, 1937

My dear Lord Linlithgow,

I find it difficult to reply to Laithwaite's letter of the 17th of February regarding the probable trend of events following the elections, as I have been out of touch with all-India politics for some time and the views I have heard about developments in the near future both from Europeans and Indians differ widely and are necessarily based on surmise. Also, I have fortunately no reason to anticipate any immediate difficulty in the Punjab, and so have not had to set my mind to the question. I have now attempted to weigh the possibilities, and give my impressions for what they are worth.

2. In several Provinces the future will depend on the attitude of Congress, and here there are two persons who obviously count a great deal, although their influence may not be decisive, namely, Gandhi and Jawaharlal Nehru.

My last talk with Gandhi was in 1931, and much water has flowed under the bridges since then, but there are one or two impressions I formed in my dealings with him which may prove to be relevant. First, Gandhi is less uncompromising than Jawaharlal. In 1931, as Nehru mentions in his autobiography (which incidentally throws a great deal of light on his character), he yielded on the question of complete independence. Second, he used often to talk of co-operation, although his idea of co-operation was a state of affairs in which Congress, meaning largely himself, was to be the mediator through whom Government were to have relations with the people. It was over the attempt to enforce this idea after the Irwin-Gandhi agreement that the chief fight was waged between us. He had, I believe, at that time occasional dreams of being the first Prime Minister of all India. Third, he was then devoted to Jawaharlal, whom he regarded as his son and sometimes, but not always, he supported action by, or proposals of Nehru which he himself did not approve. Fourth, he is far less socialistic in his views than Nehru. Fifth, he is more farseeing than Nehru, but less practical and direct in his methods.

I have met Jawaharlal once only, but then had several hours' talk with him. I have read and heard a good deal about him since, and in connection with his visits to the Punjab I have had to estimate his personality and his aims. I believe that he is intractable, uncompromising and determined to work for complete independence. He hopes for mass revolution, and will not shrink from violence if necessary. Until lately he was counting more on external events, e.g. a world war, than on internal developments, but the success of Congress can hardly fail to affect his views. He has an attractive personality, great force of character, and appeals to the mass of Hindus because he is one of their few leaders whom they can regard as a big man. Many of them dislike his socialistic views, but I have always felt that too much importance was being attached to this as a factor detracting from his influence – at an rate at this stage. The position may change if and when he attempts to put those ideas into practice. He was devoted to Gandhi, and would probably still go some way in meeting the latter's wishes, but not nearly so far as he went in 1931, and I doubt whether he will compromise on what he conceives to be vital issues. He will be more ready to face a rupture in Congress than Gandhi. The latter will do all he can to avoid a split, but, although he will go a long way in supporting Jawaharlal, I am not sure whether he will go the whole way if several of the Provinces revolt against Nehru's domination.

I regard Nehru as more dangerous than Gandhi ever was. At the same time, it would be a mistake to view the latter as a spent force. If he emerges from his retirement, he will still exercise very great influence. I am not convinced that Gandhi wants mass revolution as Nehru undoubtedly does, but, if he decides to support the latter in his wrecking policy, then he will be prepared for the consequences, except that he will again delude himself on the question of non-violence.

I know little about the other Congress leaders, but I have always understood that Rajagopalachariar in Madras and Rajendra Prasad in Bihar were comparatively moderate. They would find less difficulty in breaking with Nehru than with Gandhi.

3. I am told that the Congress party in Madras are determined to take office, and that this is likely to be the attitude in the Central Provinces if Congress succeed there. Reports in the press suggest that this may also be the case in Bihar, and the latest rumours from the United Provinces mention the probable composition of a Congress Ministry. At the moment it looks as if Congress intend to accept office. I find it difficult to believe that Jawaharlal approves of this. It will be hard for him to swallow everything he has said in the last few months and is still saying. He must know that once Congress accept office, he will find it very difficult, in practice, to control the policy of the various Congress Ministers. I remember that years ago I told him that if he would only take a constructive part in the administration, he would become so interested in it and so seized of the practical difficulties that he would soon become more bureaucratic than any one of us. He understands the implications of office as affecting his aim of complete independence, and, in spite of present indications, it seems to me that he may press strongly for non-acceptance. If he insists, there will be the prospect of a split in Congress ranks. Gandhi will do his utmost to avoid this. At any rate, in that case he will try to manoeuvre things so as to put Government as much in the wrong as possible. If there is a fight between acceptors and non-acceptors, a possible development is an attempt to make terms with Government. This may either be in the form of a uniform statement of conditions to be presented to each Governor concerned, or an all-India attempt to negotiate with Your Excellency. It is just possible that there may be a move for a discussion between Your Excellency and Gandhi with the onus placed on Your Excellency for refusing. Having gone all through the 1930 and 1931 negotiations, I have no hesitation in holding the very strong view that any discussions of an all-India character would be a very grave mistake. So far as Governors are concerned, the position seems to be clear. The prospective Ministry is bound by the Constitution. There is no room for an agreement outside it and no need for one inside it.

4. Present indications, however, suggest that Nehru is likely to find the opposition to non-acceptance so strong as to make it useless for him to pursue it with any hope of success. He will then, I think, attempt to make acceptance conditional on the aim of wrecking the Constitution from within, or, at any rate without any such declared intention, make it conditional on a uniform programme representing Congress policy. In this connection

Your Excellency might see the statement of Congress policy as enunciated in the Karachi Congress session of 1931, when a detailed list of their aims was drawn up. Many of the items relate to all-India questions. Among those relevant to provincial matters are the following:

(*a*) Freedom of association and combination.
(*b*) Freedom of speech and of the press.
(*c*) Substantial reduction in agricultural rent or revenue paid by the peasantry, and in case of uneconomic holdings exemption from rent for such period as may be necessary, relief being given to small zamindars wherever necessary by reason of such reduction.
(*d*) Imposition of a progressive income-tax on agricultural incomes above a fixed minimum.
(*e*) A graduated inheritance tax.
(*f*) Expenditure and salaries in Civil Departments to be largely reduced. No servant of State, other than specially employed experts and the like, to be paid above a certain fixed figure, which should not at any rate exceed Rs. 500 per month.
(*g*) Total prohibition of intoxicating drinks and drugs.

So long as there is no question of a Governor approving a programme as a condition by a Ministry of accepting office, I take it that the mere announcement of a programme, however extreme it may be, is no bar to the appointment of Ministers, provided that the programme is not clearly inconsistent with the Constitution itself. On this assumption there would seem to be clear advantages if office is accepted. Even although the Congress programme may, and probably will, lead to a constitutional crisis in the near future in one or more Provinces, the acceptance of office is likely to prove less troublesome than non-acceptance, because, first, if there are Congress Ministries in several Provinces, some at any rate may develop into genuine co-operators; second, Ministers will find it difficult to wreck from inside; third, some are likely to resent attempts by Congress to dominate their policy from outside; fourth, even if a Governor has to exercise his special responsibility, the crisis would occur on a specific issue and not on a general programme. I assume, of course, that the Governor would retain, as he must retain under the Constitution, complete freedom of action within his powers, and that the constitutional position would be made clear in some way or other to the public. It would, for instance, create great demoralisation in the Services if the false impression were to get abroad that the appointment of a Congress Ministry has in any way compromised the power of the Governor to protect the legitimate interests of the Services.

5. If the deliberate policy is pursued of wrecking from within, the probable issues on which a crisis will be precipitated are:

(*a*) Law and order, e.g. repeal of so-called repressive laws.
(*b*) Reduction of the police.
(*c*) Reduction in the number and pay of Government servants.

Congress, with a deliberate wrecking policy, are likely to choose the issue most favourable to themselves. In some Provinces I imagine that they will propose drastic reductions in land revenue – which of course would not touch a Governor's special responsibility – and urge that this can only be effected by a reduction in the number or pay of Government servants, in particular by reduction of the police, which would at once affect the Governor's responsibility. They will not, however, find this to be so easy as they think, and they will find themselves up against hard facts. Assuming, however, that Jawaharlal will stick to his aim of complete independence through mass revolution, he will attempt to use the acceptance of office as a means of stirring up an agrarian revolt through the refusal of a Governor to accept advice which would make relief in taxation possible only at the sacrifice of his special responsibilities. While this policy might meet with a measure of success in one or two Provinces, it is unlikely to succeed in all, and the Congress position will be weakened if their plan breaks down in some Provinces.

6. There remains the case of non-acceptance. Here there may be two classes of cases:

(*i*) where an alternative Ministry can be formed, although not commanding a majority ; and
(*ii*) where no alternative Ministry can be formed.

In the first case, the balance seems to be in favour of postponing the crisis and putting Congress in the wrong for creating one. In the second case, there seems to be no alternative to the suspension from the outset of the Constitution under section 93 of the Government of India Act.

7. Your Excellency will, of course, appreciate that the above observations are of a general character, that they are not intended to have reference to any particular Province, and that local conditions might make them quite inappropriate. They are also based on alternative assumptions, none of which may be in accordance with the development of the situation during the next few weeks.

Yours sincerely,
H.W. EMERSON

6

EMERSON TO LINLITHGOW

Private and Personal

Government House, Lahore,
February 22nd, 1937

My dear Lord Linlithgow,

In my first letter of the series written in October last I gave an account of the various parties in the Province, and attempted to make a rough estimate of their chances in the elections. Except in one important respect, namely, that Congress had more successes at the expense of moderate urban Hindus than I anticipated, the estimate has been roughly confirmed by the results of the elections. Your Excellency may wish to refer to that letter both as regards parties and personalities fully to appreciate what I now have to say.

2. The Unionist Party has done almost as well as it expected. It lost two or three seats that it expected to win, but, on the other hand, has had several successes in constituencies which were doubtful. Its final strength is not yet determined as there is still some discussion going on with independent members, but it is likely to be nearer 100 than 90, and in a House of 175 members has a clear majority over all other parties combined. The party, as at present composed, consists of one European, one Anglo-Indian, two Indian Christians, two or three members of the depressed classes, eight or nine rural Hindu members, and the rest Muslims. It held a party meeting a week ago in which very clear pledges of loyalty were given to the party by various groups and individuals, and the leadership of Sir Sikander Hyat Khan was confirmed without any dissentient note. On the surface, therefore, the party is in a strong position.

3. Among other Muslim parties or groups the Ahrars failed badly and captured only two seats, one of their most prominent leaders losing in his home constituency. The Muslim League had two successful candidates, and one of them has already joined the Unionist Party. No Ahmadi candidate was successful as such, but there is an Ahmadi member, who fought the election on the Unionist ticket. The Ittihad-i-Millet, which professed to take a prominent interest in the Shahidganj affair, obtained only two seats, and one of the members concerned has now joined the Congress. In addition, a few Muslims got in as Independents, most of whom have joined or will join the Unionist Party. One or two Muslims at

the most will join Congress, and there is one Muslim communist, a curious case as he belongs to a family with very loyal traditions and was educated at the Chiefs' College and at Oxford. His election, however, was entirely due to tribal influence, had no reference to communist tendencies, and the Unionist Party ought later to be able to get hold of him.

4. Among the Hindus, Congress was more successful than was anticipated, the total successes being about 11. These successes were obtained almost entirely at the expense of the Nationalist Progressive Party representing urban Hindus of the Hindu Sabha school. There were several reasons for this. In the first place, here, as in other Provinces, the strength of Congress in the towns had been under-estimated. Second, Pandit Jawaharlal Nehru's visit undoubtedly gave a great impetus to Congress. Third, and perhaps the most important, the Progressive Party was divided among themselves, and there was neither effective leadership nor organisation. On the other hand, Congress had few successes in rural constituencies, and this was particularly the case in the south-east, where the influence of Rao Bahadur Chhotu Ram and the organisation which he has been building up for years were the decisive factors. The Nationalist Progressive Party, with the addition of a few Independents, may ultimately number 20 as a maximum, but, owing to personal jealousies, it may split up into small groups.

5. Chhotu Ram's group of rural Hindus will number about 9 members, and will, of course, be staunchly Unionist. The failure of Congress in rural constituencies in the south-east, which border on the United Provinces, is very satisfactory, and shows that, for the present at any rate, the Jats, Rajputs, Ahirs and Gujars of that part of the Province prefer their own tribal leaders to Congressmen.

6. A few Sikhs were successful on the Congress ticket, and taking into account Muslims also, the Congress party is at present about 18. The leader will probably be Dr. Gopi Chand, a private medical practitioner. He was a member of the Legislative Council some years ago, and is not so extreme as several other Congressmen in the Punjab. He is a fairly good speaker and his presence will strengthen the Opposition.

7. The two main parties among the Sikhs were the Khalsa National Party led by Sir Sunder Singh Majithia, and the Akali party. The former did better than I anticipated, and, including some Independents, who will join the party and two or three defections from the Akalis, Sir Sunder Singh is likely to have a following of nearly 20 members. The Akalis will number about 10. This is the first time for some years that moderate Sikhs have come into the open and seriously challenged the position which the

Akalis have obtained. The results are very gratifying. Some of the Sikh contests were very bitter. Sir Sunder Singh himself only got in by a small majority, and in the Lyallpur district a very popular and loyal Sikh was defeated by an extreme Akali, almost entirely because of the unscrupulous methods adopted by the latter. The Akalis are alleged to have spent money freely out of Gurdwara funds, and corruption, which I am afraid occurred on a smaller or greater scale in many constituencies, was most pronounced in the Sikh ones. The Akali group contains four or five Communists of the extremist type, but the group generally is too small to do any harm. For purposes of opposition they are likely to work with Congress, but differences about the Communal Award will probably prevent a complete merging of parties.

8. The position as created by the elections was sufficiently clear to allow me at once to invite Sir Sikander Hyat Khan to assist me in the appointment of Ministers, and he has accepted the invitation. The Ministry will almost certainly consist of three Muslims including the Chief Minister, two Hindus and one Sikh. Of the Muslims, two will be rural and one urban, and of the Hindus, one will be rural and one urban. There is not likely to be much difficulty about the urban Muslim and the rural Hindu. There are at least three prominent candidates for the Hindu urban Ministry, namely, Sir Gokul Chand Narang, existing Minister, Mr. Manohar Lal and Rai Bahadur Mukhand Lal Puri. The position will be clearer within a few days. It seems probable at the moment that the Nationalist Progressive Party as a whole will agree to work with the Unionist Party, but will not formally accept the Unionist programme as a whole. Even if this does not happen, there are other groups in this party who are likely to work with the Unionists.

The same is true of the Khalsa National Party led by Sir Sunder Singh, with this difference that his party is likely to be much more united. The indications at present are that they also will agree to work with the Unionist Party without accepting their programme, and, if Sir Sunder Singh is willing to accept office, he seems to be marked out as the Sikh Minister. Sir Sikander Hyat Khan has, of course, not yet offered any advice in this respect. It is just possible that the Nationalist Progressive Party and the Khalsa National Party will try to impose terms in return for co-operation with the Unionist Party, which the latter are not in a position to accept, e.g. regarding the Communal Award and communal distribution of posts in the services. This would create complications, but in any case I do not think Sir Sikander Hyat Khan will find much difficulty in finding a Sikh and a urban Hindu, each with some following to accept office.

The second rural Muslim Ministry is likely to cause most difficulty. In this connection Your Excellency might refer to what I said in my first letter regarding the rivalry between the Wah Party on the one hand, and the Noon-Tiwana group on the other. The Shahpur election resulted in the victory of Nawab Allah Bakhsh by a small majority, and, as I expected, stirred up a great deal of ill feeling. There have been constant rumours that Nawab Allah Bakhsh has been attempting to form a rival group, although he proclaimed his loyalty to Sir Sikander Hyat Khan at the Unionist meeting a week ago. The Tiwana group will certainly be disgruntled if it does not get a Ministry. In the meantime, another group is pressing its claims. This consists of a certain number of Muslim members in the south-west of the Province, namely, the Multan Division, and the chief aspirant to office is Nawab Sir Jamal Khan, Chief of the Leghari Tribe in the Dera Ghazi Khan district and adjacent tribal area. Sir Jamal Khan is a Baluch who, although he has abandoned the long hair and the picturesque dress of the Baluchis, has still considerable influence among them owing to his integrity and impartiality in dealing with them. He presides over the inter-Provincial Jirga which is held every year to settle tribal disputes between Baluchistan and the Punjab. He has a fair knowledge of English, and, although he has no marked ability, is reliable and pleasant to deal with. His group base their claim to Ministry on the broad ground that the Multan Division, which is essentially Muslim, has never had a Ministry and that the Tiwana group, which they have often supported in the past, should give way to them. The two groups may reach a compromise, and at the moment there does not seem any great danger of a split in Muslim ranks that would take away more than half a dozen Muslim members. But one can never tell, and until the Ministry is appointed, the situation will remain to some extent fluid. There are, of course, many other candidates for office, and Sikander will probably have to create a fair number of Parliamentary Secretaryships to assist in keeping his party together. He is at present waiting for final developments, but I hope decisions will be reached within the next ten days. Sir Shahab-ud-Din will, I understand, be content with the Speakership.

9. On the whole, the prospects appear to be very favourable for a stable Government with an opposition sufficiently strong to exercise a salutary influence. But one cannot be unduly sanguine since there are several features which warn one against complacency regarding the future. There is first the question of personal ambitions and animosities, which are always liable to break out. Second, there is the danger of some unexpected communal dispute or a riot undermining the strength of a Coalition

Government. Third, there is the prospect of reactions on the Punjab of developments in other Provinces. The spectacular success of Congress elsewhere must have a certain amount of influence here and, if Congress accept office in other Provinces and embark on a programme of large reductions in land revenue, the Ministry in the Punjab will be placed in a difficult position. The very large measure of success achieved in the elections by stable elements in the Punjab tends to obscure the fact that in the towns Congress was largely successful, and that in some rural areas there was a good deal of talk about socialist and communist doctrines. The peasantry as a whole are at present contented and loyal, but the margin of safety is not so wide as to allow any definite assumption that the Punjab will remain comparatively unaffected by outside events. For the moment, however, there is sufficient cause for satisfaction and insufficient reason to anticipate trouble.

10. Since I last wrote, Sir William Stampe has been here as a member of a committee to advise on the extension of the Mandi Hydro-Electric Scheme to new areas. I took the opportunity of his visit to discuss fully with him the scheme of tube well irrigation in the United Provinces. We later had a conference on the subject among ourselves. The main decision is to put an officer on special duty thoroughly to examine the prospects of tube well irrigation in the Punjab. Every aspect of the question would be thoroughly investigated both generally and with reference to seven or eight tracts in which the prospects appear to be most favourable. My present impression is that, owing to climatic and other reasons, tube well irrigation will not be practicable on such a large scale as in the United Provinces, but it may be an economic proposition in particular areas. In any case, however, it was clearly necessary that we should now collect the necessary data on which to arrive at well-considered conclusions, and we hope that the material will be ready at any rate within a year.

Yours sincerely,
H.W. EMERSON

7

EMERSON TO LINLITHGOW

Private and Confidential

Government House, Lahore,
March 26th, 1937

My dear Lord Linlithgow,

I have little to report this month. The announcement of the Ministry was, on the whole, well received by the press throughout the Province, the general opinion being that, as four of the six Ministers have previous experience as Members or Ministers under the existing constitution, the administration should be efficient. Within the Unionist Party there is so far no sign of disaffection on the part of disgruntled groups or individuals, but Sikander will have to satisfy some of his supporters within the party and also within other groups, that have joined the coalition, by the appointment of Parliamentary Secretaries. His present intention is to appoint eight or so and to give them Rs. 500 per mensem. Provision for their pay will be included in the budget, and they will not receive any remuneration until the budget is passed.

2. The Hindu Urban Party is not united. Sir Gokul Chand Narang is dissatisfied with not being included in the Ministry. He is unlikely to support Manohar Lal, the Urban Hindu Minister, and may join the Opposition. As he is a forceful Speaker, he may be a thorn in the side of the Government. I am told, however, that Manohar Lal is likely to bring nine or ten Urban Hindu votes which from the Government point of view is not unsatisfactory.

3. The Opposition will have considerable debating strength: Among Muslims there are Dr. Kitchlew, Dr. Alam, Malik Barkat Ali and Mian Abdul Aziz. Kitchlew is a stormy petrel. He belongs to Amritsar, and has at one time or another taken a prominent part in Khilafat and Congress movements. He has been to jail several times. Of late years he has kept fairly aloof from anti-Government movements, but still commands considerable sympathy from the Muslim masses.

Dr. Alam is a Barrister. He was previously a member of the Legislative Council – loud-voiced and of violent speech, but nothing much behind. He represented the Muslim cause in various suits and proceedings relating to Shahidganj, and so increased his influence. Although he got elected on the Shahidganj ticket, he subsequently joined the Congress.

Malik Barkat Ali was a member of the Provincial Civil Service, but was dismissed some years ago for corruption. He has a fairly good practice at the Bar, is unreliable and self-seeking, but a fair speaker.

Mian Abdul Aziz would have liked to be the Urban Minister, but was felt to be too weak and unstable. He is a curious mixture. He was a President of the Municipal Committee of Lahore for some years and was not, I think, corrupt, but he was not strong enough to do any good. He has at times done good work for Government notably in the communal riots in Lahore in 1927; at other times he has been troublesome.

The Congress Hindu members include very few men of any substance. Dr. Gopi Chand of Lahore, leader of the party, and Lala Duni Chand, a Barrister of Ambala, are fair speakers. Congress ranks in the Punjab are still very divided.

The Sikh Opposition contains several communists and other extremists who are good at stumping the country and making violent speeches, but they have still to show that they can adapt themselves to the conditions of parliamentary debate. The leader of the Sikh Opposition is Sardar Sampuran Singh, who has got himself into a position which cannot be much to his liking. He was a delegate to the first Round Table Conference and is, by instinct, of moderate views. He is, however, unstable and vacillating. He thought he would have a better chance of being elected if he stood on the Akali ticket, although his natural place was with Sir Sunder Singh's party. Having committed himself, he has so far found it impossible to extricate himself, and, not because he wishes, but because he wiil be too weak to resist pressure, he may degenerate into the common type of anti-Government agitator. He has not sufficient character to be dangerous.

4. The pay of Ministers has not been finally settled. It is likely to be about Rs. 48,000 per annum for the Chief Minister and Rs. 40,000 per annum for each of the other Ministers, but may take the form of fixed salaries at less than these sums with rent-free houses or, in lieu thereof, house allowances. Including the pay of the Chief Whip and of Parliamentary Secretaries, the total expenditure will, I think, be about the same or possibly a little more than the present expenditure on Members and Ministers.

5. I am watching with great interest the developments in connection with the acceptance of office by Congress. It is characteristic of Gandhi's subtlety of mind that, apparently against his inclinations and intentions, he should have produced a form of words, which has temporarily at any rate failed to achieve its purpose. It is always difficult to know what is at the back of his mind, but, without inside knowledge, I am inclined to think that he himself does want a solution. At the same time, he realises the future value to Congress of any commitment by Governors which, when crises occur, can be put forward as evidence of a breach of faith or, in the meantime, can be used to show that the Governor has renounced his powers

of protection, especially of the Services. I saw so much of the game in 1930 and 1931 that it is very interesting to watch much the same moves on this occasion. I hope Gandhi will have the sense to untie the knot that he has made.

Yours sincerely,
H.W. EMERSON

8

EMERSON TO LINLITHGOW

Confidential

Government House, Lahore,
April 24th, 1937

My dear Lord Linlithgow,

My last regular monthly letter was dated the 26th of March. Since then there has been a session of the Legislative Assembly lasting about a week. The first serious business was the election of a Speaker. The nominee of Government was Chaudhri Sir Shahab-ud-Din, and this provided the first test of the solidarity of the Unionist Party, since there were in that party a certain number of members who would like to have voted against the party's nominee on personal grounds. He was, however, elected by a large majority. Sardar Daswandha Singh was elected as Deputy Speaker. He also was a nominee of the party, and is a Sikh member of the Bar of the Ludhiana district. On the day following the election, I addressed the Assembly and I attach a copy of my address.[3] It was well received by the Assembly and, on the whole, by the provincial press. Congress members absented themselves from the House.

2. The legislative business consisted of three Bills, relating to the following subjects:

(*i*) Fixation of the pay of Ministers.
(*ii*) Fixation of the pay of Speaker and Deputy Speaker.
(*iii*) Removal of disqualification of certain office holders from election to, and membership of, the Provincial Legislature. The list of office holders in question included certain village officials, Sub-Registrars and officers of the Territorial Force. It also included Parliamentary Secretaries if and when appointed. It did not contain any whole-time servants of Government.

The Bills were passed without difficulty, the Government majority varying between 50 and 60. Opportunity was taken of the Ministers Salary Bill to give the official designation of Premier to the first Minister. Public sentiment was obviously in favour of this rather than of the alternative title of Chief Minister. The pay of the Premier was fixed at the rate of Rs. 42,000 per annum *plus* a rent-free furnished house or in lieu thereof an annual allowance at the rate of Rs. 6,000. The salary of other Ministers was fixed at the rate of Rs. 36,000 per annum with a house allowance at the rate of Rs. 3,600 per annum. While there was naturally some criticism from the opposition regarding these rates of pay, the general feeling in the House was in favour of giving reasonable salaries.

The official business also included the election of several Committees.

3. Various adjournment motions were moved by members of the opposition. Two of them related to the communal riots at Panipat and Kot Fateh Khan, and it was a good sign that by the general consent of the House they were not proceeded with. The only motion that proceeded to debate was the one relating to the Secretary of State's speech regarding the non-acceptance of office by Congress. This was talked out. The general line taken by Sir Sikander was that in the Punjab the Ministers had not asked for assurances since they intended to work the Act; they were sure of themselves and would have no hesitation in resigning if the Governor's powers prevented them from working for the good of the Province; he blamed Congress for not playing the game. I think this was the best line to take. Even in the Punjab it is not a practical preposition for a Minister to attempt to defend the safeguards, &c., whatever his private opinion may be. Indeed everyone is on the lookout for an excuse to attack the Governor, and he and the Ministers have to see that no excuse is given. Although nothing has been said on the subject, I have detected signs that the Ministers themselves are sensitive in this respect. I therefore go out of my way to impress upon them their responsibility, and to make it clear to them that any schemes of the old Government they adopt must be adopted as their own schemes about which they have satisfied themselves. This does not mean that they do not freely seek my advice, but I feel instinctively that our relations would easily be impaired if I attempted to thrust my advice on them. An interesting example of this occurred when we were discussing the Schedule of New Expenditure for the current financial year. The Schedule included proposals which had been strongly recommended by the conference on cattle breeding held a few mouths ago over which I presided. Although the conference included all the official and many of the non-official experts in the Province, the Minister was obviously

reluctant to adopt several of the proposals, and I imagine that he had the support of his colleagues. I think that the underlying feeling was that the schemes were not theirs. I did not attempt to press them, but took the line that the Minister would naturally wish to examine them himself and, if and when he is satisfied about their soundness, to adopt them later on. Ultimately I think most of them will be sponsored by the Minister.

4. The first session of the Legislature was definitely a success from the Government point of view. Their supporters stuck together, the level of debate was high, and Government were on top not only as regards voting but also in debate. They found the opposition less strong in this respect than they expected, while they themselves were better. They will soon have a good team of speakers. Sikander had a Party meeting before the session began. He found some difficulty in making his supporters understand that it was no longer open to them to get up and criticise the Government, since in doing so they would be criticising their own leaders. Even the most loyal among them have been so accustomed to have a mild grouse against the 'Sirkar' that they are a little disappointed to find that this will no longer be possible. They say that the opposition has much the easier job, that it does not require much ability or eloquence to have a dig at the 'Sirkar', but it requires both to be always in the position of a defendant. However, they will soon adapt themselves to the new conditions, and, incidentally, the obligation to defend the schemes of Government will make them take a keener interest in them. Fortunately no rash promises were made during the elections, so there is little question of carrying out pledges. At the same time the people expect the new Government to do a great deal for them. This is where the chief difficulty is going to occur. Sikander has promised the appointment of a committee to enquire into:

(*a*) new financial resources;
(*b*) possibilities of retrenchment; and
(*c*) relief of the poorer classes.

There is, in fact, as he knows himself, very little scope for any of these measures. He is hoping that the hard logic of facts and figures will convince his committee. There are very few big landlords in the Punjab and, apart from the unpopularity of a tax on agricultural incomes, the yield would be very small indeed. Other new sources of taxation are very few. The only scope for retrenchment on a considerable scale is by cutting down the beneficent activities. It has indeed been clear for years that the people cannot have both relief from taxation and progressive administration. In the past, except of course during the economic depression, they have preferred Government to push ahead with beneficent schemes. It may be possible to persuade them to the same effect in future, but the golden age which is being promised to voters in other Provinces, will not make things easier here. The budget for 1937-8 will contain nothing sensational. Harvest prospects were extremely good until we had devastating hailstorms in several districts. These have seriously affected the revenue estimates for the year. Government will probably budget for a small deficit and will include in their proposals one or two new beneficent schemes and the revival of several others which had been in suspension since the slump occurred. Examples of these are the provincialisation of a few hospitals now supported by district boards, greater assistance to industry, a scheme for the encouragement of well sinking and larger grants to the Sanitary Board for the encouragement of rural and urban sanitary schemes. These do not amount to very much, but are on the right lines. The great difficulty which the Ministry has to face is that the acceptance of the Niemeyer recommendations has for the time being left the Punjab worse off so far as help from central revenues is concerned than it was before.

Government have also promised to appoint a committee to go into the question of unemployment. This is a popular move.

5. The Ministers are shaping well and are taking their work seriously. They are accessible to the people and now that the session is over they are getting out on tour. They are working well together and the spirit among them all is excellent. Four of them have previous experience as Members or Ministers and so have no difficulty in dealing with administrative questions. The other two are picking up the threads. I am particularly pleased with Nawabzada Khizar Hayat Khan, the son of Sir Umar Hayat Khan. He is showing distinct ability and common sense, and I believe that he is going to be a real success.

6. There have been no serious reactions from Panipat or Kot Fateh Khan but neither affair is yet liquidated. I gave Your Excellency the first information we received about Kot Fateh Khan. Subsequent reports show that it was a very bad affair. Considerable damage was done to the gurdwara, and one of the Sikh *sewadars* or ministers was badly assaulted while he was reading the *Granth Sahib*, which was desecrated by his blood. Fiery speeches were naturally made at Sikh meetings and there was talk of large bands of Sikhs attending the Baisakhi Fair which was held a few days after the incident. Fortunately the attendance was comparatively small, and police arrangements were sufficient to prevent trouble. There is now talk of efforts to reach a permanent settlement of the dispute, and I hope that these will be successful. The fact that there have been no immediate reactions of a serious nature shows that at present there is a feeling abroad

among responsible persons that communal matters should be kept in the background. This feeling, however, is very far from general. The question of loaves and fishes is continually cropping up in one form or another, and all the communities watch every appointment that is made. Apart from this, there is a certain number of irresponsibles who are deliberately planning to stir up communal trouble in order to embarrass the Ministry. For instance, one gang hopes to revive the Shahidganj agitation, purely for political purposes.

7. There are persistent reports that Congress intend to make a dead set against the Punjab in order to show that the constitution cannot be worked. As elsewhere, they are trying to bring in Muslims and have made an alliance with the Ahrars. Pandit Jawaharlal has also interested himself in a dispute between landlords and tenants in the Gurgaon district. The estate concerned belonged originally to the Skinners and is now owned by the Ingrams, who are related to the family. The landlords have done a great deal for their tenants, and Brayne considers that the villages of the estate are the best in the Punjab. One village has been giving a certain amount of trouble out of which a local Muslim leader saw the opportunity of making some personal profit. Apparently Congress now intend to take a hand in the affair and there may be developments. Congress have also published their intention of setting up a committee to go into the question of corruption. It is perhaps not irrelevant that I saw today an intercepted letter from the President of the Provincial Congress Committee asking a friend of his to persuade an examiner in the Intermediate Examination to cook the marks in physics in favour of the daughter of another Congressman who was afraid she had done badly in the paper!! It is a pity that one cannot always publish the information one has.

Yours sincerely,
H.W. EMERSON

9

EMERSON TO LINLITHGOW

Confidential

Camp, Barog,
May 8th, 1937

My dear Lord Linlithgow,

In my last letter of the 24th of April 1937 I referred to the speech made by Sir Sikander Hyat Khan on the adjournment motion arising out of the Secretary of State's speech regarding the non-acceptance of office by Congress. I had not then read a full report of Sir Sikander's speech which was not available at the time. I now enclose a copy.[4] While it followed the general lines I indicated, my brief account did not do justice to the speaker. It was, in fact, a bold defence of the attitude taken in the Punjab and a condemnation of the attitude taken by Congress.

2. The Coronation celebrations will be on a wide scale in the Punjab. There has so far been no dissenting note, and it appears certain that the celebrations will be held in all places of any size throughout the Province. Government have sanctioned the same expenditure as on the occasion of the Silver Jubilee of His Late Majesty King George V. Local bodies appear to be contributing reasonable amounts, and in the larger towns public funds have been opened. There will be a special programme in Simla. Lahore has a strong committee and the celebrations will be on an extensive scale. Generally, they will take the form of religious services by the various communities, distribution to children and the poor, illuminations of Government and private buildings, fireworks, &c. Boy Scouts will take a prominent part. There will be a general holiday on the 12th, and a second holiday is being given in Government offices, except Treasuries, and in educational institutions. Enquiry from banks and business firms showed that they deprecated a second general holiday under the Negotiable Instruments Act as the present time is a very busy one with the wheat about to come on the market. It may be assumed that the celebrations will be on a fitting scale and carried out in a genuine spirit of loyalty.

3. I have already mentioned that the provincial revenue for the year will be seriously affected by the remissions it has been necessary to give on account of damage caused by hailstorms. The area mainly concerned is the Multan division where a disastrous storm affected a long belt situated in the Muzaffargarh, Multan, Lyallpur and Montgomery districts, and varying in breadth from a mile or two to 15 miles. Six or seven hundred villages came in the path of the storm and in at least half of this number the crop was wiped out. Some days later there was a bad dust storm in part of this area, and this shrivelled a good deal of the wheat that had survived the hail. Prompt measures were taken to inspect the villages concerned and to give generous remissions, and the initial concessions were supplemented as soon as news came of the further damage which was not discovered until the wheat was on the threshing-floor. In addition, a lakh of rupees was sanctioned for gratuitous relief. Sir Sunder Singh, the Revenue Minister, has toured the area and was warmly received. He says that the people were very grateful indeed for the prompt action taken and for the generous scale of remissions. Government have undoubtedly got a good deal of credit out of the action taken.

What may prove to be in the long run a more serious calamity is the almost complete failure of the gram crop in the Rawalpindi division and in parts of the Multan and Lahore divisions. The cause appears to have been excessive and unseasonable rains during the cold weather. They seem to have encouraged the spread of a disease known as gram-blight. Previously the only part of the Province in which this had occurred on any serious scale was the Attock district where a few years ago it practically wiped out the crop. Preventive measures have been in force there for several years, the Agricultural and the Revenue Departments working together. Until this year the results had been very good, and it was hoped that the disease was completely under control. The preventive measures are:

(*i*) Eradication of disease-affected plants when detected during the period of growth.
(*ii*) Burning of the stubble in the affected fields.
(*iii*) Avoiding such fields for the next year's crop.
(*iv*) Use of new and pure seed.

This year the blight spread with extraordinary rapidity, and the area was so extensive that it was quite impossible to take preventive measures while the crop was on the ground. The Agricultural Department do not think that it will be practicable to deal effectively with the disease before next harvest, and they are very pessimistic. Every effort will, however, be made to do what is possible. Gram is not an important crop except in a few districts in the north of the Province, and in most places wheat can be substituted for it. There is one area, however, in which this is not possible. In the Thal tract of Mianwali district it is the main source of revenue to Government and the people. This area consists of very light soil, with many sandhills, no means of irrigation and it is dependent on a scanty rainfall. Up to 15 years ago it was almost completely barren. It was then discovered that with very little rain fine crops of gram could be produced. The blight has got into this area also, but the intention is to make special efforts here to mitigate the effects next harvest. It is possible that, if seasonal conditions are favourable next year, the area affected may be small, since the weather seems to be an important factor. The Ministers are alive to the importance of this matter.

The total amount of remissions of land revenue and water rates involved in these two calamities is likely to be Rs. 25 lakhs.

4. The Akali or extremists party of the Sikhs is steadily losing ground. As I have mentioned in previous letters, the success of the Khalsa National Party led by Sir Sunder Singh in the Assembly elections was greater than had been expected, although a good number of candidates were elected on the Akali ticket. The Akali successes would have been fewer had they

not used religious funds for the purpose of bribing the electorate. Under the Sikh Gurdwaras Act, which was passed about 1925, the control of all Sikh shrines of any importance was vested in special or local committees under the general control of the Shiromani Gurdwara Parbandhak Committee. For years the central committee and most of the special and local committees have been in the hands of the Akalis. The administration of the shrines and the funds attaching to them (which in the case of the more important are large) has been very unsatisfactory, and Sir Sunder Singh's success in the elections reflected to some extent the growing dissatisfaction of the Sikh public. It is an open secret that religious funds were used for election purposes by the Akalis. A complaint to this effect was lodged before the District Magistrate of Amritsar,[5] and, since the complaint revealed a cognisable offence, it was taken up by the police. Cases of embezzlement are now under investigation, and there will certainly be enough evidence to produce them in court. The Akali leaders are very perturbed, while the Sikh public are watching developments with the keenest interest. Master Tara Singh, who has been the outstanding figure in Akali circles for some years, is apparently involved in the embezzlements. Whatever the result of the criminal cases may be, the credit of the Akalis will be severely shaken.

Baba Kharak Singh, a very stormy petrel, has just been released from jail after serving a sentence for sedition. He is very fanatical, entirely irresponsible, unrestrained in his language and likes to be always in the limelight. He was largely responsible for the Shahidganj trouble, since the excitement he caused at a critical moment among the Sikhs gathered at Lahore made it impossible for the so-called Sikh leaders to keep their followers under control. He will probably try to cause more trouble, but is likely to bring himself quickly within the mischief of the law.

5. Congress efforts to capture Muslims continue, but there seem to me to be signs of Muslim feeling hardening against Congress. The controversy between Jinnah and Jawaharlal and the attack of the latter on Fazl-ul-Haq are not helping Congress with the Muslim public generally, although in the towns there is always a certain number of Muslims ready to take any side which will bring them into the limelight. I have heard that the All-India Congress Committee has allotted a large sum for the conversion of Muslims generally to the Congress creed, and that about Rs. 30,000 has been allotted for propaganda in the Punjab. Dr. Alam is said to be the chief agent of the Congress. If this is true, a considerable portion of the allotment is likely to stick in his pocket.

Yours sincerely,
H.W. EMERSON

10

EMERSON TO LINLITHGOW

Confidential

Barnes Court, Simla, E.,
May 22nd, 1937

My dear Lord Linlithgow,

Full reports have not been received regarding the Coronation celebrations in the Province, but it is clear that demonstrations of loyalty were on a very big scale and were spontaneous. I have been told, for instance, by several people that in Lahore the population turned out in their best clothes and in a holiday spirit, that the main street was crowded till the early hours of the morning, and that everyone was in the best of temper. Similar reports come from other towns. There were practically no attempts by any political body to boycott the celebrations, and where any such attempt was made it was a complete failure. The conclusion seems to be that the events of last December have not impaired in any way the traditional sense of loyalty towards the Throne.

2. In my last letter I mentioned that there seemed to be signs of Muslim feeling hardening against Congress. This is now definitely the case. One reason is that Congress are attempting to ignore Muslim leaders and approach the Muslim masses direct. Another is the arrogant spirit shown generally by Pandit Jawahalal, and reflected in statements made by Kripalani, the Secretary of the All-India Congress Committee. Sir Sikander Hyat Khan, in replying to a deputation of the All-India Kshatri Conference, made a strong speech against Congress pretensions. I attach a copy. This was entirely on his own initiative, and, in fact, when he showed me the draft of his speech, I advised him to tone down one or two passages which he did. He tells me that the speech was made in consequence of representations made by Muslim members of the Unionist Party among whom the feeling against Congress is greatly increasing. This feeling is shared by the rural Hindu Minister, Rao Bahadur Sir Chhotu Ram, who carries with him the Jats of the South-Eastern districts of the Province. Before Sikander spoke, Chhotu Ram had done a tour in the districts of Ludhiana, Jullundur and Hoshiarpur, where Congress and Communist parties are particularly active. He visited a number of villages and addressed informally several meetings at which the attendance amounted to two or three thousand. He spoke freely against Congress and found the people ready to listen, although the audience included a certain number of Akalis

and other extremists. The general line he took was to attack them for their lack of any constructive work and for their failure to take the chance offered to them in those Provinces where they were in a majority. This again was entirely on his own initiative.

Generally, it seems to me that history is repeating itself. Congress arrogance is increasing the apprehensions among Muslims of Hindu domination, and communal feeling will soon reach a dangerous level. Congress may be able to get a few adherents among Muslims, but every success in this direction will strengthen the feeling of Muslims as a community against them.

3. Chhotu Ram had not previously seen what was being done in the way of rural reconstruction in the three districts mentioned above. He was very greatly impressed, especially with the consolidation of holdings, the agricultural associations and private farms, and the improvement of villages. In Hoshiarpur district, for instance, there is a very keen District Officer of Health,[6] who in eighteen months has collected voluntarily Rs. 1½ lakhs, which has been spent on the paving of villages, improvement of water-supply, &c. The result of the Minister's visit is interesting. Chhotu Ram has long been an advocate of a reduction of land revenue. He now sees that there cannot be any substantial reduction and constructive work continue on the same scale. He is fast becoming a convert to the latter.

4. In the meantime, the Ministry has to anticipate attacks by the opposition on the land revenue system. A popular demand for some years has been that it should be based on the principles of income-tax assessment. Feeling that this demand would be renewed, the supporters of Government have themselves asked for a committee to examine the question. It is the present intention of Sikander to appoint a small official committee. The supporters of the demand have really only one incidence of income-tax assessment in mind, namely, the exemption of incomes below a certain minimum. They overlook other incidences of income-tax which are not so favourable, especially to big land-owners. For instance, there are the following incidences of income-tax:

(*i*) a graduated scale, the rate increasing with the income;
(*ii*) super-tax:
(*iii*) liability to increase or reduction in the rate from year to year as compared with the present guarantee of 40 years in the case of land revenue;
(*iv*) no limitation on the maximum enhancement that can be taken; and
(*v*) no limitation on the share of profits.

The Punjab is so essentially a Province of small holdings that much as one may sympathise with the small man, it is almost impracticable to devise any system which will give him appreciable relief without crippling provincial finances. In one direction a move has already been made towards basing the land revenue demand more closely than formerly on the actual income, since under the sliding-scale system the demand to be collected depends roughly on current prices and increases or decreases as these rise or fall. The system has been already introduced in the Lower Bari Doab Canal Colony and the Lyallpur district, and it is the intention to apply it in the Lahore and Amritsar districts which are under re-settlement.

5. The fortnight has been comparatively quiet. Last night there was information of a stay-in strike in the Railway Workshops at Lahore, involving six or seven thousand workers. This morning it seems probable that the strike will fizzle out. There has also been some labour trouble in two or three small factories, and agitators seem to be busy among the workers. Apart from the Railway Workshops, there are very few big industrial undertakings in the Province, and, except when railway workers have given trouble, labour problems have given little serious concern.

There has also been trouble at the Khalsa College, Amritsar. Full details are not yet available, but the following statement has been issued by the Principal:

> 'An unfortunate incident has caused some temporary excitement at the Khalsa College, Amritsar. On the 17th instant a pamphlet appeared against a professor of the Khalsa College. Some copies were thrown surreptitiously in the quarters of the staff without the knowledge of the College authorities. This was resented by the students and the staff, and in order to give expression of their feelings some students came to the Principal, who assured them that he was as much aggrieved as they and that he was ready to express his resentment in public. They were naturally satisfied with his reply and went away in good humour.
>
> 'Some evil influences began to work however, and at dead of night students in different hostels were aroused from sleep and were asked to stay away from their classes in the morning. The Principal not to lose time issued a note condemning the pamphlet in the severest terms possible and got it posted in the college and the hostels.
>
> 'The ringleaders picketed the gates, preventing the students from attending their classes. They were approached by the Principal, but they would not listen to reason and persisted in interfering with incoming students. Four of them were, therefore, rusticated for one year.

The staff in a meeting unanimously endorsed the action of the Principal both in condemning the distribution of the pamphlet and in taking action against the offending students. The meeting was resumed in the evening and two more were rusticated.

'The strike of the students was not successful, and most of them were convinced that no ground existed for any grievances. The leaders were, however, not to be deterred. They summoned men from outside, who utilised a meeting of the students held outside the premises of the college and indulged in most virulent attacks on the management of the college.

'The students, who were present, were much excited. They marched along with a number of outsiders to the house of the Principal, shouting slogans and demanding the withdrawal of the rustication order.

'This morning some students, reinforced by Akalis from outside, picketed the gates of the college. The aid of the police had to be summoned. The crowd refusing to disperse on the order of a Magistrate, a *lathi* charge was made, and the crowd dispersed. One man, an outsider, who received injuries, was removed to the hospital.

'The college is working, though some students from the city could not attend the classes owing to the disturbance at the gate. A few are keeping themselves away from the classes.'

The Chairman of the Managing Committee of the Khalsa College is Sir Sunder Singh Majithia, the Revenue Minister. Attempts have previously been made by his enemies to create trouble in the college, and it will probably be found that this is the case in the present instance also.

Yours sincerely,
H.W. EMERSON

ENCLOSURE TO NO. 10

SPEECH BY SIKANDER HYAT KHAN TO
ALL-INDIA KSHATRI CONFERENCE

Mr Durga Das and Gentlemen,

I am glad to have this opportunity of meeting you today. Your energetic and enthusiastic President apparently does not believe in allowing grass to grow under your feet. Soon after the annual session of the Conference he wrote and pressed for an early date for an interview. He followed his letter up by a personal visit and would not budge until he had got me to fix this date for our meeting. As you are aware, my time is more than full at present, but I could not resist your irresistible President. Your community deserves to be congratulated on their discerning choice of a President who will, I am confident, give a wise lead to the community and with his usual vigour and zeal put new life into the organisation which you represent.

2. Before I deal with the various matters mentioned in your address, I should like to express my gratitude and thanks for your kind reference to me and for your cordial assurance of support to the new Government. Your offer of help is doubly welcome, coming as it does from the representatives of a community which can look back with pride to its glorious traditions and achievements in the sphere of Government from time immemorial. I have no doubt that, as in the past so also in the future, your community will continue to play an important role in the administrative, economic, social, and political life of the province and the country.

3. I am at one with you in your assessment of the possibilities of the new Constitution. As you say, in spite of its limitations, it implies the transfer of power to a Government responsible to the people of the province. I would go even further and say that there is no danger of or opportunity for interference by the Governors so long as the representatives of the people entrusted with the task of administering the province, conduct the affairs of the State as a good Government should do – conscientiously, diligently and impartially. A Government which deliberately ignores or fails to protect the legitimate rights of the minorities, the services, or for that matter of any class of community entrusted to its care cannot be termed a just or even a popular Government in the true sense of the term. Again, if a provincial Government is incapable of preserving peace and tranquillity of the province or, to take an extreme example, deliberately sets about to encourage lawlessness and violence, would it be fair to the society, the province and the country to allow it to pursue, untrammelled, a course of wanton destruction and bloodshed? It is to meet such eventualities that special powers of the Governors find a place in the Government of India Act. And do not let us imagine that the inclusion of these powers marks a constitutional innovation specially devised for the benefit of India. Similar safeguards have figured in the Constitutions granted to other Dominions before us. It is true that they have been rarely, if at all, used in those Dominions and have since fallen into desuetude; but, as I have said, if the provincial Governments acquit themselves of their responsibilities as is expected of a responsible Government, there is no reason why those provisions in our case also should not prove to be equally innocuous. I

fail to understand the attitude of a section of my countrymen who are refusing to exercise their legitimate right as a majority party. To an outsider their refusal to take Office on the assurance issue seems inexplicable except on the ground that they either do not wish to see the New Constitution successfully worked in any province or else are using it as a convenient pretext to avoid inconvenient issues *vis-à-vis* the electorate. No one would be happier than myself if these conjectures turn out to be incorrect and our Congress brethren even now decide, in fairness to their constituents, to come forward and shoulder the responsibility which by all constitutional canons is theirs to bear. The suggestion that in the event of a conflict of views between the Governor and his Ministers the use of special powers should be confined to a dismissal of the Ministry followed by an appeal to the electorate shows a callous disregard for the interests and feelings of the minorities. This formula, which is sponsored by Mahatma Gandhi and seems to have the approval of other prominent Congressmen, conceals a dangerous fallacy, and, if rigidly applied, might conceivably result in relegating the minorities to a position of political *Shudras* and a state of perpetual serfdom – a result which I am sure Mahatma Gandhi does not intend or wish to produce. So long as this feeling exists it is idle to blame the minorities for evincing their anxiety and resentment over the present domineering attitude of the Congress. The recent statement of Acharaya Kripalani, the Congress Secretary, in answer to Mr. Jinnah's criticism of the Congress plan for roping in the Muslim masses surpasses all others for its arrogance and unveiled hostility to the minority interests and cannot but add to the apprehensions of the minority communities regarding the treatment which they are likely to get from the majority party in the provinces in which the Congress dominates. If we were to look at the problem from a narrow and parochial point of view, my party and I should feel tempted to welcome this formula which would give a free-hand in dealing with the minorities in our own province. But fair-play and duty to our Motherland dictate otherwise; and in spite of the provocation which pronouncements of the type recently made by Acharaya Kripalani not unnaturally offer to the majority community in our own province, we are determined to adhere unswervingly to the basic principle of our policy, viz., to give a fair deal to our brethren of the minority communities. It is our fixed conviction that if a majority party in a Provincial Legislature desires immunity from interference by the Governor of the protection of minorities, the only honourable course open to it is to try and arm itself with the goodwill and confidence of those communities in a province.

Further I fail to understand how the dignity and prestige of Ministers to which we all attach the utmost importance will be enhanced by their dismissal rather than voluntary resignation. It is an insult to Ministers, representatives of the people, to suppose that they will not zealously guard their honour if and when the necessity arises.

I trust you will forgive me for dealing at some length on this important constitutional point; but since you had referred to the constitutional changes in your address and in view of the importance of this particular aspect of the problem which is exercising the minds of all patriotic Indians at the moment, I have availed myself of this opportunity to explain my own point of view as well as the attitude of my party in regard to this important issue which ultimately concerns the minorities in the provincial sphere to whatever denomination they may belong.

Now let us proceed to consider the economic problems mentioned in your address which to us in the Punjab are of even greater moment than the constitutional problems which seem to be exercising the ingenuity of our countrymen in several other provinces. I appreciate the laudable public spirit which has actuated you to avoid a reference to past controversies. As you say, we should be content to look ahead and to plan for the future instead of indulging in the unprofitable pastime of raking up past controversies. I unhesitatingly endorse the view expressed by you that the problem which confronts us is one of balanced development so that every part in the body-politic may contribute of its best towards the general well-being of the province. The problem of debt and of agricultural finance to which you have referred are indeed of vital importance and the question of finding suitable outlets for a profitable employment of their time and money, to the professional and other classes is no less important. But the main theme of your address, not unnaturally, is the working of the Punjab Land Alienation Act and its effect on the community which you represent. I therefore propose to confine my reply mainly to an elucidation of the position regarding this measure. Let me at the outset express the view that I do not consider the Land Alienation Act as sacrosanct in the sense that like the laws of the Medes and Persians it is for all times unalterable; but at the same time I venture to remark that he would be a bold person indeed who, in view of the present circumstances and conditions, can assert that the time has come for its repeal.

Before I attempt to answer the specific points raised in your address, allow me to refer very briefly to the genesis of the Punjab Land Alienation Act. You are no doubt aware, that the agrarian riots in the Deccan in the eighties of the last century were originally responsible for focussing the attention of the Central Government and the various provincial administrations, including our own, on the agrarian problem. In the Punjab the late Mr. Thorburn, a distinguished Civilian of his period, as a result of his personal observations and enquiries had come to the conclusion, even before the matter was officially taken up, that agricultural land was rapidly passing from the possession of the tillers of the soil into the hands of the moneylender. He recorded the result of his enquiries in a series of interesting and illuminating notes which he submitted to Government from time to time. His forceful advocacy on behalf of the peasant; and the vivid picture which he presented of the likely results of a policy of inaction, and its consequent dangers to society succeeded in bringing home to the Government of the day the need for instituting an official enquiry. The result of the official enquiry which was instituted during the last decade of the last century, not only completely substantiated Mr. Thorburn's conclusions, but disclosed a state of affairs which indicated even more clearly the imperative need for early legislative action. It was then that the Punjab Government moved the Central Government to introduce a Bill which was subsequently passed into the present Act. The introduction of this Legislation in the Imperial Council was preceded by an exhaustive examination of the various provisions of the Bill by an expert committee, as also by individual executive and judicial officers of experience. The Punjab Alienation of Land Act is essentially a class-measure devised to protect the peasantry of the province against expropriation by monied classes. It cannot be denied that but for the timely enactment of this measure the Punjab peasant, who is appropriately described as the backbone of the province, might conceivably have been a source of danger to the province and a menace to society and in particular to the class which you represent. It is not difficult to conjure up a picture of what might have happened if 90 per cent. of the population of this province had been deprived of their only source of livelihood. If that was the condition nearly 40 years ago, you can well imagine the consequences of a reversal of that policy today. Apart from economic factors, other forces are at work today which aim at exploitation of the peasant, with the object of bringing about a violent upheaval in the country. Lest I may have painted too gloomy a picture, let me assure you that, as far as our own province is concerned, we need have no apprehension of any such calamity occurring so long as our present policy, of keeping the interests of the peasantry in the forefront, continues to find a prominent place in the programme of the Government of the day. You and I are agreed on this fundamental principle, because I understand that your present objective is not to undermine the efficacy of the Land Alienation Act, but to secure an examination of certain provisions of the Act, which you consider are operating harshly on non-agricultural classes without securing any substantial advantage to the classes whom the Act is meant to benefit.

I will now take up your proposal *seriatim* and briefly indicate my views with regard to each one of them.

You have suggested that the provisions of the Act should apply uniformly to cultivators and agriculturists from whichever community, tribe or group they may be drawn. As I have already explained, the Act is primarily meant to protect agriculturists against expropriation, irrespective of their community, caste or tribe. The main considerations which are kept in view in deciding whether a particular tribe or group needs protection are:

(*i*) that the tribe or group as a whole are dependent mainly on agriculture for their livelihood;
(*ii*) that they are sufficiently important both as regards numbers and the area which they own, and
(*iii*) that they are losing land to an extent and at a rate which would justify the extension of protection to them.

There is thus, no bar to the inclusion of any group or class of community in the category of 'notified agricultural tribes' provided they fulfil the main conditions which I have just enumerated.

Your next suggestion is that moneylenders, from whichever class they are drawn, should be subject to uniform standards of legal obligation. I am in complete sympathy with your views in this matter, and I can unhesitatingly give you an undertaking that the suggestion will be sympathetically and carefully examined at an early date with a view to bringing all moneylenders within the purview of the legislation affecting moneylenders.

Your third proposal aims at securing that land up to a certain limit irrespective of whether it is owned by notified agriculturists or others should be made inalienable, and you further suggest that area beyond the prescribed limit should become a commercial proposition by which I believe you mean that it should be open to sale and transfer even if it is owned by notified agriculturists. The first part of this proposal seems at first sight attractive; but there is an obvious objection which strikes one on a maturer consideration and I will try to explain it in some detail. Even if we fix the limit at the low figure of (say) 20-25 acres – and you must remember that the average holding in the Punjab is much below this figure – you would be imposing a disability, which at present is confined to notified agriculturists alone, on almost 7/8th of the land-owners in this province. I speak subject to correction, as I have not had time to verify my estimate of the number which would be affected. But assuming that my figures are approximately correct, it is obvious that you would be restricting the credit of those classes, which depend on occupations other than agriculture, to an extent which would seriously hamper trade and adversely affect the resources and income of those classes who are at present engaged in business and trade in the rural areas. These trades almost invariably obtain their stock-in-trade on the security of their landed property. However, the suggestion is one which merits examination and, without committing myself to any particular course of action as a result of that examination, I can promise you that it will receive due consideration. The latter part of this proposal, if given effect to, would strike at the very root of the Land Alienation Act, and I trust that, in view of what I have said in the earlier part of my reply, you will agree that the present time is hardly opportune to justify even a cursory examination of this aspect of your proposal. In addition to these main suggestions you have mentioned several other points on which you would like Government to make an enquiry. They are:

(*i*) That a certain economic unit may be fixed for land which is declared inalienable.

(*ii*) That where moneylending issues are not involved, land may be sold and purchased for investment purposes.

(*iii*) That land round Municipal or small towns or notified areas up to a certain mileage may be exempted from the operations of the Act to enable expansion of such towns or areas and development of healthy living quarters. Incidentally this will help the agriculturists materially.

(*iv*) That lands required for industrial purposes be free from the operations of the Act.

(*v*) That the orders of the Deputy Commissioner granting sanction for alienation of land should not be subject to review by the Financial Commissioner or any higher revenue authority.

(*vi*) That the lands of persons who have taken to professions or are in service drawing a salary subject to income-tax and of landowners paying certain amount of land revenue or above be free from the restrictions imposed by the Act.

(*vii*) That the definition of the term 'agriculturist' be made solely dependent upon actual engagement in the work of cultivation and not on hereditary rights or tribal groupings.

As regards the first point, I have already promised an examination.

Your second point has also been dealt with under general survey of the Land Alienation Act; and, in any case, it is only of academic interest as the land belonging to agriculturists which is free from debt constitutes an infinitesimal proportion of the area owned by them: and where it is free from debt you may be sure that the last thing which an agriculturist would do is to sell his land. As for non-agriculturists, the question does not arise as they have even now the fullest freedom to sell and purchase land.

Your third point deserves consideration and will be examined. As far as the municipal and cantonment areas are concerned, even now the restrictions imposed by the Act on the freedom of transfer of land are not operative.

Your fourth point will also be examined; but an obvious reply to your suggestions seems to be that even now land belonging to agriculturists can be acquired for industrial purposes with the sanction of the Deputy Commissioner or where necessary, under the Land Acquisition Act.

Your fifth point would involve an amendment of the Act in respect of an important principle and must, therefore, be ruled out for the present. Moreover, apart from other considerations, it is not likely to appeal to the Legislature as it runs counter to the established principles of law relating to appeals and revisions. You must also remember that this provision gives a valuable right to the vendor to appeal against the order of the Deputy Commissioner when permission to sell land is refused.

Your sixth point again refers to a fundamental principle of the Act. It must, therefore, be left over for consideration until there is a radical improvement in the conditions.

Your seventh and the last point, I believe, has already been sufficiently answered in a previous part of my reply where I pointed out that there is no bar to inclusion, in the category of notified agriculturists, of tribes of groups of persons who are primarily dependent on agriculture for a living if they fulfil the conditions already enumerated by me. I may for your information mention that the process of adding fresh groups and tribes to the list of notified agriculturists has been continually going on ever since the enactment of the Land Alienation Act. Some of the more important recent additions are:

1. Sainis in Montgomery and Multan.
2. Gaur Brahmans in Ambala.
3. Muhiyal Brahmans in Gujrat and Gurdaspur.
4. Mahtams in Muzaffargarh.
5. Dogars in Montgomery.
6. Indian Christians in certain colony districts.
7. Harnis in Ludhiana.

May I add for your information that non-agriculturists can freely purchase Government land earmarked for sale in the colonies. You will be interested to learn that Government has recently allotted several *Chaks* to educated grantees who have undertaken to cultivate land with their own hands. These grants were open both to agriculturists and non-agriculturists; but preference was given to those who did not own any land. I am glad you agree with me that it is of the utmost importance for a province like ours to place the interests of the peasant in the forefront before all other considerations. In the larger interests of the State, as also in the interests of those classes who like you have a considerable stake in the country, it is up to us all to make a combined effort to improve the lot of the peasant, and to devise means for increasing his purchasing power, for the prosperity of all classes whether they are engaged in business, trade or professions depends on the prosperity of the peasant. One of the urgent needs of the moment is the reformation of the moneylender. He can both be a blessing and a menace to the countryside. If he is honest and reasonable and straight in his dealings, he is a boon to the villager. On the other hand, a rapacious and dishonest moneylender is a menace to the society and the State and the sooner this type is weeded out the better for all concerned. I confidently hope that the Government can rely on you for co-operation and support in stamping out this objectionable variety of the moneylender who on account of his rapacity and dishonesty is mainly responsible for engendering prejudice and hatred against the whole class whose usefulness to the agriculturist community cannot be denied or underrated and which provides an important link in the credit machinery of the country.

I am afraid I have taxed your patience by the inordinate length of my reply to your address; but you will, I trust, concede that the importance of the subject demanded that I should attempt to elucidate the position at some length for the benefit of all concerned. If you find my reply somewhat less satisfactory than you anticipated or may be even disappointing in some respects, I hope you will not judge me too harshly as in explaining the position frankly and unreservedly I have only tried to discharge the duty which both you and I owe to the people of this province. But before I conclude let me assure you that your community can always rely on the present Government for a fair deal.

Gentlemen, I thank you again.

11

EMERSON TO LINLITHGOW[7]

Confidential

Barnes Court, Simla, E.,
June 5th, 1937

My dear Lord Linlithgow,

In my last letter I mentioned that there had been trouble at the Khalsa College, Amritsar. This is the most important educational institution of the Sikhs in India, and is run by a Managing Committee under the presidency of Sir Sunder Singh Majithia, my Revenue Minister. The trouble still continues. It has been fomented by Sikh extremists, hostile to Sir Sunder Singh, and encouraged by political agitators generally. A disquieting feature has been the sympathy given by students associations elsewhere. The root cause of the difficulties of the College for some time has been the presence on the staff of two professors of extremist views. One of these is the brother of Master Tara Singh, the Akali leader, and the Committee have hesitated to get rid of him partly for this reason. They will probably have to do so in the end. So far the Managing Committee have taken a strong line and have refused to take back rusticated students without a satisfactory apology. A day or two ago a settlement seemed likely, but this has broken down. The Committee have been promised all reasonable assistance from the District Magistrate, and, although the intervention of the police at their request may accentuate the trouble for the time being, it is very desirable on general grounds that indiscipline among students should be checked.

2. There has also been trouble at the Government Engineering School at Rasul in the Gujrat district. The cause of the trouble is communal. A Muslim member of staff took upon himself to give special coaching to Muslim students for the forthcoming examination, on the results of which appointments are to be made to a certain number of Government posts. The Hindus heard of this, suspected that he had knowledge of the examination papers to be sat and was giving the Muslim students valuable information. They went into the classroom to protest and apparently two of them went into the mosque with shoes on. The agitation then increased, and eventually about 50 students, in defiance of the orders of the Principal, left the School to proceed to Simla to lay their grievances before the Minister. Fortunately they were deterred from reaching there. It has, however, been necessary to close the School temporarily, and an enquiry

is to be held into the case. It will almost certainly be necessary to make changes in the staff. The attitude of the Ministry is, so far, sound, but a good deal of communal capital is likely to be made out of the affair.

3. In my letters of the 19th of December, 1936, and 21st January 1937, I referred to difficulties over processions in Rawalpindi. An agreement was reached in January last by which the Sikhs and Muslims were to abandon the old routes of processions after the Sikhs had been allowed to use the old route on the occasion of Guru Gobind Singh's birthday, which they did without serious trouble occurring. The next occasion for a procession was on May, 23rd, the anniversary of the Prophet's birthday. The Muslims refused to take out any procession rather than go by the new route, and the Sikhs are claiming that this is a breach of the agreement. This, however, is not the case. A Sikh procession is due in a few days and it remains to be seen whether the Sikhs will agree to the new route. In any case, they will not be allowed to use the old one.

4. While Muslims realise that, if Congress are ready to accept office in the six minority provinces, it is out of the question to refuse facilities to them, they would prefer the deadlock to continue. They are none too pleased with Gandhi's latest move. They are particularly anxious that no concession should be given to Congress.

5. Your Excellency will no doubt have seen a copy of the Haveli Project which has become practicable as a result of the recommendations of the Committee which sat on the distribution of the supplies of the Indus. A copy of all the relevant papers was also sent by the Government of India to the India Office.[8] Briefly, the scheme will provide improved irrigation in a large area in the Multan district, which is now served either by inundation canals or by partially controlled supplies, and will also give irrigation in some areas now dependent on rainfall. Provision for the scheme is included in the budget which will be placed before the Legislature in a few days. It is certain to be approved, and some work has, in fact, been started in anticipation of sanction.

6. The acceptance of the Committee's recommendations has also made possible what is known as the Thal Project. This will give perennial irrigation direct from the Indus in parts of the Mianwali and Muzaffargarh districts at present dependent on rainfall. A project has been prepared and is now under examination both on the revenue and expenditure sides. Prima facie it should be remunerative, but, until the scrutiny by experts is complete, it is premature to be definite on this point. If the project is financially sound, I have little doubt that Government will wish to start it

with the least delay, probably at the end of the cold weather of 1938. I will let Your Excellency have further information about it in due course.

Yours sincerely,
H.W. EMERSON

P.S. After writing the above, I have just been told by the Premier that the Khalsa College strike has been settled on a form of apology from the students which the Managing Committee regard as satisfactory.

12

EMERSON TO LINLITHGOW

Confidential

Barnes Court, Simla, E.,
June 19th, 1937

My dear Lord Linlithgow,

The communal situation between Muslims and Sikhs has greatly deteriorated during the past few days, and is at present the cause of considerable anxiety. The immediate cause has been trouble in the Gujrat district. For some months there has been friction between the two communities in that district, manifested by a series of incidents which, although trivial in themselves, indicated that feeling was bad. Early this month a *Nihang* Sikh was murdered in the village Ala. There was no reliable clue to the murder, and the relatives of the deceased appear to have mentioned both Muslims and Hindus as suspects. The Sikhs, however, made up their mind that it was a communal murder, and decided to trail their coats in a predominantly Muslim area. They advertised a *diwan* to be held in the village where the murder had taken place, and provocative posters appear to have been published. The Muslims of the village sent out word that their lives and property were in danger, and the countryside appears to have been greatly perturbed. At any rate on the 13th June, when Sikhs began to arrive from outside at a neighbouring railway station, attacks were made on them by Muslim mobs, and although the police did their best to give protection to Sikhs proceeding to the *diwan,* further attacks were made on them by considerable crowds at a number of points. The police had to open fire three times. As a result of attacks by Muslims two or three Sikhs were killed and about 16 injured. Five Muslims have died as a result of the firing, and eight or ten are known to have been wounded. It is probable that other wounded Muslims have concealed themselves in the villages. About 40 villages of Muslims appear to have been concerned in the rioting, and this is the most serious part of the business, since it is something new for villages to be engaged on this scale in communal fights. Great indignation was caused among the Sikhs as soon as the news of this affair got abroad. The situation in Gujrat was quickly brought under control, although I think we shall be lucky if we do not have future reactions there. But the effects outside were at once apparent in inflammatory speeches at meetings and violent articles in the press. The body of a Sikh who had died was sent from Gujrat to his home in Amritsar. Yesterday morning, the 18th, a funeral procession of about 10,000 was taken out. Although the procession was required to avoid Muslim *mohallas*, the members of it seem to have gone completely wild as it proceeded, and they attacked any Muslim indiscriminately who came in their way. Our present information is that about 60 Muslims were injured, of whom one has died and at least one more is expected to die. The communal riot scheme was immediately put into force, a Company of British troops was put into the city and precautions were taken to prevent the trouble spreading. These appear to have been successful and up to midday this morning there is no information of any reprisals by Muslims. Tense feeling, however, is likely to be caused among Muslims throughout the Province. An unusual feature of this affair is its one-sided character, and also the absence, so far as present information goes, of any provocation by the Muslims of Amritsar. Even before the Amritsar affair feeling in Lahore was reported to be tense, and it was apprehended that, when news of rioting at Amritsar reached Lahore, there might be trouble there. Elaborate precautions were therefore taken to meet this danger if it materialised. As a matter of fact, the present information is that there was comparatively little excitement in Lahore last night, but news of Amritsar events may not have reached there, and there may still be reactions. Precautions are therefore being observed for the next two or three days. The serious aspect is that events both in Gujrat and in Amritsar indicate the tense feeling existing between the two communities. The enmity between the two is of course a matter of history. It is always there and is certain to remain. The Shahidganj affair greatly embittered the situation, and events in Kot Fateh Khan and Rawalpindi increased the bitterness. In the northern districts of the Province Sikhs are in a very small minority, but this has not prevented them from being very provocative on occasions. It is now clear that Muslims in the Rawalpindi division can be very easily aroused to take aggressive action. On the other hand, although as a direct or indirect consequence of Shahidganj, there has been a number of isolated murders of Sikhs by fanatical Muslims, the Sikhs have, generally speaking, not hitherto attempted to take reprisals, but events at Amritsar yesterday show that that stage has passed. It looks as if for the next few months the situation will be tense, as both communities are itching for a fight.

2. In the meantime, the Legislature is in session. The only business transacted so far has been the presentation of the Budget, and I enclose a copy of the speech[9] of the Finance Minister, which appears to have been well received both by the Legislature and by the press. Government have budgeted for a small surplus on the revenue side, but, unless receipts are in excess of estimates (as I think they are likely to be given normal seasonal conditions), the surplus will become a deficit owing to supplementary estimates. The cost of various committees and of the allowances of members of the Legislative Assembly is likely to be more than was at first anticipated, while, if the communal situation further deteriorates, the cost of additional police will increase. The present budget provides for no relief of taxation and, although Government themselves are sound on this question, they will find it increasingly difficult to resist demands made on them. Assuming that they are able to avoid reduction of land revenue or water rates, the Province will remain solvent, but will have comparatively little scope for expansion of beneficent activities. Provincial resources are inelastic and expenditure cannot fail to increase. I am also sending a copy of the Memorandum[10] explanatory of the Budget, which explains the financial position in more detail.

3. I enclose, with his permission, a copy of a note[11] of his last tour recorded by Rao Bahadur Sir Chhotu Ram, Minister for Development. While I do not agree with one or two statements of fact and also with several conclusions, the note is of considerable interest. In particular, it shows that the people are eager for improvement of their condition, and also that, despite setbacks in one or two directions, very great progress has been made during recent years. It also shows that Ministers can do a great deal of good by touring in the villages and by frank talks with the people, and that even extreme agitators are ready to listen to them. I hope all the Ministers will carry out similar tours and give their impressions.

4. I mentioned a few weeks ago the prospect of trouble in the Gurgaon district in connection with the agitation against the Ingram Estate. Owing partly to the substitution of the then Deputy Commissioner[12] by a European[13] and partly to indirect efforts by the Unionist Party, the danger seems to have passed. A Congress Committee formed to enquire into the supposed grievances of tenants has had to confess failure, as will be seen from a copy of the letter[14] from the Deputy Commissioner to the Commissioner, Ambala Division,[15] which I enclose.

5. In connection with the relief of indebtedness, five Conciliation Boards were set up, one in each civil division. I enclose a copy of a note[16] written by Mr. Darling after inspecting all five Boards. The results on the whole have exceeded expectations, since, unlike similar Boards in the Central Provinces, there is no provision in the Act by which debts settled by the Boards can be realised as arrears of land revenue. This provision was deliberately omitted from the Punjab Act, since it was considered politically unwise to make the Executive Government the collector of agricultural debt. The omission, however, seriously prejudiced the effectiveness of the Boards, and personally I doubted whether they would do much good. I am glad to say that so far my doubts have been falsified, although even now it is too early to form a definite opinion regarding their utility. The real test will come when instalments have to be paid. If a large proportion of these is paid up to date, the experiment will be a success; otherwise not. Mr. Darling's note, however, shows that the prospects are promising, that general resort is being made to the Boards, and what is particularly encouraging, that creditors are also making use of them. Provision has been made in this year's Budget for the establishment of five more Boards, and there is likely to be pressure on the Government to go on increasing the number until there is at least one Board in each district.

ENCLOSURE TO NO. 12

NOTE BY CHHOTU RAM OF TOUR OF CERTAIN DISTRICTS, APRIL-MAY 1937 (EXTRACT)[17]

6th June, 1937

During the last two weeks of April and the first ten days of May I made a tour of certain districts. These districts were Kangra, Jhelum, Jullundur, Hoshiarpur, Ludhiana, Hissar, Rohtak, Karnal and Ambala. It will be interesting to know what I observed and learnt during these tours. I am sorry that I am recording my impressions after the lapse of a good long time. But even so, it is worth while to make a record of my observations and impressions.

GENERAL

(a) *Political.* I saw unmistakable signs of a great awakening which has already taken place and is taking place in rural areas. Ten years ago, political consciousness was, generally speaking, lacking in the countryside. But this consciousness has now come and is deepening. Probably, the last election has quickened the progress of political awakening. Apart from the political awakening of a general character, there are marked signs of a growing class consciousness. The rural population now definitely feels that it has certain claims upon the Government of the day and expects that these claims will receive due attention. This population also feels that it has been grievously neglected in the past and cannot afford to be neglected any longer.

So far as the north-western portion of the province is concerned, the Congress has not made any appreciable headway there, although signs are not wanting which show that the Congress does excite mixed feelings of esteem, curiosity and suspicion even there. The name of the Congress carries with it varying degrees of prestige and esteem in every part of the province. However, it is still true of the general masses of the north-west where the population is overwhelmingly Muslim that the Congress is viewed with a certain amount of suspicion. In the central districts the Congress seems to have established its power and influence to a degree which may be regarded as almost dangerous. In the south-east of the province the Congress, a such, is held in very high esteem. In fact, the Rohtak district is supposed to be, and perhaps with truth, the most Congress-minded district of the province. But, as the local Congress organisation is chiefly dominated by men of commercial and money-lending classes, and as the cleavage of zamindar and non-zamindar is very acute in the south-eastern districts, the Congress has failed to succeed in fixing any effective hold on the allegiance of the general population.

So far as the districts of Jullundur, Hoshiarpur and Ludhiana are concerned, socialism and communism seem to have deeply tinged the mentality of the rural population. The Congress seems to be making very vigorous efforts to capture the imagination of the countryside, and the socialist members of the Assembly, who succeeded at the last election, are taking a very active part in promoting the interests of the extreme wing of the Congress. Both the Deputy Commissioner[18] and the Superintendent of Police[19] of Ludhiana seemed to be almost panicky.

I addressed at least one gathering in every district except Kangra, and in some districts as many gatherings as three. Even in the Hoshiarpur and Jullundur districts, these gatherings had in them a noticeable number of extremist Sikhs. But everywhere the whole gathering listened to my address with commendable patience and perfect order. I explained to them briefly what the Unionist Party had done in the past and what the present Government intended to do in the future, and I observed signs of satisfaction at what we had achieved in the past and what we proposed to do in the future. I attacked the policy and ridiculed the tactics of Congress in certain respects in fairly strong language without exciting any feelings of resentment or protest among the audience. This shows that the heart of the countryside is still sound, and, if approached properly, the rural population will rally round the flag of the Unionist Party in every part of the province.

The value which agricultural classes attach to the Alienation of Land Act is not fully realised by most people. It is no exaggeration to say that if there is one thing for which agricultural classes feel really and deeply grateful to the British bureaucracy in the Punjab, it is the Alienation of Land Act. Next after the Alienation of Land Act, the three laws – Regulation of Accounts Act, Relief of Indebtedness Act and the Debtors' Protection Act – make a very strong appeal to all poor classes including the whole zamindar community, irrespective of caste or creed. Certain changes and improvements were suggested to me by certain intelligent individuals in the recent debt legislation, and there is no doubt that, if those improvements are made, this legislation will become more effective and useful and will bring further popularity to the Government. To sum up, the land laws and the debt legislation of the Punjab can, easily and effectively, serve the purpose of our stock-in-trade for some time to come. But it must be remembered that we cannot afford to rest on our oars and must do something to promote the general prosperity of the province and to relieve agricultural classes of a portion of their present burden of taxation.

(b) *Economical.* I was distressed to find that the economic condition of the rural population has suffered immensely during the last 6 or 7 years, and it does not show any satisfactory signs of amelioration. The average petty zamindar is, from a purely economical point of view, distinctly worse off than even his *kamin*, and if his good-will is to be retained – and we cannot afford to lose this good-will – effective steps will have to be taken to improve his economical condition as early as possible. The weakest feature of our present rural economy is that agricultural classes have nothing but agriculture to depend upon for their livelihood and means of income. It is absolutely essential that subsidiary professions should be found for agriculturalists to augment their usual income from agriculture.

13

EMERSON TO LINLITHGOW

Confidential

Barnes Court, Simla, E.,
July 3rd, 1937

My dear Lord Linlithgow,

In my last letter of the 19th June, I referred at some length to the communal situation. Thanks to the prompt action of the district authorities, no further outbreaks occurred at Amritsar, and there have been no immediate reactions elsewhere. Gujrat has for the time being at any rate settled down again, but further information regarding the events there of the 13th and 14th of June shows that the outbreak of lawlessness by the Muslims of about 30 villages was a very serious affair. In spite of the provocation given by the Sikhs, this could hardly have happened had there not been organised efforts to stir up the religious prejudices and hatred of the population. The most disquieting feature is the evidence it shows that feeling is so bad that a few agitators can stir up serious trouble at very short notice. Investigation into the various offences is proceeding, but it is going to be very difficult to get sufficient evidence to lead to many convictions. An enquiry held by the District Magistrate[20] immediately after the occurrences shows that the police were fully justified in firing, and that the firing was well controlled. In fact, firing was opened on six occasions and not on three as stated in my last letter. There is no doubt that had firing not been ordered, many more Sikhs would have been killed, and the small police forces present at the various places where firing took place would have been overwhelmed. The police officers in charge of the detachments did extremely well; in all cases they were Muslims acting in protection of the Sikhs. Government have appointed Mr. Innes to hold a general enquiry into the causes of the trouble.

The press on both sides has been extremely bitter about occurrences in Gujrat and at Amritsar, and reports generally show that communal tension in many places in the Province is acute. The Premier held a conference of between 30 and 40 members of all communities to consider the communal situation. Apart from the Ministers, the conference was attended only by non-officials and included members of the Legislature as well as other prominent men in the Province. A number of resolutions were passed, and I understand that it was decided to set up two small committees of non-officials to consider the question of communal dissension from two points of view: first, religious causes of friction, and second, political causes of friction. Among the first are included such controversial subjects as music before mosques, facilities for *jhatka* meat by Sikhs in prisons, &c., and religious processions. Among the political causes, there is some doubt as to whether the communal award will be included or not. From the purely political point of view the conference has been of some immediate value as helping to assuage feeling for the time being, but I am doubtful whether any lasting good will result, and I am uneasy about bringing into general prominence subjects of a highly controversial character in regard to which it will be difficult, if not impossible, to obtain any measure of agreement in a committee consisting of representatives of different communities, and still more difficult to get the masses to translate into practice any agreement which the committee may reach. It is, however, possible that the two committees will not take themselves too seriously.

2. In Your Excellency's letter of the 23rd June, I was asked to keep Your Excellency informed regarding the attitude of the Minister in charge of Law and Order towards political offences, his relations with the Intelligence and Special Branches of the police, &c. The Premier, Sir Sikander Hyat Khan is in charge of Law and Order. His relations towards the police generally and the C.I.D. Branch in particular are excellent, and, so far as political action is concerned, he has consistently supported their proposals. This attitude has the support of the Ministry in general, and I enclose a copy of a letter,[21] dated the 21st June 1937, which speaks for itself, and which was issued with the approval of the Council of Ministers as a whole. At a recent bye-election one Teja Singh Sutantar, who is a well-known revolutionary and terrorist, was elected. He is under detention under Regulation III of 1818, and the Premier has definitely refused to release him. He has also refused to consider release from restrictions imposed on certain communists under the Punjab Criminal Law (Amendment) Act. In fact, he is quite prepared to use the Act against others who are giving trouble. He has recently released a few prisoners who were convicted during the disturbances of 1919, and who are known as 'Martial Law prisoners'. They were due for release in any case in a few months, and his action had my approval. Similarly, the Premier has been quite ready to sanction prosecutions under the substantive law for sedition, &c. There is thus no ground for misgiving regarding offences of a political character.

3. If difficulties arise in the administration of Law and Order, they will be concerned more with communal than political affairs. In the communal sphere the position of the Ministry in general, and of the Premier in

particular, is one of very great difficulty. Straightforward prosecutions for offences committed are simple enough, but questions are bound to arise of deterrent and preventive action of a collective character, e.g. the imposition of additional police at the cost of the inhabitants of a particular area. Again, a communal disturbance is usually followed by agitation for the transfer of particular officers. Nothing much has so far occurred to give cause for serious misgiving, but I feel that it is in this direction, if any, that the Ministers will be faced with most difficult and delicate problems. They have, of course, ways open to them, not available to the late Government, of mitigating the effects of particular clashes, but these tend to increase the temptation to rely too much on political manoeuvring as a substitute for firm action. It is inevitable that the Ministry should be subject to great pressure from groups and individuals, and it is going to require strength of mind and character to resist this pressure. This difficulty is, however, inherent in the new constitution, and we have in the Punjab a Ministry and a Premier more likely to resist it than any other Ministry.

4. The Legislature has continued in session. Government have had no difficulty in obtaining large majorities in support both of their general policy and of particular proposals. I gather that the Ministers and their supporters have done well in debate. The opposition have attempted to make good by obstructive methods what they lack in strength and ability. At the beginning of the session, adjournment motions were continuously moved on petty and non-urgent matters. The Speaker has stopped this. In other respects he has failed to deal adequately with challenges to his authority, and there have been several unedifying scenes. Matters, however, are likely to improve in this respect. A mistake was, I think, made by the sudden appointment of a Marshal without any previous reference to the House generally. Apparently it was settled by informal discussion between the Speaker and the Ministers, and, as a temporary measure, a police officer was appointed. He suddenly appeared beside the Speaker's chair, and the Speaker made matters worse by stating that he was to perform functions similar to those performed by the Sergeant-at-Arms, and by suggesting that the Government had made the appointment over his head. Apparently he also suggested to the Premier that he had mentioned the matter to me, and that I had approved of it; and the Premier made a statement to this effect in the House. As a matter of fact, the first I heard of the matter was when I saw it reported in the press. At my suggestion a committee of the House has now been appointed to advise the Speaker regarding the appointment and duties of the Marshal. I have had to ask the Premier to clear up the misunderstanding regarding my supposed knowledge and

approval of the original proposal by stating the facts to the committee, since, unless this is put right, capital is certain to be made of it sooner or later on the ground that I acted unconstitutionally.

One line that the opposition have pursued is to attempt to make out that the Governor has been interfering unconstitutionally with the discretion of his Ministers. They have done this partly by raising the matter in debate and partly by objectionable questions. The Premier has made it quite clear that there is no basis for this suggestion, and has refused to answer particular questions, while making the general position quite clear. A particular matter which has been raised is the Governor presiding over meetings of the Council of Ministers. I have so far presided over all meetings, partly because the Premier has thought it desirable, but mainly because during the discussion regarding the form which the Rules of Business should take, it was made clear by the Secretary of State and by the Government of India that it was definitely their wish and intention that the Governor should make a regular practice of presiding at Council meetings during the early stages of the constitution. The question, however, is bound to come up again. Despite the professed views of the Ministers, I feel that they would prefer that the Governor occasionally did not preside, and personally I think it would be a good thing, after the present agitation has died down, if the practice of presiding became a little more irregular. I do not, however, want to do anything that may be cited as a precedent, and embarrass Governors of other Provinces if Congress accept office. My personal view, however, is that some elasticity in this matter is desirable. On the other hand, it has to be recognised that relaxation of the present practice will encourage the general trend to edge the Governor out of affairs, but this seems to be an inevitable result of the new constitution. The Governor's effective power in future must depend, in normal circumstances, not on any powers which he has under the Act, but on the character of his relations with the Ministers, and it seems to me to be more important for a Governor to preserve real harmony and to increase the prestige of Ministers by deliberately absenting himself occasionally from Council meetings than to insist on the regular exercise of a discretionary right. I shall be grateful for Your Excellency's views on this question which, unless I am mistaken, is likely to be taken up generally in all Provinces and to assume considerable importance.[22]

Yours sincerely,
H.W. EMERSON

14

EMERSON TO LINLITHGOW[23]

Confidential

Barnes Court, Simla, E.,
July 18th, 1937

My dear Lord Linlithgow,

In the second paragraph of my letter of the 3rd of July, I mentioned the attitude of my Premier towards political offences. There have been some developments since that was written. A resolution regarding the release of political prisoners was moved in the Legislature on the first non-official day, and the discussion will continue on the 20th. The Premier has discussed the matter with me and with the C.I.D. He is anxious to do something, since he feels that in a few days Congress is likely to release a number of such prisoners. I understand that he is likely to take the following course:

(i) He will decline to release any prisoner who has been convicted by a court. This will cover cases of sedition under section 124-A, Indian Penal Code.

(ii) There are six persons under detention in the Punjab under Regulation III of 1818. Of these, three are comparatively innocuous. Orders for the release of one have already been given. The cases of two more will probably be favourably considered. They do not include Teja Singh Sutantar, who is a member of the Legislature.

(iii) There are thirteen persons who are under some form of restriction under section 3 of the Punjab Criminal Law (Amendment) Act. The restrictions vary, but the most rigorous is a prohibition on the person concerned absenting himself from his village. Under the Act an order of restriction can last only for a year, and in several cases the period is nearing expiry. The Premier proposes to remove restrictions on nine, leaving four still under restriction.

The C.I.D. are satisfied that action on these lines will not involve any serious danger. The Premier intends to make it clear that, if any person abuses the concession given to him, there will be no hesitation in re-imposing restrictions.

2. Mr. Innes, Deputy Commissioner, Gurdaspur, was deputed to make a special enquiry into the communal rioting in the Gujrat district. His report has been received. While he holds that the Sikhs were provocative, he

expressed the strong opinion that there was insufficient justification for the action taken by Muslims, and he has recommended a strong punitive police post. His report makes it still more obvious that the rioting was of a very serious character, that about thirty villages took part, and that an excitement was deliberately organised. He has expressed the view that the police behaved very well, that firing was fully justified and that it was well controlled. It seems, however, probable that there was a certain amount of firing in the air, which is of course against orders, instead of at the rioters. The report is now under consideration by the Government.

3. The session of the Assembly will end in a few days. Since my last letter, the proceedings have been more dignified, and there has been little disorderliness. Government got the budget passed without any cut, and they have succeeded in maintaining party discipline. The general result of the session has been to consolidate their position. An apparent exception is the fact that some of the supporters of Government tried to move the adjournment of the House to discuss the report of the Palestine Commission. The Speaker failed to rule this out as having no concern with provincial affairs, and I exercised my discretionary power in doing so, action which had the full support of the Premier. I have some reason to believe that the whole thing was a piece of political manoeuvring. Government have come in for a good deal of criticism by the Muslim press and Muslim speakers, outside their own supporters in the Legislature, on the ground that in several communal riots the Muslims have come off second best. For instance, both in Panipat and Gujrat firing had to be opened on Muslim mobs. Their supporters therefore thought it necessary to show that they were staunch supporters of Muslim interests, and they chose the Palestine issue as a good pretext. First a meeting of Muslim members of the Legislature was held at which resolutions condemning the report were passed, and second, a motion for adjournment was moved by Begum Shah Nawaz. She is or will be a Parliamentary Secretary, and it is difficult to believe that Government did not countenance her action. It is possible that they thought that the Speaker would himself rule the motion out. It is also possible that he was in the manoeuvre and that it was deliberately left for me to do so. At any rate, although I believe that feeling among Muslims regarding Palestine is fairly strong, it is not necessary to attach too much importance to the action of Muslim legislators. I may have to make it clear that my own action was on the advice of my Ministers, since political manoeuvres of this kind are not to be encouraged.

4. The general impression is that Government have done very well during the first important session of the Legislature. In particular, I understand

that Sir Sikander Hyat Khan has had a great personal success and has firmly established his position as Leader without any fear of challenge. He has, however, to work under a very heavy strain, and it is already clear that in this province at any rate, the Premier will have an almost intolerable burden to bear. Apart from his regular work, he is allowed no peace by visitors, most of whom have their own axe to grind.

It remains to be seen how the acceptance of office by Congress in six provinces will affect the Punjab. I have already mentioned one result as regards political prisoners. So far as one can see, there is not likely to be any change in the attitude of the opposition, who will continue to be irresponsible critics. They know that they have no chance of turning the present Government out, and they are not interested in co-operation on its own merits. Agrarian legislation in other provinces, and especially in the United Provinces, can hardly fail to give an impetus to socialism and communism in the Punjab, and to place the provincial Government in a more difficult position regarding their policy. Until Congress took office, the feeling was increasing in strength, both among Ministers and their supporters, that there was very small scope for relief of taxation, and that the right policy was to press on with increasing the resources of the people through beneficent activities. I hope that this policy will continue to hold the field, but what is done elsewhere can hardly be without embarrassment and consequences here.

Yours sincerely,
H.W. EMERSON

15

EMERSON TO LINLITHGOW

Confidential

Barnes Court, Simla, E.,
July 31st, 1937

My dear Lord Linlithgow,

In my letter of the 18th of July, I mentioned the course the Premier was likely to take regarding the release of political prisoners. He adhered to what I said in that letter, and, although in the debate in the Assembly the Opposition clamoured for much greater concessions only 29 members voted in favour of the resolution against about 100 who supported Government. This division was a striking example of the difference between the old and the new constitution. Under the former constitution, it was often a matter of difficulty to get many non-official members to support Government in matters relating to political prosecutions or political prisoners. Although, on the whole, the old Legislative Council behaved well regarding law and order, there were usually a number of members who disliked the unpopularity attaching to the support of Government in what the agitator condemned as repressive measures. This was particularly so when elections were approaching. Under the present constitution, they are bound as a party to support the policy of Government, and common interests, combined with the confidence which solidarity gives, have helped to remove scruples which were due more to timidity than to principle.

2. On the last day of the Session there was a debate on the communal situation. I gather that the debate itself was marred by some strong partisan speeches, but the Assembly by a large vote gave authority to Government to take strong measures in regard to communal disputes. This is very satisfactory so far as it goes, but in itself will do little to improve matters. I understand that the Premier intends to take action, after a preliminary warning, against the press, which has been very bad during the past few months.

3. There was a very interesting discussion a few days ago in the Council of Ministers on the subject of Indianisation in the Indian Army. The proposal actually before the Council was that the Punjab Government should sanction two scholarships, each worth Rs. 600 per annum, to the Military Academy at Dehra Dun. Of the six Ministers, four are very closely concerned with the welfare of the martial classes, to which they themselves belong, and the discussion covered a number of questions relating to their future. It was felt that, so far as entry to the Academy through the competitive examination is concerned, the members of these classes, and especially the sons of ex-Indian officers have little chance of success with others, unless they first have the advantage of going through the Prince of Wales College at Dehra Dun. There have, in fact, been very few cases in which youths of the martial classes have succeeded in the open competition, except those who have gone through the College. So far as Y cadets are concerned, the number has been greater, but the feeling was that this also was not a certain avenue, since for social or other reasons Y cadets have so far not proved entirely satisfactory, and there have been several cases in which they have been rejected. So far as the Prince of Wales College is concerned, the course is expensive, and the number of Punjabis of the right class who apply for entry has decreased greatly during the past few years. I am Chairman of a Selection Committee which sits twice a year,

and it is now comparatively rare to have candidates, other than the sons of professional and businessmen. A great majority of the candidates are the sons of contractors or officers in the Public Works Department. The conclusions reached by the Council of Ministers were interesting. They apprehended that, if something were not done, the Punjab would have comparatively few officers in the Indian Army, that the number would tend to decline, that of the Punjabis who became officers, a decreasing number would belong to the martial classes, and that, although the Punjab would continue to supply the bulk of soldiers, it would be very badly represented in the officers' class. The Council then got on to the question of remedies, in so far as they lay in their own hands. They finally decided that scholarships to the Academy alone were of very little use, since successful candidates of the right type would not be forthcoming. They therefore decided to grant scholarships to the Prince of Wales College, so that the right class of boy could be helped at the age of 11 or 12 when he enters the College, and if he later got into the Academy, as usually happens, he could get further assistance there. The ultimate decision was therefore to grant five scholarships a year, each worth Rs. 600 per annum, for a period of nine years, which will cover a boy's education and training through the College and through the Academy. When the scheme is complete at the end of nine years, it will include 45 scholarships, and the annual cost will amount to Rs. 27,000. It was decided that of the five scholarships, two should be given to the sons of ex-Indian officers, a third to a member of the martial class, and that the other two should be open ones. The scheme cannot, of course, be put into effect until the Assembly votes the money, but there is no doubt that the proposal will be passed. It will be extremely popular with the classes from which soldiers are recruited, and these form a very large part of the rural population in the Punjab. While a scholarship of Rs. 600 per annum will materially help, it may not prove sufficient. I hope that the Government of India will be able to restore the provision for scholarships to the Prince of Wales College which was suspended a few years ago, and that, where necessary, they will supplement the Punjab Government scholarships to particular candidates. I think myself that this is one of the best schemes which the Punjab Government have sanctioned for some time, and that it merits the practical encouragement of the Military Department.

4. This particular discussion in the Cabinet illustrates the value of the presence of the Governor at its meetings. The scheme was essentially that of the Cabinet, and I had not myself thought of it. But I was able to initiate a general discussion and help the Ministers in coming to logical

conclusions, which none of us had thought out beforehand. The value of the decision to my mind lies in the acceptance of the principle that the Punjab, as a Province, is vitally interested in securing a fair share of commissions in the Indian Army, and that it is the duty of Government to help in attaining this result.

5. During the past week an announcement has been made by the Premier of the appointment of Parliamentary Private Secretaries and Parliamentary Secretaries. Eight of the former have been appointed, who will receive a monthly allowance of Rs. 250; and eight of the latter, six of whom will receive Rs. 500 a month, one Rs. 625 a month and the Chief Whip Rs. 750 a month. The Parliamentary Private Secretaries are men of independent means. The scheme is a costly one and is likely to arouse criticism. It is also going to be very difficult to find work for the Secretaries to do, but I understand that the present idea is to employ them mainly during Assembly sessions, and at other times for work in constituencies. The Premier and the Ministers are fully alive to the importance of not allowing them to encroach on the functions of Administrative Secretaries. There will no doubt be a tendency in this direction, which will require careful watching, but I do not think serious difficulties are likely to arise.

6. I am attaching the official fortnightly report for the first half of July and will try to arrange in future that the official reports correspond more closely in date to my letters. In this connection, I may mention that, in view of the fact that there are now Congress Ministries in six Provinces, it has been decided that references to Congress activities in the official report shall in future be only of a colourless character, but that a separate memorandum is to be put up for the information of the Premier and myself regarding Congress activities in the Province. It will not be sent to other Provinces, but will be attached to the copies which I send to Your Excellency and to the Secretary of State. It will also be sent to the Home Department of the Government of India, and to the Director, Intelligence Bureau, Government of India. Although the question is not likely to arise, I would request that reference should not be made to this supplementary memorandum, except in personal communications to Governors.

Yours sincerely,
H.W. EMERSON

16

EMERSON TO LINLITHGOW

Confidential

Barnes Court, Simla, E.,
August 14th, 1937

My dear Lord Linlithgow,

There is little to report for the past fortnight, but what there is relates to communal or sectarian feeling. A brief reference is made in the official fortnightly report, a copy of which is enclosed, to further trouble in the Ahmadi community at Qadian. Although internal in its origin, it is likely to have wider reactions. It appears that two or three fairly prominent followers of the head of the community have lately seceded for reasons which are not quite clear. At any rate, for some weeks past, they have been engaged in making charges against the private life of the head, and in demanding an enquiry into them. They have, I gather, not made specific charges, but the allegations have been of such a character as to cause great resentment among the Ahmadi community, together with some uneasiness. The opportunity has, of course, been seized by the enemies of the Ahmadis. The Lahore section, which broke away from Qadian many years ago, are using the difficulties of their rivals to improve their own position, while the Ahrars are joining with the seceders in stirring up trouble. The affair came to a head a week ago when a murderous assault was made on two of the seceders in Qadian by a fanatical Ahmadi. The victims do not appear to have received serious injuries, but for a few days there was great excitement, and the end has probably not been heard of the affair.[24]

2. Developments have occurred at Kot Fateh Khan where the situation between Muslims and Sikhs has been tense for some time. The immediate trouble has arisen out of the supply of drinking water to the Sikhs living at the gurdwara. They were for some time allowed to take water from a point on a neighbouring stream where Muslim women draw water and also bathe. By mutual arrangement the Sikhs were supposed to draw water at certain hours only when Muslim women were not visiting the place. The allegation is that they did not observe this agreement, and that, in consequence, there was grave danger of a breach of the peace. The District Magistrate has therefore forbidden the Sikhs under the Criminal Procedure Code from drawing water from that particular place. There is an alternative source of supply on the same stream a little distance away. On the issue of this order the Sikhs commenced to observe civil disobedience, or a *morcha* as the

Sikhs call it. For about a week, two Sikhs each day have attempted to disobey the order and have been arrested. The Akali Dal party led by Master Tara Singh is hesitating whether to take up the matter on a big scale. It is probable that they will do so since a big Muslim landlord is concerned who is a member of the Legislative Assembly and a supporter of the present Government, and for some time the extreme Akalis have been doing all that is possible to embarrass the present Government, and especially Sir Sunder Singh, the Sikh Minister. In the meantime, an application for revision has been filed in the High Court against the order of the District Magistrate. If a *morcha* on a big scale is attempted, the situation may become troublesome, as Kot Fateh Khan is in a predominant Muslim area and, however careful the police precautions may be, it will be difficult to prevent assaults on Sikhs proceeding to Kot Fateh Khan for purposes of disobeying the law. Attempts are being made to obtain a final settlement between the Sardar of Kot and the Sikhs, but in the past neither side has shown a reasonable spirit. It is possible that the District Magistrate's order may be modified by the High Court, since some months ago he passed an order, the correctness of which is open to doubt, that the Sikhs were entitled to draw water from the place now in dispute. While this need not affect the necessity of an order under Section 144, Criminal Procedure Code, it does give the Sikhs a more or less plausible cause for complaint. The case, on the whole, is a troublesome one for Government.

3. The hunger-strikes in the Andamans and elsewhere have so far had little effect in the Punjab. I have just heard that the Madras Government have asked the Punjab Government to take to the Punjab prisons three Punjabis who were convicted for terrorist crimes in Madras and who are now on hunger-strike in the Andamans. This is an obvious try-on, since beyond the fact that they happen to be natives of the Punjab we have no concern with them.

Yours sincerely,
H.W. EMERSON

17

EMERSON TO LINLITHGOW

Secret

Barnes Court, Simla, E.,
August 28th, 1937

My dear Lord Linlithgow,

The position at Qadian has changed little since my letter of the 16th of August. On pressure by the Deputy Commissioner of the district, the head of the community condemned violence by his followers, and said that he would excommunicate any one who resorted to it. Feeling is still strong at Qadian itself, but so far there have been no serious reactions elsewhere.

2. In paragraph 2 of my letter of the 16th August, I mentioned the Muslim-Sikh trouble at Kot Fateh Khan. The High Court modified the order of the District Magistrate and fixed hours during which Sikhs should be allowed to draw water from the disputed stream. On this the District Magistrate prohibited the Muslims from drawing water during those hours. The Sikhs have now abandoned civil disobedience, and for the time being the situation is easier, but there may be further trouble.

3. I have written separately to Your Excellency regarding the agitation against the abattoir at Lahore,[25] which has been the chief event of the past fortnight.

4. In my letter of the 15th of June 1937, I mentioned the trouble at the Khalsa College, Amritsar. A Committee of Enquiry was constituted to investigate the cause of the two strikes that have occurred this year. On their report, the Committee of Management have now dismissed six members of the staff, including the brother of Tara Singh, the Akali leader. There is little doubt that the persons dismissed were at the bottom of the trouble and were a very unhealthy influence in the College. The Committee of Management have shown great courage in the action they have taken. It has naturally caused some stir, but the practical reactions will not be known until the students return after the vacation about the end of September.

5. There has been very little rain in the plains during the past month, and the situation is very serious in all unirrigated tracts, especially in the south-east. The *kharif* harvest which at one time promised to be a bumper crop, will now be below average, and, if rain does not fall within the next few days, it will be a failure over large areas.

Yours sincerely,
H.W. EMERSON

18

EMERSON TO LINLITHGOW

Secret

Barnes Court, Simla, E.,
September 14th, 1937

My dear Lord Linlithgow,

Mention is made in the attached fortnightly report of communal trouble in the Sheikhupura district. It is very fortunate that the fracas, which took place some distance from the diwan and which resulted in the death of six persons, was not followed by a general fight between the Sikhs and Muslims who numbered about 6,000 and 3,000 respectively. The district officers who were present did extremely well in preventing a pitched battle. The circumstances leading to the trouble are becoming much too common. A local incident of very trivial importance occurs, the Sikhs make it an excuse for a so-called religious gathering in spite of the resentment of the local Muslims, and the almost inevitable result is a clash between the two communities. On the present occasion, the Deputy Commissioner[26] and the Superintendent of Police,[27] who are both Muslims, assumed that the mere description of the gathering as a religious one afforded sufficient reason for allowing it to be held, and their efforts were directed to appease the resentment of Muslims. This has happened on several previous occasions. District officers, in fact, have been in doubt regarding the attitude of Government, and they have obviously been influenced by the popular talk of communal unity. With a considerable section of the Sikhs determined to create opportunities to embarrass Government, this policy of drift was certain to lead to further trouble. Government have now issued a letter to all district officers, making it clear that, while their general policy is not to interfere with religious observances, the considerations of law and order are paramount, and where one party deliberately gives provocation to others under the guise of religion, the District Magistrate must consider the danger to the public peace, and, if necessary, forbid the observances, after a reference to Government if time permits. This may lead to a serious clash between the police and the demonstrators if the prohibitory order is disobeyed, but the alternative is to allow provocative acts to continue with the consequent spread of communal trouble. The policy laid down in the letter to district officers was thoroughly discussed in the Council of Ministers, and in order to remove any further ground for misunderstanding, I had the implications fully stated.

2. There have been two further communal incidents since I last wrote – one near Panipat where a body of Hindus appear deliberately to have attacked some Muslims while at prayer, and the second a murderous assault by a fanatical Muslim on Sikhs in Mandi Baha-ud-Din, a small town in the Gujrat district. The communal situation generally gives considerable cause for anxiety.

In my letter of the 3rd July, 1937, I mentioned that, if difficulties arose in the administration of law and order, they would be concerned more with communal than with political affairs. The composite character of the Government encourages unscrupulous opponents to exploit communal differences in order to embarrass the Ministers. At the same time, the dependence of Government in the legislature on the three communities, and the fact that they are all represented in the Cabinet discourage firm and swift action. The lack of this in turn puzzles district officers who do not know quite where they are. While no community is satisfied with the present position, the discontent among Muslims is steadily growing, and is finding expression both in the Muslim press and in meetings. Feeling is growing that, while the protection of minorities may be a sound principle, it has so far operated to the detriment of the major community, which has come out worst in most of the communal fights. The Muslim attitude is becoming a cause of anxiety to the Premier.

In the meantime, the proceedings of the Unity Conference continue. A sub-committee has passed a number of resolutions relating to very controversial subjects, and while the resolutions are excellent regarded as ideals to be attained, any attempt to apply some of them to particular cases would result in widespread disturbances. I have advised the Premier to go slowly in this matter and not to commit Government to the acceptance of general principles to be applied irrespective of local circumstances and the facts of particular cases. A striking example of the divorce between theory and practice is a pious resolution regarding the slaughter of animals. Its terms are such as would completely and absolutely justify the abattoir at Lahore; but among those who apparently agreed to the resolution are some of the most bitter agitators against the slaughter-house. I shall be addressing Your Excellency in a few days about the latter. Unless there are favourable developments, which are very improbable, within the next few days, I shall have to confirm the opinion previously given.

3. It seems probable that there will be a strike of students at the Khalsa College, Amritsar, towards the end of this month, when they return to their studies. Sir Sunder Singh is at present very determined to see the thing through, and to make no concession regarding the dismissal of certain

of the staff, but he told me a few days ago that the Maharaja of Patiala, who was consulted before the men were dismissed, now shows signs of going back on his agreement.

4. Government have decided to repatriate political prisoners from the Andamans, and also to take into Punjab jails three terrorists convicted in Madras. There is no question of their release. This decision has been reached with my support, because so far as the Andamans are concerned, I gather that the Government of India welcome repatriation, while, so far as Madras is concerned, there is the danger of the convicts being released, if we do not take them ourselves. The total number involved is only nine or ten.

5. The Premier is finding the burden of work very heavy, and to a less extent this is true of the Revenue Minister, Sir Sunder Singh. The other Ministers have comparatively light portfolios, and discussions are now taking place with the object of rearranging subjects so far as this is possible. It is very desirable that Sir Sikander should get relief, as at present he has no time to think out important questions of policy.

6. There has been some rain in the south-eastern districts since I last wrote, and yesterday's weather report records very good falls in one or two places. If it has been general in the south-east, the danger of a fodder famine should disappear, although the *kharif* harvest will be much below average. A more serious business, so far as provincial finances are concerned, is the appearance in very large quantities of the *tela* insect practically throughout the canal colonies. It has already done considerable damage to cotton, and unless there is good rain, the crop will be ruined, with very heavy loss to cultivators and a large deficit in the provincial budget.

Yours sincerely,
H.W. EMERSON

19

EMERSON TO LINLITHGOW[28]

Private and Personal

Barnes Court, Simla, E.,
September 22nd, 1937

My dear Lord Linlithgow,

In Your Excellency's letter of the 17th September 1937, my views were invited on the question of a visit to India of His Majesty the King. I have discussed the matter with the Premier, Sir Sikander Hyat Khan, and with

Mr. Penny, Chief Secretary. I have also had a short talk with His Excellency Sir John Anderson. As Your Excellency has observed, it is impossible at this stage to judge how the political situation is likely to develop, or what political conditions in this country are likely to be in fifteen months' time. Apart from what may be called major political issues, there is always the chance, as the Lahore abattoir agitation has just shown, of some question suddenly emerging and seriously affecting the general atmosphere. Obviously no guarantee can be given so far ahead in regard to fortuitous and unforeseen events. It is necessary to make some assumptions, and for the present purpose it may be assumed that at the time of the visit, first, there will be Congress Ministries in seven Provinces; second, that the present Ministry in the Punjab will be still in power; and third, that the personal relations between Governors and Congress Ministries will be at least as friendly as at present. These are the assumptions on which I shall proceed.

2. With regard to certain preliminary and comparatively minor issues, Sir Sikander's view, with which I agree, is that if an announcement were made at the present time from London that, owing to the international situation, His Majesty is unable to visit India next year, such a declaration would not be seriously taken as a victory for the Left. The state of international relations would in itself justify such a declaration, while such agitation as there has been against a Royal Durbar has not been sufficiently strong or widespread as to raise any presumption that the abandonment of the proposal was due to political forces in India. The effect would be still less marked if the declaration were accompanied by a statement of His Majesty's intention to visit India at some later date. The ill-effects of abandoning the proposal would be more negative than positive, that is to say, the opportunity would be lost, for the time being, of strengthening the bond between the King-Emperor and the people of India, and of making personal contacts between His Majesty and individuals who are now playing a large part in the history of India. A successful visit would unquestionably check the tendency, which is at present well marked, to undermine the imperial relationship; but in order to secure this enormous advantage, the visit must be a success. Otherwise more harm than good would result.

3. With regard to financial arrangements which Your Excellency mentions in paragraph 5 of your letter, the suggestion that guests should contribute towards certain expenditure is contrary to all oriental ideas of hospitality. Comparisons would inevitably be made between the Durbar of 1911 and the present one, and, while Government would receive little credit for economy, there would be much criticism of what would be

regarded as illiberal treatment. Obviously it would be unfair to require officers of Government to attend the Durbar at very considerable personal expense to themselves. At the least they would have to receive travelling and halting allowances even if they had to pay the full cost of board and lodging. It seems to me out of the question to make them pay a proportionate share of the cost of the stadium.

So far as non-official guests are concerned, there would appear to be no reason why the Central Government should pay their travelling allowance, but the greater the concession that can be made in regard to accommodation and entertainment, the more successful would the Durbar be from the public point of view.

4. With regard to the general question of expenditure on the Durbar, I am not clear whether this would be subject to the vote or at any rate to discussion by the Central Legislature. On principle, one would expect the Congress to oppose the expenditure, and the matter would presumably come up for consideration in the next budget session. So far as provincial expenditure on the Durbar is concerned, Sir Sikander thought that there would be no difficulty in getting the Punjab Legislative Assembly to pass a certain amount; for instance, the travelling and halting allowances of officers who had to attend. If representative members of the Assembly were invited, the Legislature would probably also vote their travelling and halting allowances. There would be, of course, opposition from the Left, and it would not be possible to avoid discussion of the advantages and disadvantages of a Royal visit. If His Majesty were to visit the Punjab, Sir Sikander believes that there would be no difficulty whatever in obtaining the sanction of the Legislature to the necessary expenditure, provided this was within reasonable limits. But, here again, a favourable vote would not be obtained without a certain amount of opposition. This must be taken as a provisional view without any guarantee. My personal view, which might later have to be qualified in the event of unforeseen developments, coincides with that of Sir Sikander. I believe that there would be much less opposition to expenditure in connection with the visit of His Majesty to the Punjab than to expenditure from provincial revenues on the Durbar at Delhi. Again in the absence of unforeseen circumstances, Sir Sikander and I are agreed that His Majesty would receive a very warm and loyal welcome from all classes in the Punjab. My Ministers would, of course, attend a Royal Durbar.

5. I now come to the really important issue namely, what the attitude of Congress Ministers and of Congress generally is likely to be towards, first, a Royal visit and second, a Royal Durbar. For reasons, which appear

later, I think it probable that the attitude towards these two may be different. I realise that in attempting to deal with these matters at all, I am to some extent going outside my sphere, since I have no personal concern with Congress Ministers, but events of the last few months and my previous knowledge of some of the Congress leaders allow me to make some assessment of the considerations which are likely to influence them. In this connection, it is relevant that, while the Durbar would not take place until late in the cold weather of 1938, an announcement would have to be made within the next few months. It is probable that Congress opinion would declare itself soon after the announcement was made, and it is prudent therefore to discount to a considerable extent the operation, during the whole period between now and the holding of the Durbar, of the favourable influences mentioned in paragraph 8 of Your Excellency's letter.[29] If it were possible to allow the natural development of those influences without the disturbance which an announcement is likely to cause, the prospects would be more favourable. Even so, I think that the following assumptions can be made:

(*i*) There would be no *hartals* or hostile demonstrations.
(*ii*) In the absence of these, the masses would give His Majesty a very loyal welcome.
(*iii*) Congress Ministers would not deliberately go out of their way to show discourtesy.
(*iv*) As Congress Ministers attended on Your Excellency in Bihar, so they would, as a matter of course, attend on His Majesty if he visited their Provinces.
(*v*) They would probably be gratified by and would accept invitations to have audiences with His Majesty.
(*vi*) Mr. Gandhi would almost certainly accept such an invitation.

Subject to what is said below, I would, for instance, expect Congress Ministers of Bombay to take part in the reception of His Majesty when he lands there. I may add that their failure to do so would in Indian opinion amount to a gross insult, which would, in my view, make it impossible for them to continue in office.

6. The main problem is concerned with the Durbar at Delhi. It seems to me extremely improbable that Congress Ministers would break with Gandhi on an issue of this kind, and it therefore comes down in essence to the attitude of Gandhi. I was greatly impressed with Your Excellency's views formed after the interview with Gandhi regarding his implacable hostility to British rule. He seems to have hardened greatly in this respect since I

knew him. He is certainly strongly opposed to pomp and circumstances as represented by high ceremonial. He might explain his opposition as based on what he would regard as an undue demand on the Indian taxpayer, but the real opposition would be to the display of imperial power. The circumstances attending the Durbar would be completely alien to the simplicity and economy which so far he has successfully imposed on Congress Ministers. He could not authorise the participation of Congress Ministers in a Royal Durbar without sacrificing his strongest convictions. I do not believe that he would do so, and whatever might be the view of individual Ministers, I think that he would be able to impose his will on them. If this appreciation is correct, then Congress Ministers would not attend the Durbar; nor, in consequence, would Congress members of the Legislatures attend, except possibly a few individuals who were invited to the Durbar as Durbaris. So far as a Congress Province was concerned, the result would be that, apart from the Governor and some officials, the Province would be represented at the Durbar by non-official Durbaris, the great majority of whom were in opposition to the Government of the Province concerned, and whose interests were threatened by the policy of the Ministry. The new political régime in seven Provinces would be almost entirely unrepresented. This would rob the Durbar of its representative character, and would make it a very easy target for the jeers and criticisms of hostile elements. Moreover, even if the difficulty were got over by leaving it open to Ministers to attend the Durbar or not as they liked, their deliberate failure to attend would have a very deplorable effect throughout India. Their absence would be more marked by the attendance of Ministers from the other four Provinces.

7. The above appreciation is, of course, based on assumptions which may be completely falsified by the Governors of Congress Provinces, but it seems to me that, unless there is a practical certainty of Congress Ministers and Congress representatives of the Provincial Legislatures attending the Durbar, the effects on the traditional reverence towards the King and on the imperial connection would be definitely adverse. Sir Sikander agrees with me in this view.

8. There is, however, an alternative which I venture to suggest and which seems to me to be free from the objections and risks which attend the present proposal. The suggestion is briefly this – that the Durbar at Delhi should be confined to what I may call the Central elements, and that it should be supplemented by short visits to as many Provinces as possible, including Congress Provinces. By 'Central elements' I mean the following:

(*i*) The Princes.
(*ii*) The two Chambers of the Central Legislature.
(*iii*) The Army.
(*iv*) The territories administered by the Central Government, e.g. Delhi and Baluchistan. This would include the tribal areas of Dera Ghazi Khan in the Punjab.

These elements comprise practically all that is picturesque and spectacular. The addition of Provincial elements adds to the size, but tends rather to detract than otherwise from the splendour. The only element in which Congress would be concerned would be the Central Legislature, and it would matter little if representative Congress members attended or not. Whether Governors of Provinces should be required to attend would be a matter for consideration. Personally, I think that there would be no necessity for their attendance provided they had the privilege of seeing His Majesty either in their own Province or in an adjacent one.

9. A Durbar of this character would have to be supplemented by short visits to as many Provinces as possible. This is an essential part of the proposal. Bombay would be included in the arrival and presumably in the departure. The other Provinces that naturally suggest themselves are Bengal, Madras, United Provinces and the Punjab. In that case two non-Congress and three Congress Provinces would be visited. The programme in each Province could be fixed with reference to prevailing conditions; for instance, assuming that there were no unforeseen developments, the programme that I would contemplate for the Punjab would be something on the following lines:

(*a*) Public arrival.
(*b*) A State function at Government House, e.g. Dinner, Ball, Reception.
(*c*) A Peoples' Fair such as was held when the Prince of Wales visited Lahore.
(*d*) State entry to the races.
(*e*) If possible, a visit to one or two institutions, or villages or canals.
(*f*) Parade of ex-military officers.

The cost of this would not be great and would be voted by the Legislature. It would enable a very large number of his subjects to see His Majesty, and it would not involve, so far as one ran foresee, any political difficulties.

So far as Congress Provinces, were concerned, it would seem to me to be necessary to avoid ceremonial functions of a command character which would place Congress Ministers in a difficult position, but, at the same time, to include certain simple functions which would enable His Majesty to get into personal touch with some of the Ministers, e.g., visits to institutions or villages, laying the foundation stone of some important building and so on. If the assumptions I have made at the end of paragraph 5 above are correct, no difficulty would then arise with regard to Congress Ministers. In fact, I believe that they would welcome visits of this kind, and, again, assuming that the attitude of Congress would not be hostile, the masses, whether Congress followers or not, would flock to see His Majesty.

10. The advantages of a scheme on the above lines would seem to be the following:

(*a*) It avoids the most difficult issue of all, and one which appears to me to be almost insurmountable.
(*b*) It ought greatly to reduce the cost of the visit.
(*c*) It does not force on Congress an immediate issue about which their attitude is most likely to be unfavourable.
(*d*) It enables contact to be made between His Majesty and Congress Ministers in their normal functions.
(*e*) It greatly widens the opportunities of the masses seeing His Majesty.
(*f*) It has the great advantage of leaving the provincial programmes fluid for at least nine months from the present time. If, as I think is not improbable, there were competition among the Provinces to pay honour to His Majesty, then the Provincial programmes could be expanded accordingly. If, on the other hand, there remained in some Provinces a strong feeling against attendance by Congress Ministers at ceremonial functions, then the programme could be adjusted as necessary.

11. The above suggestions would presumably involve a change in the original design of His Majesty's visit. There might be some difficulty in regarding the Durbar as an Accession Durbar if Provinces were not also represented. On the other hand, if it were His Majesty's pleasure, an announcement could be made that His Majesty was visiting India to see his people, that he wished the expenditure on his visit to bear as lightly as possible on the tax-payer, that he was therefore confining his Durbar within narrow limits, and that he wished to get into personal touch with the people and the Government of as many Provinces as possible.

12. There is one other point in this connection. The abandonment of the King's visit for political reasons in India after his intention had been definitely announced, would have very deplorable consequences. The political reasons which made its abandonment necessary would

continue to exist in regard to a Viceregal Durbar also, and in the situation contemplated it would probably be better to abandon the Durbar altogether than to hold a Viceregal one. It would, however, be difficult to do this if the Durbar were an Accession Durbar; but the same difficulty would not arise in the case of the smaller Durbar I have suggested.

13. There is one point mentioned to me by Sir Sikander. He thinks that Federation is likely to develop into a very controversial issue, and that an excuse for agitation might be given if the idea got abroad that His Majesty was coming to India to announce something definite about its introduction. I imagine there is no such idea, and, if this is so, it might be advisable, in announcing the intention of His Majesty's visit, to make it clear that he is not concerned with any political matter or controversy.

14. I apologise for the length of this letter, but the importance of the subject must be my excuse.[30]

Yours sincerely,
H.W. EMERSON

20

EMERSON TO LINLITHGOW

Secret
No. F.L.-5.

Barnes Court, Simla, E.,
September 28th, 1937

My dear Lord Linlithgow,

In Your Excellency's letter of the 23rd of September 1937, you ask for information regarding Service feeling in the Province. It is, of course, not easy for a Governor to ascertain what the feeling is, since he cannot have full information without making enquiries which might seem to reflect on his confidence in the Ministry. Indirectly, however, one learns a certain amount from time to time. I should say generally that, so far as their own prospects and terms of service are concerned, European and Indian officers have full confidence in the Ministers, and especially in the Premier. The mutual relations are excellent, and this applies particularly to Secretariat officers. Sikander himself has told me that among some Indian officers there is a tendency to curry favour. There is also sometimes some difficulty regarding appointments on communal grounds, but so far this has amounted to very little. A Chief Engineer, for instance, told me the other day that communal considerations enter into almost every appointment, and that the Minister concerned is continually pestered by applications from his own community; but he added that the Minister had so far always accepted his advice. General questions relating to communal distribution of new appointments are settled by the Cabinet of Ministers. There has been only one case which might have caused trouble so far as I was concerned. This referred to a campaign against a Hindu Superintendent of Police in a district where there had been a communal riot. A very strong agitation was carried on against him by Muslims, who demanded his immediate transfer. This, however, was not taken up seriously when I pointed out the inadvisability of acceding to the demand. It is difficult to make an estimate of the feelings of the Services regarding the new administration as compared with the old. A succession of communal troubles has, I think, somewhat shaken the confidence of some senior officers in the ability of the new Government to deal quickly and firmly with serious trouble, but as yet there is hardly sufficient ground to justify grave misapprehension. There is a certain amount of uncertainty among executive officers of Government as to where the policy of isolation from political affairs ends, and their duty to Government as such begins. This uncertainty is due more to their own misunderstanding than to any action on the part of the Ministry. For instance, this morning I presided at the request of the Premier who was also present, over a conference representing the three districts of Jullundur, Ludhiana and Hoshiarpur. The Commissioner of the Division,[31] and the Deputy Inspector-General, Police, of the Range,[32] were present, and also the three Deputy Commissioners[33] and the three Superintendents of Police.[34] The object of the conference was to discuss the general situation in these three districts where there has been much communist and Congress activity during the past three months. The position is not really serious, but there seemed to be rather a policy of drift, and I suspected that the district officers were not receiving the support they were entitled to receive from administrative officers. The conference proved this to be the case, and the reason was largely due to a failure to appreciate the incidental effects of the new constitution. All Government officers have been enjoined to keep clear of party politics, and especially at the time of elections. In a circular letter issued by Government towards the end of June it was, however, explained that their duties and responsibilities *vis-à-vis* the new Government were the same as under the old one. It was also clearly stated that Government intended to deal firmly with movements subversive of law and order. I found this morning that several officers present, including senior ones, were in genuine doubt as to how far they could oppose subversive movements and at the same time obey the injunction not to get mixed up with party politics. The answer was fairly clear, though of course border line cases are likely to occur. Communism, for instance, is a subversive movement opposed to Government as such. It was fought under the old constitution, and the same reasons exist how far [now for] continuing to fight it. The mere fact that some persons have the additional incentive of spreading communism because it may embarrass the present Government is no reason at all why officers of Government should not openly use their influence against it, and especially by way of propaganda. Nonetheless, officers have abstained from doing so because of the political aspect. I fancy this kind of misunderstanding exists in other districts, and I have suggested to the Premier that early in the cold weather a discussion with the remaining four Commissioners would be of value. Enlightenment is certainly necessary, for it is difficult for many officers to grasp the distinction between supporting a political party, and carrying out the policy of a party when that party becomes the Government. In any case, border line cases are likely to be sufficiently numerous as to give rise to charges of political interference, but these have to be faced. Again, as I mentioned in my last letter, executive officers do not quite know where they stand in regard to the policy of Government towards communal disturbances, though difficulties will to some extent be relieved by a letter which has since issued on my advice pointing out that, pending the decisions of Government on the proceedings of the Unity Conference, executive officers have to carry on as they have done in the past, and to regard as their main duty the preservation of the peace.

To sum up, I should say that there is no uneasiness among the Services regarding the treatment of Service questions in the Punjab, but that there is still some misunderstanding regarding the practical working of the new constitution, and a certain amount of misapprehension regarding its effects on law and order, especially from the communal point of view.

2. The reactions to the abandonment of the Lahore abattoir scheme were much as one expected. The Muslim press, forgetting that a short time before it had itself advised abandonment, regarded it as a concession to agitation. Extreme elements among the Hindus suggested pursuing the agitation in regard to existing slaughter-houses, but one or two papers that advocated this course were told at once that, if they pursued it, action would be taken immediately against them under the Press Act. For the last few days I have seen nothing on these lines, and do not think that it would have any serious backing. Hindus and Sikhs were genuinely appreciative of the action taken by the Government of India, and while there was criticism on more or less side issues, there was, I think, a general feeling of gratitude. The subject is rapidly losing its interest as a public attraction.

3. The inevitable result of the abandonment will be to encourage public agitation on other issues that may arise, and this result will not be discounted until Government have dealt firmly with some specific agitation.

The occasion may come at once, since the Khalsa College is due to open today and there are signs that there will be a big agitation over the dismissal of some members of the staff. Government are not directly interested, but if, as is probable, *satyagraha* is attempted, Government will almost certainly be asked to give assistance to the College authorities. The matter may then easily become one of law and order. I am told that the Maharaja of Patiala is either giving lukewarm support to, or has withdrawn his support from, the Committee of Management.

The general feeling is that sooner or later there must be a fight between Government and the left wing of the Sikhs. This feeling has been increased by the publication by Master Tara Singh, the Akali leader, of a truculent letter addressed to the Premier. I attach a copy of the letter.[35] Tara Singh is the brother of a professor of the Khalsa College, who has been dismissed and who has been at the bottom of trouble in the College for many years. It is, therefore, not improbable that the tug-of-war will legion at once. I hope that, in spite of the defection of Patiala, the Committee of Management will stand firm.

4. The Ministry had under consideration this week the enquiry from Delhi whether the Punjab Government would be prepared to supply electric power from the Mandi Hydro-Electric Scheme. At first sight the proposal looked attractive, although the maximum rates cited by Delhi were much too low. From the Punjab point of view, they would contribute nothing towards the cost of generating power, but they would pay roughly the cost of the main transmission line through the south-eastern districts of the Punjab, provided always that the cost of material did not rise much above existing rates. The transmission line in turn might prove of great value to the Punjab, especially if tube well irrigation proved to be practicable in that part of the Province. Our enquiry, however, has not gone sufficiently far to justify any conclusion that irrigation from tube wells will be a practicable proposition. On the contrary, the present indications, which however are not final, are that it will not pay. In the circumstances, the Ministry rightly decided that they could not commit themselves to a scheme which might prove of very doubtful benefit to the Punjab, while it would deprive the Province of power for which in a few years there may be an adequate demand.

Yours sincerely,
H.W. EMERSON

21

EMERSON TO LINLITHGOW

Secret
No. F.L.-9.

Camp, Rupar,
October 8th, 1937

My dear Lord Linlithgow,

I have been on tour since the 2nd of October 1937, and so have been rather out of touch with affairs for the past few days. I have not yet received the last fortnightly report, but am sending this letter in anticipation so as to reach Your Excellency before you yourself start on your tour through Kulu.

2. The strike of students at the Khalsa College, Amritsar, proved to be a fiasco. Less than 20 students absented themselves, and there has been no interruption of work whatever. There was a very minor demonstration on the opening day at the college itself, followed by a public meeting that evening in Jallianwala Bagh, when there was a fracas between the followers of the two parties, in which several persons were more or less seriously injured. The police took up cross cases on private complaints, and in one of them Master Tara Singh is an accused on the ground of instigation. I know nothing about the details of the charge against him, but do not think that the district officers would have arrested him had there not been a fairly strong *prima facie* case. Since the extreme Akalis headed by Tara Singh had done a great deal of propaganda in order to create serious trouble, the result is very definitely a blow to their prestige and a clear victory for Sir Sunder Singh Majithia. When I saw the latter a week ago, his satisfaction was somewhat damped by the action of the Maharaja of Patiala. Thinking that there was going to be serious trouble and also having brought over Akali opposition to himself about a year ago, Patiala had a telegram sent to Sir Sunder Singh just before the strike, saying that he was not going to allow his representatives to attend the Managing Committee, and asking that action should be taken against some other members of the staff hostile to the Akalis in the College. Sir Sunder Singh was to see Patiala personally this week, but I have not yet heard the result. The Maharaja's action, however, had the effect of allowing the Akalis to save their face on the ground that he was intervening. I hope that Sir Sunder Singh will remain firm, not only because of the immediate issue, but because Patiala has a way of intervening in Sikh affairs whenever he has a chance.

3. During the past few weeks Government have taken action against a certain number of persons, sedition-mongers, communists or communal mischief-makers. The result has been a burst of indignation in the press against so-called repressive measures, but action had been sufficiently delayed and it was necessary to show that people could not write or say what they liked regardless of consequences. There has been particular outcry against the prosecution and conviction of Baba Kharak Singh for sedition. He was at one time a prominent Akali leader, is quite irresponsible in his utterances, and at times of excitement can work up a mob to a dangerous pitch. He was largely responsible for the Shahidganj trouble; he was president of the diwan in the Sheikhupura district when a clash occurred between Muslims and Sikhs, and he presided over several meetings in connection with the abattoir. Since he came out of jail a few months ago, he has made at least half a dozen highly seditious speeches. Of late he has been in opposition to Master Tara Singh, and his prosecution was, I understand, some cause of embarrassment to Sir Sunder Singh. Nonetheless, he is well out of the way since, besides being very unstable, he is a firebrand who can cause a conflagration at times of popular excitement. The so-called repressive action, in addition to a few prosecutions, includes externment orders against two of the released Kakori prisoners who were visiting the Punjab in order to attend communist conferences, and also action under the Press Act against a Muslim newspaper for a grossly obscene attack on the Head of the Ahmadi community. The action taken by Government, so long as they remain firm, will, I think, have a very salutary effect on the general situation.

4. The attitude of the Hindu and Sikh press is illuminating. It pretends to be indignant because the law of sedition is not under suspension as in Congress Provinces. It conveniently overlooks the fact that in those Provinces the Congress organisation is supporting the Government who, if they wish, can exercise effective control over Congress speakers and the Congress press. On the other hand, in the Punjab a dead set is being made against the Government with the ultimate object of paving the way for Congress administration by undermining the influence of the present Ministry. Activities have gone far beyond legitimate party politics and there is practically no distinction between the left side of the Congress in the Punjab and those who are openly preaching communism. It was reported from Gurgaon a week or two ago that the Congress speakers there were advocating non-payment of land revenue. I have asked for this information to be amplified. If it is true, it means that, while there is a Congress

Government in the United Provinces, the Congress organisation is deliberately attempting to stir up trouble just across the river in a neighbouring province. Pandit Jawaharlal is advertised to tour in the Punjab during the next few days. It will be interesting to see what line he takes. If his speeches go beyond party politics as they are likely to do, there may be complications. In any case it will be difficult to avoid ultimate trouble if Congress, while pursuing constitutional methods in seven Provinces continues as an organisation to follow its old methods of stirring up trouble against the Governments in other Provinces.

5. The Punjab Government, although they command a large majority in the Legislative Assembly representing equivalent support in the Province as a whole, have to cope with an almost entirely hostile Press. So far as Hindu and Sikh papers are concerned, there is not a single one which is a steady supporter of Government. Owing to the fact that Mr. Manohar Lal, the Finance Minister, is a Trustee of the *Tribune,* this paper is not as virulent as it might be, but it rarely misses an opportunity of having a dig at the Ministry, and is, of course, pro-Congress in its views. Among the Muslim papers, the *Inqilab* generally supports Government, and is one of the leading vernacular dailies. Maulana Zafar Ali Khan, the editor of the *Zamindar*, is far too uncertain a quantity for any reliance to be placed on him. The *Eastern Times* is fairly sympathetic, but is uncertain and has in any case a small circulation. The other Muslim papers are almost entirely communal, and several representing the Ahrars are definitely hostile. The *Civil and Military Gazette* is a staunch supporter. There is thus the curious phenomenon of a popular Government receiving very little support indeed from the popular press. One reason is that the Hindu and Sikh press has more money behind it than the Muslim press; another and more powerful reason is that the ordinary reader wants plenty of ginger in his newspapers. He has little use for ordinary news as such. On the other hand, the more violent is the communal side the better will a paper sell. Communally, the vernacular Press of the Province is at present appalling. It has never been good, but, leaving aside special occasions of excitement such as Shahidganj, I do not think that I remember it consistently as bad as it is at present. Liberty of press in the Punjab means complete irresponsibility and licence, and the power to inflict untold harm on the community. Although the Legislative Assembly gave a mandate to the Ministry to use its powers to control the press and although several warnings have been given, little action has so far been taken. It has, however, to be remembered that, having regard to the police in Congress Provinces, the Ministry are

in a difficult position. They have indeed shown considerable courage during the past few weeks in showing that the law in other respects is not in abeyance.

Yours sincerely,
H.W. EMERSON

22

EMERSON TO LINLITHGOW

Secret Government House, Lahore,
No. F.L.-12. *October 21st, 1937*

My dear Lord Linlithgow,

In view of Your Excellency's visit to Lahore which begins tomorrow, I am writing my fortnightly letter earlier than usual and am confining it to the recent visit of Pandit Jawaharlal Nehru to the Punjab and to certain aspects of the meeting of the All-India Muslim League at Lucknow in which Sir Sikander played a prominent part. Both these events and especially the latter have considerable bearing on all-India politics, and I propose also to comment on this aspect of them.

2. With regard to Jawaharlal's visit. He attended a large political conference in the Hoshiarpur district, paid short visits to several places in the Shahpur and Gujrat districts, and was in Lahore for some hours where he addressed a large public meeting. He also made short speeches at various places on his journey. Mr. Jenkin, Central Intelligence Officer, has given a good description of his tour in a note dated the 14th October 1937, written for the Central Bureau of Intelligence,[36] and if Your Excellency has not already seen it, I would suggest its perusal. An account will also be included in the provincial fortnightly report. So far as the local and visible effects of his visit are concerned, it is sufficient to say that he was received everywhere by large crowds, that in some places these included a fair number of Muslims, most of whom had come out of curiosity, and that he himself appears to have been very unfavourably impressed by Congress organisation in the Punjab. One object of his visit was to reconcile Dr. Gopi Chand and Dr. Satyapal, who are rival Congress leaders in the Province. The former is the leader of Congress group in the Punjab Legislative Assembly, while the latter is the President of the Punjab Provincial Congress Committee. Relations between them have never been

good; they have recently deteriorated and are now extremely bad. From correspondence which I have seen it appears that Congress headquarters are disgusted with both of them. Jawaharlal's efforts to bring about a conciliation seem to have met with no success. While the Pandit's visit will probably give a temporary impetus tc communist and socialist efforts in the central Punjab, I doubt whether it will have any great lasting effect.

Generally, his speeches were more restrained than usual, and there was little, if anything, in them which would bring him within the mischief of the law even if it were wise to prosecute him. They were generally within the limits of party politics as they are understood in England, but the people are of course not yet used to party politics, and the wholesale attack which he made on the present Ministry, which is now the 'Sirkar' in the Province, has certainly caused great resentment among the supporters of Government and probably some bewilderment as to what the new order means. The resentment among my Ministers and their supporters is accentuated by the peculiar position of Congress. They have Ministries in seven Provinces, the policy of which is controlled to a large extent by the central organisation of which Jawaharlal is the head. Although Jawaharlal is himself not a member of any provincial Ministry and therefore technically his attack is not an attack by the Ministry of one Province on the Ministry of another, in the popular view it comes to much the same thing. The general interpretation of his campaign is that all the forces of Congress are to be directed against non-Congress Provinces, and in particular the Punjab. I agree with this interpretation. Apart from other forces which are at work, the result must be to encourage fissiparous tendencies as between the Provinces. With regard to the attack on the Ministry, it consisted mainly of a comparison between the Congress Ministries and the Punjab Ministry to the great detriment of the latter; people in Congress Provinces were now free while the reverse was the case in the Punjab, the police in the former were the servants of the public, while in the Punjab they were the instruments of a reactionary Government which was worse than the one which had preceded it; Sikander and his colleagues were doing nothing for the people, and there could be no real freedom or advance until they were replaced by Congress Ministers; a great deal was said about repression.

3. As regards Congress policy in general, there was little, if any, change from the policy previously advocated by Jawaharlal. The main points on which he dwelt were the following:

(*a*) Congress were out to wreck the Act rather than to work it;

(*b*) the centre of gravity of Congress had changed from the middle classes to the masses; it was now more a mass movement than at any time;

(*c*) the taking of office had enabled Congress to get into far closer contact with the people; the momentum behind Congress had enormously increased and in a few years it would be so irresistible that it would sweep everybody and everything before it; then would be the time for Congress to enforce the government they wanted. While there was not, I think, any specific reference to ousting the British, the speeches left little doubt as to what the ultimate object was to be;

(*d*) there was certain to be a big European war within a few years and the British Empire was likely to come to an end within 15 years;

(*e*) no help should be given to England in case of war;

(*f*) Congress would have nothing to do with Federation.

In short, there has been no change in the aims and objects of Congress according to Jawaharlal's interpretation of policy. The present time is merely one of preparation for a big mass revolution which will happen as a matter of course within a few years. In this estimate, however, Jawaharlal ignored two very important factors; first, the restraining and conservative influences which responsibility cannot fail to exercise on provincial Congress Ministers; and second, Muslim opposition. Incidentally, the latter is bound to encourage the former and to put a brake on the more extravagant aims of Congress. While Jawaharlal was in the Punjab, he mentioned at several places that he refused to recognise the existence of any communal problem; so far as there was one it was anti-national and therefore to be regarded as though it did not exist. He got an effective reply a few days later at Lucknow.

4. The outstanding impression left by Jawaharlal's visit was that of domination and arrogance on the part of Congress in so far as he represents its attitude. In his main speech at the political conference in Hoshiarpur he mentioned (and apparently regarded) as the supreme act of wickedness on the part of the Punjab Ministry the fact that it had had the temerity to attack Congress. There seems to me no doubt that he is or was genuinely amazed that anyone should have such audacity. It is this domineering and arrogant spirit which is causing most bitter resentment and which affected the Muslims most at Lucknow. I think it strongly influenced Sikander in taking the step which he has taken.

5. I do not know whether Sikander had made up his mind before he

went to Lucknow. He mentioned to me at Simla that Jinnah was anxious for his help in all-India politics, but the discussion was not pursued. A day or two before he left for Lucknow he told me that he was going there, but I gathered that his chief object was to attempt to influence the League against passing a resolution in favour of complete independence. When he returned, I had a long talk with him with special reference as to how his action might affect the Ministry and his support in the Provincial Legislature. I gather that he had previously mentioned the matter briefly to Sir Chhotu Ram, but that he had not taken Sir Sunder Singh and Mr. Manohar Lal into his confidence. He certainly had no discussion with the supporters of Government as a whole or with the Unionist Party as a body. As I will mention presently, he did not seem to me to appreciate the consequences of his action so far as provincial politics are concerned. Before I come to this, however, it may be of interest to Your Excellency to give an appreciation of Muslim feeling as interpreted by Sikander after his visit to Lucknow. Although this was voiced in Jinnah's opening address, the resentment was much stronger than even Jinnah represented it to be. The basis of it is the apprehension felt by Muslims regarding the future. In their view the Congress régime in Congress Provinces has been characterised by the spirit of arrogance and domination which I have mentioned above. Particular causes of offence are the non-inclusion of representative Muslims in Congress Cabinets, the flaunting of the Congress flag, the prominence given to 'Bande Mataram' and the attempt to make Hindi the universal language. To Muslims these are the outward and visible signs of the intention of Congress to create Hindu *raj*. Apparently some of the delegates from other Provinces gave concrete examples of the oppression of Muslims. I gather that this was particularly the case with delegates from Bihar. Sikander himself admitted that the complaints were probably very exaggerated, but at the moment Muslims everywhere, except in the North-West Frontier Province, are on the lookout for grievances against Congress and are in a mood to see nothing good in anything that Congress Ministries may do. Again, Muslim loyalists in Congress Provinces feel that there is no one to help them. While the more intelligent of them realise that under the new Constitution a Governor must support his Ministers and the servants of Government must carry out the Ministerial policy, they are not reconciled to these consequences of responsible government which they did not fully foresee. The less intelligent, of course, are frankly puzzled. Sikander told me that speech after speech was couched in the most bitter invective, and that feeling ran so high that, if any Congress leader had appeared in the conference, he would have been in physical danger. The words Sikander himself used were that he would have been in danger of being lynched. I asked Sikander what was the view generally of Muslims at Lucknow regarding the ultimate aim of Congress. He said that their view, which he shared, was that Congress would be in no hurry to have an open breach with the British Government, that their aim was first to get control in the Provinces and complete domination over the minorities, especially the Muslims and when that happened, to drive the British out. If they succeeded in this, they would have the minorities at their mercy. In the Muslim view this policy of Congress must result in civil war. I give this appreciation not as my own, but as that of Muslims as interpreted by Sikander. According to this view, and here I agree, the Punjab and to a less extent Bengal must be the bulwarks against Congress domination.

It is again a case of history repeating itself. After the Irwin-Gandhi agreement Muslims were very depressed and in a thoroughly defeatist mood; they had stood aside from the civil disobedience movement and many of them had given strong and invaluable support to Government. They at first thought that the agreement threw them to the wolves and were ready to make terms with Congress; Gandhi, however, missed the best chance he ever had of coming to terms with them, and gradually their confidence and courage revived. Much the same has happened now. They went to Lucknow in a defeatist mood. They left determined to fight Congress to the last or, in the alternative, to enforce favourable terms for themselves.

6. Muslims are very afraid of Federation because they believe that it will give Congress domination at the centre, and that through the centre they will be able to exercise a large measure of control in non-Congress Provinces. I give this again not as my own appreciation, but as that of Muslims. Incidentally, Sikander expressed the view that Congress intend to accept the present scheme of Federation, after the usual pretence of opposition, because they believe that it will ultimately place them in a position of domination at the centre.

7. I now come to the effect of the Lucknow agreement on provincial politics. According to Sikander, all that he agreed to do was to support Jinnah in all-India politics and to advise his Muslim supporters in the Provincial Legislature to join the Muslim League, making it clear that in provincial concerns the position of the Unionist Party would remain unchanged.[37] The Secretary of the Muslim League[38] has issued an account of the agreement which would practically mean the merging of Muslim members of the Unionist Party into the Muslim League. Sikander tells me

this morning that the statement is wrong and that he is having it corrected. I am not sure at the moment whether the views of Sikander and Jinnah coincide as to what was or was not agreed upon. Sikander has no doubt on the point, but the next few days will show whether there is any misunderstanding. If Sikander has, in fact, unconsciously agreed to an arrangement which would merge the Unionist Party into the League, then he will have to repudiate it, since he fully realises the unfortunate consequences of any such arrangement. Even assuming however, that the agreement goes no further than he intended and believes it to have gone, it is clear that there has been a big change in the position he has previously held in all-India and provincial politics. The Hindu and Sikh press at once seized on the importance of what happened at Lucknow. Sikander himself, when I talked to him immediately after his return, did not seem to realise it. He seemed to think that everything would go on much as before. He has now appreciated the change. As I pointed out to him, he is going to find increasing difficulty in assuming the mantle of a non-communal leader. He has, in fact, become a Muslim leader, and the opposition Hindus and Sikhs will, in future, refuse to regard him as anything else. His Hindu and Sikh colleagues are, I think, a little uneasy, but not seriously perturbed. Sir Chhotu Ram, however, would be very upset if there were any question of merging the Unionist Party in the League. The Premier is unlikely at present to lose any of his Hindu or Sikh supporters in the Legislature. On the other hand, his action is undoubtedly thoroughly approved by his Muslim supporters, and the danger of any split in the Muslim ranks has been removed for some time to come. It is improbable that the Unity Conference will now lead to any useful result. As I have suggested in previous letters, there was never much chance of this, while there was a real danger that, owing to the general character and wide implications of the recommendations, it would increase rather than reduce communal tension. The reason why Sikander's action is likely to have little effect at present on his non-Muslim supporters is to be found in the fact that it is generally recognised that Lucknow represents a very definite and strong challenge to Congress, and, for the moment, among non-Muslim supporters of Government, resentment against Congress is stronger than communal apprehensions. Chaudhri Sir Chhotu Ram, for instance, who is non-communal, is more influenced by the fear of Congress domination than by the fear of Muslim aggression. On the other hand, Hindus with Congress sympathies and those Sikhs who are not supporters of Sir Sunder Singh are furious with what has happened and are already making counter-plans.

The Akalis are already thinking of joining Congress, with whom they have always been in close sympathy. The Hindu Sabha may do the same, while it may be assumed that Congress will receive considerable accession to their strength in the towns. Communal feeling will certainly be increased, but paradoxically I am inclined to think that the immediate, though not necessarily the lasting, effect will be to reduce communal riots in the Punjab. One reason for them has been the growing feeling among Muslims that their interests have not been sufficiently protected. On the other hand, I have little doubt that communal troubles will increase elsewhere.

8. There is another aspect of the matter which cannot fail sooner or later to give embarrassment. Sikander is deluding himself if he thinks that provincial politics can be divorced from all-India Muslim interests. For instance, there was a very offensive resolution passed at Lucknow about Shahidganj. Sikander tells me that it was passed after he left and he did not know about it. However that may be, the Muslim League has expressed itself in favour of the return of the site to the Muslims. Sikander himself admits that this is out of the question. What are his Muslim supporters going to do in the matter? Are they going to support him as Premier responsible for law and order or are they going to press the League's views? These and other difficulties are likely to arise.

9. The League, of course, passed other, resolutions at Lucknow relating to Waziristan, Palestine, &c., but the real business which outshadowed everything else was the declaration of war against Congress. From the all-India point of view it is difficult to judge the effects of the Lucknow meeting. Tentatively I would suggest that some of the consequences are likely to be the following:

(1) It has greatly reduced the chance of Congress Ministries provoking a crisis with Government.
(2) It will put a brake on their activities. Their policy is likely to be less extreme in regard to many matters than appeared likely a few weeks ago.
(3) If it is, in fact, the aim of Congress to work for a mass revolution in a few years, then their difficulties will be greatly increased.
(4) It may gradually undermine the unnatural alliance between Muslims and Congress in the North-West Frontier Province.
(5) It will promote separatist tendencies as between Provinces.
(6) It will greatly aggravate the communal situation.
(7) It may ultimately lead to an agreement between Congress and Muslims.[39]

10. I must apologise for the length of this letter, especially as it deals to some extent with matters outside the provincial sphere, but, owing to the fact that Sikander played a prominent part at Lucknow, I have naturally had to consider the implications of his action.[40]

Yours sincerely,
H.W. EMERSON

23

EMERSON TO LINLITHGOW

Secret
D.-O. No. 16-F.L.

Government House, Lahore,
November 12th, 1937

My dear Lord Linlithgow,

In the official fortnightly report for the second half of October is a brief appreciation of Your Excellency's visit to the Punjab. I may add that the Ministers were extremely pleased with it and with the speeches which Your Excellency made. I have heard from all quarters that the visit was regarded as a great success, and there is no doubt that a ceremonial Durbar such as was held in the Fort still makes a great appeal not only to those who are privileged to take part in it and to loyalists generally, but to the ordinary man in the street. In this, as in many other matters, the vernacular press of the Punjab completely fails to represent public opinion.

2. As Your Excellency is aware, there was the threat of some trouble in connection with the Shahidganj agitation. The Durbar was held on Saturday, the 23rd of October. On Friday, the 22nd, the usual Friday prayers in the Badshahi mosque were attended by a congregation estimated at from nine to fifteen thousand, which is several times bigger than the normal congregation. A meeting was held after the prayers attended by about five thousand persons, at which resolutions were passed asking for the return of the Shahidganj site to Muslims, and in the evening the movement was revived to stage a demonstration in the mosque, which is close to the Fort, while the Durbar was taking place. This completely petered out. The C.I.D. officers and I are a little puzzled at the course which events took. Normally, one would expect that after a large meeting, a certain amount of success would have attended a subsequent demonstration, and it looks as if influences had been at work to allow the Muslims the satisfaction of passing resolutions and sending telegrams to Your Excellency on the understanding

that the face of the Ministry would not be blackened by anything worse. The immediate result, however, was very satisfactory, and, since the meeting in the mosque, little has been heard of the agitation from the Muslim side. As I suggested, however, in paragraph 8 of my last letter, the Lucknow resolution regarding Shahidganj may be embarrassing to the Premier. The Hindu and Sikh press has not been slow in taking up the point which I mentioned, namely, that there is or may be a conflict of loyalties between the professed object of the Muslim League and the duty of the Premier. I have asked that the next official fortnightly report should contain some appreciation of the position regarding Shahidganj. In the meantime, I may note that the legal position is that the courts have so far consistently recognised the right of the Sikhs, who have been in possession of the site for a hundred and seventy-five years. An appeal against the judgment of the District Judge is pending in the High Court, which will take it up when the executive authorities inform them that the time is convenient. In the normal course, a further appeal will be made to the Privy Council by the unsuccessful party. Litigation is, therefore, likely to continue for several years. Although for the moment nothing much is likely to happen, it is such a profitable source of income to professional agitators that there is always the danger of a revival of popular agitation. If an attempt were ever made to restore the site to Muslims other than by a judgment of the courts or by mutual agreement a first class crisis would arise, and it would almost certainly be necessary for the Governor in the last resort to exercise his special powers. Fortunately, there is no indication whatever that the present Ministry will countenance any such attempt and the Premier is fully aware of the very big issues that might be involved.

3. In my last letter I attempted to give an appreciation of the effects of the Lucknow agreement on all-India and provincial politics. I may supplement what I then said by subsequent knowledge. I still do not know whether Sikander went to Lucknow with the previous intention of coming to an agreement with Jinnah or whether he was carried off his feet by Muslim enthusiasm. He certainly did not realise the implications of what he was doing, nor did he appreciate the position for sometime after his return. He did not consult his colleagues previously about his action. The situation was and still is much complicated by different versions as to what happened at Lucknow. I mentioned in my previous letter that the Punjab Secretary of the Muslim League issued a statement which was contrary to what Sikander himself had published. This was followed by another statement from one Barkat Ali, a member of the Punjab Legislative Assembly and a staunch follower of the Muslim League, which showed

the agreement in a still more unfavourable light so far as the Unionist Party is concerned. These statements very seriously embarrassed the Hindu and Sikh Ministers, and especially Sir Chhotu Ram who had given a statement to the press, with the approval of Sikander, which was directly contrary in many respects to the accounts given by Jinnah's lieutenants in the Punjab. Sikander himself has so far done nothing publicly to clear up the position, although I understand that he has a statement ready for publication. I have advised him very strongly to be careful not to issue anything likely to give rise to a public controversy between Jinnah and himself, and I understand that he is in correspondence with Jinnah on the matter. In the meantime, although the Hindu and Sikh Ministers are a little uneasy, they are sticking loyally to the Premier, but I notice that Sir Sunder Singh's party (the Khalsa National Party) passed a resolution a few days ago asking that the position should be cleared. So far as urban Hindus are concerned, Sikander has been greatly assisted by the loyalty of Raja Narendra Nath, who is his close personal friend, and who has so far been able to keep the urban Hindu supporters of Government from transferring their allegiance. Chhotu Ram has of course a very firm hold on rural Hindu members. There was a movement started by Sir Gokal Chand Narang to have a big conference in Lahore, representative of all classes of Hindus, to consider the implications of the Sikander-Jinnah pact. The conference had to be dropped at the last moment because Narendra Nath would give it no support and no rural Hindu of any importance would attend it. On the other hand, I notice that Narendra Nath got a very hostile reception at a Hindu meeting a few days ago, and had to be escorted under protection.

For the present, therefore, Lucknow does not seem likely to have any appreciable effect on the following of Government in the legislature. Sikander, however, has admitted to me that it is going to increase the difficulties of Government in getting through a certain class of legislation. For instance, there is a proposal to put forward a bill for the registration of moneylenders. Had it not been for Lucknow, the urban Hindu and Sikh supporters of Government would probably have agreed to it even if they did not like it. To introduce it at present would give the enemies of Government an opportunity to try and split the party. On the other hand, if it is not introduced, the rural supporters may get restive. I may add that Sikander has a great asset in his personal popularity, and, so long as he does not place too great a strain on it, he will probably get through without much damage.

4. There has been another sign of rising feeling in political affairs. Sir Chhotu Ram is at present on a tour of the central Punjab. He had a very

rough house at one place and, I gather, precautions had to be taken at several others against hostile demonstrations. These were organised by urban Congressmen, and, although they do not represent any change in the general attitude towards the present Government, they are an unpleasant feature of democratic politics. The danger is of course that Government supporters will take means to see that the Ministers are not mobbed, or stage similar demonstrations at Congress meetings, which up to the present have been allowed to proceed without interference.

5. I do not think that I have mentioned in any of my previous letters the bitter and unscrupulous campaign that has been waged for some months against the Chief Justice[41] in connection with the proceedings he has had to take in connection with the liquidation of the People's Bank. Among other incidents, three applications were made to the Privy Council by Mr. Gauba who at present is being prosecuted on a criminal charge. There is some reason to believe that the campaign was encouraged by Sir Shadi Lal. I am glad to say that the three applications were rejected by the Privy Council, and this ought to discourage those concerned in the campaign.

6. The low price of cotton is causing much anxiety among agriculturists, and it may involve considerable relief in land revenue collections. Among the more intelligent agriculturists there is a strong feeling that their interests are sacrificed to the millowners of Bombay and Ahmedabad. They believe, for instance, that the trade negotiations between England and India might have been more successful if the non-official advisers had recognised the community of interest between the cotton grower and Lancashire. The difficulty in organising this opinion is that there are comparatively few educated agriculturists with sufficient knowledge of the subject. I have seen it stated, with what truth I do not know, that the interests of cotton growers are being further affected by the import into India of American cotton, and the suggestion has been made that in the interests of agriculturists the import duty on raw cotton should be substantially increased. I think that the Punjab Government may possibly make a representation in this respect, but I imagine that Your Excellency and Grigg have the matter under consideration.

Yours sincerely,
H.W. EMERSON

24

EMERSON TO LINLITHGOW

Secret
D.-O. No. 22-F.L.

Government House, Lahore,
December 3rd, 1937

My dear Lord Linlithgow,

I have little to report in this letter. The attached fortnightly report contains a note on the Shahidganj agitation. Since it was written the appeal has been heard in the High Court and judgement has been reserved. It will be announced on a date convenient to the executive. There has also been a further development on the political side. With the object of embarrassing Government, the Ahrars have issued a challenge to other sections of Muslims to the effect that individuals from among them are ready to start civil disobedience if others will do likewise. A week ago there was a very large congregation at the Badshahi mosque to see whether certain persons would accept the challenge, or the Ahrars stand firm if the challenge was accepted. No one, except a few men of little importance, is really anxious to go to jail and after some manoeuvring the matter fizzled out for the time being. It may, however, be revived.

2. The Premier, speaking at a meeting in the Hoshiarpur district, declared that his adherence to the Muslim League does not affect in any way the position or policy of the Unionist Party. He has, however, not yet issued the promised statement and I doubt whether he has cleared the position with Jinnah. Up to a few days ago, the Muslim members of the Unionist Party in the Legislative Assembly had not declared themselves members of the League – evidence that Sikander does not intend to burn his boats until the situation is clear.

3. The Ministers have been doing a good deal of touring and have addressed a certain number of meetings. The reception given to them was good. But there is far too little activity of this kind by their supporters, and the case of Government is allowed to go too much by default. I am always being told that the matter is in hand, but so far have seen little results.

Events in other Provinces are having their effect. The Ministers tell me that even their own supporters are getting a little restive at the absence of spectacular measures, and there have been slight signs of the Ministers themselves getting rattled – nothing serious at present, but a tendency to rush proposals through because of their political value, but with insufficient consideration of their inherent soundness. The real test is going to come in a few months when the Darling Committee reports on relief in land revenue. I am a little afraid that the temptation to gain passing popularity may influence the Ministry in giving away far more than is necessary or desirable. If they yield they will greatly restrict beneficent activities. However, for the moment there is little cause for anxiety.

4. Indeed on the side of law and order the Premier is stout and sound. He does not hesitate to sanction prosecutions and his policy has had a good effect in checking subversive activities. This is very necessary for there have been definite signs of events in the United Provinces having an effect in the Punjab, e.g. an organised campaign against the Police. There has been nothing approaching the virulence and violence of speeches in the United Provinces, only various straws showing how the wind is blowing. If Haig's action does not result in a general crisis, it will have a salutary effect everywhere.[42] If a crisis does result, I think in the Punjab we have got, and should be able to retain, control over the forces of disorder. At any rate I shall be greatly surprised and disappointed if the Ministry does not take whatever action may be necessary. They will not be slow in pointing the moral which events in the United Provinces provide – namely, that no Government in India can afford to give a free rein to political champions of violent disorder. I was greatly interested in reading the letter of Jawaharlal to Members of the Working Committee. He is beginning to realise the difficulties of either going forward or retreating. His estimate of the situation is not reassuring.

Yours sincerely,
H.W. EMERSON

25

EMERSON TO LINLITHGOW

Private and Personal
D.-O. No. 28-F.L.

Government House, Lahore,
December 18th, 1937

My dear Lord Linlithgow,

In paragraph 3 of my last letter of the 3rd December, I mentioned that there is far too little activity by the supporters of Government in the countryside and that the case of Government is allowed to go too much by default. Your Excellency remarked on this, in your letter of the 8th of December, and I may amplify my previous remarks. Previous to and during the elections the organisation of the Unionist Party was very good, and their agents and supporters were very active in the villages. Since Government took office there has been a very marked falling off in this respect. Among the Ministers, Sir Chhotu Ram has addressed a large number of meetings, and, although he has provoked considerable feeling among the urban classes, his general attitude has been very favourably received by the rural classes. It has undoubtedly done a lot of good. He has also done something to organise the supporters of Government in the south-east of the Province. The Premier and Mian Abdul Haye have also done some touring and addressed some meetings, but to a far less extent than Sir Chhotu Ram. The other three Ministers have done very little in this direction. There have been very few meetings indeed organised or addressed by supporters of Government other than the Ministers, and there is no comparison between the number of meetings organised by the Congress or communists and those organised in support of Government. District officers frequently comment on this, and unless the ministerial party wakes up, it is likely to lose ground. Similarly, nothing tangible has yet resulted from efforts made a few months ago to start a pro-Government newspaper. The impression I get is that the Premier is too [sub]merged in ordinary matters of administration to give adequate attention to party organisation.

2. Similarly, there is insufficient examination of and consultation regarding legislative measures. There have been two informal discussions in Council of proposals to legislate regarding indebtedness, the Alienation of Land Act, &c. Their general effect would be to the prejudice of the moneylending and urban classes, and some of the proposals were drastic. There seems to have been no previous discussion between the Ministers themselves, the effects had not been properly considered and there was very inadequate appreciation of the results on particular sections of the supporters of Government. There had been no previous consultation with men like Raja Narendra Nath as to the attitude which he and his friends were likely to take. It was left me to point out these matters, and I hope that my advice will have some effect. But the impression of confused thinking and lack of foresight has rather shaken the confidence of the Secretaries, who were present during the discussions, in the political sagacity and administrative ability of the Ministers. At the moment there is insufficient control and co-ordination, with the inevitable result that proposals are undigested. I may add that the Ministers did not resent the outspoken criticisms which I had to make. Indeed there is a growing tendency to refer matters to me which are not required to be referred under

the Rules of Business, and, whereas I had little to do during the first two or three months of the new Constitution, I have now a fairly full day's work.

3. The Shahidganj agitation by the Ahrars has advanced a further stage. Yesterday, the 17th of December, Maulvi Mazhar Ali Azhar, the Ahrar leader and a Member of the Legislative Assembly, offered himself with nine others for arrest. They marched from the Badshahi mosque towards the Shahidganj and a crowd of about a thousand collected. Mazhar Ali and his companions were arrested before they reached the Shahidganj and will be prosecuted in due course. After the arrest, the crowd dispersed quietly. There is no definite information whether the movement will be continued, but so far the Ahrars do not appear to have secured much Muslim sympathy, as it is generally recognised that their action has been inspired entirely by political motives.

4. I have been very much interested in developments in the United Provinces and hope that a crisis will not occur there, resulting in the resignation of the Ministry. If there is danger of this, it seems to be of very great importance that the issue should be put on as broad a basis as possible and that the case of Government should be published with as little delay as possible after the resignation of the Ministry. The broad issue is, of course, the question as to whether the Congress Ministry is going to carry out its responsibility for law and order or to allow open incitement to violence and murder. The immediate issue seems to be a much narrower one, and, if it comes to a question of resignation, the Congress will certainly try to put Government in the wrong by keeping the issue to the most narrow possible limits, namely, the question of whether a particular individual should be prosecuted before or after a warning. However, I have no doubt that they will not be allowed to choose the ground most favourable to themselves. Similarly, if a statement has to be made by Government at any time, it seems most desirable that it should not be confined to the immediate issue of a particular individual, but to the campaign of incitement to violence which seems to have been going on for several months. A statement supplemented by an account of the activities of the worst offenders, giving actual extracts from their speeches and substantiated by details of dates and places, would make it very difficult for Congress to defend their inaction, and would put them in the wrong from the outset. In fact, I do not see how the Congress could pretend to adhere to the policy of non-violence, and at the same time justify the breakdown of the Constitution because they had refused to take measures to prevent the preaching of violence. Their position from the broad point of view seems

to be indefensible. It is this fact which makes me hope that the crisis will be surmounted.

Yours sincerely,
H.W. EMERSON

26

EMERSON TO LINLITHGOW

Private and Personal
D.-O. No. 30-F.L.

Government House, Lahore,
December 27th, 1937

My dear Lord Linlithgow,

I am writing my letter earlier this week as I hope to get into camp for a few days' shooting. Craik, who is in Lahore, has told me something about the crisis in the United Provinces and its settlement. It seems to me to be a very happy issue of the affair, if, as he says, Pant is prepared to give a public warning to inciters to violence and to follow it up by action. If I may venture to say so, I do not think Your Excellency need regret the yielding of some ground on the Parmanand issue in return for the general advantage that has been obtained. My personal impression was that the Parmanand issue alone was too narrow for a first class constitutional crisis, and that, unless it could be very clearly linked up with the general question of law and order, the consequences would be out of proportion to the merits of the particular case. On the other hand, it seemed fairly obvious that, unless the United Provinces Ministry were prepared to face up to the fundamental question of law and order, a crisis would occur sooner or later. The indications from other Provinces have been in favour of Congress Ministers accepting their responsibilities, and Pant seems to be moving gradually in the same direction. This seems to me the most favourable sign since Congress accepted office. Personally, I have always thought that once Congress accepted the realities of the situation, they would not hesitate to take the necessary measures. In this connection I may mention the interception of a letter from Vallabhbhai Patel to Dr. Gopi Chand, the leader of the Congress party in our Legislative Assembly. The latter had evidently written to Vallabhbhai asking him to help towards the release of so-called political prisoners in the Punjab. The following is Vallabhbhai's reply dated the 13th of December 1937:

'I have received your letter of the 7th instant without your signature on my return from Lucknow yesterday. In the present circumstances when prisoners released from some Provinces have started preaching violence and have been rearrested on such charges it is next to impossible to hope to get the release of prisoners who are convicted for dacoity and who cannot be clearly classed as political prisoners. The workers may or may not be satisfied, but we will have to face facts. What is required is to create a favourable atmosphere for such releases which at present is sadly missing.'

This letter is a straw showing how the wind is blowing and confirms the wisdom of accommodating Pant to some extent in the United Provinces. I have little doubt myself that more has been gained than lost.

2. In Your Excellency's letter of the 22nd of December 1937, you suggested that I might give a hint to the Premier regarding better party organisation. I have in fact spoken very freely to him and his colleagues on several occasions on this matter, and shall continue to press them, since the lack of counter-propaganda to communist and other subversive activities impinges on the question of law and order. Several of our senior officers have mentioned the question in their fortnightly reports.

3. Last week the Council of Ministers sat for three days to consider the question of new expenditure during the next financial year. The results were very satisfactory from several points of view. First, their attitude indicated a return to what I have always impressed on them as their best policy, namely, the framing of a bold and ambitious constructive programme. To do them justice, they have never questioned the wisdom of this, but during the last month or two, as I have noted in recent letters, there has been a tendency to favour spectacular measures, which would have little practical results, but would react against the moneylender and the urban classes to the benefit of the rural classes. They have also been somewhat over-anxious regarding the political necessity of giving substantial relief in land revenue, thus seriously affecting the financial resources of the Province. While they recognise that relief in this direction may be necessary, much to my surprise, they now take the view that at any rate nothing need be given in 1938-39. Mr. Darling is Chairman of a Committee which is examining the matter. His report will be submitted about next April or May and the Ministers evidently hope to protract the consideration of it, so that the financial effect of any measures they may adopt will not be operative until 1939-40. Political pressure may of course force them to modify their present intentions, but their hope is that they

may be able to persuade their supporters that the right line is to increase production rather than to give relief, which, in the most favourable circumstances, can give negligible help to the small holder. In the meantime, they will explore alternative sources of taxation to make good any surrender of land revenue. This policy has my whole-hearted support.

4. Financially, the prospects for next year are favourable. There was a revenue surplus last year of 34 lakhs. It is anticipated that for the current year there will be a similar surplus of at least 24 lakhs. The estimates for the next financial year are distinctly favourable, apart from anything we may get from the Government of India. The financial proposals approved by the Council are on the following lines:

First, a generous programme of beneficent activities based on the normal expectations of 1938-9; and

Second, a special five-year programme of development to cost 50 lakhs in all, namely, about 10 lakhs a year for five years.

The Ministers will justify the latter, even although it may result in a small revenue deficit in any or all of the five years on the ground that during 1936-7 and 1937-8 there has been a revenue surplus of 60 lakhs and that they feel justified, therefore, in exceeding their revenue by this amount if necessary over a period of five years. In fact they propose to do much what the Government of India did in utilising a revenue surplus for rural development. From a strict financial point of view this course is not without its dangers, but taking the political and financial aspects together, I believe it is the right one, and it has my support. It has to be remembered that if the Ministry can successfully appeal to the imagination of the people by bold constructive efforts, they will be the better able to resist the demand for large reductions in land revenue.

5. The special programme of development has yet to be framed in detail. The present idea is to concentrate on one tehsil in each of the 29 districts of the Province, except Simla. Special importance will be attached to consolidation of holdings, the distribution of good seed, cattle breeding, better cultivation, cottage industries, &c. Efforts will be made towards a reduction of debt and the establishment of village panchayats. Fortunately, it has been possible to provide a good deal for the latter two objects in the ordinary budget. For instance, there are at present debt conciliation boards in 10 districts only. The number will be raised to 29 next year. Similarly, the number of panchayat officers is to be increased from 20 to 28, and in addition an assistant panchayat officer is to be given to 28 districts. Generous allotments in the ordinary budget will be made towards

agriculture, co-operative societies, veterinary development, industries and medical relief, and there is a big road programme. Your Excellency will be glad to hear that most of the schemes for veterinary development, which were recommended by the Cattle Breeding Conference held a year ago, are to be started next year. In particular, the schemes for the formation of pedigree herds have been approved. Unfortunately, the Veterinary Department themselves have had to postpone the scheme for increasing the outturn of bulls at the Hissar Farm, since, owing to famine conditions, the reserves of fodder are practically exhausted, and they consider it unsafe to expand the herd at the present time. On the whole, next year's budget promises to be the most progressive for some years. It should have great propaganda value and I have impressed on the Ministry the necessity of seeing that the most is made of it in this direction.

6. The Ministry have not yet decided what Bills they will introduce in the coming session of the legislature. They will have to make up their minds during the next few days, but I am hoping that they will be comparatively innocuous from the class point of view. In any case, I feel much more cheerful, as, after disquieting signs of an aberration, the Ministry are now getting back on to sound and sane lines.

Yours sincerely,
H.W. EMERSON

NOTES

1. Sheikh Abdul Ahad.
2. Mr Chaudhuri Nanak Chandra.
3. Not reprinted in R/3/1/2 (from which the present text is taken).
4. Not printed but see Enclosure to No. 10.
5. Mr A.A. Macdonald.
6. Dr R.S. Harnath Singh.
7. This report is missing from R/3/1/2 and the text has been taken from L/P&J/5/238, ff 209-12.
8. India Office papers on the Haveli Project are on L/E/9/379-80.
9. Not printed.
10. Not printed.
11. See Enclosure.
12. Mian R.B. Lal Singh.
13. Mr C.L. Coates.
14. Not printed.
15. Mr J.W. Hearn.
16. Not printed.

17. The general section of Sir Chhotu Ram's note has been reprinted in full but the detailed accounts of the places he visited have been omitted. The text has been taken from L/P&J/5/238, ff. 178-81.
18. Sardar Bawa Nanak Singh.
19. Lala Naubat Rai Sahney.
20. Mr K.B. Sheikh Khurshaid Muhammad.
21. This letter, which is not printed in R/3/1/2, has not been traced elsewhere.
22. Lord Linlithgow minuted on this paragraph: 'P.S.V. – I must look up Secretary of State's exact words. Anderson, I think, agrees with Emerson. Do we know with exactitude what is happening in Bengal? I feel sure Congress will challenge this immediately on assuming office. L.'

    Other Governors made similar comments to those expressed by Sir Herbert Emerson. As a result of an exchange of telegrams between Lord Linlithgow and Lord Zetland on 17 and 19 July 1937, it was agreed that the Viceroy should inform Governors that they should work closely to the provisions of the Government of India Act and should normally preside at Councils of Ministers. However the Secretary of State left it to the Governors' discretion as to when they should absent themselves from the Councils. They should, however, make it clear to Chief Ministers that they normally intended to preside. India Office papers on this subject are on L/P&J/9/251.
23. This report is missing from R/3/1/2 and the text has been taken from L/P&J/5/238, ff. 151-5.
24. On 16 August 1937, Sir Herbert Emerson sent Lord Linlithgow a copy of a letter from the Deputy Commissioner at Gurdaspur, dated 11 August 1937, regarding the trouble at Qadian. Sir Herbert reported that Fakhar-ud-Din, one of the seceders who was stabbed, died on 13 August. R/3/1/2.
25. More than a year previously the Government of India had decided (in view of advances in refrigeration) to modernise its methods of supplying beef to the British Army in India. It intended to close down about 27 local slaughter-houses and construct a central one. It had been agreed that this central slaughter-house would be sited some distance from the Lahore Cantonment. Hindus in the area had come to believe that cattle would become scarce and milk and butter dearer. By the time of Sir Herbert Emerson's report, several meetings on the question were being held in Lahore and Amritsar every day and feelings had become worked up. Regular committees had been formed to organise agitation and, in addition to several local *hartals*, a provincial *hartal* was proposed for 4 September 1937. Information taken from Punjab Chief Secretary's *Report for the second half of August, 1937*. L/P&J/5/238, ff. 108-9.

    In a lengthy letter of 31 August 1937 to Lord Linlithgow, Sir Herbert Emerson conveyed and supported his Ministry's recommendation that the Government of India should reach a very early decision to abandon the abattoir scheme. Emerson wrote: 'Under the old Constitution it might have been practicable to see the thing through, but it would have been unwise to do so.

With the new Constitution the difficulties and danger are far greater. Even if this course were attempted, the result would probably be negative. No contractor would be found to undertake the work, and the cold storage company would find itself in great difficulties. Labourers in the abattoir ceased to work yesterday, possibly with the connivance of the contractors.' This letter is printed in MSS.EUR.F. 125/4, section 2, pp. 259-66.

Eventually the Government of India decided to abandon the central abattoir scheme. See No. 20, paragraph 2.

26. Shaikh Nur Muhammad.
27. Agha Saadat Ali Khan.
28. This letter is not included in R/3/1/2 and the text has been taken from MSS.EUR.F. 125/4, section 2, pp. 321-7.
29. In paragraph 8 of his letter of 17 September 1937, Lord Linlithgow expressed the view that there were definite signs of a relaxation of the non-co-operative attitude of the Congress headquarters on matters like the non-attendance of Ministers at functions. He added: 'I would hope that in a year's time from now the social barriers would have been broken down or broken down to a very large extent and that the difficulty of Congress headquarters in preventing responsible Provincial Ministers from accepting invitations to a function such as the present would have very greatly increased.' MSS.EUR.F. 125/4, section 2, pp. 311-12.
30. Sir Herbert Emerson wrote again to Lord Linlithgow on the subject of the proposed royal durbar in a letter of 30 September 1937. Sir Herbert reported a conversation he had had with Colonel Shamsher Singh, a brother of Rajkumari Amrit Kaur. Colonel Singh felt that 'His Majesty's visit would be associated with politics, and, in particular, with the question of Federal Constitution, in regard to which he confirmed Sikander's view that it is likely to become a matter of acute controversy.' Colonel Singh agreed that there would be no discourtesy from Congress if the King came to India but said that: 'there would be great difficulty in regard to big ceremonial functions; he was clear that Congress Ministers could not attend an Imperial Durbar without a sacrifice of principles'.

    On 11 February 1938 it was announced that the King's visit to India had been postponed until the general world outlook had become more settled. MSS.EUR.F. 125/139.
31. Mr E. Sheepshanks, Commissioner, Jullundur Division.
32. Mr E.W.C. Wace.
33. Mr S.B. Capoor, Sardar Bawa Nanak Singh and Mr M.R. Sachdev respectively.
34. Mr H.W. Hale, Chaudhri A.S. Ram and Mr A. Unitt respectively.
35. Not printed. In this letter, dated 10 September 1937, Master Tara Singh alleged that Sir Sikander Hyat Khan's 'present efforts are directed to consolidate the Muslim position and to establish Muslim domination in the province'. He

felt that conditions had distinctly worsened since Sir Sikander had taken charge of the Government. Master Tara Singh proceeded to elaborate a number of examples he said supported his charges. R/3/1/2.

36. Mr Jenkin's note has not been traced in the India Office Records.
37. See Appendix I for the text of the Sikander-Jinnah Pact as held in the Quaid-e-Azam Papers.
38. Mr Ghulam Rasul Khan. (Secretary, Punjab Provincial Muslim League.)
39. Lord Linlithgow minuted here: 'As an alternative to the absorption of the Muslims by Congress.'
40. Lord Linlithgow minuted on this letter: 'Of great interest.'
41. Sir Douglas Young.
42. On 15 November 1937, Parmanand, a former 'revolutionary' convict from the Punjab, had delivered a speech at Dehra Dun containing clear incitements to murder and violence. On receiving reports of the speech, Sir Harry Haig (Governor of the United Provinces) felt that a prosecution should be launched but Mr Pant (Premier of the U.P.) declined to take responsibility whereupon the Governor invoked his special responsibilities. Subsequently Parmanand and his companions were arrested on a separate charge in Delhi where they deliberately disobeyed restrictive orders placed on them. At this juncture, Mr Pant argued that the U.P. prosecution should be dropped even though it related to an entirely separate matter. Finally, after Parmanand had been convicted and sentenced in Delhi, a compromise in the U.P. dispute was effected in consultation with Lord Zetland (Secretary of State for India). The prosecution for the Dehra Dun speech was given up on the condition that Mr Pant issued a severe general warning against seditious speaking in which was included a statement that no further individual warning would be given as a preliminary to prosecution. Information from MSS.EUR.F.125/142.

CHAPTER 3

Documents for 1938

27

EMERSON TO LINLITHGOW

Private and Personal
D.-O. No. 31(a)-F.L.

Government House, Lahore,
January 11th, 1938

My dear Lord Linlithgow,

There is little to report for the past fortnight. The Ahrars are continuing their campaign of civil disobedience in connection with Shahidganj. Five volunteers are sent and are arrested each day. In due course security is demanded from them to keep the peace for six months. They refuse to give it and are sent to jail. So far little excitement has been caused in Lahore itself, but I understand that a good many volunteers are coming from outside and that there is no sign of the supply running short. In the appeal before the High Court a further date was given for arguments on certain questions of law regarding which there was, I understand, some difference of opinion between the three Judges hearing the appeal. These arguments will conclude today and judgment will be announced in the near future. The postponement has naturally raised the hopes of Muslims and their disappointment will be the keener if their appeal is dismissed. This may have reactions in connection with the civil disobedience movement. As I have previously mentioned, the campaign by the Ahrars is purely political and is the direct outcome of the Lucknow conference where Sikander made an agreement with Jinnah and a resolution was passed by the Muslim League demanding the restoration of the place to Muslims. Sikander personally does not seem to be embarrassed by the situation in which this resolution placed him, but the renewal of the civil disobedience is of course an inconvenience and a source of expense to Government, and there is always the danger that it may assume more serious proportions.

2. The Assembly met yesterday and will sit until about the 25th of January. Government legislation is comparatively innocuous. The most controversial bill is one containing two amendments of the Alienation of Land Act, but the amendments are not of any particular scope or importance. The main business before the Assembly is the discussion of the draft rules of procedure about which there are a few matters of controversy. The Opposition has already tabled a number of adjournment motions, most of which will probably be turned down by the Speaker, but a few are likely to survive. I am told today that notice of a motion for adjournment has been given regarding a hunger-strike in the Central Jail, Lahore, among political prisoners. This apparently began last night and was obviously inspired by people from outside. The prisoners concerned are terrorists, and, although the grounds for their strike are not yet fully known, I understand that the old question of release is the main issue. The prisoners include several who have returned from the Andamans. I expect that Government will take a strong line and will show no inclination to discuss terms. Unfortunately, the Premier is down with an attack of influenza and is unlikely to be able to attend the Assembly for several days. The Minister, who is taking the case in his absence, wishes to discuss the matter with me before the debate, and I hope to keep him on the right lines.

3. There was a two-day conference last week attended by all the Ministers and the Administrative Secretaries and heads of departments concerned with the proposed scheme of intensive rural reconstruction. I was asked to preside over the conference which I did. The results were satisfactory in that decisions were reached and plans formulated which should permit the scheme to be brought into operation as soon as funds are voted. Earlier in the week, again by request, I presided over the annual conference relating to measures to check waterlogging. I find in fact that I am being roped in for various conferences and discussions as much as I was before the new Constitution came into force.

4. We had good rain at the end of December in most districts of the Province and the prospects for the spring harvest are now reasonably good, although we should like more rain within the next few weeks.

Yours sincerely,
H.W. EMERSON

28

EMERSON TO LINLITHGOW

Private and Personal
D.-O. No. 37-F.L.

Government House, Lahore,
January 27th, 1938

My dear Lord Linlithgow,

Since I last wrote, the civil disobedience movement by the Ahrars with regard to Shahidganj has continued and five persons daily have been arrested without incident. Yesterday a full bench of the High Court delivered its appellate judgment. The Judges were the Chief Justice, Mr. Justice Bhide (a Hindu I.C.S. Judge), and Mr. Justice Din Muhammad. The last named wrote a long dissenting judgment, of which so far I have only seen an abstract in the press. The majority decision was in accordance with the previous findings of the civil courts. Here again I have not seen the full judgment, but the press abstracts published this morning give the main decisions as follows:

> 'The personal law of the Muhammadans has been modified by the Punjab Laws Act and the Limitation Act. Muhammadan Law regarding wakfs, and the lack of any rule of limitation within that law, cannot apply to this suit. The Limitation Act and article 144 of the Act apply. A mosque is immovable property. Every suit is subject to the Limitation Act and the Act applies without distinction to suits concerning both sacred and secular property; nor does it make any difference if the plaintiffs in such suits are divine or human.
>
> 'It, therefore, follows that the Muslims and the mosque at the end of 12 years' adverse possession by the Sikhs lost all rights in the land and building, including the right of worship. The Sikhs, on the other hand, by virtue of Section 28 of the Limitation Act obtained a good title to the land and building thereon and have full rights therein as owners. The building under the circumstances cannot be held to have maintained its sacred character as a mosque, nor is there any duty cast upon the present proprietors to maintain its original sacred character or to maintain it as a building.
>
> 'Property dedicated to God can be alienated if adverse possession of the property is obtained and kept for 12 years. There was no subsisting right in the plaintiffs at the date of suit and, therefore, no action lay.
>
> 'In addition, the subject matter of the suit was *res judicata* and the

suit was also barred by the provisions of the Sikh Gurdwaras Act and the decision of the Sikh Gurdwaras Tribunal.'

The decision justifies the attitude which has hitherto been adopted by the executive Government, namely, that however embarrassing the task might be, its action must be based on the rights of the parties as determined by the civil courts. It has refused to accept the demand made by Muslims that Muhammadan Law can overrule the law of the land.

It is too early to give an accurate forecast of the results of the judgment, but I may attempt a tentative appreciation of its effects:

(*a*) The immediate effect has been to give much greater momentum to non-constitutional agitation. On the pronouncement of the judgement yesterday a *hartal* was held in some Muslim quarters and Muslim newspapers have come out with black headlines and borders. The Ahrar volunteers start daily from the Wazir Khan's mosque in the city. Up till yesterday the daily congregation had been small and the same was true of the crowd accompanying the five volunteers. Yesterday there was a large crowd in the mosque and the people accompanying the volunteers are said to have amounted to about one thousand. The situation was troublesome for some hours, but eventually the arrests were made without much difficulty. There is to be a Muslim meeting today and another tomorrow at the Badshahi mosque. Tomorrow's meeting will probably determine the nature of the immediate reactions in Lahore. The present indications are that other Muslim bodies may join the Ahrars in the civil disobedience movement and the situation may develop along dangerous lines. At any rate, the issue has again become a very live one.

(*b*) A factor which may prove to be of some stabilizing value is the dissenting judgment of the Muslim Judge. It will be used by moderate Muslims as an argument in favour of an appeal to the Privy Council. It remains to be seen whether moderate counsels will prevail over the fanatical exhortations of those in favour of direct action.

(*c*) It appears almost certain that the demand by Muslims will be revived that Muhammadan Law should prevail over the law of the land. It may take an all-India form and is likely to receive considerable support in northern India including the North-West Frontier Province and possibly the tribal areas. Both the majority and minority judgments will reinforce this demand. The first because of the clear and uncompromising statement of the law as it now stands, and the second because of the encouragement it gives to the claims of those who support the Muhammadan Law. This part of the agitation will probably be accompanied by a demand for a change in the law, a question which raises very big issues indeed.

(*d*) While there may be an increase of communal feeling and possibly a communal clash, the feeling is more likely to take an anti-Government form. Signs of this are already evident. The situation cannot fail to be embarrassing to the present Government.

If serious developments occur, I will inform Your Excellency.

2. Next in importance to the Shahidganj agitation is the question of the so-called political prisoners. There are at present 20 convicted prisoners on hunger-strike, of whom 11 are in the Lahore Central Jail, 7 are in Montgomery and 2 in Multan. The majority are terrorists convicted of crimes of violence, some of which were of a very grave character. The chief demand of these convicts is that they should be released immediately. On the 24th of January it was proposed by those supporting their demand that a sympathetic demonstration should be held outside the Assembly Chamber. With the approval of Government, the District Magistrate of Lahore[1] issued an order under Section 144, Criminal Procedure Code, forbidding an assembly of persons within a certain distance of the Chamber, while the Chamber was sitting. A meeting was held in the city but the Police held up the subsequent procession. The instructions to the Police were that they were to use the minimum of force and were to hold the crowd unless dispersal was necessary. It is generally agreed that the Police behaved with the utmost restraint and patience. The sitting of the Assembly concluded at 6-30 p.m. and the cordon of Police in the city was then withdrawn. Sections of the crowd, consisting mostly of students, then proceeded towards the Assembly Chamber, which is a part of the Secretariat buildings. This was not anticipated and the special guard of Police at the Chamber had been withdrawn. Several of the Ministers were still working in their offices. The Police force was sufficient to prevent the crowd entering the Secretariat compound, but there was a very unruly demonstration outside by a crowd estimated at about one thousand. Brickbats were thrown, some windows were broken, slight damage was done to Government property, and the Ministers were abused in the foulest language. Great indignation has been caused by this demonstration; and the political effect has been excellent, far outweighing the consequences

of defective Police arrangements. A large number of supporters of the Government have asked for time to discuss the demonstration, to condemn the action of those responsible for it and to impress on Government the necessity of taking strong action to prevent similar demonstrations in future. The resolution is to be discussed this evening and there is likely to be some very strong speeches by the supporters of Government. Meanwhile, the question of the release of prisoners was discussed in the Assembly on the 25th of January. The Premier, in winding up the debate, made a very good and courageous speech. He said that while Government were prepared to consider with sympathy the cases of State prisoners, if they gave the necessary assurances, he could hold out no hope of clemency whatever to those who had been convicted in the courts for crimes of violence. He carried the ministerial party with him and the Congress resolution was defeated by a large majority. This is all to the good, but the difficulties are not yet over. I do not think that the prisoners concerned will abandon their hunger-strike and there is a fair chance that some of them may carry it to the extreme length of committing suicide. As their condition becomes critical, agitation will increase. Pressure will be brought to bear on the Premier by the press, public meetings and a general increase in the agitation. One at least of his colleagues is already showing signs of uneasiness. In order to relieve the Premier of some of his duties, the subject of Jails, among others, was taken over a few months ago by the Finance Minister, Mr. Manohar Lal. Before the hunger-strike began he was interesting himself in some of the so-called political prisoners, and he made recommendations with regard to some of them which the Premier, I think, will not be able to accept. He has been inclined to regard as an ordinary matter of Jail administration a question which vitally concerns law and order and which, of course, is the business of the Premier. This confusion has to be cleared up. While at first he was staunch on the question of the hunger-strike, his later attitude gives rise to some misgiving. The general support, however, given to the Premier by the ministerial party in the Assembly and the clear enunciation of policy made during the debate will make it difficult for Government to change their position.

Pandit Jawaharlal was in Lahore a few days ago. He made one public speech, the gist of which has probably been seen by Your Excellency. It differed a great deal from the speeches made by him on his previous visits. He appears to have been depressed first by the state of Congress politics in the Punjab and second by the general situation. He spoke at considerable length on the international situation, his tone being less confident than usual, and so far as Indian affairs are concerned, he suggested by implication that the chief difficulties of Congress Ministers were from their own followers. Sikander had a talk with him for more than two hours. They had not previously met. Sikander found him more moderate than he had expected, but vague and undecided on important issues. In regard to Federation, for instance, the two agreed that a Constituent Assembly was impracticable and Jawaharlal admitted that he had no scheme to replace that embodied in the Government of India Act. His general line was that, as a matter of tactics, federation was a good subject on which to attack the British Government, and that when the present scheme had been scrapped there would be time to think about a substitute. He seemed to hope that if agitation was strong enough, the British Government might themselves come forward with alternative proposals. He was equally hazy about independence. He admitted that so far as defence was concerned, India could not possibly stand alone and he was uncomfortable about Japan, but he talked loosely about an independent India making an alliance with Great Britain. He was uneasy about his own left wing. Sikander tackled him about Congress Ministers going into non-Congress Provinces and attacking the Government of those Provinces. Jawaharlal admitted that a convention might be desirable to avoid this. On the communal question he adopted the usual attitude that the Congress were prepared to concede everything to Muslims, but he could not make out what Jinnah really wanted. Sikander naively admitted that he also did not know. Sikander's general impression was that of a man tired, uncertain and worried.

I had John Gunter staying with me for a couple of days. He had seen Jawaharlal on several occasions, and independently he gave much the same appreciation as Sikander. He described him as 'troubled' – an idealist incapable of coming to grips with the hard facts and problems of practical administration. Gunter had an idea that some of his doubts were due to his complex feelings as to what will happen when Gandhi is no longer here to control affairs, and how he will use the greater freedom he will then have.

I found Gunter very shrewd and interesting in his appreciation of men and affairs.

Yours sincerely,
H.W. EMERSON

29

EMERSON TO LINLITHGOW

Private and Personal
D.-O. No. 39-F.L.

Government House, Lahore,
January 30th, 1938

My dear Lord Linlithgow,

In looking through my fortnightly letter D.-O. No. 37-F.L. of the 27th of January, I find that the statement regarding the release of prisoners was not sufficiently explicit. In paragraph 2 of my letter was the following:

> 'Meanwhile, the question of the release of prisoners was discussed in the Assembly on the 25th of January. The Premier, in winding up the debate, made a very good and courageous speech. He said that while Government were prepared to consider with sympathy the cases of State prisoners, if they gave the necessary assurances, he could hold out no hope of clemency whatever to those who had been convicted in the courts for crimes of violence.'

I should have made it clear that there are no State prisoners on hunger-strike, and that the Premier's statement in regard to them related to the general policy of Government and did not imply any consideration whatsoever towards a State prisoner should he go on hunger-strike. Government are at present quite sound on this question and there is no intention whatever of yielding to the threats of hunger-strikers. I have thought it advisable to clarify this point, particularly since the Bengal Government is anxious that they should not be embarrassed by any action of the Punjab Government. There is so far no risk of this and I do not think any should occur. Should there be any unfavourable developments in this respect I will let Brabourne know direct. In the meantime perhaps Your Excellency will give him the gist of the relevant portions of this and my previous letter.

2. On the whole, the situation regarding Shahidganj is as favourable as could be expected. There were big meetings of Muslims in the Badshahi Mosque on the 27th and the 28th, but there was no mob action afterwards and no clash between crowds and the Police. The excitement, though considerable, was less than might have been expected. Maulana Zafar Ali Khan, M.L.A. (Central), fortunately discouraged precipitate action. Other bodies are expected to join the civil disobedience movement, but, so long

as this proceeds along non-violent lines, it will not cause much trouble. The immediate danger of serious trouble seems to be over but the agitation generally has been given a new lease of life and vigour.

Yours sincerely,
H.W. EMERSON

30

EMERSON TO LINLITHGOW

Private and Personal — Camp,
D.-O. No. 41-F.L. — *February 12th, 1938*

My dear Lord Linlithgow,

The only development in connection with the hunger-strike is that one under-trial prisoner has abandoned it, leaving twenty convicts still on strike. Their condition is reported to be satisfactory, but they are being forcibly fed and will not allow themselves to be weighed, so that it would be unsafe to make any assumption about their health. There is no sign at present of any tendency on their part to abandon the strike. In this connection, it is necessary to remember that the Punjab is in a different position from that of Congress Provinces. In the latter, it is in the interests of the Governments concerned that efforts should be made by Congress organisations to persuade the prisoners not to proceed to extreme lengths. Here, whatever may be the public statements of Congress, local politicians are not displeased to see the Government embarrassed, and for this reason there is little prospect of any effective pressure being brought to bear on the prisoners from private sources. Meanwhile, the Premier is quite firm on the matter, and there is no sign of dissension among Ministers.

2. As regards Shahidganj, the local situation in Lahore is much the same as when I last wrote. Some impetus has been given to the civil disobedience movement and on one or two days the number offering themselves for arrest has been considerably larger than in the initial stages. There has also been a tendency for them to create more excitement. So far, however, there has been no clash between the police and the public. Some anxiety was felt regarding proceedings on the occasion of the Id, which occurred yesterday, Friday, the 11th of February, since there were rumours that a mob orator might come from Rawalpindi and incite the large crowd in the Badshahi mosque to march on Shahidganj. There was

also the danger that some local fanatic might urge them to do the same. As I am now in camp, I have received no official account of yesterday's proceedings, but from press reports it appears that there was no serious incident and that the day passed off fairly quietly. A new departure appears to have been the attempt of Pathans to picket the residence of the Premier, but again from press reports it appears that they were arrested without trouble, before they entered the civil station. February the 18th has been fixed as Shahidganj day, but if that passes quietly, the chances are that the civil disobedience movement at Lahore itself will become a matter of routine and ultimately fade away, although it may take some months before the supply of volunteers is exhausted.

3. Meanwhile, there have been developments outside Lahore, which are of considerable interest both from the communal and political point of view. The Muslim League held a meeting of its council at Delhi, which was presided over by Jinnah. The Unionist Party was represented by several members, while the Punjab branch of the Muslim League was represented mainly by Malik Barkat Ali and Pir Taj-ud-Din. I think I mentioned the former in one of my letters dealing with the Lucknow session, at which the so-called Sikander-Jinnah Pact was concluded. Since he may attain some prominence, I may give Your Excellency some further information about him. He was originally in the Punjab Provincial Civil Service, but was dismissed for corruption. He then took up practice at the Lahore Bar, and without any special attainments is now doing fairly well. He was elected to the Provincial Assembly on the Muslim League ticket, being one of the very few League candidates who were successful. Before the Lucknow sessions he was, therefore, more or less in the wilderness. When Sikander and Jinnah came together, Barkat Ali found himself in danger of being side-tracked and shortly after the Lucknow session he issued a statement to the effect that the Muslim members of the Unionist Party had now become absorbed in the Muslim League and that Sikander had become a disciple of Jinnah. It was this statement, more than anything else, which prevented the agreement being translated into effect, the present position being that, although many Muslim Unionist members have signed the League ticket, they have all attached the proviso that membership is subject to the Sikander-Jinnah agreement, and I believe that their forms of membership have either not been handed in, or have not been accepted with this condition attached. I do not know what Jinnah's views are on the matter, but it is obviously not to his interest to have an open breach with Sikander, and I imagine that he does not wish to force the issue. Meanwhile, Barkat Ali is doing his best to create mischief. A few days ago I saw an

intercepted letter from him to Jinnah, in which he abused Sikander and the Unionist Party, claimed that about twenty Muslim Unionists were prepared to join the League without any condition, and invited Jinnah to agree to his proposal to create a cave in the party by a sudden announcement to this effect. I do not expect that Jinnah will be foolish enough to agree. He probably knows, in the first place, that Barkat Ali is thoroughly unreliable, and, second, that the statement about the Muslim Unionists is untrue or greatly exaggerated. It is however, clear that Barkat Ali, for his own ends, is doing his best to embarrass the Punjab Government. His attitude at the Muslim League meeting at Delhi was consistent with this object. His speeches consisted of either a personal attack on myself or of a demand that the Muslim members of the Ministry should resign. This latter proposal received some support, but was not favoured by Jinnah or by the Unionist Party representatives, who were not slow to point out that, far from helping Muslims, such a course would make their position worse. Sikander himself tells me that the idea would not find favour with a single one of his Muslim supporters. The League meeting ultimately passed a resolution reaffirming the pledge to secure restoration of the place [the mosque at Shahidganj], and deciding to call a full session of the League in the near future. The reaffirmation of the pledge is stupid and may prove embarrassing, since it implies that what may become the most powerful Muslim association is pledged to something that can only be achieved in face of the fierce opposition of the Sikh community as a whole, who, it may be observed, attach more genuine sanctity to the place than do the Muslims, strong as the feeling of the latter may be. The resolution, taken at its face value, therefore, closes and bangs the order to [?door on] any agreed solution. The date and place of the full session of the League have not been fixed, but efforts, which will probably prove successful, are being made to prevent it being held at Lahore. Meanwhile efforts are also being made to delay the [Shahidganj] issue, by an appeal to the Privy Council.

The difficulty of this very troublesome case has always been the fact that the only satisfactory solution is an agreed one between the Muslims and the Sikhs. Various efforts have been made, from time to time, towards this end, but have been frustrated either by the obstinacy of the Sikhs or by the ill-timed agitation of the Muslims. The former have consistently taken the attitude that they will agree to nothing while an active agitation is being carried on, and the civil disobedience movement is probably an insuperable bar. Sikander, however, is alive to the desirability quietly of opening the way to a renewal of negotiations when a favourable opportunity occurs.

4. Sikander and Sir Chhotu Ram have done a tour of about a week through the south-eastern districts of the Province. They held many meetings and received very great ovations from the rural classes. The tour was a big success and suggests that even in that part of the Province where Congress has been particularly active, it has achieved little success with the rural elements. Reports to the same effect have been received from several Commissioners. There has, it is true, been a large increase in the paper membership of Congress in the villages, but an analysis of this increase goes to show that it is largely from the non-agriculturist element combined with some increase among the menial castes. There is no serious sign of the Unionist Party having lost its grip on the countryside. On the other hand, the tour emphasizes the value of more personal contact between Unionist leaders and members and their constituents.

Yours sincerely,
H.W. EMERSON

31

EMERSON TO LINLITHGOW

Secret — Government House, Lahore,
D.-O. No. 43 — *February 24th, 1938*

My dear Lord Linlithgow,

In your telegram No. 271-G, dated the 19th of February 1938, Your Excellency asked for information regarding the behaviour of the so-called political prisoners that have been released in the Punjab. In all fifteen convicts of this class have been released since the new Constitution came into force. Under the Jail Rules, when a convict sentenced for transportation for life has done the equivalent of 14 years' imprisonment including remissions earned, his case is examined by the local Government, and the principle has been adopted by the present Government, that, unless the circumstances are exceptional, release should be ordered. All the convicts were released under this procedure and all had done long terms of imprisonment. The most notorious of these was Parmanand, who, in fact, had served nearly 23 years.[2] The behaviour of Parmanand has, of course, been most objectionable, but his case cannot be regarded as one of premature release. While one or two of the others have engaged in political activities, it cannot be said that their conduct has caused any real embarrassment, or has given sufficient justification for the view that their release was a mistake.

In addition, four persons, interned under Regulation III of 1918, have been released. I understand that two of these, Chaman Lal Azad and Karam Singh Dhut, have been engaging in agitation in Delhi, and it is probable that they will continue to make nuisances of themselves, but I have no information to show that their conduct has been so bad as to be of any real value as an argument against the release of the others.

Yours sincerely,
H.W. EMERSON

32

EMERSON TO LINLITHGOW

Secret
D.-O. No. 44

Government House, Lahore,
February 24th, 1938

My dear Lord Linlithgow,

I am sorry not to have given Your Excellency before this an appreciation of the situation in the Punjab following the constitutional crisis.[3] I was on tour when it occurred and returned to Lahore only on the 20th, so that I had little opportunity of discussing it with persons whose views might be of value. I have since had a fairly full discussion with the Premier, with the Chief Secretary (Penny), the Inspector-General of Police (Orde) and the D.I.G., C.I.D. (Bennett). I have also had some talk with several non-officials and with other officers. These discussions were mostly before the issue of Your Excellency's statement on the 22nd. First, as regards the views expressed in the press, I have sent Laithwaite several batches of press cuttings which are fairly representative. Except in one or two Muslim papers, the view that one might have expected has been taken, namely, of strong criticism of the action taken by Your Excellency under Section 126 of the Act, the lines of criticism generally following those taken at Haripura. The few Muslim papers that have not taken this line have suggested that the action of the Congress Ministries in Bihar and the United Provinces was prompted by other motives, but even in these papers there has been no serious attempt to examine the principles involved. At the same time there has been very clearly evident in the Hindu and Sikh papers a general feeling of regret that the crisis should have occurred, and of anxiety to find a way out of the suspension of Congress office in these two Provinces.

Although the danger of a general upheaval has been appreciated, the hope has been very evident that a solution might be found and that in any case the crisis might be localised. Generally, I feel that on this occasion the views expressed by the press more correctly represent Indian public opinion than is usual in such circumstances.

2. Sikander regrets that the action should have been necessary, particularly as he thinks that the result has been to bring the right and left wings of Congress together at a time when they were drifting apart. He also regards the issue as one on which the Congress can make out a plausible case. He has, of course, no sympathy himself with terrorist or revolutionary prisoners, and he fully realises that their wholesale release in the United Provinces and Bihar would be embarrassing to his Ministry, but this was the case also with the release of Kakori and other prisoners. He has been a little perturbed with the suggestion that has appeared in some sections of the press and was put forward by Vallabhbhai Patel at Haripura, that the action of Your Excellency was taken at the instance of the Punjab Government. He feels that the prestige of his Government might be affected if this belief gained ground, his attitude in this matter being that the Punjab is prepared to stand on its own legs. Your Excellency's statement, however, should dispel this idea, while, in any case, two short notice questions on the matter put in by the Opposition have been answered by the Premier. Were the Punjab Government now to be asked whether the wholesale release of the so-called political prisoners in the United Provinces and Bihar would create a situation in the Punjab which made action on its behalf by Your Excellency desirable, I think that the line taken by the Premier would be somewhat as follows: The premature release of political prisoners in any Province must be a source of embarrassment to the Punjab Government, since their own policy has been to avoid the release of prisoners convicted by the courts. A different policy elsewhere must, therefore, intensify the agitation in the Punjab in favour of release there also, and must make it more difficult to justify the Punjab policy. At the same time, it cannot be said that such release elsewhere would constitute a grave menace to the peace and tranquillity of the Punjab, or that the situation that would arise would be sufficiently serious to justify the Punjab Government in asking Your Excellency to take action which might create an all-India crisis and which might lead to the indefinite suspension of the Constitution in seven Provinces.

Whether a reply of this nature would have been given a fortnight ago before the crisis occurred is not so certain, although, on the whole, I think, it would have been. But there is no doubt that the very thorough examination and discussion of the various issues and consequences involved, which have followed the crisis, have led to very careful thought on the matter. In illustration of this, I may mention the views expressed by the Inspector-General of Police (Orde) and the D.I.G., C.I.D. (Bennett). These are both strong officers who have had long and troublesome experience of terrorist and revolutionary movements in the Punjab. They would greatly regret the wholesale release of our own prisoners, they would regard it as an embarrassment and a danger, and they know that it would involve a lot of extra work to the Police. None the less each independently expressed the view that, if the matter came to the test, he could not advise that it would be a menace so grave to the peace and tranquillity of the Province as to require the exercise of the Governor's special powers, at the risk of a break-down of the Constitution. They take the line that to admit this would be a confession of the inability of the Police to deal with a limited number of individuals. This view is not only interesting in itself but reflects, I think, the new attitude of Government officers towards particular problems. They are getting into the way of studying the constitutional issues.

3. Bengal is a different proposition, and I can well appreciate Your Excellency's difficulties having regard to the position of that Government. I think Your Excellency's statement has made the situation much clearer than it was before. If the crisis is not resolved by the statement and the subsequent instructions to Governors, then it seems to me most desirable that the Bengal aspect should be developed and emphasized. Reference is made in Your Excellency's statement to further revolutionary tendencies in that Province. I suggest that, if necessity arises, more should be said of this.

4. I hope, however, that the statement will have the effect of bringing together again the Governors of the two Provinces and their Ministers. If they come together, there should be a solution. Indications in the press this morning are favourable, but Congress headquarters has still to show its hand, and I am not at all sure what line they will take. They have committed themselves fairly deeply to their original demand, and Gandhi may not be prepared to compromise. There appear to be several favourable factors. First, most of the other Congress Ministries apparently wish to retain office. Second, Congress do not appear to be ready for a mass civil disobedience movement. A significant factor has been the absence of any popular demonstration or excitement in the United Provinces and Bihar in connection with the resignations. Third, Gandhi does not seem to want an upheaval. He must appreciate the great power which the new Constitution has given Congress in the seven Provinces. He is also, I

believe, genuinely keen on social and economic reform. On the other hand, if the two Premiers concerned are obstinate, Gandhi will not let them down. There must then, I imagine, be a suspension of the Constitution in the United Provinces and Bihar. I find it very difficult to form a definite opinion whether this would be followed by resignation of the Ministries in the other five Provinces. My own estimate of Gandhi's attitude so far is that he would like to avoid a crisis but that he is prepared to face one, in the meantime preparing the way, by attempting to strengthen his position in world and especially British opinion. If he thought himself successful in this and if there were no chance of Congress obtaining more favourable terms then I would expect him to call out the other five Ministries, unless there was serious danger of this involving a split in Congress. If there were serious risk of this, he would avoid it. Thus, although the present indications are more favourable than they were a few days ago, I do not think that the danger of a general crisis has passed. On the other hand, even if all the Ministries resign, some time must elapse before civil disobedience is attempted on a big scale. Congress have not yet attained the position even in their own Provinces where a mass movement can be started at short notice. If it is started, then it is bound to suffer from lack of organisation which should render more immediately effective, prompt and strong measures by Government. There are very few, however, who want a mass movement at the present time and there will be an almost general feeling of relief if the crisis can be avoided, provided, of course, that from the point of view of Government supporters no surrender of essential principles is involved. If I may say so, I do not think that the course at present proposed involves any such surrender, having regard to the present attitude of the Bengal Government.

Yours sincerely,
H.W. EMERSON

33

EMERSON TO LINLITHGOW

Secret
D.-O. No. 45

Government House, Lahore,
February 24th, 1938

My dear Lord Linlithgow,

In Your Excellency's telegram No. 299-G., dated the 22nd of February 1938, I have been asked for my views regarding the degree of menace to the Punjab involved in the release of Yashpal. I have consulted the Premier and also Bennett, the D.I.G., C.I.D. Your Excellency is, no doubt, aware, from the records of the Central Bureau of Intelligence, of the very dangerous character of this terrorist, and in accordance with the policy of the Punjab Government there would be no question of releasing him, were he imprisoned in the Punjab. He has many associates here and his return to the Province would be embarrassing and might be dangerous. If he did return, restrictions would certainly be placed on him. At the same time, the Premier feels, and I share that view, that the Punjab Government would not be justified in standing out against his release if their opposition were likely to make a solution of the constitutional crisis more difficult. The Punjab Government would hope, although not insist, that if he were released one of the conditions would be that he kept out of the Punjab. In this connection Your Excellency has no doubt seen the order which the Madras Government passed in the case of Nitya Ananda, the relevant condition being that he would not enter the Punjab during the remainder of his sentence without the permission of the Punjab Government. This order has been communicated officially to the Punjab Government by the Madras Government, which, however, have asked that it should be treated as confidential, as they do not wish the conditions to be made public.

2. In my separate, letter of today's date, written before I had discussed this particular case with the Premier, I suggested what I thought would be his attitude in general. Your Excellency may assume that my appreciation correctly represents his view, as illustrated by the present instance, which has also the support of the executive officers directly concerned, namely the Inspector-General of Police and the Deputy Inspector-General of C.I.D.

Yours sincerely,
H.W. EMERSON

34

EMERSON TO LINLITHGOW

Secret
D.-O. No. 46

Government House, Lahore,
February 27th, 1938

My dear Lord Linlithgow

I attach a copy of two bills relating to the Shahidganj,[4] which private members propose to introduce in the present session of the provincial legislature. The first, which is to be introduced by Mr. K.L. Gauba, provides for the compulsory acquisition of the site by Government, for its recognition as a mosque, but, at the same time, for its maintenance as an open site. The second bill, to be introduced by Malik Barkat Ali, provides in effect for the application of the Muslim Law to all buildings, which have at any time been a mosque, and is to have complete retrospective effect in this respect. The result of it becoming law would be to nullify the relevant provisions of the Limitation Act and to enable the Muslims to secure possession of the Shahidganj. It would similarly enable them to obtain possession of any other building which had, at any time, been used as a mosque.

2. The provisions included in Gauba's bill would form a satisfactory settlement of the matter if they were accepted by both communities on a voluntary basis. Indeed, attempts have been made at various times to secure a solution of this kind, but always without success. To enforce such an arrangement by legislation is a course open to the gravest objections. It would be totally unacceptable to the Sikhs, and it is no exaggeration to say that the situation created by legislation of this kind, if passed, would amount to a state approaching civil war. The bill seeks to deprive the Sikh community of rights which have been recognised by one civil court after another and only recently by the High Court.

3. Malik Barkat Ali's bill is open to the same objections and also to others. It seeks to obliterate, so far as Muslim religious buildings are concerned, the events of history and to give a legal right to Muslims to any building ever used as a mosque, however many centuries may have elapsed since its use as such. If the same principle were applied to the religious buildings of other communities, utter confusion would be created and a bitter and endless struggle started between Muslims, Hindus and Sikhs.

4. For these reasons it is clear that the bills cannot be allowed to pass into law. They have been introduced partly to make a popular appeal to Muslim sentiment, but mainly to embarrass the Ministry. The position, in fact, is likely to prove very embarrassing to the Muslim Ministers. There is strong feeling among Muslims about the Shahidganj and there are signs that the feeling is increasing rather than abating. Some of the Muslim supporters of Government are affected and there is a danger of religious sentiments conflicting with political loyalty. Sikander has had two talks with his Muslim supporters, and, although he has been able to get the majority to take a fairly sensible view, there are some dissenters, and the position may be troublesome.

5. I asked that the matter should be discussed in the Council of Ministers

yesterday. There was general agreement that the bills could not be allowed to become law. There was a long discussion regarding the best procedure to follow in order to prevent this, but no final conclusion was reached, and the matter is to be discussed again in a week's time. As the bills in any case cannot be introduced before the 1st of April, the matter is not immediate, and I made it clear that I did not wish to rush the Premier. At the same time, I explained that since issues might possibly arise which would make it necessary for me formally to consult the Governor-General, the advice of the Ministers could not be indefinitely postponed. I mentioned as a further reason for this the fact that if the bills were discussed and passed into law in the Legislative Assembly, my successor might have to deal with the question, and, therefore, it was necessary, in fairness to him, that we should all know where we were.

6. It is not necessary for me at present to discuss the different ways in which the situation could be met if, as Governor, I had to take action contrary to the advice of my Ministers. There is no reason to suppose that a situation will arise in which such action will become necessary. Both bills, as it happens, require the previous sanction of the Governor acting in his discretion under Section 299 (3) of the Government of India Act. It was round this point that the discussion mainly centered yesterday. I think the Ministers would have been relieved if I had said that I would take the responsibility and odium, on my own initiative, of refusing sanction. I made it clear, however, that the necessity of sanction was largely accidental, that the question was one which the Ministers had to face, that it was not possible for them to escape their responsibility and that before I thought of taking any action at all I must have their definite advice. Further, I said that if I withheld sanction on their advice under the provisions of Section 299 (3), it would have to be made quite clear publicly that in doing so I had accepted their advice. Without coming to any final decision as to what advice they should tender, the Ministers unanimously accepted the constitutional position and agreed that it would be wrong on all accounts for them to attempt to shelter themselves behind any special powers which the Governor might possess. The discussion then related mainly to tactics, as to whether it would be better for the Governor to kill the bills at once by withholding sanction on the advice of the Ministers publicly announced, or whether it would be better to allow the bills to be introduced and thrown out by the Assembly. There is something to be said for each point of view, although my own view at present inclines towards the refusal of sanction, although not so strongly as to justify me in rejecting the advice of the Ministers, should they prefer sanction to be given. The position would be

different if the Ministers contemplated the introduction of the bills and their passing into law if the legislature passed them. There is no such idea at present. The alternative to the refusal of sanction is introduction of the bills and definite opposition to them from the outset. Here again, I told the Ministers that if they advised me to give sanction to the bills, I would desire their advice to be accompanied by a clear statement that it was intended to oppose the bills, and I explained that if there were no such clear declaration of policy, the situation would then require very careful consideration by me.

7. Here the matter at present rests. So far as the relations between the Ministers and myself are concerned, I do not contemplate any difference of opinion and the discussion yesterday was carried out in the most friendly way, but I thought it very necessary to state my own position and the constitutional issues in such a way as to leave no room for doubt or misunderstanding, and in this respect the results were very satisfactory. I will keep Your Excellency informed of the results of further discussions and, in the meantime, Your Excellency may wish to show this letter to Craik in case of unforeseen developments.

Yours sincerely,
H.W. EMERSON

35

EMERSON TO LINLITHGOW

Private and Personal
D.-O. No. 47-F.L.

Government House, Lahore,
February 28th, 1938

My dear Lord Linlithgow,

I have written to Your Excellency separately regarding the constitutional crisis in the United Provinces and Bihar. Since that letter the Ministers have returned to office in those two Provinces and the crisis has come to an end. So far I have seen few press opinions, but the predominant note of those which I have seen is one of relief, and I do not think that there will be any tendency on either side to claim a victory. One satisfactory feature of the crisis has been the comparative restraint exercised by the press and a genuine desire to appreciate the constitutional issues, even although there has been necessarily considerable misrepresentation of them. Another feature that has struck me is the change in the attitude towards Governors. While there has of course been an attempt to minimise their functions and powers, they are no longer regarded, as they were during the first few months of the Constitution, as the enemies of the Ministry, and even Gandhi has admitted their function of guiding and advising Ministers. In the long run, I think, the crisis will be found to have done more good than harm.

2. I have also written separately to Your Excellency regarding one troublesome feature of the Shahidganj agitation, namely, the submission of private bills. These cannot fail to incite feeling on both sides. Meanwhile, the civil disobedience movement continues on routine lines.

3. All the 'political' prisoners on hunger-strike have now abandoned the strike. The immediate cause of this appears to have been a message from Gandhi, who has promised to do his best to secure their release, and, if necessary, to visit the Punjab. I notice that in the press the Premier is credited with a statement that the abandonment of the strike would make it easier for the cases of the convicts to be considered. I doubt if he has been correctly quoted, but the publicity given to the general question by events in the United Provinces and Bihar will undoubtedly make it more difficult for the Ministry to maintain the rigid attitude they have adopted in the past. There is one direction in which some reasonable concession might well be allowed. In a recent letter to Your Excellency I mentioned that according to the Jail Regulations the cases of all life prisoners are examined as a matter of course after they have done a period of 14 years, less remissions earned. Unless the circumstances are exceptional, they are then released. In the past it has been the practice to regard the cases of revolutionary and terrorist prisoners as exceptional and to keep them in prison for almost indefinite periods. I doubt whether this system can be continued under the new régime; at any rate not to the same extent. I contemplate that the Ministry may wish, while examining individual cases, to take a view more favourable to the convict.

4. Your Excellency will remember that there was some telegraphic correspondence between the Secretary of State and the Punjab Government regarding the case of one Kiroo, who was convicted by the Sessions Judge of the murder of a constable, but was acquitted by the High Court on the ground that he acted in self-defence, having been cruelly tortured by the Police. The Chief Justice made some very strong remarks about the case which was taken up in the British and Indian press. The Punjab Government at once suspended the Police officers who were implicated and ordered an investigation to be carried out with a view to placing them on their trial, if there was sufficient evidence against them. The Police enquiry is now almost complete, and I have seen the preliminary report, although I have not checked it by reference to the Police diaries, which were not available.

There is at present reason to suppose that the chief witness to the torture, one Pipe Major Stewart, was bought by the defence and gave false evidence. There is also reason to suppose that the defence approached a sergeant of the same regiment with the same object. The question of further procedure may thus present some difficulty. The objects of the Punjab Government are: (*a*) to ascertain the truth and to bring to justice anyone who has committed an offence, and (*b*) to satisfy British and Indian opinion that no attempt has been made to burke the case. At the same time it has to protect its officers if they have been wrongly accused. The best procedure to attain these objects has still to be considered, but, subject to examination of the case when it is ready, I am at present inclined to think that it will be necessary to put on a senior executive or judicial British officer, preferably the latter, to carry out a further enquiry and to advise Government as to the facts and the persons, if any, against whom criminal proceedings should be filed. It seems to me that it is only by some such method that justice can be done to everyone concerned and at the same time public confidence satisfied as regards the facts.

5. There has been good rain during the past fortnight practically throughout the Province, and, provided that we have a long spell of sunshine, the *rabi* harvest should be a bumper one.

Yours sincerely,
H.W. EMERSON

36

EMERSON TO LINLITHGOW

Secret
D.-O. No. 48

Government House, Lahore,
March 4th, 1938

My dear Lord Linlithgow,

I am writing to inform Your Excellency of developments regarding the situation created by the two private bills relating to Shahidganj, about which I wrote to you on the 27th of February. Sikander and his two Muslim colleagues have had at least three long discussions with their Muslim supporters in the Assembly during the past week, and he tells me that he is having great difficulty in keeping them in hand. In all, 24 Muslim members of the Assembly have put in motions for leave to introduce a bill in the same terms as that sponsored by Malik Barkat Ali, and although I gather that several of these will be prepared to withdraw if asked to do so by the party, there are some who will not be willing to withdraw in any case. Meanwhile, increasing attention has been given to the bills in the press and on the platform by both Muslims and Sikhs, and feeling on them has grown very considerably. Muslim members of the Assembly have been subjected to great pressure, one device being for a small party to appear before them with a Quran and to ask them to sign the bill, or to be considered unbelievers. On the Sikh side, there have been strong statements and speeches by Sardar Tara Singh and other Akali leaders with demands that the Governor should refuse sanction to the bills.

2. The above was the general position in which the Council of Ministers resumed discussion of the question this morning (Friday, the 4th of March). Sikander at once started off by saying that the position was becoming so difficult that he thought that ultimately he, and with him, the Ministry would have to resign. He said that he was as firmly convinced as ever that the bills could not be allowed to become law, and that it would not be even in the interests of the Muslim community to allow this; but he said that he had used every sort of argument with the Muslim members of the Assembly, and that he had been unable to convince them so far to this effect. He, therefore, thought that what he would have to do would be to resign on the ground that, since he could not carry his Muslim supporters, he and the Ministry had better make way for somebody else. At the same time he would make it clear that he was definitely opposed to the bills and that he would continue to oppose them. I asked him at what stage he thought that such a step might become necessary, but he was indefinite and I got the impression that he thought that he might have to do so without his Ministry giving any clear advice to the Governor as to what should be done about the bills. His two Muslim colleagues might perhaps have had some previous warning of what he was going to say, but his three non-Muslim colleagues had none and were very surprised and perturbed. The view very strongly expressed by them throughout has been that the Ministers should advise the Governor to withhold sanction and should face the music afterwards in the Assembly on a motion of adjournment, or a vote of no confidence. They stuck to that view this morning, while, of course, desiring to find a way out, if one was possible. I suggested that the line proposed by Sikander was open to criticism on several grounds: first, that it did not appear to be the right way for a popular Ministry to meet their responsibility; second, that it did not pay sufficient regard to the interests of the Province; and third, that it was unfair to the non-Muslim supporters of the Government. Although the three non-Muslim Ministers naturally did not say very much, it was quite clear from what they did say that they thought that this way of

escape was a wrong one and was lacking in courage. In particular, Sir Chhotu Ram had no hesitation in expressing his opinion, namely, that if a responsible Government is not going to face boldly a direct communal issue, the only rule governing politics in the Punjab will be the domination of the communal majority. Moreover, they expressed the opinion, which I share, that if the Ministry took a bold course, most of the Muslim members would support the Premier. Indeed Sikander admitted to me after the meeting that he thought that at least 75 per cent. would support him out of personal loyalty, if for no other reason.

3. In the course of discussion in Council Sikander mentioned that his position would be much stronger in dealing with Muslims, if there were any sign of a gesture from the Sikhs that if sanction was refused to introduce the bills, they would be prepared to consider an amicable settlement. For reasons which I will mention later, this is obviously the case, and I have pressed on the Council for some time that serious attempts should be made to get a settlement between the two communities, however unfavourable the prospects may appear. One obstacle in the way of a settlement, and a very important one, is that Tara Singh, the leader of the Akali party, on whom at present a settlement depends more than on anyone else, is a very bitter enemy of Sir Sunder Singh, and it would please him very much if the Ministry, including Sir Sunder, resigned on this issue. This makes it impossible for Sir Sunder to get into direct touch with Tara Singh, but he agreed this morning to bring certain influences to bear on Tara Singh and to explore the chances of a settlement. The only settlement that appears possible is one by which the place would be walled in and accepted by both communities as absolutely neutral territory accessible to no one. Sikander gave a practical guarantee to Sir Sunder that if the Sikhs agreed to this, the solution would be accepted by Muslims, except a minority of extremists.

4. The discussion could proceed no further today and will probably be resumed early next week. So far as it has gone, it amounts to a definite warning by Sikander of the action he may have to take. My first impression, and it was shared by Penny, the Chief Secretary, who was present as Secretary of the Council, was that it was a manoeuvre by the Muslim Ministers to force my hands to use my special powers, but on reflection I am inclined to think that a more powerful motive is to bring pressure to bear on the Sikhs to come to an amicable settlement. A third influence, which was weighing with Sikander, was anxiety regarding his position as a Muslim outside the legislature if he had to advise that the bills should be turned down. On the other hand, as I have said, the non-Muslim Ministers

obviously thought that if a courageous stand were made, Sikander would get the support of the great majority of Muslim members of the legislature.

5. I am not yet able to form a firm opinion whether Sikander is serious about taking the action he suggested. He will probably have a private discussion with me on Sunday. Meantime, it is necessary to recognise that a very grave crisis may develop. If the present ministry resigns in connection with the Shahidganj issue, I see no alternative Ministry able to carry on, except possibly a purely Muhammadan one, pledged to the restoration of Shahidganj to the Muslims, and in their case I do not see how the Governor could avoid making it clear from the outset that this would almost inevitably bring the Ministry into direct conflict with the Governor's special responsibilities. In any case, there was no doubt in the mind of anyone present this morning that if Sikander took the course he proposed, there would be very great danger of grave trouble in the Province and perhaps beyond.

6. In my private discussion with Sikander I should be able to talk more freely than I could this morning and to impress forcibly upon him that the line he suggested is not only fraught with great danger to the Province, but is likely to damage his political reputation. I may also be able to disabuse him of the vague idea which he now seems to have that as the result of the Ministry resigning Barkat Ali would be placed in an impossible position, since either he could not form a Ministry, or, if he was able to do so, he would be quickly defeated. The most probable result, in fact, would be the suspension of the Constitution, with the odium on the Governor.

7. There is one aspect of the position which merits consideration. The action of the Muslims in bringing forward these bills is opposed to their own interest, because, assuming, as one must assume, that they cannot be allowed to become law, the result will be to place the Sikhs in such an extremely strong position that they will never agree to a settlement. But so long as no irrevocable step of this kind is taken there is always the chance that a settlement may be reached, although some time may elapse before conditions become favourable. If political motives had not inspired Barkat Ali's action, it ought not to have been difficult to persuade him to this effect, but Sikander is convinced that no consideration of this kind will affect him. None the less, whether sanction is refused to the bills or the bills are thrown out after introduction, or whether they are allowed to pass, the situation so created will make any settlement almost impossible. It is undoubtedly in the interests of everyone that, if it can be avoided, a situation should not arise where some positive action has to be taken in regard to these bills, unless of course there is a gentleman's agreement

between the Muslims and the Sikhs that if sanction is refused to the bills, the Sikhs will make a corresponding gesture. This is Sikander's proposal, and it may be that the Muslims are using these bills in the hope that they will thereby force the Sikhs to come to a settlement. I doubt whether this method will succeed at this juncture, and if it does not and the Muslims continue to insist on the bills, sooner or later action must be taken in regard to them, which will place the Sikhs in an impregnable position and which will inflame Muslim feelings by making them desperate. I had been considering even before today's meeting of the Council whether there was any escape from this position. There may be one possible way of avoiding it, but it may not be possible of adoption because of constitutional objections. It is clear that until the sanction of the Governor is given under Section 299 (3) of the Government of India Act, the bills cannot be introduced in the Legislative Assembly. There is nothing in the Act which requires the Governor to give or withhold consent within a specified period, and one can conceive circumstances in which a Governor would require considerable time before he could form a proper opinion on what was the right course for him to take in regard to a particular bill. He might, for instance, wish to ascertain the reactions of public opinion to it. Thus a possible course in the present instance would be for the Ministers to advise the Governor that for the present he should neither give nor withhold consent, but that he should take further time before reaching a decision. The advice in this case could justly be based on the grounds that I have already given, namely, that positive action is likely permanently to reduce, if not destroy, the chances of an amicable settlement without which the peace and tranquillity of the Province is likely to be gravely disturbed. If this course were followed, it would be necessary for the Governor or the Ministers to make the reasons perfectly clear. For the time being it would postpone the issue and might be even welcomed by a large body of opinion of all communities. It would give time for Muslims and Sikhs to get together. The objection to it is of course that unless an amicable settlement were reached, the issue would ultimately have to be faced in the same form, and the conditions might be even more difficult than they now are. None the less, the course is worth consideration as a last resort. I have been very careful not to mention it to the Premier or any of the Ministers and so far the idea has not suggested itself to them. Even if it were suggested to them they might be able to advance good reasons for turning it down and might not be prepared to agree, but I would greatly welcome Your Excellency's advice from the constitutional point of view, the issue being not merely whether it would be within the Governor's legal powers, but whether it would be constitutional and proper for the Governor in certain circumstances to defer giving or withholding his sanction to a bill under Section 299 (3) of the Government of India Act.[5] Meanwhile, I do not propose to put the idea forward even as a tentative proposal.

8. I shall be grateful if Your Excellency will let Craik see this letter at once. He is, I believe, coming to Lahore on the 12th. I may ask him to come earlier as he is closely concerned. While I think that, at the worst, a crisis can be deferred for a fortnight or so – and at present I do not anticipate the worst – Your Excellency may think it advisable to inform the Secretary of State by cable of the developments that have occurred.

9. I have thought it desirable to send Cunningham a copy of my letter of the 27th of February and of the first six paragraphs of this letter, as developments may affect his Province.[6]

Yours sincerely,
H.W. EMERSON

37

EMERSON TO LINLITHGOW

Government House, Lahore,
D.-O. No. 49 *March 7th, 1938*

My dear Lord Linlithgow,

In my Demi-Official No. 31 of the 4th of January 1938,[7] I discussed the necessity of giving Government servants guidance as to their conduct under the new constitution. I mentioned the doubts and difficulties of some of our officers. In illustration of these, I now enclose a copy of a letter from the Deputy Commissioner of the Attock district, to the Commissioner, Rawalpindi, and a copy of the latter's letter to the Chief Secretary. The Premier has made the following observation on the file:

> 'The difficulty is that open and filthy abuse of officials and Government by paid propagandists and irresponsible persons, who carry on propaganda, is gradually but surely undermining the prestige and authority of both the Government and its officers; and where the district officials are indifferent, out of ignorance or otherwise, the process is rapid.'

I agree with the Premier in this respect. At present the issue of instructions by the Punjab Government is held up for the reasons given in paragraph 4 of my letter to Your Excellency of the 4th of January 1938.[8] I shall be grateful if Your Excellency can advise on the matter as soon as convenient.

Yours sincerely,
H.W. EMERSON

ENCLOSURE 1 TO NO. 37

KING TO PENNY

Confidential

Commissioner's Office,
Rawalpindi Division,
February 3rd, 1938

D.-O. No. 113-H.Q.

My dear Penny,

I enclose a copy of Eustace's Demi-Official letter No. 26-L., dated the 1st February 1938, in which he is asking for guidance. It is not very easy to visualise the exact nature of his difficulties, but apparently he feels that he needs some moral support in dealing with subversive propaganda, which does not actually come within the scope of the law. Can you suggest a reply that is likely to help him and at the same time is in conformity with the policy of Government? I do not think I have yet received any clear official statement of Government's attitude towards subversive propaganda, and I know that some members of His Excellency's Council, certain[ly] Mr. Manohar Lal, are inclined to raise a difficult academic query as to what exactly constitutes subversive propaganda. But I do agree with Eustace that sooner or later the Congress propaganda which is being carried on in the rural areas will bear its inevitable fruit of civil disturbances unless some effective measure is taken to discourage it. I should have thought that no Deputy Commissioner would have needed detailed instructions and it is obviously difficult to give detailed instructions in the absence of a detailed statement of the difficulties. You however will know best what kind of advice will meet the case.

Yours sincerely,
C. KING

ENCLOSURE 2 TO NO. 37

EUSTACE TO KING

Deputy Commissioner's Office,
Attock District, Campbellpur,

D.-O. No. 26-L. *February 1st, 1938*

My dear King,

As you know, a good deal of anti-Government speaking has been going on in this district for some months. I do not think it has yet had much result – certainly it has had none so far amongst the zamindars. There was however as you know a formal anti-Government conference on a fairly considerable scale at Pindigheb at the end of December, and another is proposed for Talagang this week. I feel that in the circumstances I should now ask for instructions as to what action if any I should take. If violence or the non-payment of rent or revenue were to be advocated, the position would be simple because such speaking is or can be made a punishable offence – so also speaking which comes under Section 124-A. The kind of speaking which is going on at present is not however illegal – I refer to the general blaming of all the zamindar's troubles including his poverty on Government and the large landowners, and the socialist speaking generally. As.I have said, there has been no result so far; the refusal of many of the Tamman tenants to pay rent which has been going on since the spring seems to be due to the old quarrel accentuated by the Assembly elections between the Pir of Makhad and the Awans, and has so far shown no signs of spreading. The kind of unsettling speaking which I have mentioned is however still going on, and if the refusal of rent were at any time to extend to further areas or if there were to be civil difficulties of other kinds, I should not like it to be said that I had allowed this speaking to go on for months without reporting the matter formally. It is clearly better to take orders in advance as to the line to be followed, and that is why I am writing to you.

2. Nobody would wish to interfere with free speech or ordinary criticism of Government. Politics in this Province have however a way of impinging very definitely on the question of law and order. For example, if the Awans of Talagang were to get certain ideas into their head, they might spread very rapidly; and of course in the Chhachh the people are a wild lot, and the whole 80 villages could be infected in a day by disorderly ideas if the people were sufficiently impressed by what was stated by them. Something

of the sort I believe happened in your time when Abdul Ghaffar Khan came to Hazro. I saw myself in 1931 the greater part of Sialkot tahsil rise and march into Jammu against orders and against the law when the people got the idea that Muhammadans in the State were in difficulty through the practice of their religion. There are the difficulties into which the Frontier Government got in 1931 on account of unrestricted Red Shirt speaking. Going further back still there was the case of Jhang in 1915 when the people I understand got the idea that we had lost the war and that sahukars could be robbed with impunity. The lesson of these events would seem to be that it is possible for ill-disposed people to stir up the villages, and if that is so, the question of the present socialist speaking, &c., deserves consideration. I would add at this point that from the 21st to the 28th January from Hazro I rode over the whole of the Chhachh, and visited probably 40 villages. It is in the Chhachh (with Talagang) that difficulties could most easily be caused by persons against Government. Sykes has been much in Talagang during the winter, and I shall try to go there myself in March. I have had to cancel the tour in that tahsil which I had contemplated for February on account of the visit of His Excellency and the Land Revenue Commission.

3. I have stated what the present position is and what have been the results in other places of continuous evil propaganda. At this stage you will I think want to know what action I have taken so far in this district, and the answer is that I have done practically nothing for fear of incurring the charge of interesting myself in politics. When zaildars have asked for orders as to whether they should oppose (for example) the Congress, I told them up to December to please themselves. From a discussion which I had with you in December I understood however that this was not the correct line, and I have since when spoken to by zaildars or maliks told them that they should give no encouragement to anybody who seems to wish to change the existing forms of Government or who advocates arrangements which would probably lead to disorder or the break up of our present rural system. It has seemed difficult to go further without incurring the charge of going against one political party.

4. There is then the question whether any action ought to be taken. So long as the speakers keep within the law it is difficult to see how any action can be taken against them. There remains the question of counter-propaganda, &c., amongst the people. Men of the zaildar and malik class with whom I have discussed this point say that few zamindars go to these meetings (which is true) and that they have control over their people. That may be so. On the other hand, it is a fact that in Sialkot the people defied

their zaildars – I do not know about the other cases I have mentioned – and as we saw at the Assembly elections the influence of the zaildars and maliks if the issue can be distorted so as to bring in religion is not all they think it is. The Muslim League now shows signs of getting going in this district but only in towns. Whether the zaildar and malik class would do much effective work if instructed I doubt. I also think that except in the Chhachh it will at present suffice if the zaildars keep their people away from these subversive meetings as they are doing at present. In the Chhachh however my feeling is that something more is desirable, and that general suggestions to rural leaders that they should impress upon the people the beneficence of Government (if not of the maliks), their anxiety to do everything they can for the people, and the duty of the people in the circumstances to support Government, be well behaved and pay their revenue and rents is not sufficient. To speak plainly I feel that in view of past experience in the Chhachh counter-propaganda ought definitely to be organised. It is not of course for me to meddle in politics to the extent of suggesting that the Unionist Party should get a proper organisation going in the Chhachh. But if they did and tried to counter some of the ideas which are at present put about, it might be a good thing from the point of view of law, order and the general stability which is all I am concerned with. It is always necessary to remember that in Attock tahsil which adjoins the Frontier Province men's minds are unquestionably affected by what happens there.

5. The question on which I would ask for orders is whether any action should be taken with regard to the present anti-Government speaking which is going on in this district. The more one considers the matter the more difficult it seems in a case of this kind to find any half-way house between non-interference as between political parties and interference. I have of course no concern with political parties as such, but I am concerned with civil order, and it is difficult to discuss that question in the Province without bringing in political parties. There is one final point. In May last when I wrote to you about certain difficulties in Kot Fateh Khan, you replied that I seemed distressed. I most earnestly hope that you will not take this view on the present reference. There is no question whatever of that kind of thing. I have been reluctant to write this letter at all for fear of being written down as an alarmist, but I feel that if now that regular conferences are being organised I do not make a reference, I may be written down as remiss. The district is at present entirely quiet and in hand; I can myself scarcely imagine anything which would set our villages against Government except an idea that their religion was being interfered with, and that none

of the speakers have so far suggested, though Shahidganj or the Nikki shooting case may give an opportunity later. Leaving aside however all questions of the people being turned in large numbers against Government, I do feel that this socialist speaking does no good and might do harm especially amongst the semi-educated classes of the people everywhere, and amongst all classes in the Chhachh.

Yours sincerely,
E.A.R. EUSTACE

38

EMERSON TO LINLITHGOW

Secret
D.-O. No. 50

Government House, Lahore,
March 7th, 1938

My dear Lord Linlithgow,

In continuation of my letter of the 4th/5th of March, I write to say that I had a very reassuring talk with Sikander last evening. He told me that he was to meet his Muslim supporters this evening (Monday), that he intended to tell them that he was going to recommend that sanction to the bills should be withheld (or, as a possible alternative, which is very unlikely, that, if they were allowed to be introduced, it was on the understanding that he would strongly oppose them at the first stage), and that he was prepared to make this an issue on which to resign if he did not have the support of the Muslim members. While he thought that there might be a dozen Muslims who would not accept his policy, he felt pretty confident that the great majority would be loyal. Following the meeting this evening, he intended to have a meeting of the Unionist Party tomorrow and he thought he would be in a position to give definite advice within the next three or four days. He himself realised the importance of avoiding further delay. He anticipated that as soon as it became known that sanction had been refused to the bills, either an adjournment motion or a motion of no-confidence would be moved and that he would then make a full statement giving the reasons for his action and particularly stressing the constitutional aspect, the necessity of protecting the minorities and the fact that the bills were not in the interests of the Muslims themselves, since they would close the door to an amicable settlement. Unless, therefore, he changes his intentions or his Muslim supporters revolt, which is improbable, there should be no crisis. There may be reactions outside, when it is known that the bills are to be refused sanction, and these will have to be dealt with as they occur.

2. I told Sikander that I was very relieved at what he said, as his attitude in Council on Friday had perturbed me. He said that his line has always been the same and that I must have misunderstood him. I think the explanation is that on Friday he was tired and depressed, was particularly worried about the position of Muslim members outside the Legislature and that he failed to make himself clear. Certainly both Penny and I were left with the impression that he was very uncertain about the issue and that he had not then made up his mind regarding the avoidance of further delay. We also felt that he might seek the easy way out of resigning without putting up a stiff fight, although he himself would have the courage of his convictions. Manohar Lal also tells me that he left Friday's meeting confused and bewildered as to the Premier's intentions. It is a great relief to me to find that these impressions were wrong, as I have no doubt they were, and that Sikander is prepared resolutely to take the right line. Failure to do so would have had the most deplorable effects constitutionally, since it would have meant the failure of ministerial responsibility on a communal issue.

3. I hope that the point mentioned in paragraph 7 of my last letter will be academic so far as the present occasion is concerned, but, since it might easily arise in future, I shall still be grateful for Your Excellency's views.

4. I let Craik know on the telephone last night the result of my talk with Sikander, but he will be interested to see this letter.

Yours sincerely,
H.W. EMERSON

39

EMERSON TO LINLITHGOW

Government House, Lahore,
D.-O. No. 51 *March 9th, 1938*

My dear Lord Linlithgow,

In continuation of my letter of the 7th of March, I write to say that Sikander had a very long discussion with his Muslim supporters lasting till the early hours of the morning on Monday, the 7th, and that in the end they left it to him to take what course he thought right. I understand that he was very pleased with their attitude, since, although there may be a few seceders, the great majority will support him. There was a meeting of the Council of Ministers yesterday when the position was discussed. The Ministers considered that it was not necessary or desirable to have a meeting of the Unionist or Ministerial Party on the subject, but that the Premier should himself meet the groups concerned. It was also considered that owing to the Muharram holidays, which occur at the end of this week, it would be inopportune to communicate the refusal of sanction to the bills until the holidays are over, first, because the local reactions would be greater if the fact became known during Muharram, and, second, because the legislature will not be sitting, and, if there is an adjournment motion or a vote of no confidence, it is desirable to have it as soon as possible after the facts become known when the supporters of Government have returned from their homes. The present plan is, therefore, that the Ministers will advise me formally on Monday, the 14th, to withhold consent, and that this will become known on the 15th. There will probably be a motion of some sort by Barkat Ali on the 16th.

2. There is a possibility that Gauba will give notice that he does not wish his bill to be balloted for this session. In that case it will not be necessary for me to give any order regarding that bill.

3. Should there be any unexpected developments, I will keep Your Excellency informed.

Yours sincerely,
H.W. EMERSON

40

EMERSON TO LINLITHGOW

Private and Personal
D.-O. No. 52-F.L.

Government House, Lahore,
March 17th, 1938

My dear Lord Linlithgow,

The centre of interest during the past few weeks has been the Bill of Malik Barkat Ali regarding the Shahidganj in particular and mosques in general. I have written separately to Your Excellency from time to time regarding this matter. Your Excellency will have seen from the press that, on the advice of my Ministers, I withheld consent to the Bill, and that yesterday the Premier made a very good statement in the Assembly. There was an attempt to move a vote of no confidence against the Government, but only two members stood up. The local reactions so far have not been serious.

There is, I believe, a partial *hartal* in Lahore City today among Muslim shopkeepers. I will write to Your Excellency in a day or two dealing fully with the question when reactions in the press and elsewhere are known. For the present the outstanding fact is that the Ministers have faced their responsibility with great courage and that, so far as can be seen, there is no danger of a constitutional crisis.

2. In my last letter I mentioned the torture case of Kiroo. I have since seen the Police diaries, and, although, pending its examination by the Legal Remembrancer[9] and a discussion of the action to be taken, I have not come to any final conclusion, my impressions are that the man was ill-treated, although possibly not to the extent suggested, and that, although Pipe Major Stewart was paid to give evidence and is generally a very unsatisfactory person, part of his evidence is true. It also appears certain that attempts were made to bribe a Sergeant of the Regiment concerned to give evidence for the defence, although he knew nothing about the case. The evidence is so meagre and conflicting that it is going to be difficult to get anyone convicted, and the proper course to take will have to be very carefully considered.

3. A few days ago there was a very serious incident in a village of the Amritsar district. It appears that the Congress attempted to hold a meeting there some weeks ago against the wishes of the local inhabitants, who heckled the speakers severely. The Congress arranged to hold a further meeting and went there in large numbers. They say that the meeting was again interrupted, but it appears fairly clear that if there were any interruptions, they were of a minor character. The meeting lasted several hours and, according to the public statements of Congressmen themselves, was successfully completed. When the meeting was over a section of the Congress followers appear to have lost all control. They attacked the villagers, chased them into their houses, broke open the doors, killed one man on the spot, injured four or five others seriously, of whom one has died, and generally were guilty of the most brutal violence. There is no complaint from Congress that a single member of their party was injured in any way, and when the Police arrived at the village some hours after, the *shamiana*, chairs, &c., used for the meeting were in complete order. The villagers had fled. Two members of the Assembly, one a Muslim and the other a Sikh woman member, were present during the meeting. The Congress were quick in getting out their version of the affair and had the audacity to move an adjournment motion last evening in the Assembly. The debate seems to have roused very strong feelings on both sides and the Speaker had to suspend discussion for a few minutes. The Police enquiry

is proceeding, but there seems to be little doubt about the main facts of the attack. This is the first serious affair of its kind arising out of political meetings, but, I am afraid, it will not be the last.

4. Except for this adjournment motion and the Shahidganj affair, the present session of the legislature has on the whole been uneventful. The Finance Minister made a good budget speech and the budget received a favourable reception in the House and in the press. Voting on the demands for grants is now proceeding. There is little controversial business at present, but Government are exploring the possibilities of drafting a Bill, without retrospective effect, but applicable to the places of worship of all communities, which will prevent their conversion to other purposes. The question is a very difficult one. It is comparatively easy to draft an innocuous Bill which will, however, give little satisfaction to anyone. As soon as attempts are made to go further than this, one finds oneself in a morass of difficulties. The present idea is to obtain the advice of an informal committee representative of all communities in the Assembly.

5. Except for a little trouble at Kasur, the Muharram passed off peacefully. We are lucky to get through so lightly. At one time it looked as if there would be serious trouble in the Jullundur district, but this was averted at the last moment by an agreement between the Shias and Sunnis. The Shias, who have fourteen or fifteen members in the Assembly, are becoming more insistent in their demands and are pressing for innovations as regards processions, &c. Two such innovations have been arranged with the assistance of Muslim supporters of Government, one at Kasur last year and another this year in the Jullundur district. Representatives go down to the place concerned, get a so-called agreement from unwilling parties, which is promptly repudiated, and the district officers have then to deal with the difficult situation which results. The old practice, and, to my mind, the only safe one, was to allow no innovation unless there was clear and complete agreement between both sides. Deviations are certain to lead to trouble. The Ministry, however, is becoming wise from experience and the difficult situation that arose in the Jullundur district a few days ago will, I hope, have the salutary effect of making them more chary of trying to please everybody by action, which, however laudable its motives, often produces most undesirable results.

Yours sincerely,
H.W. EMERSON

41

EMERSON TO LINLITHGOW

Secret
D.-O. No. 54

Government House, Lahore,
March 31st, 1938

My dear Lord Linlithgow,

In my last fortnightly letter I mentioned briefly the immediate reactions to Sir Sikander's statement on the Shahidganj and said that I would write later to give my considered impressions. Owing to illness, my letter has been delayed, but I now take the opportunity of placing on record one or two points which may be of importance later.

2. All sections of the press gave a good reception to the line taken by Government. There was much approval and little criticism of the fact that I consulted my Ministers, although I had discretion to refuse sanction to the Bill of Barkat Ali without consulting them. In one or two articles I noticed the assumption that the fact that I did consult them implied that I would have been prepared to follow their advice whatever that advice might have been. This assumption is, of course, wrong. It was quite clear to my Ministers that my consultation with them did not in any way fetter my discretion. There was also some misunderstanding apparent in the press regarding my reasons for consulting them, and, since I do not think that I had stated them fully, I may now do so. In the first place, it has been my practice to consult the Ministers in all matters. Second, this particular issue raised very big questions of policy with which the Ministry was intimately concerned, and the fact that my discretion was involved was almost incidental. Third, although at first some, if not all, of the Ministers would have preferred me to act without consulting them, it was clear that this would have placed both them and myself in an impossible position. Had I refused sanction to the Bill on my own initiative, there would have been a general and almost irresistible demand from Muslims for the resignation of the Muslim Ministers. Further, a matter which I had constantly to consider, Muslim resentment would have been concentrated solely and very strongly against the British Government, and there would have been serious danger of trouble in the Punjab and North-West India generally.

There was thus never any doubt in my own mind that I must insist on the advice of the Ministers, and that, if I had to act contrary to it, it must be because they had failed to meet their responsibilities.

3. I have said that the reception given by the press to the statement has been good and for the time being not only is the crisis over but the position of Sikander has been greatly strengthened. It is, however, necessary to make some qualifications. While the Sikh press has been full of gratitude, there has been practically no sign of any response in the nature of an agreed settlement. In fact I see from the papers that only a few days ago the executive committee of the S.G.P.C. declared that there could be no talk whatsoever of any compromise. Last week I had a long and serious talk with Sir Sunder Singh about this aspect. I told him plainly that it was up to him and his friends to make a gesture, that I was certain that there were plenty of moderate Sikhs who would welcome a settlement, but that at present no one had the courage to come forward to suggest it. I asked him what he was doing or proposed to do in the matter. He was not very promising and was inclined to point out the difficulties, which are admittedly very great, rather than get down to the matter in hand. The impression he left on my mind and also on that of Sikander, who was present for part of the talk, was that the Sikhs are content to let matters drift and that it is going to be difficult to get them to do anything practical. Political considerations are continually clouding the issue. I thought it right to tell Sir Sunder that in my view the matter had only been tided over and not solved, and that unless there was a mutual agreement between the Muslims and the Sikhs the question was bound to come up again. I said that I thought that the Muslims might be content to wait for a few months to see whether the Sikhs were willing to do anything at all, but that if there was no move at all from their side there would then be a demand for legislation by Government and that Sikander and the Muslim Ministers would find themselves in a very difficult position. I also suggested that it was going to be difficult for the Sikhs continually to claim the special protection of the Governor when, contrary to public opinion, they would not budge an inch in the way of reconciliation. Sir Sunder promised that he would try to get a move on, but I am not sanguine about the result.

4. As Your Excellency will have seen, the Council of the Muslim League at a meeting held at Delhi approved the action taken by Sikander and his Government. Sikander himself went to Delhi in order to talk to Jinnah and others before the meeting of the Council. He tells me that Jinnah took a very reasonable view and that the members of the League present were, with one or two exceptions, amicably disposed. The full session of the League is to be held in Calcutta during the Easter holidays. My impression is that the line it will take is not to press matters for the present but to give a fairly definite hint that if a solution cannot be found within a reasonable

time by a mutual settlement, then the Muslims will expect Sikander's Government to introduce legislation for the purpose. I do not know whether Sikander held out any hope of this when he was at Delhi. Before he went I particularly asked him to be careful not to commit himself in any way on this matter. Since he fully realises the difficulties that it might raise both with his colleagues and with the Governor, I imagine that he was careful in what he said. Since at sometime or the other the matter may be of importance, I should like to make it clear that I have been very careful to keep the discretion of the Governor completely unfettered should such a situation arise.

Yours sincerely,
H.W. EMERSON

42

EMERSON TO LINLITHGOW

Private and Personal | Government House, Lahore,
D.-O. No. 60-F.L. | *April 5th, 1938*

My dear Lord Linlithgow,

With reference to my last letter regarding the Shahidganj, Sikander tells me that he saw Master Tara Singh secretly on the 3rd of April. While the meeting did not lead to any positive result, Sikander found Tara Singh to be on the whole less adamant regarding a settlement than he expected. He emphasised his personal difficulty, namely, that if he made a move opponents would use it against him to oust him from his position in Akali circles; and it is in fact the conflict in personal and party interests among the Sikhs that mainly stands in the way of a compromise. In this connection Tara Singh specially mentioned the activities of Sardar Mangal Singh, M.L.A., who is hostile to him, but who does not carry sufficient influence among the Sikhs to do any good. However, it is a good thing that Sikander and Tara Singh have got into personal touch. I gather that for the present, at any rate, Sikander is keeping the fact strictly secret.

2. With regard to the Kiroo case, there was a conference, before I fell ill, attended by the Premier, the Home Secretary,[10] the Advocate-General,[11] the Legal Remembrancer, the Inspector-General of Police and myself, at which decisions were reached regarding the procedure to be adopted. It was decided to prosecute under the Criminal Law an Anglo-Indian Inspector, a Head Constable and two Constables of Police and a non-

official, who is alleged to have been concerned in the ill-treatment. The case will be tried by Mr. J.D. Anderson, who is just returned from leave and gone as Commissioner to Rawalpindi. He is a senior officer, who, for several years, worked as a Sessions Judge, so that his impartiality and experience are above criticism. The Crown will be represented by the Advocate-General. It appears doubtful whether the case will end in conviction, but the issues will be fought out in open Court.

3. The Fatehwal case, which I mentioned in my previous letter, has gone into Court, but a number of accused are still absconding, including the two principal culprits. Congress have formed a defence committee and unscrupulous attempts are being made to give the case a political colour. I was told today that this defence committee intends to tour villages in the Amritsar district for propaganda purposes and to hold meetings in and around Fatehwal. It is almost certain that action will have to be taken to stop this after a few meetings have been held, since with feeling running high as it is, there would be serious danger of a breach of the peace. The object is probably to obscure the merits of the original case in a fog of political side-issues.

4. There was a bad communal riot about ten days ago in Hissar, when two Hindus were shot dead including an Honorary Magistrate, whom I had invested a few days before with a Rai Bahaduri. He was the most respected man in the town, non-communal and very quiet. The riot was a sequel to previous trouble that had occurred a few weeks before, and, although the last trouble was quickly brought under control, the feeling is said to be very tense. As usual, there is clamour for a European Deputy Commissioner and European Superintendent of Police, but, even if the transfer of the present officers were justified, which is not the case, we simply have not got European officers available.

5. This is the last letter I shall write before I go on leave in two days' time. As it also synchronizes with the end of the first year of the new Constitution, I may perhaps give some brief general impressions. In spite of certain tendencies and difficulties, which I have brought to Your Excellency's notice from time to time, there can be no doubt that the Ministry have come through the year very well. Inside the Ministry there has been good co-operation and full recognition of the spirit of joint responsibility. So far as I know, there have been no internal differences of any kind. This has, of course, been largely due to the success of the Premier, who is greatly respected and genuinely liked by all his colleagues. He has kept the team together very well. In spite of occasional difficulties, he has also held his party together, and, if anything, is stronger now than when he

took office. His handling of the Muslim members over Barkat Ali's Bill was, so I am told, very masterly, and in the end he turned into a personal triumph what threatened to be a very difficult situation. There has been little, if any, sign of any defection by the Noon-Tiwana group. On the contrary, Nawabzada Khizar Hyat is a most loyal colleague, and the father of Sir Firoz Khan Noon volunteered to me the other day the statement that while, as I knew, Sikander was at first viewed with some suspicion by that group, they now held him in the highest respect and were determined to support him. Sikander has also been able to hold the Hindu and Sikh supporters of Government, while, so far as rural Hindus are concerned, Sir Chhotu Ram exercises great influence over them in spite of the strenuous efforts of Congress, especially in the south-east.

The Ministry has on the whole been very stout on the question of law and order, and, although there has sometimes been hesitation in dealing firmly with communal troubles, and the communal situation is still difficult, I do not myself think that it is quite as bad as it was in July last.

The relations between the Ministry and officers and between individual Ministers and their Secretaries have been excellent. There is no apprehension among Government servants, who are serving the new Government loyally and well. There has been no attempt at victimization. The Premier is very popular with officers of Government, whom he always treats with great consideration and courtesy.

The policy of the Ministry has been sound without being spectacular. It has avoided making rash promises, which could not be fulfilled, and recently there has been a distinct tendency to tell the people plainly that there cannot be big sacrifices of revenue without serious detriment to the Province. The Government, however, will be faced with a difficult situation when the report of the Darling Committee. regarding land-revenue comes to be considered. At times there has been a danger of the Ministers. rushing into hasty legislation, but, generally speaking, this has been surmounted. On one or two questions a surrender has had to be made to popular sentiment contrary to the merits of the case. For instance, Government have accepted the principle of trying prohibition in one district. They have also promoted amendments of the existing Compulsory Education Act, which admittedly will have very little, if any, practical effect. Such instances, however, are rare and some concession to public opinion on matters of this kind was almost inevitable.

6. Finally, my own relations with the Ministry as a whole, with the Premier and individual Ministers, could not have been better. They have gone out of their way to consult me and have almost invariably accepted

my advice, although, except where my special responsibilities were concerned, I have always made it quite clear that there was no obligation on them to do so. On the whole, therefore, in spite of some temporary set-backs, the year has been a very good one. I would be sanguine regarding the future were it not for two elements of instability: success has depended very largely on the personality and popularity of the Premier. It would be very difficult to replace him, if for any reason he were not able to carry on. Second, there is always the danger of some communal question causing a division in the ranks. On the other hand, a factor of growing importance is the value which members of the Legislature attach to their position, and their unwillingness to sacrifice that position except on very big issues. Supporters of Government are not going to turn Government out without very good reasons.[12]

Yours sincerely,
H.W. EMERSON

43

CRAIK TO LINLITHGOW

Secret Government House, Lahore,
D.-O. No. 62-F.L. *April 18th/19th, 1938*

Dear Lord Linlithgow,

I took over charge here on April the 7th[13] and Emerson and his wife left for England the same evening. I have been surprised and deeply touched by the warmth of the welcome I have received from everyone whom I have met at the various functions connected with my assumption of office. There has been a long and exhausting list of such functions and I have been kept busy renewing old friendships after an absence from the Province of just about four years.

2. On the whole, I see singularly little change in the general tone of the administration. There has probably been some slight, but not disturbing, loss of efficiency, and I should say that the pace of the administrative machine has slowed down a little, but my first impression is that the general principles of sound and prudent administration are being as closely observed as under the old régime.

3. The Assembly session was still in progress when I took over and did not terminate till the evening of April the 11th. It was the longest session in the history of the Punjab Legislature and all the Ministers were more or

less exhausted at its close. Immediately the session concluded all of them, with the exception of the Premier, left Lahore on tour or on a brief holiday, and the Premier himself has since left to attend the session of the Muslim League in Calcutta, where he is to be joined by his two Muslim colleagues and by several of his supporters in the local Assembly. I have thus not been able to see much of my Ministers, though I have had several long talks with Sikander and have presided at one Cabinet meeting. This was summoned at my request in order that I may exchange formal greetings with the Ministers and renew my acquaintance with them. Four of them, including the Premier, were at one time my colleagues under the old Constitution, and the other two are old friends. I am confident that our relations will be of the happiest description. So far, as I have observed, the Ministers are working well together as a team and there is no lack of confidence between them. The Ministry has, I think, undoubtedly acquitted itself with credit in the Budget session that has just concluded. The Budget itself was passed without any material modification and, indeed, without provoking any serious criticism.

4. I have made it a point to ask all officers I have met how they feel they are getting on under Provincial Autonomy and whether they find that its introduction has made any material change in their position. The officers in question have naturally been mostly those working in the Secretariat or at the headquarters of Government. The answer has invariably been that Provincial Autonomy has brought about very little actual change in their position, that their relations with the Ministry are excellent and that there is little or no tendency to ignore the advice or dispense with the assistance of the permanent staff; nor is there any tendency to curtail the rights and privileges of officers.

In these circumstances I was rather surprised to find that among almost the first set of official papers that came to me were two cases of retirement on proportionate pension, both the officers concerned being comparatively senior Executive Engineers in the Irrigation Department. I asked the Chief Engineer concerned how many cases of this kind there had been recently and I enclose, for Your Excellency's information, a copy of his reply.[14] It is not very enlightening as to the reasons underlying the applications for premature retirement, but when the Chief Engineer returns from tour I will have a further conversation with him on the subject.

I was also surprised to have, a day or two later, a similar application from a young officer of the I.C.S., E.P. Moon, who has between 8 and 9 years' service. Moon will be a great loss, as he is an exceptionally brilliant young man and, I believe, the only serving member of the I.C.S. who is a

Fellow of All Souls. I am making enquiries as to the reasons for his application, but I think it is quite possible that he has received some offer of an appointment in England. I know that Geoffrey Dawson is interested in Moon and it is possible that the latter may have been offered an appointment on *The Times*. I have no reason to think that he has any special cause for dissatisfaction with conditions in India.

5. One of the questions which I discussed at length with Sikander was that which was considered in Council a day or two before I left Delhi, viz., the problem of checking speeches discouraging recruitment to the Army. I have written at length to Cassels on this matter and I have no doubt that he will show my letter to Your Excellency. Its purport is that while Sikander is quite ready to enforce Central legislation, either in the form of an Act or an Ordinance, on the subject, he does not think that the problem can be dealt with under Section 3 of the Punjab Criminal Law (Amendment) Act, 1935. So far as the Local Government is aware, there has hitherto been no difficulty in securing adequate numbers of recruits of all classes.

6. Communal tension is unfortunately still acute, though there has been no incident of any importance since my assumption of charge. I am not happy about the situation at Hissar, where, Your Excellency may remember, there was a serious Hindu-Muhammadan riot about March the 26th, in which a Hindu Honorary Magistrate and one or two other Hindus were killed by gun-fire. A few arrests have been made, but the general belief is that the real culprits have not yet been arrested, and the local Hindus are reported to be in a vindictive mood. Strong reinforcements of Police have, however, been drafted to the District and the Deputy Commissioner,[15] though apprehensive as regards the future, has not asked for further assistance either in the form of additional Police reinforcements or troops. The Deputy Commissioner is a comparatively young Sikh I.C.S. officer and the Superintendent of Police[16] is a Muslim promoted from the Provincial Service. On the occasion of the riot at the end of March they were both absent from headquarters on tour. This in itself was a serious error of judgement, as there had been previous rioting on the occasion of the Muharram festival and the Deputy Commissioner and the Superintendent of Police should so have arranged their touring that both were not absent from headquarters simultaneously. The Commissioner[17] visited Hissar immediately after the riot of the 26th of March and sent in a long report, in which he recommended that the Superintendent of Police, who has certain defects, should be replaced, if possible by a British officer. This is being arranged. The Commissioner did not recommend the transfer

of the Sikh Deputy Commissioner, as he did not think he was in any way to be blamed for the manner in which the situation was handled. Sikander, however, advised me that he should be transferred, as the local Hindus had urged on the Premier, through their representatives in the Assembly, that the Deputy Commissioner had lost their confidence and had pressed for a British officer to be sent to take charge of the district. After some discussion with Sikander and the Chief Secretary (who took the same view) I agreed, and arrangements are being made to replace the Sikh Deputy Commissioner early in May by a young British officer, who will then become available. The Sikh Deputy Commissioner is being transferred to Ambala, a better district than Hissar, which is in accordance with his own wishes, and will avoid giving the transfer the appearance of a punishment.

7. As regards the Shahidganj affair, I have no change to report. Your Excellency may have noticed that in a speech delivered at a recent dinner in my honour I referred briefly to my own willingness to do anything in my power to bring about a settlement of this difficult problem satisfactory to both communities concerned. I purposely avoided going further than this and particularly suggesting any specific form of solution. I told Sikander beforehand what I meant to say and he agreed. He was present at the party himself. At the moment and until the conclusion of the Muslim League session in Calcutta he feels – and I entirely agree – that no further move should be made. He has gone to Calcutta, as mentioned above, with a considerable body of his Punjabi supporters, and I do not think that he anticipates that Jinnah will allow the League to come to any decision that would be embarrassing to Sikander's Ministry. I, of course, gave Sikander a full account of my own conversation with Jinnah, which took place the day before I left Delhi, when Jinnah certainly gave me the impression that he wished to be helpful to Sikander. Meanwhile I understand that Sikander has been secretly in touch with various Sikh leaders and that their reactions, though not very "forthcoming", have not been wholly unfavourable. As soon as Sikander returns to Lahore I will discuss the matter again with him.

8. It may interest Your Excellency to know that in one of our conversations Sikander repeated an opinion, which he had expressed to me before, to the effect that the Congress are not genuine in their opposition to Federation. There was a debate on this question during the recent session of the Punjab Assembly, but the resolution that was unanimously passed was in an agreed form and considerably milder than that which had been originally tabled. So far as I can judge, Sikander on that occasion managed

a somewhat difficult position adroitly. He seems to have a flair for parliamentary tactics.

9. I am staying at Lahore, save for a brief visit to Amritsar, till May the 2nd, when I start on a short tour to the north of the Province. I hope to reach Simla on May the 13th.

10. I enclose the provincial fortnightly report for the second half of March and also that for the first half of April.

Yours sincerely,
H.D. CRAIK

44

CRAIK TO LINLITHGOW

Secret
D.-O. No. 65

Government House, Lahore,
April 25th, 1938

Dear Lord Linlithgow,

I had a long talk this morning with Sikander about the Muslim League meeting in Calcutta, and he gave me some information which may be of interest to Your Excellency.

The opening (public) session of the League was held on the evening Sikander and his party arrived in Calcutta. The tone of Fazl-ul-Haq's address of welcome to Jinnah (which was printed in Urdu and also recorded for radio purposes) was, in Sikander's view, completely irresponsible. Sikander himself listened to it with increasing embarrassment and so, I gather, did the Bengal Home Minister, Sir Nazim-ud-Din. Indeed, the latter expressed the opinion to Sikander afterwards that the speech offended against about six Sections of the Indian Penal Code! This was not the speech which contained certain very impertinent references to Your Excellency as regards the praise you had bestowed on Congress Governments and your invitation to Gandhi. These references were contained in a later speech by Fazl-ul-Haq delivered after Sikander had left Calcutta.

At the opening session Jinnah's speech was also calculated to keep the communal temperature at a high level. Sikander thought the speech a bad one and I rather infer from something he said that he had remonstrated afterwards with Jinnah, but Jinnah explained that he had deliberately adopted this tone, as he thought it might secure him some tactical advantage in his approaching conversations with Gandhi. Incidentally I may mention that Sikander has very little hope that anything will come of these conversations.

The heat generated at the open session was, in Sikander's opinion, calculated to produce a very unfavourable atmosphere for the Shahidganj discussion, which took place in the Subjects Committee next morning. The Subject Committee's discussion was, of course, not open to the public or reported in the Press. As Sikander had anticipated, the discussion started with feeling generally hostile to any settlement of the Shahidganj dispute except by 'direct action'. There were between 250 and 300 delegates present and Maulana Zafar Ali Khan, the leader of the Ittihad-i-Millat, and Barkat Ali, the author of the notorious Bill, spoke in a sense strongly hostile to Sikander. Other speakers in this sense were one Lal Din Kaisar, a third-rate agitator from the Punjab, a Maulvi from Bihar whose name Sikander did not remember, and another whom he described as 'some other nondescript'. Sikander's position during this session must at first have been very unhappy, as before the discussion began some of the Bengal delegates had suggested some kind of a compromise resolution, which Sikander considered most unsatisfactory from his point of view, and even Jinnah was in two minds whether it would be possible to pass any resolution that would leave the settlement of the matter in the hands of the Punjab Ministry. However, after these three or four hostile speeches, Sikander himself spoke at great length and apparently with such success that in the end Zafar Ali, who was the protagonist of direct action, only secured four votes and the resolution that was eventually adopted and passed next day in the open session of the League without any dissent was, from Sikander's point of view, highly satisfactory. I gather the general line which Sikander took in his speech in the Subjects Committee was to make it plain that no 'half-way house' measure was possible and that only two courses were open to the League – (*a*) direct action, which must lead to an aggravation of bitterness between the two communities and eventually to bloodshed, or (*b*) to express confidence in the line taken by the Provincial Government and to encourage them in their efforts to bring about an amicable settlement. Sikander was particularly pleased that his speech commanded general support, especially from the North-West Frontier Province delegates and from those representing the United Provinces, the leader of the latter being Khaliq-uz-Zaman, who eventually moved in the open session the adoption of the resolution approved by the Subjects Committee.

When we had finished discussing what happened at Calcutta, I asked Sikander whether he thought it was possible at the present moment to take any further step towards bringing about a reconciliation and how much importance he thought should be attached to the extremely stubborn statement issued by Tara Singh, the Akali leader, which appeared in the Press simultaneously with the report of the Muslim League's decision. Sikander told me that Tara Singh's statement was actually based on a false report published in a Lahore newspaper, the *Milap,* to the effect that Sikander had stated at Calcutta that the Sikhs had agreed, or were willing to agree, to a settlement. As a matter of fact, of course, Sikander said nothing of the kind. On Saturday last Sikander saw at Lahore one of Tara Singh's leading supporters, who expressed the view that it would take some time to bring Tara Singh into a more reasonable frame of mind. The question of the correct tactical approach to the Sikhs is one of considerable delicacy, largely because of the bitter feeling between the Khalsa National Party (i.e. the moderate Sikhs led by Sir Sunder Singh Majithia, the Revenue Minister), and the Akali Party led by Tara Singh. Each party is afraid that if it comes out with any kind of public statement in favour of a settlement involving any sacrifice by the Sikhs of their legal rights – and of course any settlement must involve some such sacrifice – the other party may make capital out of it and denounce their rivals as traitors to the community. Hitherto the Khalsa National Party has not come forward with any statement, though I believe that most of them would really welcome a settlement. I am now trying to think of some way of inducing some moderate and influential Sikhs, who are not directly connected with politics, to make some kind of conciliatory gesture. On the whole, I think this would probably be better tactics than trying to persuade the Khalsa National Party, to make a statement.

I think it is probable that the so-called civil disobedience on the part of the Ahrars and followers of the Ittihad-i-Millat will now stop. An Ahrar deputation has gone to see their leader, one Mazhar Ali, who is now in the Shahpur Jail. No arrests were necessary either on Friday or Saturday last.

Sikander told me he had a very good reception at Lyallpur yesterday from the local Sikhs of the Khalsa National Party, who presented an address to him in which he was described as the 'first ruler of the Punjab since Maharaja Ranjit Singh who enjoyed the confidence of the Sikhs and Muslims alike'! I told Sikander that I hope this would be published and he said it surely would be. One Gyani Sher Singh, a leader of one section of the Akali Party but not friendly to Tara Singh, made a speech in somewhat similar terms, and the general atmosphere was extremely friendly. Sikander replied to the address in Punjabi, which pleased the Sikhs, and the speech was punctuated with cheers and shouts of 'Sat Sri Akal'.

Many thanks for Your Excellency's letter from Peshawar of the 22nd of April. I am in correspondence with Moon and will let you know the result in due course.

I am so glad to hear you have had so good a reception in the North-West Frontier. It was very satisfactory that the Ministers should have attended the formal arrival and the State Banquet and should generally have been so friendly.

Yours sincerely,
H.D. CRAIK

45

CRAIK TO LINLITHGOW

Secret
D.-O. No. 66

Camp,
May 3rd, 1938

Dear Lord Linlithgow,

Your Excellency wrote to me the 26th of April about a case in which you rejected the petitions for mercy of four prisoners (Sher Bahadur, Khuda Bakhsh, Shera and Ali Sher) who had been condemned to death, and in which after the receipt of your orders the Home Secretary[18] to this Government referred the case back to Your Excellency with his letter No. 825-Judl./D.C. of the 8th of April with a further recommendation for the commutation of the capital sentences.

Your Excellency asked me in your recent letter whether in fact this reference back had been seen and approved by the Governor, as was the case with the original reference from the Local Government, in which it was stated that similar petitions from the convicts had been considered and rejected by the Local Government.

I have now sent for and read the papers connected with this case and am almost certain that it was one on which my advice was sought by Your Excellency when I was still in Delhi. I find that on the 24th of March last, i.e. a day or two after your orders rejecting the petitions had been received, the Home Secretary to the Punjab Government wrote demi-officially to the High Court, stating that the Punjab Government were disposed, if the Hon'ble Judges saw no objection, to recommend to the Governor-General that the capital sentences should be commuted on the grounds – (*a*) that four capital sentences for a single and unfortunately common type of murder were perhaps unnecessarily severe, and (*b*) that the father of one of the convicts had an altogether exceptionally fine record of military service. The High Court replied on the 1st of April, stating that the Judges had no objection to the proposed commutation, but desired to point out that the case had originally come before them in the shape of an appeal by the Local Government against an acquittal in the Sessions Court and, further, that the Crown Counsel had in the High Court pressed for the infliction of capital sentences. I cannot find that Sir Herbert Emerson actually saw the papers after the High Court's reply was received (he was, as you will remember, unwell at the time and was unable to attend to work), but there is a note on the file by Sikander, dated the 5th of April, stating that he had discussed the case with Sir Herbert and it had been decided that the High Court should be consulted and if the Judges did not object, a recommendation might be made to the Government of India for commutation. Sikander added that he was, of course, aware that the case was one of appeal by the Crown against the original acquittal and that it was for this reason that he suggested a reference to the High Court before proceeding further with the matter. As the High Court had intimated that they had no objection to the course proposed by the Local Government, Sikander gave instructions that a letter should be sent recommending commutation.

The other Minister concerned, Mr. Manohar Lal, who ordinarily deals with petitions for mercy, saw and concurred in this note, and a letter was accordingly addressed to the Governor-General's Secretary in accordance with the Premier's instructions. Sir Herbert did not see the letter either before or after its despatch, nor did I.

As I think I have mentioned in conversation with Your Excellency, there is a general tendency in the Punjab – and indeed throughout India – to regard it as rather harsh to hang three or four men for the murder of one. Sircar [?Sikander] himself has occasionally taken this line in discussing death sentences with me. Personally I entirely agree with you that this is a wholly mistaken notion, and I propose to explain both to the Premier and to the other Minister concerned your view on this question and further to point out that in the particular case now under discussion you have informed me that you do not consider that there was any justification for a further reference by the Local Government.[19]

Yours sincerely,
H.D. CRAIK

46

CRAIK TO LINLITHGOW

Private and Personal
D.-O. No. 67-F.L.

Camp,
May 10th, 1938

Dear Lord Linlithgow,

I am afraid this letter is written a few days after the due date, but I have been on tour since the beginning of May and I have had a pretty full programme to get through at the various places visited.

2. The last fortnight has not been an eventful one from a purely provincial point of view. I have already sent you the account given me by Sikander of the Muslim League meeting at Calcutta. As the result of what happened at Calcutta there was a general expectation that the silly farce of so-called civil disobedience at the Shahidganj Mosque would cease and for some days no volunteers offered themselves for arrest. The Ahrar party has now announced its decision of abandoning civil disobedience, but unfortunately Maulana Zafar Ali Khan's rival party, the Ittihad-i-Millat, has decided to continue the process, their decision being based, in the words of their resolution, on 'the irreconcilable attitude adopted by the Akalis and Master Tara Singh and the wayward policy of the Majlis-i-Ahrar'. The Ittihad-i-Millat's decision was announced at a public meeting at Lahore and had a very mixed reception at the meeting itself, opposition being voiced even by some of Zafar Ali Khan's own followers. The decision has had a bad Press and I enclose as an example of this a cutting from the *Eastern Times* of May the 7th.[20] This is as a rule a newspaper of almost fanatical pro-Muslim tendencies but on this occasion I think the line taken in the article reflects the views of all sober-minded Muslims. I am afraid the Ittihad-i-Millat's adherence to this foolish policy is likely to stiffen the Akalis' opposition to any settlement by agreement on the Shahidganj affair. Meanwhile, a formal application has been made to the High Court for leave to appeal to the Privy Council against the High Court's decision. The High Court has ordered notice to be served on the Sikhs and has granted an interim injunction that the *status quo* is not to be disturbed at present. I anticipate that leave to appeal to the Privy Council will be given and that the injunction will be extended pending decision of the appeal, which may, of course, take many months.

3. The Congress has gained a notable victory in a bye-election in the Amritsar-Sialkot Rural Constituency, the successful candidate being

Dr. Satyapal, one of the two rival leaders of the Provincial Congress party (the other leader, Gopi Chand Bhargava, is already an M.L.A.). Satyapal beat a strong and wealthy opponent, Sardar Ganda Singh Uberoi of the well-known Sialkot sports firm, by a large majority, and I am afraid the result of this bye-election is pretty clear proof that the Congress have greatly strengthened their hold on the rural Hindus in the Central Punjab. The constituency is that in which Fatehwal village is situated, see paragraph 3 of Emerson's letter to you, No. 60-F.L., of the 5th of April 1938.

4. The recording of prosecution evidence in the Fatehwal case is still proceeding and, I imagine, will take a very long time. A good many of the absconding accused have been arrested or have surrendered.

The trial of the Police officers involved in the Kiroo case has commenced before J.D. Anderson, the Commissioner of Rawalpindi. So far he has only recorded the evidence of the local witnesses, but, I believe, is to take that of the Sikanderabad witnesses, including the Pipe Major, about the 17th of this month.

5. I have visited three districts, Shahpur, Gujrat and Rawalpindi, during my present tour and have obtained some interesting sidelights on the working of Provincial Autonomy from the District Officers' point of view. I am afraid I must, as a result of this, somewhat modify the opinion expressed in paragraph 2 of my letter to Your Excellency, No. 62-F.L., of the 18th April. I there said that I saw only a slight, but not disturbing, loss of efficiency and a little slowing down of the pace of the administrative machine. I fear the loss of efficiency and of pace is rather greater than I was at first inclined to think. I need not trouble you with details, but I find that local officers complain that there is considerably greater delay in obtaining orders on important matters and a pronounced reluctance on the part of the Ministry to decide questions which might affect the interests of influential supporters. In one or two instances I find that the local M.L.As. managed to use their pull with the Ministry in a manner that is distinctly discouraging to a keen District Officer. Such tendencies are, however, I suppose, an inevitable result of any form of democratic government.

6. I had an interesting time at Sargodha, the home district of the Tiwanas, Noons and other considerable landed gentry. I renewed many old friendships among these Maliks, whose traditional loyalty to the British *raj* and to service in the Army I find completely unimpaired. They have, of course, their local grievances and two or three of them mentioned to me that they thought Congress doctrines were permeating among the Hindu and Sikh personnel of the provincial and subordinate services. I am, however, a little sceptical of this.

I also had some interesting talks with various officials. The local Deputy Commissioner,[21] a young English officer of 7 or 8 years' service, tells me he has no apprehensions as to his future, though in the ordinary course he has at least 20 years of service in front of him. He does not think there is much depression among the younger British members of the Indian Civil Service though there are one or two exceptions. Men recruited before 1921 naturally feel the recent changes more than those recruited since that date. The latter generally feel that the introduction of Provincial Autonomy has made practically no change in their daily work or life.

I also met two young British recruits to the Indian Civil Service who joined only a few months ago. Both told me that they were interested and happy in their work and, on the whole, found India a better place than they had been led to expect. I also had an opportunity of meeting two senior Muslim Deputy Commissioners of neighbouring districts, both promoted from the provincial service to 'listed posts'. One is a member of the well-known Noon family and the other a man who has made his own way in the service by his capacity and hard work. Both of them confirmed what the English Deputy Commissioner told me, viz., that Provincial Autonomy has made little, if any, difference in their daily work, and both seem completely confident as to their future.

On the other hand, I am told there is a good deal of depression among British officers of the Irrigation Department, and this confirms what I wrote to you in a previous letter of premature resignations in that department. The feeling of depression has recently been intensified by the new Income-tax Bill, which has aroused – as I anticipated it would – considerable resentment among the services. I am told that one at least of the Service Associations is likely to submit a formal representation on the subject. Officers with technical qualifications, such as fairly senior officers of the Irrigation Department possess, usually have some prospect of obtaining employment in England or other parts of the Empire, but premature retirements from whatever cause are calculated to prejudice recruitment in England, and I understand that there has recently been considerable difficulty in obtaining the one or two British recruits required annually for this service. It would be a disaster if the small British element in this vitally important branch of the administration should disappear altogether.

7. The Deputy Commissioner of Gujrat is Moon, about which I wrote to you in a previous letter. I found him quite fixed in his decision to resign the Service, but he has agreed to stay on till the autumn. He has also accepted an offer I made to him to act as my Secretary from the beginning

of June, when Lawrence (who has been far from well lately) goes on four or five months' leave. It is possible that a change of work and environment may modify Moon's views, but I doubt it.

The Deputy Commissioner of Rawalpindi[22] is also a comparatively junior English officer of only six years' service. He told me that when on leave last year he had been offered a teaching fellowship at his old College, Selwyn, but he had refused it. I dare say he was influenced by the fact that he married at a comparatively early age, but he told me he definitely preferred service abroad to work in England; and though he has a difficult and responsible charge for his years, he likes his work and, so far as I can judge, is doing it well.

8. I am leaving today for a couple of weeks with George Cunningham at Nathiagali. It will be rather a relief to get away from the extreme heat we have had during this tour. I reach Simla on May the 13th.

9. I have not yet received the fortnightly report for the second half of April in print, but will send it on as soon as I do receive it.

Yours sincerely,
H.D. CRAIK

47

CRAIK TO LINLITHGOW

Secret — Barnes Court, Simla,
D.-O. No. 71 — *May 20th, 1938*

Dear Lord Linlithgow,

I had an opportunity today (the first since the beginning of this month) of having a talk with Sikander and think one part of it may be of some interest to you.

I asked Sikander if he had any information about the Jinnah-Gandhi conversations and he said he had none at all. The reports that have appeared in the Press about Jinnah consulting Sikander on the telephone are entirely untrue and Sikander does not think that Jinnah has in fact consulted any one so far. He did have some talk with Sikander when they were both at Calcutta in April about his forthcoming conversations with Gandhi, and Jinnah then, I gather, expressed the view that the conversations would lead to no real result. Sikander, speaking to me this morning, told me that his own view was, and still is, identical.

You may have noticed a statement in the Press that Jinnah has called a meeting of the Muslim League Executive at Bombay early in June. Sikander will probably have to attend this meeting. He agreed with me that Jinnah had appointed a very unrepresentative Executive Committee. The Punjab has only two members, Sikander himself and Barkat Ali, M.L.A., the author of the notorious Shahidganj Bill, who is a bitter opponent of Sikander's.

Sikander volunteered that his main object in going to the Bombay meeting would be to keep Jinnah straight on what he described as 'Defence'. In reality what he means is that there must be no agreement on Jinnah's part with any proposal for a reduction in the representation of the Punjab martial classes in the Army. This is a point which Sikander considers of primary importance from the point of view of both Muslims and Sikhs in the Punjab, and I gather that he doubts whether Jinnah appreciates how much importance Punjab opinion attaches to this question. Sikander evidently anticipates that the Congress will press for the abolition of the distinction between the martial classes and other classes and for recruitment to the Army being spread more or less evenly over all Provinces.

Should I hear anything more of interest about this matter, I will, of course, let Your Excellency know.

Yours sincerely,
H.D. CRAIK

48

CRAIK TO LINLITHGOW

Private and Personal
D.-O. No. 72-F.L.

Barnes Court, Simla,
May 26th, 1938

Dear Lord Linlithgow,

I have not very much to report this fortnight. Your Excellency will have noticed the result of the by-election for the Amritsar Urban Muslim seat. This by-election was due to the unseating on petition of Dr. Kitchlew, who won by a large majority at the general election defeating Shaikh Muhammad Sadiq, who stood as the Unionist candidate. On the present occasion Shaikh Muhammad Sadiq, standing as the Muslim League candidate but with the support and approval of the Unionist Party, easily defeated Dr. Kitchlew, who stood as the Congress candidate, and also Chaudhri Afzal Haq, the Ahrar candidate. This is regarded by the Unionist Party as a notable success and a rebuff to the Congress, as the general expectation was that Muhammad Sadiq and Dr. Kitchlew would have a close fight and that the Ahrar candidate would be easily beaten. The election was keenly contested and there was a certain amount of disorder, but not of a serious character.

2. There is a good deal of labour trouble in Amritsar and I believe that the latest figures are that about 50 factories are closed and over 1,100 labourers are on strike. The causes of the strike are somewhat obscure, but there is little doubt that it has been fomented by communist influence. No disorder has so far been reported, and the Director of Industries[23] has been instructed to go to Amritsar and see if there is any possibility of a settlement.

3. The communal situation is, I think, a little easier. The use by the Rawalpindi Muhammadans of the new processional route on the day of the 'Id-i-Milad' (vide page 2 of the Provincial Fortnightly Report enclosed) was a notable and satisfactory incident. There is to be a Sikh procession on June the 2nd and if the Sikhs will also agree to use the new route (which is at the moment doubtful), that would undoubtedly be a genuine contribution to communal peace in that city.

As regards Shahidganj, the High Court have granted the Muslims leave to appeal to the Privy Council and, what is more important, have granted an injunction against any building being erected on the disputed site pending the decision of the appeal. This is distinctly satisfactory, the more so since I understand that Counsel for the Sikhs consented to the issue of this injunction. Another satisfactory feature of the Shahidganj situation is that the Ittihad-i-Millat have now reversed their decision to persist in civil disobedience (see paragraph 2 of my letter to you No. 67-F.L. of the 10th May).

During the last few days there has been acute communal tension in Raja Jang, a large village in the Kasur sub-division of the Lahore district, between the Sikh proprietors and the local Muslims, who mostly belong to the menial classes, over the calling of the *Azan* from various mosques in the village. Some neighbouring villages were involved in this dispute, and it was necessary to send a fairly strong force of Police to Raja Jang. The situation seems, however, to have been well handled by the local officers and the parties have now come to an agreement, which has been reduced to writing, on the question of the dispute. One can only hope that the terms of the agreement will be observed.

4. The visit of V.D. Savarkar, President of the All-India Hindu Maha Sabha, to the Punjab was a notable event of the fortnight. As you will see from the printed report, he had a somewhat mixed reception; but to my mind the most interesting aspect of his visit was that he was treated as an

honoured guest by such respected leaders of Hindu opinion as Raja Narendra Nath and Sir Gokul Chand Narang. I can hardly believe that these two gentlemen know what Savarkar's real history is. So far as I remember, he was strongly suspected of complicity in the murder of Sir Curzon Wyllie,[24] though there was not enough evidence against him to justify his being charged with this crime. Some years later he was identified as the consignor of some revolvers sent from Europe to India, one of which was the weapon by which Jackson a District Magistrate in Bombay, was murdered. As a result of this Savarkar was arrested in England and sent under Police escort to India. You may remember that he escaped from the steamer in Marseilles harbour, but was secured by a French gendarme and handed back to his Police escort.

5. The trial of the Kiroo case at Rawalpindi is still proceeding and I believe the hearing of the prosecution evidence is nearly concluded. You will probably have seen the daily reports appearing in the press. At the Secretary of State's request I have arranged with Reuters to telegraph a summary of each day's proceedings to the English newspapers. I understand that Reuters' reports go direct to Joyce.

Yours sincerely,
H.D. CRAIK

49

CRAIK TO LINLITHGOW

Confidential
D.-O. No. 74

Barnes Court, Simla,
June 5th, 1938

Dear Lord Linlithgow,

I owe Your Excellency an apology for not having replied earlier to your confidential letter of May the 7th, in which you asked for an appreciation of the atmosphere and the position, as I judge it, in the Punjab in regard to the introduction of Federation. The delay was in part due to the fact that although the question of Federation was debated in the Punjab Assembly on the 8th of April last, I have only recently succeeded in obtaining a typed copy of the official report of the debate, which has not yet, so far as I am aware, been published in print.

2. The debate took place on a resolution tabled by a non-official member of the Congress party. The resolution recommended the Assembly to record its 'firm resolve to be no party to the inauguration of the proposed

Federation'. It contained a further recommendation 'that no money be spent out of Provincial revenues and no further arrangements be made by the Provincial Government in connection with the inauguration of the Federal Scheme, whether in the matter of holding elections to the Federal Legislatures or in any other matter connected with it'.

The mover made a speech on the lines of the conventional Congress opposition to Federation. He attacked in particular the method of indirect election to the Lower House; the nomination by the Princes of the representatives of the States; the limitations on the financial powers of the Legislature and on its power of control over the Railways and the Reserve Bank. He further criticised the protection given to British capital invested in India and the provisions regarding the security of the Services. Curiously enough, he made no reference to the reservation of Defence or External Affairs.

Several members had tabled amendments to this resolution, but the only one moved was that of the Premier, which was in the following terms:

> 'This Assembly considers that the Federal Scheme formulated in the Government of India Act, 1935, is unsatisfactory, and in view of the urgency of the problem recommends to the Government that the earliest possible steps should be taken radically to revise the scheme in full consultation with all sections of the people concerned.'

I understand that this amendment was framed after protracted private discussion between the Premier and his supporters in the House. It was eventually adopted by 99 votes to 32, the voting being apparently strictly on party lines.

3. Sikander's speech in moving this amended resolution is of considerable interest. It began with an expression of his scepticism as to the genuineness of the Congress opposition to Federation. He twitted the Congress with its original opposition to and ultimate acceptance of office in the Provinces and expressed the view that 'there is a large section of *bona fide* opinion in the country which suspects that after using this opposition or criticism as a lever for getting certain concessions from the British Government, the Congress may again agree to work the Federal portion of this scheme'. He then went on to say that although the scheme as at present formulated does not come up to the expectations of the people of this country and every possible effort should be made to have it modified in accordance with their aspirations, yet some sort of Federal Government at the Centre is necessary, and he expressed the belief that there was general agreement on that point. After some somewhat academic remarks on the

objections to what he called a 'unitary form of government' for the whole country (by which he seems to have meant a strong Central Government with the Provincial Governments relegated to the role of mere administrative agents of the Centre), he observed that 'no patriotic citizen today will welcome any proposal which is likely to impair the power of the units and the autonomy of the units as constituted under the Government of India Act', and he further emphatically opposed the view that the Indian States can be omitted from any Federal system.

Then followed a somewhat ambiguous passage about the reservation of certain important subjects such as Defence and External Affairs. In this connection Sikander observed:

> 'I think that from a purely national point of view the criticism about the exclusion of these subjects from the purview of the centre is most unsatisfactory. But practically all constructive public men in India have expressed their willingness to some sort of a differential treatment with regard to these subjects, provided it is on a specified transitional basis with possibility of growth from precedent to precedent.'

I imagine that in this passage Sikander meant to hint his personal agreement with the reservation of Defence and External Affairs.

4. As regards the method of election to the Federal Assembly, the Premier expressed his 'individual personal point of view' in favour of indirect election on the ground that the Federation should be truly representative of the various federating units. The following is an interesting extract from this part of his speech:

> 'We should have representatives of the various federating units with a view to bring about solidarity and cohesion. Unity of voluntary co-operation should not be superimposed by anybody. If you superimpose any conditions, then you may be sure that instead of bringing about that cohesion and solidarity, which we all desire, it would engender conflict and unfavourable conditions, which unfortunately are even now perceptible. What we want to avoid is a domineering central government, a central government which is likely to interfere with the provinces so as to put the provinces in a position where they may eventually find it difficult to take any big action because of the conflict with the centre. This is a thing on which every patriotic citizen and everybody who has considered this question carefully will agree with me. That is the position which I take. I visualise a federation in which the representatives of the various units will constitute the central

government with a view to see that provincial autonomy is not in any way trenched upon by the central body; and with the safeguarding of the interests of their respective units or province, they may also serve the common interests of the country as a whole in the federal sphere . . . . If you have direct election, what would happen? You will be sending in representatives chosen by an electorate with higher franchise than at the moment. Unless you get down to the level of adult franchise, you will be sending an independent body of men who are likely to think differently from your provincial legislature. What would happen in that case? Nothing but a tug of war between the two and a break.'

5. As regards the method of securing some modification of the Federal Scheme, Sikander poured scorn on the Congress suggestion for a Constituent Assembly based on universal adult franchise. He quoted, with apparent approval, the view of one of his supporters (Raja Narendra Nath) that the Scheme of Federation embodied in the Act should be worked to the best advantage of the country, while efforts should continuously be made to improve the Constitution, both Federal and Provincial, and he went on to say:

'I am almost certain that I am voicing not only the opinion of this House or the majority of this House, but the province as a whole or the majority of the province as a whole, when I say that we should not irrevocably commit ourselves to any action at this stage which we might have to eat back later on. The Congress did it last time. They ate back their decision. We do not want to take that position. I am prepared to work for the earliest possible revision of the present scheme which nobody seems to like in its entirety and which I do not like either in all its bearings, but, as I have said, there are differences of opinion, differences on detail, and it may take time to get that revision. I think that in the meantime my amendment makes the position of the province quite clear and I think that in this I am reflecting the opinion of the province as a whole. We do not like the scheme, we should like it to be revised as soon as possible in consultation with all sections of the people and we want it to be changed radically.'

After alluding to the fact that he had prepared an alternative Scheme of Federation, which he would be prepared to put forward at the proper moment, he concluded his speech with the following passage:

'But for the moment I would content myself by saying that I cannot possibly associate myself and my party, knowing the views of the various sections of the people in the province, to an absurd position or commit them to any step which might either lead them into the wilderness of destructive criticism or the barren and arid deserts of non-co-operation. We are not prepared, at any rate the Punjab is not prepared, to take that attitude at the moment. But at the same time I am not going to commit this province that we will work the federal portion of the constitution whether it is revised or not. (An Hon'ble Member: Neither one way nor the other ?) Yes, for the simple reason that I should like to be quite clear in my mind what kind of revision the various schools of thought want. If that revision suits me and my province, we will support whole-heartedly that body which puts forward that revision. If the revision proposed is something different from what I think will suit our province, then we will have to oppose it and support an alternative scheme. In view of all these circumstances I cannot at this moment, as I said, commit the province or this House to any irrevocable decision.'

After the speech of the Premier a Congress member followed and criticised Sikander for sitting on the fence. The last speech was delivered by Malik Barkat Ali, who won a seat at the general election on the Muslim League ticket and is usually a strong opponent of the Premier. On this occasion, however, he endorsed the Premier's attitude and gave his support to the amended resolution.

6. I think it may be taken that the resolution passed correctly represents the general attitude of the party now in power in the Punjab to the Federal Scheme embodied in the Act. The Unionist Party do not like the scheme, because they apprehend that it will mean a Congress government in power at the Centre or, at any rate, predominantly Hindu government with a strong Congress tinge; and they anticipate that such a government would be strictly controlled by the Congress High Command and would be inclined to interfere in Provincial matters and to impose its authority on the Provincial Governments, and more particularly on the Punjab Government with a view to strengthen the Congress hold on the Punjab. On the other hand, I think it is clear that the Unionist Party has no intention whatever of opposing the introduction of Federation by any form of direct action ; nor would it countenance or sympathise with direct action by any other party in the Province.

7. I have already reported to Your Excellency the substance of two confidential conversations I have recently had with Sikander on this subject

and you have yourself had a talk with him and are aware of his views. But it may be convenient for your purpose to have them in written form and I accordingly summarise below the gist of what he has said to me on this subject.

8. He began by saying that his original impression was that the Congress opposition to the Federal Scheme was not genuine and that they would in the end be prepared to accept it. He now takes a somewhat different view and thinks that the Congress are waiting to see how strong the Muslim opposition to the scheme will be. The more Muslim opposition intensifies, the higher will the Congress demands for modification be pitched. But he adheres to his view that, in spite of their protestations, the Congress opposition to the introduction of the scheme will not take the form of direct action.

9. As regards his own objections to Federation, these are founded on the apprehension that it will place the Hindus permanently in power at the Centre (in this connection he put forward an interesting but academic point that, apart from the depressed classes, the Hindus are not a majority in India as a whole). Judging by what has happened in the case of the Congress Provinces, he apprehends that a Hindu Ministry at the Centre will be predominantly a Congress Ministry and will be very rigidly controlled by the Congress High Command. The tendency will be for the party in power at the Centre to interfere in Provincial matters, and their efforts in this direction are likely to be specially directed against the Punjab as being the one Province in India where at present the Congress exercises comparatively little influence. He thinks it likely that this interference will be specially aimed at 'clipping the wings of the Punjab as the dominant partner in the Indian Army'. Although 'Defence' will be a reserved subject, he feels that a Congress Ministry at the Centre will be continually trying to make its influence felt in regard to Defence questions and will work steadily against the reservation of the existing large share of recruitment for the martial classes of the Punjab. The Congress have already made it clear that their policy is to make the Indian Army a truly national army, i.e. to open recruitment to all classes and to spread it more or less evenly over all Provinces. This policy is obviously most strongly against the economic interests of the Punjab peasantry, whose prosperity is so largely due to its connection with the Army. He pointed out that in taking this view he was not making a communal point and he was confident that Sikhs, Dogras and Hindu Jats would stand by the Punjabi Muslims in this matter.

(I may here add that another of my Ministers, Chaudhri Sir Chhotu

Ram, who represents the Hindu Jats of the south-east Punjab, takes the same view as the Premier in regard to this point.)

10. Sikander's next point was that, while he recognises the anomalies and difficulties of the existing situation, i.e. the combination of autonomous Provinces with an irresponsible Executive at the Centre and an even more irresponsible Central Legislature prepared to refuse all supply on the flimsiest pretext, he was disposed to think that under the Federal Scheme there would be an almost equal possibility of crises and difficulties. He felt sure that a Congress Ministry at the Centre would be continually pressing for the establishment of a convention by which the Governor-General would be bound to accept the advice of the Ministry even in regard to reserved subjects. He evidently visualises a situation when the Ministry would threaten to resign whenever the Governor-General took his own line on such subjects. The only safeguard against such a situation that he could see would be 'a central Executive so constituted as to reflect the opinion of those elements who are not prepared to surrender completely to the Congress or purely Hindu policy'.

He went on to say that if His Majesty's Government and the Government of India feel that they are strong enough to resist such encroachment by the Central Ministry on the reserved side and to face the inevitable crisis which such resistance would provoke, then let them go ahead with the introduction of Federation. If, however, they are not prepared to face such a crisis, then in his view it would be better tactics to postpone the introduction of Federation, taking advantage of the Congress claim that the Constitution must be revised, and to carry on for some time longer as at present. In spite of the anomalies of the present Constitution it has worked for more than a year and can continue to work for some time longer. His view seems to be that His Majesty's Government would be committing a tactical mistake in insisting on the introduction of Federation in the near future in face of general opposition. He expressed his belief that should His Majesty's Government decide that revision of the Constitution is desirable, they would find a large volume of opinion both in British India and in the States, which would support revision on what he called 'sound lines'. He was not very clear on what he meant by this expression,[25] but I rather gathered that he would be in favour of giving the Central Executive a certain share of responsibility for the subjects now classified as reserved, provided the Federal Scheme was so recast as to secure a Federal Executive that would be more representative of the stable elements in the country and would not be almost inevitably of a predominantly Congress character.

In this connection he mentioned that he regarded the following as the vital Central subjects – and I think his view is that these should be the only subjects with which the Centre should deal:

(1) Defence;
(2) Customs, because they pay for Defence;
(3) External Affairs;
(4) Relations with the States; and
(5) Communications.

11. Sikander then unfolded to me in outline his own ideas on the subject of Federation. His main purpose is to secure a Centre in which both the Legislature and the Executive would be really representative of the different federating units, i.e., each Federal unit would have an equal share of representation both in the Legislature and in the Ministry. For this purpose he would divide the whole of India into the following 7 units with a total population of roughly 5 crores each:

(1) The Madras Presidency and the Southern India States other than Hyderabad;
(2) Bombay, the Central Provinces and the Hyderabad State;
(3) Bengal;
(4) Bihar, Orissa and the Eastern States;
(5) The United Provinces and the States within the borders of those Provinces, such as Rampur, Tehri-Garhwal and Benares;
(6) A Central unit consisting of the Rajputana and Central India States;
(7) A North-Western unit consisting of the Punjab, the North-West Frontier Province, Sind, Kashmir and the Punjab States. It might be desirable to add to this unit one or two of the Rajputana States bordering on the Punjab, such as Bikaner and Alwar, in order to avoid the appearance of creating a 'Pakistan' or too predominantly Muslim unit.

He claimed that an incidental advantage of this system would be that it would tend to blur the line of cleavage between British India and the States. He also claimed that it would tend to secure a stable Federal Government inasmuch as the Central and the north-western units would be definitely conservative in their outlook; the Bengal unit would be, from the communal point of view, a stabilising element, while none of the other four would be of a purely Hindu or Congress complexion, as all of them would include a moderating State element.

12. Sikander concluded his observations by saying that he thought His

Majesty's Government should decide at an early date (but should not necessarily publish their decision) whether they are prepared to give India Dominion Status and within what period. When this vital question of policy has been decided, they should then devote their attention to a revision of the Federal Scheme so as to secure a Government at the Centre that could be relied on to maintain the British connection, which, in his opinion, all the minority communities desire to see maintained.

13. I must apologise for the length of this letter. Much of its contents are, of course, already within your knowledge, but I thought it best to record Sikander's views and projects at length. One must, of course, recognise that in many respects they are impracticable and indeed visionary. Nevertheless, they deserve serious consideration on account of the influence and personality of the man who puts them forward and the importance of interests which he represents. He is in my judgment by far the most thoughtful and far-seeing Muslim in public life at the moment and his criticisms and suggestions are actuated by the most sincerely friendly feeling to ourselves.

Yours sincerely,
H.D. CRAIK

50

CRAIK TO LINLITHGOW

Private and Personal
D.-O. No. 75-F.L.

Barnes Court, Simla, E,
June 7th, 1938

Dear Lord Linlithgow,

I have seen Your Excellency so recently that I do not find I have much of interest to report for this fortnight.

2. I recently presided at a Council meeting at which we discussed certain legislative measures that will be put before the Assembly that commences in Simla on June the 20th. These are all measures designed for the benefit of the cultivator. The first is a Bill for the compulsory registration and licensing of moneylenders. It leaves Government discretion to fix the scale of license fees. The second is a Bill designed to liquidate on very favourable terms to the mortgagor all mortgages with possession executed before 1901, the date of the passing of the Punjab Land Alienation Act. The third Bill Proposes to amend the Land Alienation Act in two particulars, both of them designed to prevent what are known as 'benami' transactions, i.e. the sale or mortgage of land by agriculturists to persons who are in

reality non-agriculturists but pose as members of agricultural tribes. The fourth is a Bill to regulate marketing, designed to do away with the innumerable small customary deductions from produce brought to the market.

There was no disagreement within the Council as to the general principles of these Bills, but the fourth as drafted was admitted to be unnecessarily elaborate, and the Minister concerned has promised to attempt to simplify it. It will be interesting to see what attitude the Congress opposition in the Assembly adopt to these Bills, most of the Congress members being Banias or Khatris by caste and the Bills being distinctly prejudicial to the economic interests of these castes.

3. Two incidents have occurred during the fortnight, which are, I think interesting illustrations of the way Provincial Autonomy is working in the Punjab. The Premier was very keen that I should address the Legislature at its opening session, and I have agreed to do so. I thought it courteous to write to the speaker, informing him of my intention, and received a reply to the effect that he was delighted at my decision. The second incident occurred on the day the Premier left Simla to attend the meeting of the Executive of the Muslim League called at Bombay by Jinnah for the 4th of June. The Premier rang me up and asked me if I would very kindly deal with his work during his absence, adding that he had instructed the Secretaries concerned to send all cases requiring his orders direct to me. Although this request was a pleasant illustration of our mutual confidence, I have, of course, in practice to be very careful how I word my decisions, as, if the arrangement became known to Sikander's political opponents, it would be distinctly embarrassing to him.

4. The hearing of the prosecution evidence in the Kiroo case has been concluded and Anderson has asked the Government Advocate, who appeared for the prosecution, to argue before him the case against the accused persons before he decides whether to frame a charge or not. In view of the interest this case has excited in England, I think I should let you know that I have seen a private letter from Anderson to a personal friend in Simla, saying that it is practically certain that he will discharge all the accused. The only evidence that Kiroo was tortured by the Police is the evidence of Kiroo himself and of the Pipe Major of the A. and S. Highlanders, and Anderson does not regard either of them as a truthful witness. Should Anderson decide to discharge, his order is likely to create a considerable sensation, as it will, of course, imply that the view taken by the High Court was completely mistaken. I have reason to believe that Sir Douglas Young wrote the judgment in this case in a moment of irritation and showed it to an officer of my Government, who is in his confidence.

The latter urged him to reconsider the terms of the judgment, but Young disregarded this advice.

5. The papers in the case of Prithvi Singh, who surrendered to Gandhi in Bombay a short time ago, have not yet come to me but I have had some conversation on the subject with the Premier and found the latter very disinclined to agree to Prithvi Singh's release. As is mentioned in the Provincial Fortnightly Report (of which I enclose two printed copies), Prithvi Singh's surrender is generally regarded here as a clever move designed to force the hands of the Punjab Government to release his partner in crime, Gurmukh Singh. I will, of course, keep you informed of developments in this case.

Yours sincerely,
H.D. CRAIK

51

CRAIK TO LINLITHGOW

Private and Personal
D.-O. No. 76

Barnes Court, Simla, E.,
June 10th, 1938

Dear Lord Linlithgow,

I am glad to say that Sikander was well enough to have a talk with me today. He caught a chill after being drenched at a public meeting held in pouring rain in Bombay.

2. I gather that the only business put before the Council of the Muslim League at Bombay was the correspondence between S. C. Bose and Jinnah, the purport of which you already know. The main point for decision by the Council was whether the League should insist on the position that it must be regarded as the sole representative of Muslim opinion. All members present in Bombay were agreed that the League must take up this attitude, and eventually a resolution was passed containing the following three parts:

(*a*) An answer was to be sent to Bose's note to Jinnah, stating that the Muslim League was agreeable to continue the negotiations with Congress, but only on the clear understanding that Congress should recognise the Muslim League as the sole representative of Muslim opinion.

(*b*) Gandhi had written to Jinnah, suggesting that Jinnah should see and deal with Maulana Abul Kalam Azad, who is, of course, a member of the Congress Working Committee. (I am not sure whether Azad was to take Bose's place, or whether the idea was that both should represent the Congress.) As regards this suggestion, the Council of the Muslim League considered that it would 'not be desirable' to deal with any Muslim representative of Congress, should the negotiations eventually reach a stage at which a conference between Congress and League representatives would be useful.

(*c*) The third part of the resolution was suggested by Sikander himself. It was to the effect that since the Muslim League is committed to the policy of safeguarding the interests of minorities other than Muslims, it should be made clear to Congress that the League would consult other minorities and other interests should negotiations with Congress be resumed. (I asked Sikander if he had in mind the Sikhs as one of the other minorities, but I gathered that the reference was rather to the scheduled castes, Anglo-Indians and Europeans. It appears that there is a clause in the constitution of the Muslim League pledging it to safeguard the interests of all other communities.)

3. I asked Sikander whether Bose and Jinnah, had really got to grips with the problem of an agreement between Congress and the League, i.e. whether any specific terms for such an agreement had been discussed. Sikander thought that there had been no discussion at all of detailed terms, but he gathered from Jinnah that Bose had told Jinnah that Congress would be prepared to go a very long way towards meeting Jinnah's demands, should the League agree to join a 'united front' with Congress in its opposition to Federation.

Apparently this was as close as the two negotiators got to the real question at issue. The comic part about it is that there is, of course, a 'catch' in the 'united front' condition, the League's main objection to Federation being that it will put the Congress in power at the Centre.

Anyhow, this was as far as the two negotiators got before they fell out on the question whether Congress could accept the League as the sole representative of Muslim opinion.

4. I asked Sikander what was the point of summoning the whole Executive Council of the League to Bombay and what was the net result of its meeting. To this his reply was that the meeting merely endorsed the attitude already taken up by Jinnah in the conversations and threw the onus on the Congress of breaking off negotiations.

5. I then told Sikander I had been rather puzzled by Jinnah's savage

attack on Congress at a public meeting in Bombay held (I think) on June the 6th. Sikander was present at this meeting and said that Jinnah's attack was quite deliberate. Jinnah considers Congress is suffering from swollen head and that the only way to deal with it is to adopt a truculent attitude, or, in other words, to treat Congress as *de haut en bas*. Evidently there is no genuine desire on the part of Muslims to come to terms.

6. The Shahidganj affair was not discussed at the Bombay meetings, except in connection with the venue of the Muslim League session to be held next Xmas. On this point Sikander expressed the view that the session should not be held in the Punjab till the Shahidganj question is finally settled. He thinks the session will probably be held either in Bihar or Madras, but the intention is to hold a further special session after Xmas in the North-West Frontier Province.

7. Sikander mentioned an interesting piece of news about Sind, where he thinks there is likely shortly to be a change in party alignments. Sir Abdullah Haroon, who is a supporter of Allah Bakhsh, the present Sind Premier, was at Bombay and so also was Abdul Majid, who is by common repute a close supporter of Sir Ghulam Hussain Hidayatullah. Abdullah Haroon said there was a possibility of Allah Bakhsh trying to reconstitute his Ministry so that it would rely mainly on the Muslim vote (I take it this means discarding the present Congress element in the Ministry.) Abdul Majid announced on behalf of Sir Ghulam Hussain Hidayatullah that the latter would support such a rearrangement. Haroon suggested that Sir M. A.K. Dehlvi, a Bombay ex-Minister, should be sent to Sind to prepare the ground for this change, and I gather that Abdul Majid agreed to this.

Yours sincerely,
H.D. CRAIK

52

CRAIK TO BRABOURNE

Private and Personal — Barnes Court, Simla,
D.-O. No. 80-F.L. — *June 24th, 1938*

My dear Brabourne,

I enclose herewith the provincial fortnightly Report for the first half of June.

2. The agitation in Lyallpur regarding the remodelling of canal outlets on certain distributaries (to which reference is made in the last paragraph

on page 2 of the printed report) is causing some embarrassment to my Government. In theory the intended remodelling is designed to secure to all irrigators on the distributaries their fair share of the water available, but it has naturally involved some curtailment in the supply to irrigators using the outlets on the upper reaches of each distributary. I have some reason to think that in carrying out the remodelling the canal officers acted in a somewhat hasty and possibly tactless manner, and it is alleged that the reduction in the supply on the upper outlets has been in excess of what is allowed by the canal rules and that the irrigators on these outlets are left with only enough water to irrigate 17 of the 25 acres that make up each 'square'. On the other hand, there is no doubt whatever that the grievance has been deliberately exploited by Congress with an eye on an impending by-election to a neighbouring seat in the Provincial Assembly (to which a Congress candidate has just been returned unopposed). The demonstration that took place on the 10th of June at the district headquarters did not result in any disorder, but there was a somewhat regrettable demonstration in the Civil Station. I am afraid we shall hear more of this grievance.

3. The Legislative Assembly session commenced on June the 20th, on which day, at the suggestion of the Premier, I addressed the Assembly. My speech consisted for the main part of a review of the work done by the Assembly during the past year. There was not very much to say on this subject, as the year has necessarily been one of preparation and the actual legislative enactments passed dealt only with such matters as the salaries of Ministers, the Speaker and Deputy Speaker and the allowances for members. Much time has been spent on the consideration of rules of procedure, which is not yet concluded. From this subject I passed on to review the working of the Provincial Government in the administrative field, dealing more particularly with projects for the development of irrigation and schemes of rural reconstruction. I also alluded to the improvement in communal relations which has taken place during the last few months, and concluded by a reference to the legislation to be placed before the Assembly this session, particulars of which I gave in my private and personal letter to Lord Linlithgow, No. 75-F.L. of June the 7th.

4. My address was well received by the Assembly, though the Congress members, in accordance with expectations, absented themselves. I have good reason for believing that it gave considerable satisfaction to the Ministers and their supporters, and it has been favourably reviewed in such English papers as the *Times of India,* and the *Civil and Military Gazette*. The Nationalist Press, e.g. the *Tribune* and the *Hindustan Times*, have criticised it as being a speech more suitable for delivery by the Premier

than by a constitutional Governor. I rather expected some such criticism, as my deliberate object in reviewing the administrative performances of the Local Government was to bring out the point that the Unionist Party has really done something substantial for the rural classes. From some remarks which Sikander had made to me in the course of recent conversations, I had gathered that he and his colleagues are a little inclined to resent the 'bouquets' thrown at the Congress Ministries in recent public speeches at home, e.g. by Zetland and Lothian, and feel somewhat hurt at the absence of any commendation bestowed on their own achievements, which they themselves feel – and I think with some justification – are really more solid than those of most of the Congress Ministries. Unfortunately the Unionist Government in the Punjab is under a considerable handicap owing to the facts that most of the provincial Press is definitely under the influence of Congress and that they have no organ of their own.

5. You may have noticed in the Press allusions to a new group or rather a 'cave' being formed within the Unionist Party by about 12 members of the Party, who are for various reasons disgruntled. Some of these 12 members announced their intention of forming a separate group, and though the accuracy of this announcement was denied by the Chief Secretary of the Unionist Party, there is certainly a tendency for some at any rate of these 12 members to break from the party. I have not had an opportunity of talking the matter over at any length with Sikander owing to his preoccupations with the Assembly session, but I have had a few words with him and two or three of the Parliamentary Secretaries and all are inclined to treat the matter lightly and to take the view that Sikander will be able to persuade the errant members to return to the fold. I can only hope that this view is correct.

There does not seem to be any difference in regard to questions of policy between those taking part in this revolt and the party as a whole. The grievances of the former are, according to my information, purely personal and in some cases of a petty nature. They consider, for example, that two of the Ministers, Manohar Lal and Abdul Haye, are off-hand in their manner to their supporters and apt to keep them waiting on their door-step when they come for interviews. There are complaints against the Chief Secretary of the party, Ahmad Yar Khan Daultana, and one of the Parliamentary Secretaries, Afzal Ali Hasnie. The former is considered unreliable, bumptious and something of a bully, and the latter is supposed to be making money 'on the side' in the course of his duties. Another personal reason for the split is said to be that Khan Bahadur Raja

Muhammad Akram Khan, the leader of the revolt (who is a retired member of the Provincial Civil Service) is a disciple of the well-known spiritual leader, the Pir of Makhad, who is now standing his trial for conspiracy to murder. Muhammad Akram Khan is said to believe that the Premier, who resides in the same district as the Pir, is making special efforts to secure his conviction. I believe this is a completely mistaken belief. Other members who have joined in the 'cave' consider that they have been unfairly treated in respect of the loaves and fishes of office or that in other respects their material interests have not been forwarded by the Ministry. I have also reason to believe that the split is to some extent a reflection of a feeling among members of what may be called the well-to-do yeoman farmer class that the bigger land-owners of the Province and more especially the Tiwanas and the Noons, have received more than their fair share of seats in the Assembly and in the Ministry. This feeling was reflected in a recent by-election in the Shahpur district (the home district of the Tiwanas and Noons), in which Major Sardar Khan Noon suffered a narrow defeat by some 300 votes on a very heavy poll, his successful opponent being a yeoman farmer.

This indication of an incipient revolt against the larger land-owners is distinctly disquieting as such a revolt might ultimately lead to serious dissensions in the Unionist Party, which even Sikander, in spite of his general popularity, might find it difficult to reconcile.

For the moment, however, I do not think the incipient split is likely to be widened by the dissentients taking a different line from the party as a whole on any business that is coming up during the present session of the Assembly.

6. I have great doubt whether the settlement of the Congress differences described in paragraph 1 of the printed report is likely to prove permanent. It may, however, bring about the temporary strengthening of the relations between the Congress and the nationalist Muslims. Efforts are being made to persuade the Ahrars to join with thc Congress, but the Ahrar Party seem to be reluctant to merge themselves entirely in the Congress and insist on maintaining their separate entity.

Yours sincerely,
H.D. CRAIK

53

MOON TO PUCKLE

Confidential
D.-O. No. G.S.-257

Barnes Court, Simla,
July 2nd, 1938

Dear Mr Puckle,

As desired in Laithwaite's confidential D.-O. No. 2448-G.G., dated the 17th June, I forward a note recorded by His Excellency the Governor on the various Punjab Ministers.

Yours sincerely,
E.P. MOON

ENCLOSURE TO NO. 53

NOTE BY CRAIK

Confidential

July 1st, 1938

There has been no change in the personnel of the Ministry since its formation in April 1937 and I do not think I can usefully add anything to the confidential reports on Major Khizar Hayat Khan, Mr. Manohar Lal and Mian Abdul Haye sent to Private Secretary to the Viceroy with Lawrence's letter of the 1st of July 1937.[26]

Since I assumed office I have found the Ministry working well together as a team. I fancy Mr. Manohar Lal is not really in sympathy with the legislative measures recently put forward by the Ministry with the object of releasing the cultivator from the clutch of the moneylender, but he has not voiced at Cabinet meetings any opposition to these measures.

2. As regards individual Ministers, Sir Sikander Hyat Khan has certainly increased his reputation for statesmanship and impartiality by his skilful handling of recent developments of the Shahidganj problem. Sir Sunder Singh Majithia is, I think, rather overwhelmed by the very heavy portfolio and it is possible that some readjustment will be necessary. He is an elderly man and not a quick worker.

Sir Chhotu Ram is perhaps the most effective and combative platform speaker in the Ministry and shows plenty of courage in attacking the Congress.

I find Mian Abdul Haye genuinely interested in educational and medical reform. His own ideas on these subjects are sensible and he is amenable to advice and works in harmony with the official heads of departments.

I have seen perhaps less of Major Khizar Hayat Khan's work than that of any other Minister, but so far as I can judge, he is an efficient administrator and has plenty of brains. He is in charge of Local Self-Government and Public Works Department (Buildings and Roads, Electricity and Communications). Mr Manohar Lal is now in charge of the Jail Department and is inclined to press proposals for the release of 'political' prisoners. The Premier is not as a rule sympathetic to such proposals.

H.D. CRAIK

54

CRAIK TO BRABOURNE

Private and Personal
D.-O. No. 83-F.L.

Barnes Court, Simla,
July 8th, 1938

My dear Brabourne,

I enclose the provincial fortnightly Report for the second half of June.

2. I referred in paragraph 2 of my letter No. 80-F.L. of June the 24th to the agitation at Lyallpur, regarding the remodelling of outlets on certain canal distributaries. This agitation still continues, though I have had no report of any further organised demonstrations. Some of the irrigators are still refusing to take canal water which, in view of the recent rains, is not really required.

A similar agitation is in progress in one part of the Amritsar district in connection with the remodelling of outlets on a certain distributary of the Upper Bari Doab Canal. I have gone pretty fully into the circumstances of this remodelling and am convinced that it was necessary in the interests of certain Muslim villages at the tail end of the distributary. The grievance here is certainly a purely manufactured one and my Government will probably shortly issue notices to the Sikh irrigators on the upper reaches of the distributary who have refused to take water, that their outlets will be closed either permanently, or at any rate till the end of the present harvest, if they do not make use of them within a date to be indicated in the notices. I trust this action will bring the irrigators to their senses.

3. The result of the Kiroo Case (see paragraph 4 of my demi-official letter No. 75-F.L. of June the 7th) has now been announced, all the accused being discharged. Somewhat to my surprise I have seen no comment on

Anderson's judgment in the Press; indeed it is somewhat difficult to see what line such comment could have taken, as Anderson's judgment is in effect a finding that the very severe strictures passed by the High Court on the Police were ill-considered and unjustified.

4. During the whole of the past fortnight the Legislative Assembly has been in session in Simla and its proceedings have attracted considerable interest. I think the Premier has taken up a wise attitude in regard to the Bill for the suppression of mischievous and defamatory statements (see paragraph 1 of the printed report). The Bill when published was adversely criticised by practically all sections of the Press, including even the *Statesman* and the *Civil & Military Gazette*, and it would, in my opinion, have been bad tactics on the part of the Ministry to force the Bill through in the teeth of this attitude. Sikander has, however, made it perfectly plain that if there is no improvement in the tone of the more irresponsible newspapers before the Budget session of the Assembly, he intends to proceed with the Bill.

5. The other legislative measures placed before the Assembly, all of which are designed to improve the economic position of the peasantry, have aroused keen controversy. The Marketing Bill, a long and complicated measure, has been referred to a Select Committee, which will not report till the next session. The Bill for the registration of moneylenders has also been considered in Select Committee, and the Ministry hope to secure the passage of this Bill before the end of the session. The debate on the Bill for the amendment of the Alienation of Land Act so as to extinguish 'benami' transactions is not yet concluded. The most controversial Bill of all, that for the extinguishment of mortgages effected before 1901 (i.e. before the Alienation of Land Act became law) has emerged from Select Committee after a stormy passage, and motions that it be taken into consideration and passed will be made today or early next week. All these measures have the enthusiastic and practically unanimous support of the Unionist Party and have, I think, had the effect of pulling the party together. They now feel that they are doing something really practical for the benefit of the peasantry and that when these measures are passed their position in the constituencies will be considerably strengthened. The Congress party in the Assembly have, on the other hand, been placed in a difficult position. Most of the Congress members represent urban constituencies, where trading and moneylending interests are strong, and in their hearts they are strongly opposed to all the Bills, which are unquestionably prejudicial to the interests of the moneylending classes. They have, however, received stringent orders from the Congress High Command that they are not to oppose the Bills, and the result has been that the majority of the Congress

members have remained neutral on all divisions, while the comparatively few Congress members who represent rural constituencies have voted for the Bills. The attitude of the urban Congress members is, of course, anomalous and difficult to explain away, and the Ministerial Party have not failed to make capital out of it. The urban Congress constituencies on the other hand are furious at the attitude of their representatives and a movement has been started to call upon them all to resign their seats in the Assembly.

Raja Narendra Nath, the leader of the small party of non-Congress Hindus in the Assembly which generally supports the Unionist Government, has also been placed in an embarrassing position by these Bills. He and two of his supporters, who were members of the Select Committee on the Bill for the extinguishment of old mortgages, 'walked out' of the Committee, because they thoroughly disliked the Bill and none of their amendments was accepted. The Raja has since issued a statement to the Press, appealing for advice and guidance to the Congress High Command, but he is not likely to receive any help from that quarter. He and his supporters constitute the comparatively small minority that continues to oppose the Bills, but it is too early to say whether this will result in his withdrawing his support of the Ministry on other questions. It is possible that his excellent personal relations with the Premier will prevent this consequence.

6. The split in the Unionist Party, to which I alluded in paragraph 5 of my letter No. 80-F.L. of June the 24th, has, I understand, been composed, though how exactly the Premier has managed to satisfy the personal grievances of the twelve dissentients, I am not aware.

7. I have myself gone on two occasions to listen to the debates in the Assembly. As compared with the old Legislative Council the tone of the Assembly strikes me as having lost greatly in dignity and decorum: in fact it is hardly an exaggeration to say that when controversy flares up, the place degenerates into a bear-garden. The Speaker, who is now 72 years old, is, I think, rather losing his grip on the Assembly. He is so anxious to maintain an appearance of fairness to all parties that he permits far too many interruptions on trivial points of order or 'personal explanation', and he has recently given a ruling, which I believe he admits is contrary to the terms of Section 85 of the Government of India Act, that any member who likes can speak in the vernacular, whether he is acquainted with English or not. The result of this is that practically all speeches are now delivered in Urdu or Punjabi.

Yours sincerely,
H.D. CRAIK

55

CRAIK TO BRABOURNE

Private and Personal
D.-O. No. 84-F.L.

Barnes Court, Simla,
July 22nd, 1938

My dear Brabourne,

I enclose the Provincial Fortnightly Report for the first half of July.

2. The Legislative Assembly session has continued throughout the fortnight and there have been some stormy debates on the Ministry's agrarian legislation. The session is expected to conclude today, when the passage of all the Bills, with the exception of the Marketing Bill, will be completed. As I mentioned in paragraph 5 of my letter No. 83-F.L. of July the 8th, the most controversial of all the Bills was that for the extinguishment on easy terms of mortgages with possession effected before the passing of the Alienation of Land Act in 1901. As originally drafted and as it emerged from Select Committee, this Bill was to apply only to mortgages effected before 1901, which would have been illegal under the Alienation of Land Act., i.e. to mortgages by agriculturists in favour of non-agriculturists for a period of more than 20 years. An important change has, however, been introduced since the emergence of the Bill from Select Committee at the instance of the Ministerial Party, making the Bill applicable to all mortgages effected before 1901, whether the mortgagee is an agriculturist or a non-agriculturist. The effect of this is, of course, to put all mortgagees, whether they belong to agricultural tributes or whether they are professional moneylenders, on the same footing. This to a great extent meets the main criticism against the Bill that it was a discriminatory measure directed against the moneylender and especially the Hindu and Sikh moneylender.

3. The other two Bills (*a*) for the extinguishment of 'benami' transactions, and (*b*) for the registration and licensing of moneylenders, have, I believe, been passed practically without change. But the Ministry have themselves introduced and passed yet another Bill, which is designed to check the rapacity of the agriculturist moneylender. It prohibits an agriculturist from alienating any portion of his land to another agriculturist, who has lent him money, until after a period of five years has elapsed from the extinguishment of the debt. I am somewhat doubtful as to the practical wisdom of this measure and fancy it will be difficult to work, but I could see no reason why I should not give my sanction to its introduction,

which was required under Section 299 (3) of the Government of India Act. I gather this Bill was passed without any opposition.

4. During the fortnight I gave an interview at his request to Raja Narendra Nath (see paragraph 5 of my letter to you of July the 8th) in connection with these Bills, and more particularly with the Restitution of Mortgages Bill, which he considers a most inequitable and confiscatory measure. He made two requests, first, that I should try to persuade the Premier to postpone further consideration of this Bill till next session; and secondly, that if I was unsuccessful in this endeavour, I should, before assenting to the Bill in the event of its being passed, give him (Raja Narendra Nath) an opportunity of trying to convince me that my assent should be withheld in the exercise of my special responsibility for safeguarding the legitimate interests of minorities. As regards the first request, I did not give the Raja any indication that I agreed to it, but I did subsequently suggest to Sikander that it might be wise to postpone further consideration of the Bill till next session and in the meantime to collect statistics of the total number of mortgages effected before 1901, which are still in force, and showing by communities what mortgagees would be affected by the Bill. I made this suggestion, because I feel that in this particular case the Assembly is legislating 'in the dark', as we have only the most vague ideas as to the number of mortgages to which the Bill will apply. Sikander, while admitting my point, said he did not think he could persuade his Party to postpone further consideration of this measure unless the necessity of concluding the session during the present week made it absolutely impossible to get the Bill through.

As regards Raja Narendra Nath's second request, I told him that I would certainly take some time for careful consideration before giving my assent to important legislation of this character and that I would gladly give him an opportunity of stating his views. I pointed out, however, that in view of the definition of 'minorities' given in paragraph IX of the Instrument of Instructions[27] I could not see how my special responsibility under Section 52 (1) (*b*) of the Act was attracted. The question whether I should have to reserve the Bills for the consideration of the Governor-General was, of course, an entirely different one, into which I had not yet looked.

5. These agrarian measures have, as pointed out in paragraph 1 of the printed report, aroused very considerable opposition among the Hindu non-agriculturist and moneylending classes throughout the Province. On the other hand, they have all been passed by very large majorities in the Assembly and have been enthusiastically welcomed by the agriculturalist interests both inside and outside the Legislature. They will all, I am afraid,

present considerable practical difficulties when they come to be applied and will throw a very heavy extra burden of work on the Revenue officers who have to administer them. Indeed, I imagine that it is not unlikely that the Revenue establishment in many districts will have to be strengthened for this purpose.

6. I alluded in paragraph 5 of my letter of July the 8th to the difficult position in which the Congress party in the Assembly have been placed by this legislation owing to the fact that they had received stringent orders from the Congress High Command not to oppose the Bills. I have just learnt from our C[entral] I[ntelligence] O[fficer] that on the 16th of July Dr. Gopi Chand Bhargava, the leader of the Congress party in the Assembly, received the following telegram from Abul Kalam Azad:

'Hope you have decided to vote for Bills according to my instructions.'

To this Dr. Gopi Chand sent the following reply:

'Your orders will be obeyed. Permit me to resign from the Assembly. Cannot lead the party.'

It is also reported that 14 of the more prominent urban members of the Congress party have decided to resign their seats, as they find it impossible to obey the instructions of the Congress High Command. This information has not yet been made public.

7. You will probably be interested to know what ultimately happened in the case of the three Ootacamund Bank convicts, whose release was ordered by the Madras Government. You are aware that Erskine was unable to persuade his Premier[28] to agree to our suggestion that the three convicts should be sent in custody to Madras to be released there. When I informed my Premier of the refusal of the Madras Government to agree to this proposal I found him quite unshaken in his determination to extern these convicts from the Punjab. Accordingly when they were released from the Lahore Central Jail on the evening of the 18th of July, they were immediately served with orders under Section 3 of the Punjab Criminal Law (Amendment) Act of 1935, directing them to remove themselves from the Punjab by the first available train. They were sent in a Government car to Moghalpura, a suburban railway station just outside Lahore, whence they left for Saharanpur by the Calcutta Mail an hour after their release. They were given their third class fares to Saharanpur and Rs. 15 in cash each. The orders served on them are in force for 12 months and if they attempt to re-enter the Punjab within that period, they will render themselves liable to imprisonment for a year.

8. I referred in paragraph 2 of my letter No. 80-F.L. of the 24th of June to the agitation in Lyallpur regarding the remodelling of outlets on certain canal distributaries. On July the 15th an attempt was made to hold what was called an 'anti-canal day' throughout the district as a protest against the remodelling, all villagers being exhorted to refuse to take canal water on that date. The appeal was only successful in the case of 50 Sikh villages and even in these it was only partially successful. Nothing untoward occurred, careful precautions being taken by the Police and Canal staff to ensure that no damage was done to the canals. In some cases small bands of Congressmen more or less forcibly insisted on the villagers closing their outlets and in one case the bank of the distributary was cut, which led to a few arrests being made. The Congress members of the Assembly moved the adjournment of the House about this incident, making wild allegations of 'lathi' charges by the Police, &c., but the charges were ably refuted by the Premier and the motion was easily defeated.

9. A somewhat more serious incident took place at Amritsar on the afternoon of the 20th instant. Various conflicting accounts have appeared in the newspapers of this incident, but I attach to this letter a statement[29] compiled in the Secretariat from the reports received from local officers. Yesterday, the 21st, another small *jatha* of 25 men tried to enter the civil station, but was quietly arrested. It is probable that there will be some further demonstration today. The Tear Gas squad from the Police Training School at Phillaur is now at Amritsar and can be employed, if necessary. An adjournment motion will probably be moved in the Assembly in regard to this matter today.

Yours sincerely,
H.D. CRAIK

56

CRAIK TO BRABOURNE

Private and Personal
D.-O. No. 86-F.L.

Barnes Court, Simla, E.,
August 9th, 1938

My dear Brabourne,

I enclose the Provincial Fortnightly Report for the second half of July.

2. The three Bills dealing with agrarian subjects have now been submitted for my assent. As I explained in paragraph 4 of my letter to you No. 84-F.L. of July 22nd, I propose to take time for careful consideration

of these important measures and more specially of the point whether it is my duty to reserve the Bills for your consideration. I have not yet thoroughly examined this question but I am at present inclined to think that at least 2 and possibly all 3 of the Bills will have to be so reserved.

3. As you will have seen from the newspapers these Bills have aroused very considerable opposition from the non-agriculturist classes and a special Association has been formed for this purpose. This was inaugurated at a Conference held on July 30th and 31st at Lyallpur of which an account is given in the first paragraph of the Provincial Report. It was attended by about 6,000 persons and was 'splashed' in practically all the Hindu and Nationalist papers. I have read carefully the reports of this Conference and the speeches delivered at it and I have also received an interesting report on the subject from the Central Intelligence Officer. According to certain of the press reports the Conference passed a resolution in favour of immediate civil disobedience, but I have been assured by Sir Gokul Chand Narang, M.L.A., who presided at the Conference, that this is incorrect. Indeed it is difficult to say what form civil disobedience to legislation of this character could take. One resolution that was passed requested all non-agriculturists to withdraw their deposits in the Co-operative Banks. If this is acted upon it may have troublesome consequences, but I doubt whether the advice will actually be followed.

4. On the whole I do not think that this Conference was the complete success which the Hindu newspapers make out. Two awkward incidents occurred, first when Sir Gokul Chand was asked why he did not resign his knighthood, he made the somewhat ineffective reply that he was prepared to lose his knighthood and his head when the occasion demanded. The second incident was in regard to a resolution passed by the Reception Committee deploring the attitude of neutrality of members of the Congress Party in the Assembly and the resolution of the Congress Working Council banning agitation against the Bills by members of the Congress. This resolution should have been brought forward in the open session of the Conference, but as members of the Congress had mustered in considerable numbers and there was some likelihood of disturbance if this resolution had been moved, Sir Gokul Chand refrained from putting it forward.

The appeal for funds for opposing the Bills made at the Conference resulted in promises of Rs. 11,000 while a sum of about Rs. 600 was collected in cash. Sir Gokul Chand and the Hon'ble Rai Bahadur Ram Saran Das (Leader of the Opposition in the Council of State) each promised Rs. 1,000.

5. In spite of the publicity given to the Lyallpur Conference and similar

gatherings elsewhere, I doubt whether there is really very much 'drive' behind the opposition to these Bills. I had a talk for two hours today with Sir Gokul Chand, who is an old friend and was a colleague of mine in the local Government for 3 or 4 years. He put the case against the Bills with great skill but assured me that he intended to do all in his power to keep the agitation against them on constitutional lines. The Bills are unquestionably very unpopular for the moneylending and trading classes and no doubt test cases will be fought up to the highest court. On the other hand, they are certainly popular with the agriculturists generally and three of my Ministers are now touring in the Province explaining how they will help the peasantry. The Premier told me the other day that he has received innumerable messages congratulating him on their passage.

6. In paragraph 6 of my letter to you of July 22nd I mentioned that information has reached me regarding the probable resignation of 14 members of the Congress party in the Assembly. No further statement on this subject has been published and I am not aware at the moment of writing what the exact position is. Sir Gokul Chand told me today that there is to be a meeting of the Provincial Congress Committee on August 12th to discuss the question. There is certainly a very general feeling that the Congress has betrayed the interests of the Hindu non-agriculturists who have hitherto been its principal financial supporters. Dr. Gopi Chand, the Leader of the Congress party in the Assembly, has issued a singularly unconvincing explanation of the attitude of his party which has not improved matters. There is no doubt that at the moment, as a result of its attitude on this question and on the crisis in the Central Provinces, Congress stock is very low in the Punjab.

7. The trouble about the remodelling of the outlets of certain canal distributaries in the Lyallpur district has fizzled out and all the outlets are now being used. An agitation on the same question on the Raya distributary in the Amritsar district has also terminated in the same way.

8. The trouble at Amritsar to which I alluded in the final paragraph of my last letter unfortunately still continues, though on a somewhat minor scale. Small *jathas* of peasants are being sent daily to demonstrate in the Civil Lines and are being either dispersed or arrested. On two occasions recently these *jathas* were in a reasonable mood and accepted an invitation from the District Magistrate[30] that, after laying aside their flags and agreeing not to shout slogans, they should come to his house where he discussed their alleged grievances with them and then allowed them to return to the City. Both these *jathas* were, however, abused by those who are running the agitation for their action. A few days ago it looked as if the

agitation was about to die down, partly owing to dissensions amongst those who are organising it and partly because some of the organisers had been arrested. This expectation has, however, so far not been fulfilled. The daily despatch of *jathas* continues. The real cause is the Gurdwara elections which are about to take place next spring. The Akali party who are now in a majority in the Gurdwara Committees and thus control the considerable funds of the Gurdwaras, realise that this influence has recently declined and are determined to make every effort to regain the ground they have lost, especially in the rural areas. They are therefore deliberately maintaining the agitation though the alleged grievances of the peasantry are entirely imaginary. But the more prominent leaders are keeping in the background in order to avoid arrest, the consequences of which might prevent them from standing as candidates at the coming elections.

9. The Premier is at the moment visiting Amritsar and I believe he is to address a public meeting at Ajnala, a tehsil headquarters some 15 miles from Amritsar, today. The local officers apprehend that the agitators might try to organise a demonstration at this meeting. But full Police precautions have been taken and I have no doubt that Sikander will be completely equal to the situation.

10. During the fortnight I presided 'by request' at a Conference regarding possible methods of checking corruption in the public services. The Conference was attended by all the Ministers, Heads of Departments and Secretaries to Government. The discussion was interesting though the conclusions reached were necessarily of a somewhat general nature. It was, however, unanimously agreed:

(*a*) that nothing was to be gained by the appointment of any Parliamentary or official committee to consider the subject;

(*b*) that the establishment of an 'anti-corruption department', such as has been recommended by the Committee recently appointed by the United Provinces Government on this subject, would be a mistake as it would tend to convey the impression that Heads of Departments and local officers controlling large establishments were to be relieved of responsibility for checking corruption amongst their subordinates;

(*c*) that a central staff to investigate *prima facie* cases of corruption would be useful, but this should be purely an investigating agency to which local officers and Heads of Departments could apply for assistance;

(*d*) that the power at present exercised by the local Government to retire certain classes of officials on the completion of 25 years' service without assigning any reason should be extended. At present this power can only be exercised in respect of non-gazetted establishment; and

(*e*) that more care should be taken in compiling confidential reports on officials and particularly that fuller notes should bem recorded in regard to their reputation for integrity or the reverse.

There is no doubt that the Ministers are genuinely keen on checking corruption but are somewhat at a loss to devise practical measures to this end. Unfortunately, while public opinion generally condemns the bribe-taker, the giver of a bribe is tolerated and condoned.

Yours sincerely,
H.D. CRAIK

57

CRAIK TO BRABOURNE

Private and Personal — Camp,
D.-O. No. 87-F.L. — *August 24th, 1938*

My dear Brabourne,

I have not very much to add to the Provincial Report for the first half of August, which I enclose herewith. You will see from page 3 of this that the Kisan demonstrations at Amritsar came to an abrupt and somewhat ridiculous conclusion on August the 9th, and the fact that their termination coincided with the Premier's visit to Amritsar is a distinct feather in his cap. As a matter of fact the credit for this result is in the main due to the excellent and sensible way in which the situation was handled by the District Magistrate, Macdonald, who is a first class officer, and Sikander with characteristic generosity has admitted this in a note written to me. Nevertheless, I have no doubt that his presence in the place contributed materially to the collapse of the agitation.

2. The Premier's visit to Amritsar and the simultaneous tour of his colleague, Sir Chhotu Ram, in some of the western districts of the Province were marked by tremendous enthusiasm. Such opposition as the opponents of the recent agrarian legislation were able to organise was feeble and ineffective, though, as usual, it has been grossly exaggerated in the Press. On, I think, two occasions the Premier carried the war in his opponents' camp by addressing meetings organised in opposition to his own and on both occasions he was listened to with attention and respect.

3. There can be no doubt that the prestige of the Ministry and its supporters has been greatly increased by the passage of the agrarian legislation. In the two districts I have visited during the course of my present tour, Ambala and Karnal, I have found that a great majority of my visitors, and all who are either owners or cultivators of land, are enthusiastic in their support of the Bills, and there is no doubt that they command the approval of the majority. In several of the addresses presented to me by local bodies reference was made to this fact, though of course I had to be carefully non-committal in my replies.

4. As regards the question of my assent to the Bills, I am still awaiting the official reports of the debates, the publication of which has been most annoyingly delayed. I have, however, now had an opportunity of examining all three Bills with some care in consultation with my legal advisers, and I have provisionally come to the conclusion that there is no reason why I should not assent to the Moneylenders' Registration Bill. No question of 'repugnancy' or *vires* seems to arise as regards this Bill, and there is not really so much opposition to it on the part of the non-agriculturists as there is to the other two. As regards the Bill to amend the Alienation of Land Act so as to extinguish 'benami' transactions, a question of repugnancy does arise, and I am pretty clear that I shall have to reserve this Bill for your consideration. The third Bill for the restitution of lands mortgaged before 1901 is that which has aroused the keenest opposition. In regard to this Bill, my provisional conclusion is that there is no question of repugnancy, though I think some sort of a case (but not a very strong case) could be made out against the competency of the Provincial Legislature to pass the measure. I am not yet clear in my own mind whether I shall have to reserve this Bill for your consideration or not.

5. I had a most cordial reception in both the districts I have visited and on three or four occasions my car has been stopped in remote places by a large and apparently quite spontaneous gathering of the local peasantry, who gave me a really warm welcome. My general impression is that the attitude of the rural people is distinctly more cordial and contented than it was in 1931 and 1932. There seems to be a wide-spread impression that the tillers of the soil are now beginning to get a square deal.

In the greater part of the Ambala District, which is submontane, the monsoon has been good and the crops are satisfactory. In Karnal the rainfall hitherto has only been about one-third of the average and sowings have been very limited in area. Further south in Hissar (which I have not visited) I hear the monsoon has failed completely, and there is already an acute shortage of fodder and considerable distress. I think we shall very shortly have to open famine test works in that district.

6. I have, of course, been away from Simla during the debates on the Bill penalising anti-recruitment speeches, but many of my visitors on tour have displayed in conversation considerable interest in this Bill and have expressed the view that its passage from the Punjab economic point of view is to be welcomed. I know Sikander is very keen on it and I understand he played a considerable share in bringing about the attitude which the Muslim League party in the Assembly adopted.

7. I return to Simla on the 26th and must admit I shall be glad to escape from the heat, which has been trying.

Yours sincerely,
H.D. CRAIK

58

CRAIK TO BRABOURNE

Barnes Court, Simla,
D.-O. No. 89 *September 2nd, 1938*

My dear Brabourne,

I have reserved the Punjab Alienation of Land (Second Amendment) Bill for your consideration, as I am advised that owing to repugnancy it requires your assent under Section 107 (2) of the Government of India Act. A copy of the Bill duly endorsed by me has been forwarded formally and officially by Moon to Thorne. But as this is one of the three agrarian Bills which have aroused such a storm of opposition, I imagine that you will desire to have my considered opinion on the question whether you should or should not assent to it.

2. The Bill has two objects:

(1) To secure that the ultimate decision whether a person is or is not a member of a statutory agricultural tribe for the purposes of the Land Alienation Act shall rest with the revenue officers instead of, as at present, with the Civil Courts.

(2) To render void all *benami* transactions whereby the land of statutory agriculturists has passed or may pass to non-agriculturists in contravention of the provisions of the Land Alienation Act.

3. Though it is in connection with (1) above that I have had to reserve the Bill, this part of it has not in fact excited much opposition. I have had to reserve it for the reason that a provision of law which debars Civil

Courts from determining whether a man is or is not a statutory agriculturist is repugnant to Section 42 of the Specific Relief Act (an existing Indian law) in regard to a matter, viz., the mode of determining civil rights, which is included in the Concurrent Legislative List (Item 4, Civil Procedure). But so far as this question of repugnancy is concerned, I do not think that you should find any difficulty in giving assent. I do not consider that there is any objection in principle to giving revenue officers authority to determine a man's tribe; indeed there is much to be said for it. For, in many ways, they are better qualified to give correct decisions on such matters than the Civil Courts.

4. It is against the second part of this Bill that most criticism has been directed, and you may like me to indicate the forms which this criticism has taken. I have given the opponents of the Bill ample opportunity of stating their objections. The ablest of them, Sir Gokul Chand Narang, had a lengthy interview with me, while Raja Narendra Nath has sent me several written representations and has also seen me personally.

5. A *benami* transaction is one whereby a statutory agriculturist alienates his land, ostensibly in favour of another agriculturist, but in reality in favour of a non-agriculturist; generally a moneylender. What usually happens is this. A, an agriculturist, owes money to C, a moneylender. C prevails upon B, another agriculturist, to pretend to purchase land from A. B is now shown in the revenue records as owner of the land, but he has not really purchased it nor does he take possession. A, the original owner, usually continues in possession, ostensibly as a tenant under B, but in reality paying rent to C, the moneylender. Either this arrangement continues indefinitely, or perhaps after the lapse of some little time B, now the nominal owner, asks the Deputy Commissioner for permission to sell this land to C, the moneylender. He will represent that he has had no financial dealings with C and that to sell this land which he had previously purchased will be in his interest, for instance, that he will be able, with the sale money to redeem a much larger area of ancestral land which is mortgaged. This affords good ground for permitting the sale and the Deputy Commissioner therefore, deceived as to the real facts, gives permission and C now becomes in name as well as in fact owner of the land. Ostensibly the land is passing from B to C, but in reality it is passing direct in settlement of debt from the original alienor and debtor, A, to the creditor, C.

6. Such transactions are, of course, essentially fraudulent in so far as they are deliberately designed to evade the provisions of the Land Alienation Act. The present Bill enables the Deputy Commissioner to set them aside and put the original alienor in possession again. In principle

there seems no reason why such fraudulent transactions should not be set aside. But it has been represented to me that assent should not be given to the Bill for the following reasons:

(1) It is only non-agriculturists, Hindu and Sikh moneylenders, who will be adversely affected, and they are a minority for the protection of whose legitimate interests I am responsible. As the Bill stands, they will be deprived altogether of the rights in land, which they have acquired through *benami* transactions, without any compensation whatever except for 'improvements' which are narrowly defined. *Benami* transfers should not, it is argued, be set aside altogether, but should be transformed into some form of mortgage permissible under the Land Alienation Act, e.g. a mortgage up to 20 years. Unless this is done, the moneylender will be put to heavy loss and will have no remedy. It will not be open for him to proceed against the debtor in some way for the recovery of his dues, as at the time when the *benami* transaction was completed he will have signified to the debtor that the debt was discharged.

To these arguments there are two answers. In the first place, the non-agriculturists are clearly, in my opinion, not a minority within the meaning as explained in clause IX of the Instrument of Instructions. My special responsibilities are not therefore attracted. Secondly, a *benami* transaction is essentially fraudulent and the moneylender may be justly penalised for this fraud. It can, of course, be argued that the alienor is just as much guilty of fraudulent evasion of the Land Alienation Act as the moneylender and there is some force in this. But it is probably the fact that in the majority of cases the alienor is uneducated and ignorant and has been induced to agree to the transaction by the threats or skilful cajolery of the moneylender, and under the pressure of a load of debt the greater part of which is represented by interest charges at usurious rates.

(2) It is argued that in many cases the land will have changed hands several times since the date of the original *benami* transaction, and the present holder may have acquired it in perfectly good faith. The Bill makes no provision for compensation in such cases. To this objection no wholly satisfactory answer can be given. It is possible that the present holder will be able to obtain some redress in a Civil Court from the person who knowingly transferred to him an imperfect title; it is also possible that in most cases in which the land has changed hands several times it will in fact be difficult to

prove to the satisfaction of revenue officers that the original transaction was really *benami*. Indeed, conclusive proof of this would be practically impossible to obtain except when the 'dummy' purchaser can be persuaded to 'give away' the real alienee (i.e. the moneylender) and this he will, in my opinion, very seldom be induced to do.

(3) The Bill is said to be invalid under Section 298 of the Government of India Act. It is, I think, true that the Bill falls within the purview of Section 298, for, though the immediate reason why the beneficiaries of a *benami* transaction are being deprived of their rights is that they have deliberately evaded the provisions of the Land Alienation Act, ultimately the only ground for preventing them from retaining these rights is that they are members of non-agricultural tribes. Thus it is arguable that they are being prohibited from holding land simply on grounds of 'descent'. But, though falling within the purview of Section 298, the Bill, like the original Punjab Land Alienation Act which it seeks to amend, is protected by the saving clause 298 (2) (*a*), and therefore does not appear to be invalid. It will be open to its opponents to challenge it in the Courts – and doubtless they will do so – but there does not at present seem to be adequate reasons for refusing assent on the ground that it is invalid.

7. There are certain other objections to this Bill, which, though they have not been mentioned by its opponents, are nevertheless of some importance. In the first place, it will add very greatly to the work of revenue officers, who already have more than enough to do. In all probability a very large number of false and baseless applications will be submitted and there will be much suborning of witnesses to support false claims or rebut true ones. Increased opportunities for corruption will be offered to the subordinate revenue staff; for in deciding whether a transaction is *benami* much depends on the entries in the revenue records in the columns of cultivation and rent, and these entries, which are made every harvest by the Patwari, are inevitably not very closely checked by superior officers. Lastly, the difficulties of deciding whether or not a transaction is *benami* are usually so great that decisions will often depend on the bias of the particular officer hearing the application.

8. But, in spite of the objections enumerated in the two preceding paragraphs, the force of some of which cannot be denied, I do not think that there are adequate grounds for refusing assent to this Bill. It has been promoted by the present Ministry as an essential part of their agrarian

policy, it has been passed in the Assembly almost without a division and it does, I feel sure both from what I have heard from my visitors and from the messages which I have received from various parts of the Province, really meet with the enthusiastic approbation of a large majority of the population. My considered opinion therefore is that assent should be given to this Bill, in spite of the fact that it may in a limited number of cases have an inequitable effect.

9. Before concluding this letter, there is one other matter to which I must refer. In paragraph 29 of Lord Linlithgow's letter of June the 14th, 1938, it is stated that the Secretary of State is to be made aware at the earliest possible moment of the promotion of any Bill for the ultimate disallowance of which by the Crown (if it were to be passed and assented to in India) any material pressure is likely to be exerted. Within the last three weeks I have more than once seen the suggestion made by opponents of these agrarian Bills that they should approach the Secretary of State if they can obtain no satisfaction here. I am doubtful whether they would in fact be able to exert any really embarrassing pressure, but I think it is well to let you know at once that there is a possibility of the Secretary of State being approached to move His Majesty's Government to intervene and disallow these Bills. Indeed I have some reason to believe that steps have already been taken with this object.[31]

Yours sincerely,
H.D. CRAIK

59

CRAIK TO BRABOURNE

Private and Personal Barnes Court, Simla,
D.-O. No. 90-F.L. *September 6th, 1938*

My dear Brabourne,

I have not very much to report this fortnight. The recent agrarian legislation continues to be the principal subject of discussion in the Press and in political circles generally. I gather that the Non-Agriculturists' Association is to some extent weakened by internal dissensions and certainly the so-called 'Black Week', which was to have been held from the 15th to the 21st of August as a protest against the three Bills, was a practically complete failure. The Congress organisation in the Province is also suffering from severe internal friction and its prestige is probably lower than it has been for many months. It has, however, now come down pretty definitely on the side of the non-agriculturists and against the Bills. This move is certainly not likely to increase the Congress' chances of strengthening its hold on rural areas.

All my Ministers, except one, are on tour at the moment and have received enthusiastic welcomes in the districts they have visited. The culmination of their tours has been the great Zamindara Conference at Lyallpur, where Sikander and Chhotu Ram made fighting speeches, which were well received, in defence of the agrarian Bills and the anti-recruitment Bill recently passed by the Central Assembly. According to the Press reports this Conference has been in every way successful and I should say that the prestige of the Ministry among its supporters stands higher at the moment than ever before.

A rival demonstration was organised at Lyallpur, which was called the 'Kisan Conference'. This was a misleading title, as the Conference was in fact organised by the Non-Agriculturists' Association with the aid of the Congress and other opponents of the Ministry. It is said in the newspapers that the attendance was as high as 15,000, which I doubt. In any case, I imagine most of those present must have come from the urban classes. The numbers attending the Zamindara Conference have been put as high as 1½ lakhs.

2. The Non-Agriculturists' Association are understood to have formed what they call a 'War Council', of which Sir Gokul Chand Narang is a member. Its object is to raise 10,000 volunteers and a sum of Rs. 25,000 in order to start civil disobedience. Sir Gokul Chand has declared at meetings of the Association his readiness to go to jail, but I am sceptical about this.

3. Agitation about Palestine affairs is certainly on the increase, promoted by the Majlis-i-Ahrar and the Jamiat-ul-Ulema of Delhi. A good many meetings have been held and some violent speeches have been delivered. I am afraid it is possible that this agitation may grow in strength, but so long as the Muslim League holds aloof it is unlikely to prove a serious embarrassment to my Ministers.

4. I enclose the Provincial Report for the second half of August.

Yours sincerely,
H.D. CRAIK

60

CRAIK TO BRABOURNE

Private and Personal Barnes Court, Simla,
D.-O. No. 93-F.L. *September 23rd, 1938*

My dear Brabourne,

I enclose the provincial fortnightly report for the first half of September, to which I really have hardly anything to add.

2. The fortnight has been a quiet one apart from the anxiety in regard to the situation in Europe. European affairs are in fact occupying not only all our thoughts, but the greater part of the columns of the daily Press. The situation is being very closely watched by the educated classes.

I have had several talks with Sikander on the grave responsibilities that would fall on all of us should the Empire become involved in a world-war, and I am confident that he and his Ministers fully realise that the security of India as a whole will in a great measure depend on the loyalty of the Punjab; and that under their leadership the martial classes in the Punjab would make as splendid and loyal a response as they did in the Great War. We have also discussed, though only of course in a general way, the immediate measures that would have to be taken on the outbreak of war, and I do not think that my Ministry would raise any difficulties about taking firm action in respect of such matters as the control of aliens, press and postal censorship and the suppression of seditious speaking and writing. I know it is the Ministry's intention to bring the anti-recruitment law into force in the Punjab at the earliest possible opportunity.

3. You may have noticed in the newspapers a report that the trial of the Pir of Makhad on a charge of conspiring to murder the Nawab of Kalabagh has ended in the conviction of the Pir and certain of his associates, who have been sentenced to long terms of imprisonment. The Sessions Judge presiding at the trial was an Indian I.C.S. officer a Christian named Cornelius. I believe he is one of our best younger Sessions Judges. Owing to the personality of the two protagonists in this affair the trial, which has lasted a long time, attracted a great deal of publicity. The Pir is not only a Member of the Punjab Assembly, but also the spiritual head of one of the most important shrines in the North-West Punjab and he has a very large number of disciples in that part of the Province and also in the North-West Frontier Province. The Nawab of Kalabagh on the Indus is one of our larger landowners and a man of considerable local influence and

importance. The two have, I believe, been on terms of enmity for some time. The conviction of a spiritual leader of this importance of so heinous a crime may cause some unrest among his disciples, but on the whole I am inclined to think that more excitement would have been caused had he been 'dishonourably' acquitted.

Yours sincerely,
H.D. CRAIK

61

CRAIK TO BRABOURNE

Private and Personal
D.-O. No. 95-F.L.

Government House, Lahore,
October 11th, 1938

My dear Brabourne,

I enclose the Provincial report for the second half of September. The delay in sending this letter is due to my having been on tour since I left Simla on October the 5th. I only arrived in Lahore this morning and have not yet had an opportunity of seeing any of the Ministers.

2. The chief event of the fortnight has, of course, been the agreement reached at the Munich Conference, which has saved us from the horrors and suffering of a world war. So far as I can judge from conversations with my visitors, both in Simla and on tour, this result has been received with enormous relief by all thoughtful men. On the other hand, I fancy that the agricultural masses would rather have welcomed a war, which would have had the immediate effect of sending up the prices of primary products and increasing employment among the martial classes. Sikander's speech at the dinner given in my honour by the Ministers in Simla on the 26th of September made it quite clear that the Punjab was prepared, in the event of a war, to stand by the cause of the Empire as fully as it did in the Great War. Even before the date of that speech I had received numerous messages from associations and individuals placing their personal services and all their resources at the disposal of Government in the event of war, and after his speech I received every day till I left Simla a very large number of messages to the same effect. I think there can be no doubt that the Province as a whole, with the exception of a few disaffected elements, thoroughly endorsed the attitude taken by Sikander. There has been a certain amount of captious and ill-informed criticism of his speech in the nationalist

press, but I do not think that on this question it represents any real body of feeling.

3. I think the Provincial report is correct in saying that the agitation against the recent agrarian legislation is steadily losing force, and I shall be surprised if that agitation takes the form of any kind of civil disobedience. There are, however, rumours of the possible secession from the Ministerial Party in the Assembly of five members of the Hindu National Progressive Party and possibly two or three Sikhs of the Khalsa National Party, but these rumours have not yet received any kind of official confirmation from the members concerned. There are also rumours that Congress are prepared to spend large sums in an attempt to alienate from the Ministerial Party the six or seven representatives in the Assembly of the Scheduled Castes, but here again it seems doubtful whether these efforts will be successful.

4. There has been a lull, possibly only temporary, in the agitation about Palestine, but I think it probable that this agitation will be intensified after the Cairo Conference.

5. The agitation against Kalsia State, to which reference is made on page 3 of the Provincial report, seemed likely to die down on the conclusion of the Chirkh cattle fair in the State, but since then some rather ill-advised attempts have been made by officers of the State to come to terms with the leaders in British India of the agitation. I am afraid that these attempts may only have the result of prolonging the agitation, as they will be interpreted as a sign of weakness on the part of the State authorities. The situation will be carefully watched.

6. One of the places I have visited on my recent tour was Ludhiana, where I received addresses of welcome from the Municipal Committee, the District Board and the District Soldiers' Board. In the course of my reply to these addresses I took the opportunity of warning these bodies against the insidious dissemination of communistic ideas in the district. I particularly stressed the point that communism aims at the abolition of all religious sanctions, as I believe that this [is] the aspect of communism which is most open to attack and which, if properly realised, will be most likely to deter the Punjab peasantry from adopting communism as their political creed. My remarks were well received and have attracted considerable publicity in the Press.

7. The condition of the south-eastern districts of the Province, where the monsoon has been a complete failure, is giving rise to great anxiety. Several testworks have been opened in Hissar and arrangements are being

made to import fodder on a large scale to this and other districts. I am afraid that unless there are early and ample winter rains, the area sown for the *rabi* harvest will be very small in a considerable part of the Province.

Yours sincerely,
H.D. CRAIK

62

CRAIK TO BRABOURNE

Secret
D.-O. No. 98

Government House, Lahore,
October 17th, 1938

My dear Brabourne,

I have read with great interest and a good deal of sympathy the representation recently made by the Raja of Sangli with reference to the activities of Congress and their supporters, especially in the smaller States, a copy of which you sent to me under cover of your secret letter of October the 6th.

2. I fully appreciate the difficulties presented by agitation directed from British India against the authorities of States. We have in the past had various instances of such agitation in the Punjab, of which perhaps the most serious example was the incursion of *jathas* organised by the Ahrars into Kashmir in (I think) 1931 or 1932. I was Home Member of the Punjab Government at the time and the agitation reached such serious proportions that it became necessary to send British troops to assist the Maharaja's Government in the Jammu province and a British civil officer (Jenkins) was sent to take over temporarily the administration of that province.

Since then other instances of a similar, though less formidable, type of agitation have occurred. These have been directed against several States, including at various times Patiala, Bahawalpur, Kapurthala, Nabha and Malerkotla. None of these movements have been sufficiently formidable to justify the use of armed forces from British India to assist the State authorities, though several of them were for the time being distinctly embarrassing to the States concerned. I think it would be correct to say that in dealing with all of them there has been cordial co-operation between the Provincial Government and the State authorities.

3. At the present moment the only State which is being subjected to an agitation of this kind is the small Sikh State of Kalsia, the main portion of whose territories lies in the Ambala district of the Punjab. There is also a

small 'island' of State territory, consisting, I think, of only five or six villages, in the Ferozepore district, and the present agitation has been mainly in regard to certain alleged grievances of the residents of this 'island'. I have kept you informed in my recent fortnightly letters and in the Provincial Reports enclosed with them of the course of this agitation, see in particular paragraph 5 of my letter No. 95-F.L. of the 11th of October 1938. This agitation still persists and the latest form it has taken is the despatch of a *jatha*, which proposes to march through various Punjab districts to the capital of the State, Chachrauli, while there are rumours that another *jatha* is to be despatched to interview the Raja at his residence in Mussoorie. The Resident[32] has recently written to the Chief Secretary to my Government, asking the Provincial Government to consider the advisability of bringing into force the Provisions of the Indian States (Protection) Act of 1934. I have spoken to the Premier on this subject and he expressed himself in favour of notifying this Act in certain Punjab districts, and the question is to be considered in Council in a few days. I will let you know the decision arrived at.[33] Should the Act be introduced, it will be possible to pass orders prohibiting the assembly of *jathas* (Section 4) and also orders restraining the leaders from action in furtherance of the agitation (Section 5). Disobedience or failure to comply with these orders will be punishable with imprisonment for six months (Section 6).

4. As regards the more general questions raised in the Raja of Sangli's note, I have had an informal conversation with the Premier and I find him in general sympathy with the attitude taken up by the Raja, particularly in regard to the point made in paragraph 9 of the Raja's note regarding the difficulties created by the separation between Provincial Governments and the authorities of States lying within the borders of provinces. The difficulties which this separation has caused lie not only in the political, but also in the economic sphere, and in the Punjab this difficulty is particularly likely to arise in connection with the administration of our great irritation schemes, some of which irrigate areas in the States as well as in British India. Should there be any considerable expansion of irrigation in the future, e.g. should the Bhakra Dam Project come to fruition, the claims of certain States to a share in the benefits of such expansion may give rise to very difficult and delicate questions. I certainly think that should this contingency arise, the States would feel that their claims are likely to receive less sympathetic consideration than they would have received under the old régime when the Lieutenant-Governor was the Agent of the Governor-General in regard to all States lying within the Punjab.

In this connection I note that you are instructing Residents to maintain, where the necessity occurs, as close touch as possible with Provincial Governors and you express the hope that Governors will give Residents all practical assistance should occasion arise. I will, of course, do all that I can in this direction. My relations with the Resident for the Punjab States are close and cordial, but this is hardly the same thing as the maintenance of cordial, personal relations with the Rulers themselves. Although I am personally acquainted with nearly all the Rulers of the Punjab States, they now very seldom visit Lahore, and I naturally have fewer opportunities of coming into personal contact with them than my predecessors in the past have had. This is, I think, a somewhat unfortunate effect of the recent changes under which all the States have ceased to have any direct political relations with the Head of the Provincial Government.

5. As regards practical suggestions for protecting States from agitation fomented and controlled in British India, I think that so long as the Punjab has a Ministry of the same political complexion as the present Ministry, the Provincial Government would certainly be prepared to co-operate in a sympathetic spirit with the State authorities concerned. But I fully recognise that in Congress Provinces the same co-operation cannot be expected, and I imagine that in those provinces should circumstances arise that would attract the Governor's special responsibility under Section (52) (1) (*f*) of the Act, the Governor might find considerable difficulty in discharging his responsibility, or rather might find that insistence on discharging that responsibility brings him into conflict with his Ministry. Here I confess that I cannot see any solution in existing conditions except possibly by means of the cumbrous device of establishing some kind of Federal Police force, which would be entirely independent of provincial control and would act directly under the orders of the Governor as the Agent of the Governor-General. But this device, even if it were practicable in other repects, would not diminish the possibilities of friction between the Governor and his Ministry.

In the course of our conversation Sikander made an interesting suggestion that the best form of countering Congress agitation against the States would be for the States to retaliate by sending paid agitators into the province concerned with instructions to do everything possible to embarrass the Ministry. This method of retaliation would, however, only be within the capacity of the more powerful and wealthier States. It would obviously be useless for a small or comparatively poor State to endeavour to protect itself by such means.

Yours sincerely,
H.D. CRAIK

63

CRAIK TO LINLITHGOW

Private and Personal
D.-O. No. 100-F.L.

Government House, Lahore,
October 26th, 1938

Dear Lord Linlithgow,

As this is my first letter to Your Excellency since your return, may I begin by offering you my welcome back to India?

2. The Provincial Fortnightly Report (which I enclose) refers at some length to the tours of the Premier and other Ministers in the south-eastern Punjab. I have since received Sikander's own impressions of this tour and of a subsequent tour they made to some of the northern districts such as Gujrat, Jhelum and Attock. I enclose also an article[34] from the *Civil and Military Gazette* of October 22nd, giving an interesting account of this tour. Sikander told me that at every single place they had an extraordinarily enthusiastic reception. At Campbellpur, the headquarters of Attock which is the Premier's own district, the meeting was the largest that has ever taken place in the memory of man and the enthusiasm was tremendous. It culminated in the Secretary of the local Congress Committee ascending the platform and announcing that he intended to resign his office and his connection with the Congress! Sikander was greatly struck by the growth of political consciousness among the rural masses in all districts which he visited and also by the fact that the European crisis and its reactions in India have had the effect of drawing the martial classes very closely together. He assured me of his own confidence that in the event of a world war the Punjab would readily supply a million fighting men, thus more than doubling its contribution during the Great War.

3. There is no doubt that the prestige of the Ministry at the moment stands extremely high throughout the Province. This is largely, of course, due to their recent agrarian legislation and also in part to the very generous measures of relief taken to deal with the famine in Hissar and the neighbouring districts, measures which are on a scale considerably more generous than would have been taken under the old famine procedure. It is also, I think, largely due to the fact that the Ministers are now devoting a great deal more of their time and energy to these propaganda tours, where they address huge audiences and find it comparatively easy to work up enthusiasm. Ever since I took over as Governor I have been impressing on them the necessity for more propaganda of this kind to counteract the

influence of the Nationalist Press, which is of course mainly in the hands of their political opponents, and they have been quick to appreciate the point. Naturally these tours impose a considerable strain on their energy and mean some delay in the disposal of administrative work, but this is a comparatively minor point. Both Sikander and Chhotu Ram, who are the most frequent and popular speakers, seem to stand up to the physical strain extraordinarily well.

4. The prestige of the Congress, on the other hand, is still at an extremely low ebb. I notice that in the recent election to the District Board of Gurgaon the Congress succeeded in capturing only one out of 30 elected seats in spite of the fact that Gurgaon is so exposed to visits from the leading Congressmen of Delhi and members of the Central Assembly.

5. With reference to what I stated in paragraph 3 of my letter to Brabourne, No. 95-F.L., of October the 11th, the agitation against the recent agrarian legislation seems to be steadily declining in force. I saw a C.I.D. account of a meeting of the Working Committee of the Non-Agriculturists' Association held on the 13th of October with Sir Gokul Chand Narang, the ex-Minister, in the Chair. There was considerable internal dissension, but the interesting point brought out in the report was that the total expenditure of the Association up to date was only Rs. 2,800 and the balance in hand only Rs. 4,500. The Association appears to have no definite policy of civil disobedience or anything of that kind, and its present efforts are apparently concentrated on attempts to detach from their allegiance to the Unionist Party certain of its individual supporters. No authoritative instance of successful detachment has been reported so far.

6. The Punjab has been having a visit recently from Chaudhri Jug Lal, the Harijan Minister from Bihar, who has addressed a number of meetings. Sikander dealt with this potentially embarrassing visitor with considerable skill. He wrote him a letter of welcome and said that he had arranged for an officer to be detailed to see after his comfort in each district visited. He trusted that Chaudhri Jug Lal would respect the convention which the Punjab Ministers had decided to observe in visiting other Provinces, that they would indulge in no public criticism or attacks on the Ministry in power. Judging from the newspaper reports of his meetings Chaudhri Jug Lal has faithfully observed this convention. Indeed on one occasion he reproved certain people who presented an address to him which contained attacks on the Unionist Ministry, and on another occasion he deplored that the Congress in the Punjab had done practically nothing for the depressed classes.

7. All my Ministers and a large number of other distinguished persons from the Punjab were invited by the Maharaja of Patiala to attend the recent Dussehra celebrations and all with whom I have talked are loud in their praises of his courtesy to his guests, his accessibility to his subjects and his high sense of duty. Cordial references to the traditional and close relations between Patiala and the Punjab were contained in speeches made by His Highness and by Sikander at a banquet on this occasion, and I believe that there was a certain amount of informal discussion on the idea of a separate Federation for northern India, but I have no precise information on this point.

8. One effect of the European crisis has, I think, been to widen the breach between the Punjab and the Congress Governments in other Provinces. Sikander's speech in Simla on September the 26th regarding the loyalty of the Punjab has been bitterly criticised by various Congress speakers and writers, but he has made several effective replies to such criticisms. The Congress creed of non-violence has been the target of a considerable amount of ridicule in connection with the European crisis even in Hindu papers. An interesting article in this connection appeared the other day in the *Partap,* an influential Hindu daily of Lahore, written by Mahasha Krishan, the proprietor. He said that 'the situation in India is that the Muslims of the north greatly predominate in the Army and their political leaders are in alliance with Great Britain. While this is so Britain's position is assured and Congress and Hindus are impotent, for any situation in the country could be controlled immediately with the greatest of ease. Hindus must therefore arouse themselves in their lethargy, recognise facts as they are, and not rest till they have fitted themselves to repel the aggression of the north.'

9. As regards the agitation against the Kalsia State, which still continues, I informed Brabourne in a recent letter that my Ministry had accepted the suggestion made by the Resident to bring into force the Indian States (Protection) Act of 1934 in certain districts. The Act has now been notified as in force in Ferozepore, Ludhiana, Jullundur, Amritsar, Hoshiarpur and Ambala, the last-named being the district within whose limits the main portion of Kalsia State territory is situated. It is hoped that this will enable the Magistrates of these districts to take effective steps to check the activities of the agitators.

10. The famine in the south-eastern Punjab is, I fear, a very serious matter. The worst district is Hissar, where conditions are estimated to be worse than they have been since the great famine of 1899-1900. Rohtak, Gurgaon and Karnal are also suffering from a more or less complete failure

of the monsoon. Relief works have been opened in about a dozen places in Hissar and I believe the daily average of attendance of labourers is at present in the neighbourhood of 6,000 and steadily increasing. Elaborate arrangements have been made for the import of fodder for cattle at concession rates, but I fear that a large number of good quality stock have already been sold off at minute prices. I need not go further into details, but a very rough preliminary estimate of the cost of relief operations is in the neighbourhood of Rs. 25-30 lakhs. The provincial budget for the year anticipated a small balance of revenue over expenditure of a few lakhs, but the Finance Department now fears that this is likely to be converted into a deficit of somewhere about Rs. 50 lakhs.

11. The communal riot of October the 13th at Multan (described at the foot of page 3 of the Provincial Report) is the first serious incident of this kind that has occurred since my assumption of office. The local Officers appear to have dealt with the situation promptly and efficiently, though they were somewhat handicapped by the inadequacy of the Police force. I have suggested to Sikander that a careful enquiry should be made into the strength of the force to be maintained in future at Multan, which is a place with a particularly bad record for communal rioting. A few days after the riot two of the Ministers (Mr. Manohar Lal and Mian Abdul Haye) visited Multan at the request of the Premier in the hope of being able to compose the tension between the two communities. I am not sure that their visit was in its effects quite so successful as they themselves consider. The District Magistrate[35] reports that their inspection of the burnt-up shops and other buildings attracted large and excited crowds and the Ministers' enquiries were so protracted that they began to assume almost the form of a Police investigation, resulting in an intensification of communal feeling, which was beginning to die down. However, I fully sympathise with the motive which prompted the Ministers to make this visit. They know, of course, that they are likely to be bombarded with questions on the Multan incident at the next session of the Assembly and their visit will provide them with ammunition for their replies.

The last report I have seen about Multan is to the effect that the situation is improving and tension is declining.

12. The next session of the Legislative Assembly commences on the afternoon of November the 10th. On the morning of that day I have agreed to open formally the new Legislative Assembly Chamber, which has just been completed. This ceremony will probably be made the occasion for a considerable gathering and some military display. The Brigadier here is

anxious that his troops should have any opportunity that may occur of taking part in a ceremonial parade.

Yours sincerely,
H.D. CRAIK

64

CRAIK TO LINLITHGOW

Private and Personal
D.-O. No. 101-F.L.

Government House, Lahore,
November 10th, 1938

Dear Lord Linlithgow,

I have seen you so recently that I really have practically nothing to add to the Provincial Report for the second half of October, which I enclose herewith.

The fortnight has been a comparatively quiet one. The success of the Unionist and Muslim League candidate in the recent by-election for the Provincial Assembly from the Multan Division was a striking success for the Unionist Party, the successful candidate's majority being over 3,000.

In paragraph 6 of my last letter I mentioned the recent tour in the Punjab of Chaudhuri Jug Lal, the Harijan Minister from Bihar. I am told that this gentleman informed one of our Scheduled Caste M.L.As. that in his opinion the Harijans should in every province give their support to the party in power, as it was only in this way that they could secure any material advantages for themselves or office for their leaders. This advice was in fact 'carrying coals to Newcastle', as in the Punjab all the Harijan representatives are, I think, supporters of the Unionist Party and two of them are Parliamentary Secretaries.

The autumn session of the Legislative Assembly opens today in its new Chamber, the ceremonial opening of which I performed this morning. It was a successful and effective function, as I had a guard of honour and an escort of cavalry. There was some talk of demonstrations being organised at this ceremony by the Non-Agriculturists' Association and by the Akalis, but careful Police precautions were taken and there was nothing to mar the success of the function. I have not yet heard whether any attempt was made to hold a demonstration.

Yours sincerely,
H.D. CRAIK

65

CRAIK TO LINLITHGOW

Private and Personal
D.-O. No. 102-F.L.

Government House, Lahore,
November 22nd, 1938

Dear Lord Linlithgow,

The Assembly has been in session since November the 10th. On the opening day there was a great deal of disorder and deliberate defiance of the authority of the Chair by some leading members of the Opposition, and since then the proceedings have been marked by a number of disorderly scenes. I am afraid there can be little doubt that the Speaker is rather losing his grip and his tendency to argue about his rulings does not contribute to decorum. Very little progress has been made with the principal Government measure of the session, viz., the Marketing Bill, owing to the dilatory tactics of the Opposition. The Congress party dislikes this measure, but is unwilling to oppose it openly and on the only division that has taken place, abstained from voting. The session seems likely to continue, with a brief break for the Id, till well into December.

2. I attended the usual Armistice Day Service at the Cathedral on November the 11th and noticed that three of the Ministers, the Premier, Sir Chhotu Ram and Malik Khizar Hayat Khan, sat in the pew behind me. After the Service I was asked to inspect a contingent of 40 or 50 ex-service men, all of whom were Europeans, and I noticed with pleasure that the Premier and Khizar Hayat Khan, both of whom have held Commissions in the Army, fell in in the rear rank of this parade. The incident is significant.

3. When I saw Your Excellency in Delhi the other day I mentioned to you my anxiety regarding European recruitment for the Irrigation Branch of the Public Works Department. Last year we required one European recruit and though there were very few applicants, we succeeded in obtaining a man who will, I think, be suitable. His father served in India for many years. This year we asked the High Commissioner[36] to recruit two more Europeans. Only four applied and only three of these turned up for the interview. Two of them were considered suitable, but one of these eventually declined the offer. The only one who has accepted and who has arrived in India is the son of a retail grocer in Liverpool, and the impression of the Chief Engineer, who has seen him, is that he is entirely unsuitable for service in India. I think there is little doubt that the comparatively low

initial salary offered and the exceptional opportunities now open in the United Kingdom for Engineers are going to prejudice seriously the prospects of European recruitment for this branch of the service. I am taking the matter up with the Ministers and, as you know, I have to report to you fully on the matter early next year.

4. The situation as regards the famine in the south-eastern part of the Province continues to grow graver. There has been no rain during November, and it is now too late for *rabi* sowings; so it is practically certain that famine conditions will prevail till August or September next year. The latest figures I have seen regarding test-works in the Hissar district give a daily average of labourers of over 20,000, and it is proposed to open several new test-works in the near future. It is satisfactory that the local officers report that the people appreciate the efforts which Government is making to help them.

The local Congress organizations are, as usual, trying to exploit the situation for political purposes. A Congress relief committee is trying to collect funds, but has so far done no effective work of any kind, while its criticism of the Government measures is described by the Deputy Commissioner of Hissar[37] as 'unfair and at times mischievous'.

As regards the cattle situation in Hissar and the neighbouring districts, I have recently seen a report by the Director of Veterinary Services[38] after a visit to the area. At recent fairs in Hissar over 50,000 head of cattle were sold at an average price of Rs. 24-1-0 per head. Last year the numbers sold at these fairs were 34,170 and the average price was Rs. 32-10-0. The estimated decrease of the cattle population in the *barani* areas of Hissar is 50 per cent, but a census is to be held this month and thereafter at intervals of two months. The prices of good milking cows and buffaloes have not, however, fallen. Additional veterinary staff has been posted to the district.

In Rohtak district the number of cattle sold at fairs this year was over 42,000 as compared with about 25,000 last year. The average price has fallen from Rs. 47-5-0 to Rs. 34-8-0 per head.

I think I mentioned to you the Congress scheme to export cattle on a large scale from Hissar and Rohtak to grazing areas in the United Provinces (Saharanpur and Dehra Dun), which the United Provinces Government had agreed to throw open for the purpose. The Punjab Government have, in my opinion rightly, refused to help in this ill-considered scheme by paying the cost of transporting the cattle by rail. Our Director of Veterinary Services reports that the grazing available in the United Provinces is very poor in quality and cattle would have to be fed with fodder and grain if they are to survive there during the winter months. Some thousands have already been sent to these areas by private agencies and I imagine that few of them will ever return to the Punjab. But from the Rohtak district, which is not so hard hit as Hissar and where the people are very keen cattle breeders, there has been no large scale emigration to the United Provinces and the few that were sent have been brought back, because the grazing is so poor in quality.

It is reported that there has been no mortality of cattle in Rohtak or Gurgaon. There is no accurate information on this point from Hissar, but undoubtedly a considerable number of poorer quality cattle have been slaughtered for the value of their hides.

It is still difficult to make an estimate of the financial burden which the famine will throw on provincial revenues but I have little doubt that it will be at least 50 lakhs of rupees, in addition to the large remissions of land revenue and canal dues that will have to be given, and the total may amount to a considerably larger sum.

5. You asked me at Delhi whether my Government had decided to introduce in the Punjab the Criminal Law Amendment Act of 1938, directed to stop anti-recruitment propaganda, and I told you that Government had decided to await the report as regards anti-recruitment meetings held during October. This has now been received and shows that the number of meetings during October was 82 only as compared with 187 in September and 113 in August. Most of the meetings during October were held in areas where there is little or no recruitment and have had no adverse effect on recruitment. I have little doubt that the decline is due to the passing of the Act as the persons who run this agitation have no desire to be sent to jail. After considering this report my Ministry has decided to wait and choose their own time for applying the new Act.

6. It is difficult to estimate what effect the recent announcement of His Majesty's Government regarding Palestine has had in the Province. I fancy the better-informed public appreciates the decision to hold a conference, though there is considerable criticism of the exclusion of the Arab leaders. I do not see much change in the tone of the Press comment on this subject, but hitherto there has been no intensification of agitation. The Ahrars, the party most likely to take up this question, have not yet decided on any definite programme or line of action.

7. At a recent Cabinet meeting we discussed at some length the problem of agrarian unrest among the tenantry of certain areas on the Sutlej Valley Project. As you are possibly aware, large areas of land on this Project are leased by Government on temporary leases for three, four or five years

pending their allotment to permanent settlers. This system has been in force for some years, because it is for obvious reasons uneconomical to put a large area on the market simultaneously. These temporary leases are allotted on a system of calling for tenders and in some cases are taken up by capitalists who secure very large areas. The lessees put in their own sub-tenants and naturally enough are anxious to make as much profit as they can out of the land in the comparatively short period available. There is no doubt that in many cases they more or less rack-rent the sub-tenants, who usually pay in kind. The commonest form of rent is half the produce, calculated after considerable deductions in favour of the landlord have been made from the common heap, and the sub-tenant has to pay all the canal dues. In these days of low prices this is a very severe rent and it is a fact that the sub-tenants have a substantial grievance in this respect. The local Congress and Communist organisers have been doing their best to exploit this grievance with the result that there is considerable unrest among the sub-tenants. Government have accordingly decided to insist on the lessees granting the sub-tenants substantial reductions, corresponding reductions being made in the rent charged by Government from lessees. Any lessee who will not accept the new conditions will be at liberty to abandon his lease.

The system of these temporary leases is, however, an uneconomical one and as the land has not only to support the sub-tenant (who in present conditions makes a bare subsistence), but also to provide the rent due to Government and the middle-man, lessee's, profits, Government have decided to take steps to bring this system gradually to a close and, in spite of the present low value of land, to dispose of considerably larger areas than hitherto either by auction or by settlement of permanent peasant colonists. In the meantime, such temporary leases as continue to be granted will be subject to a comparatively restricted maximum area in the case of each individual lessee. The Ministry decided to make an early announcement regarding its intentions in this respect in order that the Congress and Communist agitators might not claim this result as a victory for themselves, but I have not hitherto seen any announcement.

8. I enclose the provincial report for the first half of November.

Yours sincerely,
H.D. CRAIK

66

CRAIK TO LINLITHGOW

Secret and Personal
D.-O. No. 103

Government House, Lahore,
November 25th, 1938

Dear Lord Linlithgow,

This is in reply to Your Excellency's secret and personal letter to me of the 23rd of November.

Douglas Young does not reach the age of 60 (when High Court Judges are compelled to retire) till April 1943, but I understand that the additional pension which he earns as Chief Justice matures in 1941, and I have reason to think that he speaks to his intimates of the possibility of retirement in 1941. Personally, I am rather sceptical if he will retire before the age of 60, as he is strong and physically energetic and interested in his work.

As regards my view of Zafrullah as a possible successor to Young as Chief Justice, I knew that Zafrullah had ambitions in this direction and I find that he wrote a long letter to Emerson in August 1933, asking to be considered for the post and at the same time making it clear that a Puisne Judgeship had no attractions for him. Emerson replied in September 1933 to the effect that he could not hold out any hope of Zafrullah's appointment as Chief Justice. In a letter of December the 24th 1933, to Lord Willingdon about the selection of a successor to Shadi Lal, who was due to retire in May 1934, Emerson mentioned the agitation in the Muslim Press in favour of the appointment of a Muslim Chief Justice and expressed the view that there was not any strong feeling behind it. He went on as follows:

> 'In this connection Chaudhri Zafrullah Khan has been mentioned as a possible candidate. While I have great regard for his abilities and character, I consider his appointment as out of the question. Apart from the general objection mentioned above (viz., the apprehensions that would be aroused among Hindus by the appointment of a Muslim from outside the Court as Chief Justice) it will give the greatest offence to the present Judges of the Court to have placed over them a member of the local Bar who has never acted as a Judge. Several of the Indian Judges would probably resign. The appointment, moreover, would not be acceptable to Muhammadans as a body, since Zafrullah is an Ahmadi, and feeling between members of that sect and orthodox Muslims (which is always bad) is worse at the present time and [?than] for many years.'

I have given the matter most careful thought and in my judgment the objections stated by Emerson five years ago still have great force. Like Emerson, I have great regard for Zafrullah's abilities and character and I also have a considerable personal liking for him. I fully recognise his great value as a Member of Your Excellency's Council and he is, of course, a considerably bigger figure in public estimation now than he was in 1933: but we cannot overlook the fact that he has never held judicial office and that, although his practice at the Lahore Bar was considerable and I believe lucrative, he has never been one of the recognized leaders of that Bar mainly because his practice his been so often interrupted by other calls. But the principal objection to his appointment lies, in my opinion, in the fact that he is an Ahmadi and, I am afraid, a fanatical and leading adherent of that sect. I do not think his appointment as Chief Justice would in existing circumstances lead to resignations among the present Judges, but I do feel that it would be regarded by the Hindus and Sikhs as made on communal grounds, and I am convinced that it would not be popular with Muslims generally. The relations between orthodox Muslims and the Ahmadis, though less tense at the moment than they were a few years ago, are still very far from cordial and mutual recrimination is still a common feature in certain organs of the Press.

I should add that although Zafrullah's great abilities are generally recognised and admired, I do not think he is on cordial terms with Sikander or, indeed, with any of my present Ministers.

I would myself infinitely prefer – and I believe most responsible persons in the Province would prefer – to see an Englishman succeed Douglas Young. The Province has unhappy recollections of Shadi Lal's lengthy tenure of the office of Chief Justice. Shadi Lal was generally regarded even by such leading and responsible Muslims as Sir Fazl-i-Husain, Sikander and Zafrullah himself as strongly pro-Hindu in his administration of the Court.

I should add that by a curious coincidence I received yesterday evening a telegram from the Shiromani Gurdwara Parbandhak Committee, the statutory body set up to administer the Sikh shrines, protesting against 'the proposed appointment of Sir Zafrullah Khan to the Judicial Committee of the Privy Council in view of the pendency of the Gurdwara Shahidganj appeal in the Privy Council and the antecedents of Sir Zafrullah as a communist'. I expect you have received a similar telegram. I do not attach much importance to this protest, but it does go to show that the Sikhs do not regard Zafrullah as impartial on communal questions.[39]

Yours sincerely,
H.D. CRAIK

67

CRAIK TO LINLITHGOW

Secret
D.-O. No. 104

Government House, Lahore,
November 25th, 1938

Dear Lord Linlithgow,

Moon has forwarded to Laithwaite on the 23rd of November in a demi-official letter a recommendation for the conferment of the hereditary title of 'Nawab' on the head of the Qizilbash family of Lahore, but there is one point in connection with this proposal which I did not think it would be appropriate to include in Moon's letter, as that will doubtless have to be examined in the Political Department, but which I think it is right that I should mention privately to Your Excellency. The point is that Sikander is strongly in favour of the revival of this hereditary title. In a note which he sent me, recommending that the question of this title should be reopened, he wrote as follows:

> 'Nawab Nisar Ali Khan is not brilliant, but he is steady and means well. He is thoroughly loyal and is a staunch supporter of the administration. The family, as His Excellency is aware, has a long and continuous tradition of steadfast loyalty to the Crown and is one of the leading families of the Punjab. It is desirable that the influence and prestige of this family should be restored both on account of past services and its meritorious record of loyalty and also in the interests of the administration. It is in the interests of the Province that as far as possible the influence and position of old families of proved loyalty and merit should not be allowed to suffer.'

I would also like to emphasise my personal agreement with Sikander's point of view. The British *raj* in the Punjab is under very great obligations to these old families which have for generations used their influence in support of the administration. In recent years the tendency has been for their influence to decline, partly owing to the falling off in their income from land, but mainly because it is not nearly as easy now as it was a generation ago for their sons to secure appointments in Government service. I have been distressed to see in recent years that many of the old families which in the early days of my service carried great influence, which they exerted loyally in the interests of the administration, have now sunk into comparative insignificance or poverty. This is far from being the case with the Qizilbash family, but I hold strongly the view that anything we can do to uphold the position and influence of these old families is well worth doing; and for these reasons I venture to express the hope that Your Excellency may find it possible to accept my recommendation.

Yours sincerely,
H.D. CRAIK

68

CRAIK TO LINLITHGOW

Private and Personal
D.-O. No. 106-F.L.

Government House, Lahore,
December 8th, 1938

Dear Lord Linlithgow,

The Assembly Session ended abruptly and somewhat dramatically on Friday, the 2nd of December. The progress with the principal measure of the session, viz., the Marketing Bill, had been so slow that on Friday, Sikander, after securing the oral agreement of the Opposition leaders, moved that the House should sit till late that night and should sit again on Saturday, December the 3rd, and continue its sitting till the Bill was passed. The Opposition, however, double-crossed the Premier by putting up a member to raise the question whether this motion was in order, i.e. whether the House was competent to order a sitting on Saturday. There was a prolonged discussion on this and the Speaker at first took the line that the question was so difficult that he preferred not to give a ruling on it, but to leave it to the decision of the House. The Premier took objection to this suggestion on the ground that it would not be proper for the majority party in the House to decide a point that was purely one of interpretation of the rules and pressed the Speaker to give a ruling. Ultimately (and apparently after considerable havering) the Speaker ruled that the House had no power to decide that it could sit on a Saturday, and Sikander thereupon moved that the House should adjourn *sine die*, the motion being carried by a considerable majority. The Speaker is reported to have then said that on reflection he thought his ruling was wrong!

I saw Sikander next day and he told me that though he is a man of equable temperament, he very nearly lost his temper on this occasion; not, as I had expected, with the Speaker, but with the Opposition leaders, who had agreed to have two long sittings to complete the business of the House and then went back on their word. I gather his motion to adjourn the House *sine die* was prompted by the fact that he had an important engagement in

Delhi on the Monday and engagements in Multan and Montgomery later on during the present week, and he thought it would be impossible to secure the passage of the Marketing Bill within a reasonable time.

The Opposition have hailed the success of their dilatory tactics as a substantial Congress victory. As a matter of fact it was nothing more than a piece of clever manoeuvring, but it was successful in that it has delayed the passage of the Marketing Bill, which is strongly opposed by the Bania community. The intention is, I gather, to call another Session about the 10th of January to pass this Bill.

2. The Congress newspapers have announced with considerable glee that there are signs of the Unionist Party breaking up. Four of the representatives in the Assembly of the Scheduled Castes have announced that they are leaving the Government benches, but not that they are joining the Congress or any other party. Sikander informs me that one of these four has since apologised and rejoined the Unionist Party, while another has sent a message to say he is prepared to do so, but Sikander has so far refused to see him. Sikander suspects that the four members in question were paid by the Congress Party.

Another sign of disagreement in the Unionist ranks occurred during the discussion of a non-official resolution urging that the charge for canal water should be reduced by 50 per cent. This was opposed by the Ministry, but a member of the Unionist Party moved an amendment suggesting a 25 per cent. reduction, and in the course of his speech admitted that in doing so he was acting contrary to the instructions of his Leader, but under pressure from his constituents. His conduct was subsequently discussed at a party meeting, at which he said that he had been wrong in disobeying his leader's instructions, but would not admit that the principle embodied in his amendment was wrong. I understand that no disciplinary action has been taken against him.

Sikander does not seem to be in the least dismayed by either of these incidents or to anticipate that they will have any permanent effect on the voting strength of the Unionist Party. But it is reported that Pandit Gopi Chand Bhargava, the leader of the Congress party in the Assembly, has consulted Maulana Abul Kalam Azad as to the advisability of moving a motion of no confidence in the Ministry. It is not known what advice he has received from the Maulana.

3. As regards the famine in the south-eastern Punjab, the number of workers on the various test-works in the Hissar district is steadily increasing and must now have passed the 30,000 mark. Hissar has been declared a 'Famine district', the effect of which is that allowances will now

automatically be paid to the dependents of workers on the test-works and the test-works now automatically become known as 'relief works'. Owing to practically no rain having fallen anywhere during the last three months, it is certain that *rabi* sowings will be considerably below the normal in area.

4. Reference is made in the fortnightly report (enclosed) to the collection at Lahore of volunteers by the Non-Agriculturists' Association with the idea of picketing the houses of certain members of the Assembly. No picketing, however, took place, and I fancy that we shall hear little more of this Association. There certainly does not seem to be any prospect of civil disobedience or any other form of defiance of the law.

5. As regards anti-recruitment meetings, I recently noticed a report from the Jullundur district, which is an important recruiting centre for Sikhs, that zamindars had boycotted meetings designed to hamper recruitment and on two occasions had refused to let them be held at all.

6. The fortnightly report refers at some length to Subhas Chandra Bose's visit to the Punjab during the latter part of November. He actually spoke in 12 districts and laid considerable stress on the desirability of Muslims joining the Congress. In private conferences he is reported to have said that the Punjab Provincial Congress should have a Muslim President. He also gave prominence in most of his speeches to the Congress opposition to Federation and professed his own anxiety to force a crisis on this issue and to launch 'a countrywide campaign' if the demand of Indians to be allowed to frame their own constitution is denied. I gather that in most places which he visited his audiences, though large, were considerably smaller than those that collected on the occasion of Jawaharlal Nehru's last visit to the Punjab, and it does not appear that Bose himself excited any great enthusiasm. In private conferences he is reported to have done his best to encourage all groups outside the Unionist Party to do everything possible, by fair means or foul, to embarass the present Ministry and to have been lavish in his promises of financial support for this object. He does not appear to have had any success at all in his efforts at composing the existing internal differences in the Congress ranks.

7. You will, of course, have read in the newspapers of the recent meeting of the Muslim League in Delhi, at which a resolution was moved criticising the speech delivered by Sikander in Simla on September the 26th, in which he pledged the complete support of the Punjab to the Empire should war take place. The *Hindustan Times* of Delhi has, according to Sikander, gravely misrepresented what took place at this meeting. The newspaper stated that Jinnah administered 'a stern rebuke' to Sikander. Sikander

himself told me that nothing of the sort occurred and that in fact Jinnah during the course of the meeting spoke in praise of Sikander's speech (as did several other speakers), and further that he (Jinnah) took the earliest possible opportunity of closing the discussion by insisting on the withdrawal of the resolution moved by Lari (the latter, according to Sikander, was paid by the United Provinces Congress to move the resolution). Sikander in defending himself emphasized the point that when he spoke at Simla he was not speaking as a Muslim, but as the representative and leader of the martial classes generally and that his offer of loyal co-operation with the Empire had been fully endorsed by those classes, including the Sikhs, Jats and Dogras as well as Muslims. His attitude was in no way apologetic and he made it quite clear that he fully adhered to his Simla speech.

8. My Revenue Minister, Sir Sunder Singh Majithia, has had an unfortunate accident and broken his ankle. He expects to be confined to his house for six weeks, but is able to deal with administrative business.

Yours sincerely,
H.D. CRAIK

69

CRAIK TO LINLITHGOW

Private and Personal
D.-O. No. 109-F.L.

Government House, Lahore,
December 23rd/24th, 1938

Dear Lord Linlithgow,

I enclose the provincial fortnightly report for the first half of December. The report is short for the fortnight has been on the whole quiet; but there are one or two matters which I think I ought to report to Your Excellency.

2. In paragraph 2 of my letter No. 106-F.L. of December the 8th, I mentioned the secession from the Unionist Party of four members of the Assembly who represent Scheduled Castes, but noted that one of the four had since rejoined the Government Party. The other three are reported to have promised Subhas Chandra Bose during the course of his tour in the Punjab that they would join the Congress Party in the Assembly provided the Congress agreed, if and when it comes into power, to grant three demands, viz.:

(*i*) that the Harijans should be declared to be statutory agriculturists for the purposes of the Punjab Alienation of Land Act;

(*ii*) that they should be given the benefit of free education; and (*iii*) that they should be allowed a proportionate share of representation in the Army and Government services.

The Congress President is reported to have given a promise to consider these demands favourably.

It is also reported that the Ahrars made an offer to Subhas Chandra Bose, through their leader Ch. Afzal Haq, that they were prepared to join the Congress if they were not called upon to pay the usual four annas subscription. I do not know what reply was given to this proposal.

3. I have now seen reports from the District Officers in most districts which Subhas Chandra Bose visited during the course of his tour. Nearly all of them describe his speeches as 'ordinary' or 'moderate' in tone, and it is generally agreed that his visit excited no great enthusiasm. But it has certainly stimulated efforts by the Opposition to seduce from their allegiance some of the supporters of the Ministry.

4. In paragraph 7 of my letter No. 102-F.L. of November the 22nd, I referred to the agrarian unrest among the tenantry of certain areas on the Sutlej Valley Project and mentioned that my Government had decided to grant the sub-tenants substantial reductions in their rent, making corresponding reductions in the rent charged by Government from its own lessees. These concessions have now been announced and there has in consequence been a considerable improvement in the situation, both in the Nili Bar Colony of the Multan district and in the Lower Bari Doab Colony in Montgomery. Three meetings which were recently called to discuss Kisan grievances were very thinly attended and the agitation has, at any rate for the time being, subsided. Nevertheless, the concessions announced are generally regarded as a triumph for the Congressmen who promoted the agitation.

5. As regards the famine situation in the south-eastern Punjab, the daily average of workers on the 17 test-works in the Hissar district about the 10th of December was over 52,000 and it is rapidly increasing. It is anticipated that by March the total number of labourers on test-works in this district will be 90,000 a day. In Rohtak only one test-work has been opened and on the 12th of December there were 1,750 labourers at work there. I saw a report the other day from Dr. Aykroyd, the Nutrition Expert from Coonoor, who had visited one of the test-works in Hissar and examined a large number of labourers. Although he saw some sign of malnutrition due to lack of vitamins, he saw no cases of serious under-nourishment. Our own officers also report that there are no signs of starvation among the people.

As regards cattle, the census taken towards the end of November in

Hissar showed that the total decrease in the number of cattle due to deaths was only between 5 and 10 per cent. Enormous quantities of fodder are being imported into the district, partly by Government agency and partly by private contractors, and the people are reported to be satisfied with the arrangements. The scheme for the purchase of young breeding stock of good quality by Government with a view to subsequent resale to its owners is now in working order.

The Financial Commissioner (Dobson) has recently paid a fairly long visit to the famine areas and has reported that all relief measures are working smoothly. We are fortunate in having two most able and energetic young Indian Civil Service officers at Hissar – Brander, the Deputy Commissioner, and Bryan, a young Assistant Commissioner of 4 or 5 years' service. Both these officers are doing admirable work. I hope to be able to pay a short visit to the famine areas myself next month.

6. In paragraph 8 of your letter to me of the 3rd of December you asked me to keep you in touch with Congress activities in regard to the affairs of Indian States. I have called for a special report from the C.I.D. on this subject, which has only just reached me. I have not yet had time to study it, but I will write to you separately about this matter. There is certainly at the moment very little overt activity of this kind, and I have heard nothing at all for some time of the agitation directed against the Kalsia State.

Palestine affairs are attracting a diminishing amount of public attention.

7. I have during the last week presided at three lengthy meetings of the Cabinet to discuss the preliminary edition of the Budget for 1939-40 and more particularly the Schedule of New Expenditure. The financial situation created by the famine is most serious. Expenditure on various forms of famine relief (including *taccavi* advances, very little of which will ultimately be recovered) will probably amount to 56½ lakhs during the current financial year and is estimated at 75½ lakhs during 1939-40. Had it not been for the famine our financial position at the end of the current year would have been strong and we should certainly have ended the year with a surplus, but the heavy expenditure necessitated by the famine has upset all our calculations and we are now confronted with a situation which will require drastic economies and probably some increase of taxation.

I was considerably impressed during the course of our discussions by the courageous and statesmanlike view which my Ministry took of the situation and also by the very able and lucid exposition of the financial situation given by the Finance Minister, Manohar Lal. It was also noticeable that the whole course of these lengthy discussions was entirely harmonious and indeed I do not remember a single point on which there was the slightest disagreement between my Ministers.

I need not trouble you with the details of the decisions taken, but will content myself with a very short summary. It is proposed to make considerable cuts in contingencies, expenditure on travelling allowances, Irrigation Branch working expenses, i.e. maintenance and repairs, repairs to buildings and communications and certain less important items. I do not personally like the idea of reducing expenditure on travelling allowances, which of course involves some curtailment of touring, but I see no adequate alternative. No proposal has so far been made to reduce the rates of travelling allowance. Altogether the economies expected to be effected by these measures in recurring expenditure amount to something between 27 and 30 lakhs. It is also proposed to bring in a Bill for the imposition of a small tax on the sale of petrol and lubricants, the rate mentioned being one anna per gallon on petrol, which is estimated to produce 7½ lakhs a year (such a tax is within the competence of the Local Government under the recent decision of the Federal Court). There is also an important proposal, which will require the approval of the Auditor-General, to charge famine expenditure (over and above the comparatively small amount available in the Famine Relief Fund, which is already exhausted) as 'Extraordinary Expenditure', i.e. to set it off against what are known as our 'Extraordinary Receipts'. These extraordinary receipts represent instalments on the sale price of Crown land in the canal colonies and have for the last 10 or 15 years not been included among our revenue receipts. The change contemplated in treating famine expenditure as extraordinary charges is a drastic one, but it does not seem to me to be contrary to the canons of sound finance, as famine is essentially an extraordinary incident. I hope Burdon will not raise any objection to this change, which is indeed the only way in which we can present a balanced budget for the current year and for 1939-40.

8. So far there has been practically no Press comment on the terrible Nowshera tragedy,[40] nor has the matter been mentioned to me, except with conventional expressions of regret, by any of my visitors. But I have just received a secret and personal letter[41] from the Commander-in-Chief, telling me of the results of the enquiry held (of which I had already learnt something from a conversation with the Northern Army Commander[42]) and of the action which Government has decided to take. I have not yet thoroughly digested the contents of Cassels' letter, which only reached me an hour ago, but my first feeling is one of some dismay as to the possible political consequences of the action contemplated. I am writing separately to Laithwaite about this matter.

Yours sincerely,
H.D. CRAIK

NOTES

1. Mr F.C. Bourne.
2. See No. 24, paragraph 4 and No. 26, paragraph 1.
3. The constitutional crisis occurred over the question of the release of political prisoners. At the start of 1938 there were 23 such prisoners in Bihar while in the U.P. there were 15. Early in February 1938 the Premiers of these two provinces pressed their Governors for immediate and unconditional release of the political prisoners. However, acting on the basis of powers vested in him under Section 126 (5) of the Government of India Act, Lord Linlithgow instructed the Governors to stand firm no matter what the consequences were. On 15 February both provincial Ministries tendered their resignations although these were not immediately accepted.

   On 22 February Lord Linlithgow issued a statement explaining that Governors were still prepared to consider releases after examination of individual cases and stressing the importance of the Governors' special responsibilities. He assured Congress of the continued co-operation of Governors and ended by expressing the earnest hope that the Ministries would resume their tasks.

   Both Ministries resumed work on 26 February. The Governor of Bihar agreed to the release of ten prisoners forthwith while the Premier agreed to get an assurance of renunciation of violence from each one and guaranteed that there would be no demonstrations. The Governor of the U.P. agreed to the release of six prisoners who duly made a public statement that they abjured violence. Information from MSS.EUR.F. 125/142.
4. The texts of the two bills are not printed.
5. Lord Linlithgow minuted: 'I should have thought the course suggested would be to strain the sense of the Section beyond reasonable limits; that is, if any prolonged delay is contemplated. – L.'
6. Lord Linlithgow minuted on this letter: 'P.S.V. – Evidently we are faced with a crisis of the first magnitude. Sikander's fibre is under most severe test. What line will the Muslim League take? Jinnah owes little to S., but he cannot desire the collapse of the mainly Muslim Government. – L.'
7. Not printed.
8. In paragraph 4 of his letter of 4 January 1938, Sir Herbert Emerson had asked for Lord Linlithgow's advice on whether the instructions by the Punjab Government should issue. Evidently a reply had not been received by 7 March. R/3/1/59.
9. Mr R.B. Beckett.
10. Mr A.V. Askwith was Punjab Home Secretary until 30 March 1938 when Mr C. King assumed the office. The present reference is almost certainly to Mr Askwith.
11. Diwan Ram Lal.
12. Although it was only intended that Sir Herbert Emerson should go on home

leave in April 1938, in fact he did not return to the Punjab. Between 1939 and 1946 he served as High Commissioner for Refugees, League of Nations. When he left India, as this document shows, Sir Herbert was in poor health. In another letter to Lord Linlithgow, dated 5 April 1938, he explained that he would consult a specialist on his arrival in England. He concluded that letter with the following passage: 'May I also express my great admiration of the manner in which Your Excellency has directed affairs especially during the past year, when one difficulty after another has arisen and when clear guidance was so necessary.' R/3/1/59.

13. The civil lists give 8 April 1938 as the date when Sir Henry Craik assumed charge of the Governorship of the Punjab.
14. Not printed.
15. Mr Nawab Singh.
16. Mr K.S.S. Hamid Mukhtar Shah.
17. Mr J.W. Hearn, Commissioner, Ambala Division.
18. Mr C. King.
19. Lord Linlithgow minuted on this letter: 'P.S.V. – It seems to me that Craik is going past his brief in letting Ministers know my views at this stage. So far as I am concerned, the case is *sub judice*, no doubt I shall see papers again. I wish you would have a talk to Maxwell on this. I feel rather strongly that Ministers have been thoroughly wobbly and that they ought not to have put the G.-G. in the position in which he now stands. – L.' Mr Reginald Maxwell served as Home Member of the Viceroy's Executive Council from 4 April 1938.
20. Not printed. The article stated: 'The Majlis-i-Ittihad's resolution will afford the Akali firebrand [Master Tara Singh] much-needed aid for the maintenance of his sinister influence among the Akalis and persistence in his irreconcilable attitude.' It urged the organisation to suspend its civil disobedience and strengthen the hands of Sir Sikander Hyat Khan and Sir Henry Craik in their efforts to make a satisfactory settlement of the knotty problem.
21. Mr K.V.F. Morton.
22. Mr A.A. Williams.
23. Rai Bahadur Lala Ram Lal.
24. Sir Curzon Wyllie was shot dead by an Indian student at the conclusion of a function at the Imperial Institute in London on 1 July 1909. Sir Curzon had held senior posts in India and at the time was political aide-de-camp to the Secretary of State for India.
25. Lord Linlithgow minuted here: 'I pushed him hard on this and am entirely satisfied that he has not the very least idea what he does want!'
26. Not printed.
27. The relevant section of paragraph IX of the *Instrument of Instructions to Governors* (1936) reads:

'Our Governor shall interpret his special responsibility for the safeguarding of the legitimate interests of minorities as requiring him to secure, in general, that those racial or religious communities for the members of which special representation is accorded in the Legislature, and those classes of the people committed to his charge who, whether on account of their smallness of their number or their primitive condition or their lack of educational or material advantages or from any other cause, cannot as yet fully rely for their welfare upon joint political action in the Legislature, shall not suffer, or have reasonable cause to fear, neglect or oppression. But he shall not regard as entitled to his protection any body of persons by reason only that they share a view on a particular question which has not found favour with the majority.'

Parl. Papers, H. of C. paper No. 1, vol. xx, 1936-7, pp. 1031-8.

28. Mr C. Rajagopalachariar.
29. Not printed.
30. Mr A.A. Macdonald.
31. In telegram 1378-G of 13 October 1938, Lord Brabourne sent Sir Henry Craik the reactions of Lord Zetland to the Punjab Alienation of Land (Second Amendment) Bill. The Secretary of State felt that the retrospective provisions of the Bill relating to *benami* transactions were objectionable. The transactions, though morally fraudulent, had been tolerated by the government for 37 years and in many cases it would be subsequent transferees who would suffer from the legislation. Lord Zetland asked for views on a number of alternative options he suggested including cutting out certain words from the Bill relating to retrospection.

In his letters of 15 and 16 October 1938 to Lord Brabourne (D.-O. 96 and 97), Sir Henry Craik said he felt that the Secretary of State might have been got at by his Advisers, in particular Sardar Bahadur Mohan Singh. Craik said that Sardar Mohan Singh's 'fortune (which is considerable) was founded on moneylending, and in fact it is generally believed in the Punjab (and I think actually stated in Thorburn's book on the subject) that the Alienation of Land Act of 1901 was passed largely in consequence of a notoriously usurious transaction, in which S.B. Mohan Singh's father or grandfather was the "Shylock"'. In a lengthy exegesis, Sir H. Craik argued that Lord Zetland's alternative options did not commend themselves on their intrinsic merits. More important politically, the Ministry was likely to resign if assent to the Bill was refused. R/3/1/60.

On 7 December 1938, Lord Zetland wrote again and told Lord Linlithgow that he was still unconvinced that the Punjab Bill was acceptable. He remained concerned about a measure which proposed to alter retrospectively the substance of rights in property. He therefore suggested two further alternative ways in which the Bill might be amended. Sir Henry Craik, however, continued to press for the Bill to be enacted as it had been passed by the Legislature. The crux of his argument was that the transactions to be cancelled by the Bill were admitted evasions of the law. L/E/9/567. See No. 76 and its note 12 for subsequent developments.

32. Lieutenant-Colonel Sir H. Wilberforce-Bell, Resident of the Punjab States.
33. In his letter D.-O. 99 of 22 October 1938, Sir Henry Craik informed Lord Brabourne that the Council had, the previous day, resolved to apply the 1934 Act to the districts of Ferozepore, Ludhiana, Jullundur, Hoshiarpur, Ambala and Amritsar. Craik added: 'There was no difficulty in reaching this decision. Sikander stated at the outset that he considered it the Punjab Government's duty to assist the State and the proposition was not questioned by any one.' R/3/1/60.
34. Not printed.
35. Mr I.E. Jones
36. Sir Firoz Khan Noon.
37. Mr G.M. Brander.
38. Captain U.W.F Walker.
39. Lord Linlithgow minuted: 'Oh dear!'.
40. Early in the morning of 24 November 1938, Dost Muhammad, a sepoy of the 4th Battalion, 2nd Punjab Regiment, ran amok in the camp near Nowshera where the Battalion was stationed. Dost Muhammad killed four British officers and three Indian officers and was himself shot while attempting to escape from the camp. A Court of Enquiry found that the behaviour of the Quarter Guard (which took no steps to apprehend Dost Muhammad) was highly discreditable and that the general discipline of the Battalion left much to be desired. The communiqué giving the Court's findings did not detail the punishments proposed, but it is evident from No. 73, paragraph 2 that it was intended to pay off two Muslim companies and return the sepoys to their homes.
41. Not traced.
42. General Sir John Coleridge.

CHAPTER 4

Documents for 1939

70

CRAIK TO LINLITHGOW

Secret
D.-O. No. 110

Government House, Lahore,
January 3rd, 1939

Dear Lord Linlithgow,

In paragraph 8 of your letter of December the 3rd, in reply to my fortnightly letter of November 22nd, 1938, you said that you would be glad to be kept in touch with facts regarding the development of Congress activities within the boundaries of Indian States. Our Criminal Investigation Department have now, at my request, prepared a note on the subject and though it goes into rather great detail, I enclose a copy of it, as you may be glad to have it on record. The upshot of it is that, though Congress workers and Left Wing Organisations have been showing some interest in State affairs, the only serious agitation directed against any of the Punjab States during the last two or three years was the agitation against Kalsia in September and October last, and this collapsed as soon as the Indian States (Protection) Act of 1936 [1934] was enforced by the Punjab Government.

Yours sincerely,
H.D. CRAIK

ENCLOSURE TO NO. 70

NOTE BY AHMED

December 20th, 1938

It may be observed at the outset that in this province the Congress as a body has refrained from taking a direct part in political movements directed against the Indian States' Rulers and administrations. This abstention from interference in State affairs has been due to several causes. Firstly, the Congress in the Punjab is torn by internal dissensions, and the energies of its leaders have been fully absorbed in setting their own house in order. Secondly, the Congress, owing to its internal weakness, commands limited influence in the Punjab, and still more restricted influence in the Punjab States. Thirdly, most of the Punjab States are non-Muslim States, and the Congress, which has a definitely Hindu bias in this province, is not prepared to incur the displeasure of its Hindu supporters by fomenting disaffection against non-Muslim Indian Princes. Congressmen in the Punjab, therefore, have taken shelter behind the resolution passed at the Haripura session of the Indian National Congress regarding non-interference in the Indian States' affairs, and have maintained an attitude of benevolent neutrality towards political movements started in recent years in the States of the Punjab. Individual Congressmen, however, have taken a more or less prominent part in recent State troubles. For instance, during the agrarian agitation in the Kalsia State, Dr. Gopi Chand Bhargava, M.L.A., was reported to have remarked: 'Though it is a State matter, yet we should try to influence and guide co-workers in the freedom of our Motherland'. It is on record that Dr. Gopi Chand visited Moga on 16th September 1938 and recorded the statements of persons injured during the *lathi* charges by the State Police. At the same time, he complained to the All-India States Peoples' Conference, Bombay, that the Kalsia agitation was started without his knowledge and consultation. On the whole, it appears that Dr. Gopi Chand was 'peeved' at having been ignored by the organisers of the agitation against Kalsia State. There is reason to believe that among other Congress leaders Master Kabul Singh, M.L.A., Master Hari Singh, M.L.A., S. Harjap Singh, M.L.A., L. Duni Chand, M.L.A., and Master Raja Ram, were directly or indirectly interested in the Kalsia agitation. A number of Congressmen actually organised an emergency hospital in the Ferozepore district and provided medicines and first aid to the persons injured during the Kalsia disturbances. These Congressmen were, however, careful not to enter the State territory. Reports received from other sources indicate that discontented State subjects have from time to time sought the advice and assistance of Congress leaders in the Punjab in matters affecting the internal administration of the States and in the formation of Congress Committees in States' jurisdiction. Such requests emanated from agitators in Patiala, Jind, Malerkotla, Nabha and Chamba States.

2. The oldest and most important organisation, which has taken an exclusive interest in State affairs, is the Riyasti Parja Mandal. The Mandal

was formed in July 1928, by certain Sikh extremist leaders like S. Sardul Singh Kavishar, Jaswant Singh of Danewal and Bhagwan Singh of Longowal, with the ostensible object of organising the States' subjects with a view to forcing the Rulers to grant full political rights to their subjects. The real object of the organisers was to incite the people of the Patiala State against the late Maharaja and thereby avenge the abdication of the ex-Maharaja of Nabha, for which the organisers held the late Maharaja of Patiala to be largely responsible. Among the declared aims of the Mandal were the establishment of responsible Government in the Indian States under the aegis of the Indian Princes; the removal of the grievances of the State subjects and the protection of their legitimate rights; the establishment of self-governing local bodies in the States; and the separation of the executive and the judiciary in the States of the Punjab. The Mandal consisted almost exclusively of Sikh agitators and deportees from the various Indian States. Branches of the Mandal were formed in the States of Patiala, Dujana, Pataudi, Kalsia, Loharu, Nahan, Bilaspur, Mandi, Suket, Kapurthala, Malerkotla, Faridkot, Chamba, Nabha, Jind, Bahawalpur, Kashmir and the Hill States of Simla. For years the activities of the Riyasti Parja Mandal were directed wholly against the Patiala State. With the demise of the late Maharaja of Patiala, the *raison d'être* of the Mandal disappeared and the Mandal almost ceased to possess the strength and influence it did in past years. It is consequently passing under the influence of a stronger and more dangerous organisation, to which a reference is made later in this note.

3. The present office-bearers of the Punjab Riyasti Parja Mandal are:

1. Master Hari Singh, M.L.A., of Baddon (Hoshiarpur district) (Congress) – *President.*
2. L. Achint Ram of Lahore (Congress and Servant of the Peoples Society) – *Vice-President.*
3. Master Taj Din, Municipal Commissioner, Ludhiana (Ahrar-Congress) – *Vice-President.*
4. Hira Singh Bhathal (Nabha State exile) (Socialist) – *General Secretary.*
5. Bhagwan Singh Longowalia (Patiala State) (Socialist) – *Secretary.*
6. Mansa Ram of Patiala (Socialist) – *Propaganda Secretary.*
7. Giani Sardara Singh Yuthap (Socialist) – *Financial Secretary.*

The composition of the directorate of the Mandal is significant.

4. The body which now controls the destinies of the Riyasti Parja Mandal and which is likely to have a dominant voice in State affairs in the not too distant future, is the Servants of the Peoples Society. This Society was

formed in 1920 by the late L. Lajpat Rai, who was a strong advocate of the formation of a permanent and financially sound institution which should furnish the country with trained missionaries for social and political work. The services of the Society were lent to the Congress in 1921 and 1932, when more than half of its life members went to jail for participating in the Civil Disobedience movement. As time went on, it became clear that the avowed objects of the Society were identical with those of the Congress. The Servants of the Peoples Society is perhaps the most dangerous organisation we have in the Province at the present moment. It has funds; it employs the services of some of the cleverest paid propagandists in the province; and its members include several able and intelligent persons who have connections with all the important political organisations in the country and have a voice in the counsels of political leaders of all classes. The accredited representatives of the Society have been working, since its inception, in practically every form of subversive movement in India. The present office-bearers of the Society are:

1. B. Purshotam Lal Tandon, M.L.A., (U.P.) – *President.*
2. Feroze Chand of Lahore – *Vice-President.*
3. Dev Raj Sethi, M.L.A. – *Secretary.*
4. Mohan Lal of Lahore – *Assistant Secretary.*

Among the Punjab members of the Society are Achint Ram, Principal Chhabil Dass, Jagan Nath and others. The Society has ramifications all over India.

5. It was some time in 1934 that the Servants of the Peoples Society, under the influence of Balvantray Mehta of Bombay first started taking an interest in State affairs. States' work was allocated to L. Achint Ram, one of the best propagandists in the Punjab, who combines in himself the dual authority of an important provincial Congress leader and the Vice-President of the Riyasti Parja Mandal. Achint Ram has set to work with characteristic energy and it is due entirely to his efforts that the Riyasti Parja Mandal is being rapidly subordinated to the dictates of the Servants of the Peoples Society.

6. The third important organisation, which is taking an active interest in the Indian States, is the Punjab Kisan Committee. The Committee is a composite body consisting of terrorist ex-convicts, revolutionaries, socialists, Sikh exiles from Indian States and the more extremist Congressmen. It, therefore, derives its influence from many sources and uses it as effectively as possible towards the subversion of authority both in the Punjab and in the Punjab States. For some time past it has been maintaining a very close touch with the States' peoples and their ambitions

and disabilities through the agency of the Riyasti Parja Mandal leaders such as Bhagwan Singh of Longowal and Jagir Singh Joga of Phagusinghwala, ex-deportees of the Patiala State. Reports received in 1938 showed that the proceedings of the meetings held by the Riyasti Parja Mandal in the various States were invariably reported in some detail to the Punjab Kisan Committee.

7. Mention must be made here of the All-India States Peoples' Conference which is a specialist body dealing exclusively with Indian States' matters and which operates from Bombay. The President of the Conference is the well-known all-India leader, Dr. Pattabhai Sitaramayya, and its Secretary is the able, if disgruntled, Balvantray Mehta, who was expelled from the Bhavanagar State some time ago. The Conference has no recognised branch in the Punjab, but it has appointed a Provincial Secretary in the person of Talib Husain, a deportee of the Malerkotla State, who is a man of little importance. All the States' work in the Punjab has, however, been entrusted by the conference to Achint Ram of the Servants of the Peoples Society. In February 1938 another political body, known as the Central India, Rajputana and Northern Indian States Peoples' Association, was formed at Delhi under the presidentship of Shankar Lal, with Bhagwan Singh of Longowal as one of its Vice-Presidents and Satya Narayan Saraf, a deportee of the Bikaner State residing in Hissar, as one of its members. The declared object of the Society was the establishment of a 'Republican Government in the Central and Northern Indian States', the organisation of opposition to the Federal scheme and the enlistment of the assistance of the British Indian people in fomenting agitation in the Indian States. This body was organised principally because Bhagwan Singh of Longowal and his friends suspected that the All-India States Peoples' Conference had been bought over by the Patiala officials to suppress the Patiala Enquiry Report. The Association, therefore, merely represents a faction and there is little evidence that it commands any influence in the province.

8. As has been stated before, the Riyasti Parja Mandal has in the past directed its energies entirely towards vilifying the late Maharaja of Patiala. The All-India States Peoples' Conference, at the request of the Riyasti Parja Mandal leaders, held an inquiry into the conduct of the late Maharaja of Patiala and the States peoples' grievances generally. On the death of the late Maharaja, the President of the Conference, acting on the advice of M. Gandhi, declined to publish the Patiala Enquiry Committee's report on the ground that it was improper to malign a dead man. This created a schism in the ranks of the Conference and Bhagwan Singh of Longowal

and other leaders interested in the Patiala State affairs broke away from the All-India States Peoples' Conference early in 1938. The Riyasti Parja Mandal, however, did not remain inactive in other directions. During the year (up-to-date) it organised 20 meetings in the districts of Lahore, Amritsar, Hissar, Ludhiana, Ambala and Karnal. Most of these meetings were held on the borders of the Indian States and attracted fairly large numbers of malcontents from the States' territory. Among the Congress and socialist leaders who participated in these meetings were Dr. Gopi Chand Bhargava, M.L.A., Dr. Satyapal, M.L.A., S. Hari Singh, M.L.A., S. Kartar Singh, M.L.A., Bibi Raghbir Kaur, M.L.A., Master Kabul Singh, M.L.A., Sohan Singh Josh, M.L.A., S. Lal Singh, M.L.A., Pandit Muni Lal Kalia, M.L.A., and Munshi Ahmad Din. Speaking at the Lahore meeting on the 21st January, 1938, Dr. Gopi Chand Bhargava said that the suppression of civil liberties in the Indian States was made possible only because one of the greatest Imperialist powers in the world was at the back of the autocratic Rulers of the States. The Chhappar fair in the Ludhiana district, which has for some years past been made the occasion of a yearly re-union of the Riyasti Parja Mandal leaders, took place in September and was attended by 1,500 persons. The usual speeches were made and resolutions were passed protesting against the *lathi* charge by the Malerkotla State Police on members of a meeting at Ahmadgarh, demanding the formation of elected Assemblies and the release of political prisoners in the States, and condemning the interference of the Jind State authorities in the enlistment of Congress and Kisan members.

9. The part played by the Servants of the Peoples Society, represented by Achint Ram, in the organisation of the Riyasti Parja Mandal conferences and meetings during 1937-38 deserves special mention. In September 1937, in a communication to Achint Ram, Balvantray Mehta of the All India States Peoples' Conference laid down the lines of propaganda against the Indian States in the following terms:

> 'It is much better to hold States' Conferences in the States territory. It creates a sense of reality and responsibility . . . However mild, this sort of conference will be able to organise public opinion in the States on the right lines, and will make real headway after some time. Failing this, we might hold such conferences in British India, where people from the States could gather and become members. I wish you could, in co-operation with progressive-minded Rulers, start working from within the States on constructional lines and on mild constitutional lines. That will be more paying in the end.'

This policy was followed by Achint Ram as closely as was permitted by the circumstances obtaining in the Punjab States. In September 1937, he organised a Riyasti Parja Mandal conference at Mahlam in the Jind State territory. In September and December 1937 two further Riyasti Parja Mandal conferences were organised by Achint Ram at Sangrur (Jind State) and in a village in the Malerkotla State. The conference in the Malerkotla State was banned by the State authorities but the organisers succeeded in holding it on the borders of the State in British territory. In April 1938 another Riyasti Parja Mandal conference, for which Achint Ram was responsible, was held at Bichwana in the Hissar District and was attended by a considerable number of the residents of the Indian States bordering on the Hissar district. Still another conference was held at Amritsar in June 1938, under the presidentship of Narain Dass Bechar, M.L.A., of Karachi and was attended by prominent workers of the Congress and the Servants of the Peoples Society. At the same time, Achint Ram was active in other directions during these years. In December 1937 he held an inquiry into circumstances of the police firing at Qila Hakiman in the Patiala State and corresponded with the authorities of Patiala and Malerkotla States over specific grievances of the States' subjects. In All-India States' affairs, Achint Ram took an equally important part. Along with other representatives of the All-India States Peoples' Conference he assisted in drafting the Haripura resolution of the Indian National Congress on States' affairs. He was one of the members of the sub-committee appointed by the Navasarai States Peoples Convention, held in February 1938, and signed the 'mass memorial' prepared by the sub-committee against Federation. Preparations for the All-India States Peoples' Conference, which is to be held at Ludhiana on the 4th, 5th and 6th of February 1939 under the presidentship of Pandit Jawaharlal Nehru, are solely in the hands of Achint Ram and his friends. His services in the interests of the States' peoples during 1937 were gratefully acknowledged by the Servants of the Peoples Society in their annual report for the year in the following terms:

> 'As Vice-President of the Punjab Riyasti Parja Mandal, Shriyut Achint Ram concentrated on work within the Punjab States. Agitation was carried on through the Press and the platform for redress of grievances in Jind, Malerkotla, Nabha and Patiala States. Conferences of States' people attended by thousands were organised in Jind, Malerkotla and other places.'

10. The Punjab Kisan Committee remained particularly active during 1938 in enlisting the States' subjects as its members and in forming

branches in the Indian States' territory. Information was received in January that workers of the Committee were busy in the Patiala, Kapurthala and Jind States in distributing membership forms among the peasants. Minor grievances and the alleged highhandedness of the Patiala Police authorities continued to be exploited by the Punjab Kisan Committee for propaganda purposes throughout the year. During 1938, the committee was interested in the following incidents which occurred in the various Punjab States:

(*i*) The dispersal of a Kisan meeting by the State police at Ahmadgarh in the Malerkotla State in the month of September. (A case of obstruction and attempted murder was registered by the Ahmadgarh Police against the Kisan agitators.)

(*ii*) The ban placed by the Nabha authorities on the hoisting of the 'National Flag' in State territory.

(*iii*) Grievances against the Irrigation Department in the Jind State and the alleged enhancement of land revenue which, it was stated, was 1¼ times more than the rates in force in the neighbouring States and twice the rates in British India.

11. The most important accomplishment of the Punjab Kisan Committee during the year was the organisation of a serious agitation in the Kalsia State. This agitation started with the formation, in April 1938, of a branch of the Kisan Committee in Chirak by a dismissed Sessions Judge of the State with the object of ventilating local grievances and of pressing forward the well-known agrarian demands of the committee. Four members of the committee were arrested for sedition by the State Police and this was the immediate cause of the agitation which subsequently assumed serious proportions. The Punjab Kisan Committee, under the influence of Baba Rur Singh, M.L.A. (who is now one of its Vice-Presidents) and Baba Jawala Singh, at once took the agitation in its hands and organised two *jathas* which toured about 50 villages in the Kalsia State in the month of June and made propaganda against the State authorities. The cry of excessive land revenue was raised and demands were made for its immediate reduction. In September the Kisan leaders decided to boycott the Cattle fair at Chirak. The fair took place between 11th September 1938 and 20th September 1938 and Moga became the centre of the agitation. Picketing was started on 6th September 1938 and action against several of the ringleaders in the British territory had to be taken under the Criminal Law (Amendment) Act. A number of arrests of the pickets was made, but the boycott was sufficiently successful and the fair was a failure. Agitation continued to increase and on 22nd October 1938 the Punjab Government

enforced the Indian States (Protection) Act of 1934 in the Ferozepore, Jullundur, Hoshiarpur, Ludhiana, Amritsar and Ambala districts. A *jatha* of 25 persons, which left Moga under the leadership of a Moscow trained student on 6th October 1938 was arrested in the Ambala district on 26th October 1938. Another *jatha* of 25 persons, which left Moga on 24th October 1938, to demonstrate in the Kalsia State territory, was arrested by the State Police while attempting to enter Chirak. Since then agitation against the Kalsia State has ceased, but the Kisan Committee has not lost hope of reviving trouble in the State and of extending it to other parts of the country.

12. Recent events in the Kashmir State aroused little interest in this province, except among the Ahrars whose efforts to organise 'Kashmir Day' on 21st October 1938 were a miserable failure. About 65 emigrants of the Kashmir State reached Rawalpindi in October and attended two socialist meetings. They were, however, disappointed with the poor reception extended to them and most of them returned to Kashmir within a fortnight. The only signs of interest evinced by the Congress in Kashmir affairs was a vague and platitudinous statement issued to the Press by Dr. Gopi Chand Bhargava on 11th October 1938. In this statement he welcomed generally the desire of the State subjects to replace the present irresponsible executive by a responsible government in the Kashmir State. Again, in December 1938, Dr. Gopi Chand made a request to Bhulabhai Desai to raise in the Central Assembly the question of redressing the grievances of the *British Indian people* in the Kashmir State. Apart from these somewhat academic and futile efforts designed to prove its solicitude for the States' people, the Congress has taken no interest in Kashmir affairs.

13. The present agitation in the Hyderabad State has aroused no interest in the Punjab Congress circles.

14. 'All-India States Day' on 7th December 1938 evoked no enthusiasm in this province. Two small meetings, addressed by Congress and socialist workers, were held in the Multan and Gurdaspur districts. The speakers concentrated on local grievances and references to Indian State matters were infrequent and incidental.

16. [15.] Before I close, I must again emphasise the point that although the Congress as a body is not taking a direct part in political agitation in the Indian States, prominent Congressmen, working under the cloak of one political organisation or another, are trying all they can to stir up unrest among the Indian States' subjects. The attitude of the All-India Congress Committee towards the States is stiffening unmistakably. A comparison of the Haripura resolution on Indian States and the resolution

passed by the Congress Working Committee at Wardhaganj on 14th December 1938 will indicate the way the wind is blowing. Recently Dr. Gopi Chand Bhargava made a special reference to the General Secretary[1] of the All-India Congress Committee on the subject of Congress policy regarding the formation of Congress Committees in the Indian States. He was informed that the States Congress Committees should be affiliated to the Provincial organisation and should work under its control provided the rules framed for the guidance of the States Committees conformed to the terms laid down in the Haripura resolution. The point was further to be discussed at a special meeting of the Punjab Congress Working Council at Lahore on 19th December 1938 but the meeting had to be postponed. On the whole, it is clear that as time goes on, the Congress will more and more come out into the open and show its hand more clearly. At the present moment it is not fully prepared to carry on a fight against 'British Imperialism' and 'Indian autocracy' simultaneously.

G. AHMED
(A.D.I.G., C.I.D.)

71

MOON TO LAITHWAITE

Confidential
D.-O. No. G.S.-677

Government House, Lahore,
January 5th, 1939

My dear Laithwaite,

As desired in your confidential D.-O. No. 2448-G.G., dated the 17th June 1938, I forward a note recorded by His Excellency the Governor on the various Punjab Ministers.

Yours sincerely,
PENDEREL MOON

ENCLOSURE TO NO. 71

NOTE BY CRAIK

January 4th, 1939

There has been no change in the personnel of the Ministry since I last reported and I have little to add to my confidential note of the 1st of July last on the work of the Ministers.

The Premier, Sir Sikander Hyat Khan, continues to enjoy great personal popularity among his supporters and his prestige has, in my judgment, been enhanced during the last six months by the passage of the Ministry's agrarian legislation and by his advocacy of the retention in full of the Punjab's share in recruitment to the Army, which has been ardently endorsed by the martial classes throughout the Province. His declaration during the height of the crisis in September last in favour of India's supporting the Empire in case of a European war was also fully endorsed by the martial classes. Although there have been some defections from the Ministerial ranks in the Assembly, caused by the agrarian legislation and other causes, Sir Sikander does not appear to regard these very seriously. He is optimistic and equable by temperament and is not easily perturbed, and he has a flair for overcoming difficulties of this kind, largely owing to his popularity and his skill in handling men.

Sir Sunder Singh Majithia continues to work harmoniously with his colleagues, but though he is greatly respected by reason of his high character and social position, he seldom takes part in popular demonstrations or political meetings organised by the Ministerial Party. He is not an effective platform speaker, nor has he really much administrative ability. But his views are sound and he is personally a most likeable man. His weakness is his excessive partiality to his own community in the manner of patronage.

Sir Chhotu Ram continues to be the most combative and on the public platform the most effective champion of the agrarian policy of the Ministry. On the other hand, he is more unpopular than any other Minister among his opponents, i.e. in Congress and urban circles, as he is prone to indulge in unrestrained attacks on his opponents. His prejudice against non-agriculturists sometimes makes him unfair in dealing with members of the services who come from that community.

In dealing (in the Cabinet) with the difficult financial situation created by the famine in the south-eastern Punjab, Mr. Manohar Lal has shown great skill and a gift for lucid exposition. His views on public finance are conservative and sound, and he is not in the least inclined to indulge in such 'stunts' as prohibition.

I have been favourably impressed with Mian Abdul Haye's administrative work and, so far as I can see, there is no friction between him and the Secretaries and Heads of Departments working under him. A somewhat unsavoury story came to my ears regarding his alleged interference with the course of justice in a criminal case. It was reported that he had approached a stipenduary Magistrate and put pressure on him to acquit a certain accused person. But he assured me most solemnly that there was no truth in the story and I have accepted his denial.

Major Khizar Hyat Khan has continued to do excellent work. He is developing into a first-class administrator and is in my opinion thoroughly straight. So far as I am aware, his relations with his colleagues and with their supporters are entirely cordial.[2]

H.D. CRAIK

72

CRAIK TO HALLETT[3]

Secret

Government House, Lahore,
January 12th, 1939

My dear Hallett,

I apologize for the delay in answering your secret Demi-Official letter No. 32-GB of January the 7th,[4] but Sikander has been very busy with Assembly business since his return to Lahore and it was only last night that I had an opportunity of having a talk with him about the Patna meeting of the Muslim League.

2. I told him frankly that you had written to me about his speeches there, which had rather puzzled you, and had asked me if I could throw any light on his attitude. He said that he hoped you had not taken all the published reports of his speeches as accurate and that the only accurate report he himself had seen was that of the A.P.I. He believes, however, that the report given in the *Searchlight* was a fairly accurate version, though he had not seen it himself.

3. As regards the resolution on civil disobedience, Sikander claims that it was only owing to his intervention that the amendment was accepted to the original resolution laying down that the decision as regards starting civil disobedience should be left in the hands of the Working Committee. Jinnah himself would not have succeeded in securing an amendment to this effect without Sikander's help. Indeed, Sikander claims that throughout the conference he himself acted as the principal moderating influence and this statement has been confirmed by what I have heard separately from other members of the Punjab party who went to Patna.

4. Sikander explained in some detail the circumstances in which he spoke on the resolution about 'direct action'. Considerable excitement had been created by the recital of alleged Muslim grievances in the

Congress provinces, particularly the United Provinces, Bihar and the Central Provinces, and a speaker from the United Provinces had taunted the Muslims in the majority provinces (the Punjab and Bengal) with not having given any proof of their sympathy with their co-religionists elsewhere. Jinnah then sent down a note to Sikander, saying that he thought Sikander had better speak on this point and accordingly he intervened in the debate, which he had not intended to do. He does not admit that he said that he accepted the view that the grievances and complaints of the Muslims in Congress provinces were fully justified, as was stated in paragraph 7 of your letter to the Viceroy. In fact he says that he began his speech by referring to the convention set up by himself that Ministers of one Province should not criticise the action of other Ministries, but he appealed to the Congress Ministries to take immediate steps to rectify the alleged grievances *if they were genuine.*

5. I told Sikander that in your view the attack on the Congress Governments was not justified and asked him whether he thought that the grievances brought to notice at Patna were in fact genuine grievances. As regards this point, Sikander says that some very unpleasant stories were recited in the speeches made by delegates from the United Provinces and Bihar and particularly referred to a case in which a Muslim had bought beef for distribution to a marriage party and had been severely assaulted by the local Hindus and had pork forced into his mouth. It was admitted that the offenders had been prosecuted and convicted in this case, and Sikander claims that he pointed out in his speech that this being so, there was no case for blaming the Provincial Government. But in connection with the alleged grievances he mentioned three other points:

(*a*) a circular issued by a local Education Board or an Inspector of Schools in the Central Provinces, printed in Urdu and addressed to Madrissas (i.e. Muslim schools), directing that Gandhi's portrait should be worshipped on his birthday in all schools;

(*b*) allegations that subordinate officers and even some gazetted officers in Bihar did little to check acts of repression committed by Hindus on Muslims;

(*c*) He formed the impression from speeches by and talks with Bihar Muslims that there is a genuine feeling of pessimism and apprehension among them.

6. Sikander gave me one interesting piece of information, which he said I could convey to you in confidence, viz., that the Central Working Committee of the League have advised the Bihar Committee to make every

attempt to secure the redress of Muslim grievances by constitutional methods before starting anything in the nature of direct action. By "constitutional methods" I gather what was meant was deputations to the Ministers, then to the Governor and, if necessary, to the Governor-General, and if all these methods proved ineffective, the Local Committee is to report the result to the Working Committee of the League, who will then consider the matter further.

7. As regards the reference to the possibility of civil war by Sikander, he explained to me that what he said was that if these grievances were genuine and if no redress could be obtained, feelings between the two communities might be so exacerbated that there must be a danger of civil war.

8. I quite agree with you that passions may have been dangerously aroused by the Patna session of the League, but at the same time I do think that Sikander genuinely did what he could to exercise a moderating influence. The atmosphere was, however, clearly one of considerable tension and I am sure you realise, as well as I do, how easy it is in such conditions for the spirit of fanaticism to be aroused and how difficult it is to allay it.

You may perhaps be interested in a note recorded by me on the 10th of January (before I received your letter) of an interview with Nawabzada Khurshid Ali Khan, a member of the Council of State and a strong supporter of Sikander's, who formed one of Sikander's party at Patna.

Yours sincerely,
H.D. CRAIK

ENCLOSURE TO NO. 72

NOTE BY CRAIK

January 10th, 1939

Nawabzada Khurshid Ali Khan:

He gave me some interesting information about the recent Muslim League meeting at Patna, where he said Sikander was a very strong moderating influence. In the public proceedings Sikander trounced Barkat Ali, M.L.A., as a traitor with considerable effect; and later in the Working Committee Jinnah 'ticked' off Barkat Ali with great severity and said he would expel him from the League if he did not accept Sikander loyally as his leader. Barkat Ali apologized profusely and since his return to Lahore has attended a meeting of Muslim Members of the Unionist Party at the Premier's house and again expressed abject contrition. I gather the Premier accepted his apologies, but he is very much suspected by most of the Unionist Party, as is also Nurullah.

At Patna Sikander told Jinnah quite plainly that he could not tolerate constant interference by the Muslim League in purely Punjab affairs or resolutions condemning Sikander's public pronouncements. There was some plain talking on this question and Sikander made it quite clear that the strength of the League depended mainly on the support it received from the Punjab, which had the only stable Muslim Government in India. Khurshid Ali Khan felt that this plain speaking had cleared the air to a considerable extent.

As regards the allegations made at Patna concerning acts of repression by the Congress governments in the U.P. and Bihar against Muslims, Khurshid Ali Khan said they mostly related to such things as the prohibition of kine slaughter, stoppage of the Azan, etc. Certain gross acts of repression were also alleged, but were possibly considerably exaggerated.

73

CRAIK TO LINLITHGOW

Private and Personal

Government House, Lahore,
January 12th, 1939

Dear Lord Linlithgow,

Very many thanks for your private and personal letter of the 4th of January, in which you told me about your talk with Sikander in Calcutta.

I think you will be interested to know that although the communiqué about the Nowshera tragedy[5] duly appeared on January the 5th, there has been absolutely no Press comment about it in any newspaper that has come to my notice. I asked Sikander last night whether he had seen any comments and he replied in the negative. I also asked whether there had been any local reactions, i.e. in the district from which the two Muslim Companies are recruited. He said he had heard of none, but he believed that the men of these two Companies had not yet actually been paid off and returned to their homes. So far as his own district (Attock) is concerned, he mentioned that one of the Indian officers murdered was a Khattar (Sikander's own tribe) of a well-known and respected family, and he thought that this fact would alienate popular sympathy from those suspected of any complicity in the murders.

I think the fact that there has been no comment in the Press on the communiqué is a matter for satisfaction, and I have little doubt that if the communiqué had been published as originally drafted, it would have given rise to considerable controversy.

As regards Sikander's attitude at the Patna session of the Muslim League, you will by now have received Hallett's account of this session, a copy of which he sent to me under a covering letter of the 7th of January.[6] I think you will be interested in my reply to Hallett, of which I enclose a copy.[7]

I am very glad that you gave Sikander a hint as to the necessity of mingling caution with politics in a rather larger degree, and I am sure that he will take the hint. At the same time, I have no doubt, both from my talks with Sikander himself and from what others have told me, that although he may have been somewhat carried away by the excitement engendered at the session, he was on the whole able to exercise a strong moderating influence.

Yours sincerely,
H.D. CRAIK

74

CRAIK TO LINLITHGOW

Private and Personal
D.-O. No. 113-F.L.

Camp, Jullundur,
January 15th, 1939

Dear Lord Linlithgow,

I am afraid my letter this fortnight is a little late, but I have only just received the provincial fortnightly report (which I enclose), as its preparation was somewhat delayed by the Christmas holidays. I have not much to add to it.

2. Our main anxiety at present is the prolonged drought. Over by far the greatest part of the Province there has been no rain whatever since the premature cessation of the monsoon, and the outlook is now most grave, not only in the famine districts, but over the whole unirrigated area of the Province. Unless rain falls within the next ten days or so the *rabi* harvest will, I fear, be an extremely bad one.

As regards the famine-stricken areas, I think Your Excellency may be interested in the enclosed note of the 7th of January,[8] written by Dobson, the Financial Commissioner, who has recently spent some days in Hissar. It is on the whole quite satisfactory as regards the efficacy of the measures of relief that have been taken. I am, as I told you, hoping to visit Hissar and Gurgaon during my present tour, and I also hope to have an opportunity of speaking to Guthrie Russell or some other Member of the Railway Board regarding the difficulty of obtaining sufficient wagons for the transport of fodder, to which Dobson has alluded in paragraph IV of his report.

3. There have been no further developments as regards Congress agitation against the States, but I found that the Maharaja of Kapurthala, with whom I have just been spending two days at his capital, is distinctly nervous regarding the effects of a meeting announced to be held in Ludhiana early in February of States' subjects from all over India. It has been stated that Pandit Jawaharlal Nehru has accepted an invitation to preside at this meeting and if he does come, it is certain to be a large one and to be made the occasion of a good deal of wild speaking. I do not think the people of Kapurthala have any particular grievance, as the general pitch of the land revenue there is, I believe, little, if at all, heavier than that in the adjoining British districts, and the Ruler's 'civil list' is drawn almost entirely from his Oudh estates and not from the revenues of the State. But the Tikka Sahib of Kapurthala told me that he had some conversation on his voyage out to India with Pandit Jawaharlal Nehru, who was travelling in the same ship and who was a contemporary of the Tikka's at Harrow. Jawaharlal attacked the Tikka Sahib, because his father employs as Chief Minister an Englishman (Sir John Coldstream, a retired Indian Civil Service Judge of the Lahore High Court) and said that the Ruler should get rid of him at once. Coldstream is, I believe, in any case leaving the State service at the end of this year.

4. A special session of the Legislative Assembly commenced on January the 9th with the object of completing the passage of the Marketing Bill. The opening days were marked by scenes of disorder and rowdyism, which are all too common in the Punjab Assembly, but the Premier succeeded in passing a motion appropriating all private members' days for Government business and also a second motion prolonging the daily sitting an hour or two beyond the usual time. Hitherto, however, comparatively little progress has been made with the Bill, which is the only business of the session, considerable time being wasted every day over adjournment motions. The Speaker, Sir Shahab-ud-Din, has not sufficiently recovered from a recent attack of influenza to preside and the Chair has been occupied by the Deputy Speaker, Sardar Dasaundha Singh, who, so far as I can gather, has done pretty well in a position of great difficulty.

5. I have just seen a telegram, reporting what seems to have been a really bad business in the New Central Jail at Multan. The telegram runs:

'Two prisoners who offered resistance succumbed to multiple injuries last night. Detailed report follows.'

I have heard no further details, but the inference one naturally draws is that the two prisoners were 'beaten up' by the Jail staff. I believe notice has been given of an adjournment motion regarding this incident.

6. In writing to Your Excellency on January the 12th I said that there had been no Press comment regarding the Nowshera tragedy. I have since seen one article in a Lahore *Hindu* paper, but it merely repeated the gist of the communiqué and added something to the effect that the rumour that certain men had been shot by way of punishment was false. There was no editorial comment.

7. Sir Firoz Khan Noon, the High Commissioner, arrived in Lahore on leave early this month, and I understand he had a great ovation at the railway station from his friends, including all the Ministers. He spent a day or two in Lahore and came to lunch with me, when he was in high spirits and very pleased with life. I received information that some of the local Congress and Ahrar leaders contemplated approaching him and trying to induce him to cause dissension in the ranks of the Unionist Party, the inducement to be offered being the Premiership for Firoz! I doubt whether any approach to him was actually made, but I feel confident that if these intriguers do approach him with any such suggestion, they will receive a first class 'raspberry'. There was at one time a certain amount of jealousy between Sikander and Firoz, but I believe that is entirely a thing of the past and that Firoz and his family are now loyal supporters of Sikander's Ministry.

Yours sincerely,
H.D. CRAIK

75

CRAIK TO LINLITHGOW

Government House, Lahore,
January 20th, 1939

Dear Lord Linlithgow,

With my letter of January the 12th I enclosed a copy of a letter I had sent to Hallett about Sikander's attitude and utterances at the Patna Session of the Muslim League. I think you may be interested to see the reply I have received from Hallett, and I enclose a copy of it herewith.

Since my return from tour this morning, I have shown Hallett's letter to Sikander, who, I think, was very pleased with its cordial tone and is glad that any misapprehensions that Hallett may have entertained regarding his attitude at the Session have been cleared up.

Yours sincerely,
H.D. CRAIK

ENCLOSURE TO NO. 75

HALLETT TO CRAIK

Camp,
January 15th, 1939

My dear Craik,

I am most grateful to you for your reply to my letter of 7th January 1939, No. 32-G.B., about the Muslim League Session. I am very glad that you told Sikander of what I had said: I am still more glad that he has been equally frank in his reply. I am writing this in Camp, so have not to hand a copy of my letter, but I hope I did not convey the impression that I resented or was distrustful of the action that he has taken. I realised, even before I received your letter, that he had been put in an extremely difficult position at the Session and I agree that his claim that he exercised a moderating influence on the extremists is entirely true. He was, I think, particularly helpful over the 'direct action' resolution, and it is very satisfactory for me to get the information given in paragraph 6 of your letter that the League contemplate constitutional action in the first instance.

2. I was interested to get Sikander's account of the 'atrocities'. Of the three points mentioned by you in paragraph 5, (*a*) concerns the Central Provinces. I have not myself seen any indication of (*b*), but some of my Muslim friends here have put the matter in much the same way as Sikander did and have told me that it is not so much what Government have done as the fact that under the present Government, Hindus are encouraged to commit atrocities on Muslims; they have referred to the criminal case to which you refer, but as you and Sikander recognise Government did all that was possible in that case by prosecuting the accused, in spite of the fact that at an early stage a stupid police officer had tried to compromise it. In another recent case where some Muslim houses were burnt down by Hindus, Government gave money for rebuilding them, which I do not think we should have done in the old days. I will, however, watch and see

that officers do not take action hostile to Muslims, but, as you will recognise, there are cases when we must stop cow sacrifice and the policy in this respect followed by my Ministers is really the same as we adopted in the old days. I shall feel happier when the Id is over.

3. I hope you will assure Sikander that I am most grateful to him for the action which he took at the Session and for the information which he has given me. I feel sure that his action improved the situation. Again with best thanks for your letter.

Yours sincerely,
M. G. HALLETT

76

CRAIK TO LINLITHGOW[9]

Private and Personal

Government House, Lahore,
January 26th, 1939

Dear Lord Linlithgow,

I have written to you today[10] fully regarding the Punjab Alienation of Land (Second Amendment) Bill, and have explained in detail why Sikander and the Ministry are not prepared to accept the amendments proposed by the Secretary of State.[11] But there is some further information which I think I ought to give you privately. Sikander told me that from a political point of view he would not particularly mind if the Secretary of State continued to oppose the Bill, although this.would mean the resignation of the Ministry, which would presumably be followed by the dissolution of the Assembly, as no alternative Ministry could command its confidence, and a general election. This sequence of events would, in Sikander's view, have the effect of rallying his party both in the Assembly and in the constituencies. He and his colleagues would take a firm line and gain considerable credit by representing themselves as sticking to their guns and boldly refusing to accept dictation from Whitehall. I mentioned in my letter No. 96 of the 15th of October 1938 to Brabourne that there was some suspicion that Mohan Singh might be influencing the Secretary of State. Sikander told me that he had definite information that the opponents of the Bill had approached Mohan Singh. If the Bill were turned down, considerable capital would, of course, be made out of this.

2. I have no doubt in my own mind that a campaign on these lines would have most unfortunate consequences. It would of course enormously

exacerbate the conflict between the rural and urban interests, quite apart from the political difficulties with which it would confront us and the exultation which it would create in Congress circles all over India. It is not necessary for me to emphasize how very unjudicious it would be to precipitate anything of this kind, especially when no important principle is at stake.

3. I confess I cannot understand what is troubling the Secretary of State. As Sikander put it, 'having swallowed a camel (the Restitution of Mortgaged Lands Bill) he is straining at a gnat'.[12]

Yours sincerely,
H.D. CRAIK

77

CRAIK TO LINLITHGOW

Government House, Lahore,
D.-O. No. 114-F.L. *January 26th/27th, 1939*

Dear Lord Linlithgow,

In paragraph 7 of Your Excellency's letter to me of the 4th of January you said you were looking forward with interest to receiving my impressions of the famine areas when I visited them. During the course of a tour which I completed a few days ago I visited Hissar, which is the district worst affected by famine, and Gurgaon, a considerable part of which is similarly affected. I did not go to Rohtak on this tour, as I had paid a short visit there in October.

2. I inspected one of the 25 relief works in the Hissar district at a place called Agroha, some 15 miles from district headquarters. The attendance there on the day of my visit was about 6,000 including dependents, and there were actually a number of new arrivals on the day in question who were waiting to be allotted to gangs. The labour is employed in the construction of a road from Agroha to Adampur, where there is a railway station and a market, a distance of about 7 miles. The people at work were of all classes and included a considerable number of peasant proprietors, both Hindu and Muhammedan, but a much larger proportion of menials. The rates of pay are 2 annas a day per man and 1 anna a day for old men and women, and children unable to work are, I think, allowed half an anna. I was able to make a fairly close inspection of the majority of the

people and paid particular attention to the state of the women and children. Speaking generally, the appearance of the people was good and their bearing alert and cheerful. There was no sickness of any sort except that a few of the children were suffering from colds. I saw no cases of obvious under-nutrition and only a small proportion of the children were insufficiently clad. Warm clothing will be provided for these out of the Charitable Relief Fund. It was noticeable that many of the women were wearing silver bangles, both on wrists and ankles, as well as silver ornaments on their heads and breasts.

Only a few of the people stay on the work for the night most of them returning to their villages. In some cases it was said that they came from a distance of 9 or 10 miles. Only the small permanent staff in charge of the camp remain there at night. This particular work had only been started about a fortnight before my visit and the staff in charge had hardly yet settled down. The whole thing is run by a Christian Naib Tahsildar candidate with a clerk in charge of each gang, which number from 300 to 400, and a few Chaukidars. A Public Works Overseer is responsible for the technical side of the road construction, which is of the simplest nature, but the Naib Tahsildar candidate is responsible for everything else, viz., sanitation, the supply of drinking water, the daily payment of wages, the distribution and collection of implements, &c. This is a heavy responsibility for a very junior officer, but the people are tractable and no trouble of any kind had occurred or was expected. There is ordinarily only one Police constable at each such camp.

I walked slowly down the greater part of the completed road with the gangs of workers and dependents drawn up on each side. There was every opportunity for anybody who wished to make a complaint or to represent a grievance to come forward, but actually only two or three did so. One or two men said the daily wage was not high enough, but this is certainly not true with grain at its present price. One explained the difficulty of bringing small children daily to the camp from considerable distances in order that they may receive the dependents' allowances; but arrangements are being made which should render this unnecessary in many cases, e.g. in the case of children attending school the teacher's certificate that they have attended the school will be accepted, provided that they come to the camp once a week.

As I have already stated, there was no sickness, but a District Board dispensary is within a hundred yards of the camp.

3. I also visited the cattle concentration camp close to Hissar itself. Here there are collected between 4,000 and 5,000 cows and heifers bought

by Government at an average price of somewhere about Rs. 7 a head and selected as suitable eventually for breeding purposes. Each animal bought is marked (not branded) with the number: the seller's name is recorded in a register and the seller is given a voucher entitling him to buy the animal back from Government when he can afford to do so. This scheme was started only a few weeks ago with the object of preserving the famous Hariana breed. The Superintendent of the Civil Veterinary Department,[13] whose officers were responsible for the purchase of the animals, assured me that they had on the whole improved in condition since they came there a week or two before my visit. The site is well-chosen and excellent stabling of a simple character, but on a good plan, has been erected quickly and cheaply. I am satisfied that this scheme is working well and it reflects great credit on the local officers. The people fully appreciate its object and advantages.

As regards the condition of cattle generally in the famine areas, I took the opportunity of going round the 'home farm' of the Hissar Cattle Farm. All the cattle I saw there were in good or at any rate fair condition. In every very dry year there is, of course, some falling off in condition, but none that I saw looked debilitated or really poor. The majority are still turned out daily in what is called the Bir, i.e. the farm grazing grounds, and roam over considerable distances in search of anything to eat: so their condition is harder and finer than that of stall-fed animals. The small reserves of fodder at the Farm had been completely exhausted and it now depends entirely on fodder imported from elsewhere. The officers in charge of the Farm have for years been begging to be allowed to build up really big reserves of fodder in good years, but the Minister concerned has, with regrettable lack of foresight, not allowed them to do so on financial grounds.

I had expected to see many emaciated or even starving cattle during my tour in these two districts, but was agreeably surprised to find most of those I saw, whether returning from grazing or working in carts or on the wells, in pretty fair condition. I was particularly struck with this in Gurgaon, where I did not see a single animal that showed signs of privation.

4. I also inspected one of the fodder dumps run by a contractor adjoining the Hissar railway station and watched the working of the system for the distribution of fodder to individuals. The organisation so far as the local Government is responsible, seems to be working well, but the contractor complained of great delays in deliveries by the various Railways owing to shortage of wagons and pilfering and corruption on the part of railway subordinates. These complaints were fully endorsed by the District Officers at Hissar and Gurgaon and by our Fodder Adviser[14] (a very senior and

reliable Indian officer of thc Agricultural Department), who is responsible for the whole arrangements for the importation of fodder into the famine-affected districts. This officer supplied me with a long and detailed note on this subject, and I had a full discussion at Delhi with Hawkes, the Member of the Railway Board responsible for transportation. His attitude was helpful and sympathetic and I trust that there will soon be a considerable improvement. But I am afraid there is no doubt that corruption is terribly rife among the railway subordinates.

5. I gave as many interviews as time permitted during my visit to Hissar and was able to see a large number of leading non-officials. I was much impressed by the unanimity with which they praised the arrangements made by Government for famine relief, for which they are, I think, really grateful. All of them admitted that there was nothing more that could be done and all of them spoke in the highest terms of the Deputy Commissioner (Brander) and his Assistant (Bryan), the two officers to whom I referred in paragraph 5 of my letter No. 109 -F.L. of the 24th of December 1938.

In Gurgaon, where the famine is more partial and on the whole less severe than in Hissar, I did not find quite the same gratitude or approval. In fact, some of those to whom I granted interviews were inclined to grumble and one rural notable alleged that people were dying of starvation. I told him flatly that I did not believe this and he then said that the deaths were due to pneumonia caused by cold and insufficient nutrition. I have had enquiries made into this and believe that his statement is grossly exaggerated, if not completely false. I am afraid, however, that there is not the same confidence in Gurgaon in the good intentions of Government or in the capacity of the District Officers. The Deputy Commissioner of Gurgaon[15] is an Indian member of thc I.C.S., a Kashmiri Pandit with plenty of brains, but I am afraid he has not yet fully established himself in the confidence of his district. I wish I could send an English officer to the district, but unfortunately there is none available.

On the whole, however, I am satisfied that the situation is being adequately tackled in Gurgaon and that everything possible is in fact being done.

6. I had not seen a famine relief work since my first winter in the country in 1899-1900, when there was a very severe famine over much the same area. My recollections of visiting a relief work in what was then part of the Delhi district are naturally somewhat vague after an interval of about 39 years, so I cannot really compare the conditions then existing with those on our present relief works. But I am confident that on the present occasion we have at any rate tackled the problem in good time, i.e. before

the morale of the people had begun to decline. There are many anxious months still ahead, more particularly as we must now face the probability that the winter rains may fail; but I have at any rate the satisfactory feeling that we have made a good start and that everybody concerned, from the Ministers down to the local officers, is doing his best.[16]

Yours sincerely,
H.D. CRAIK

78

CRAIK TO LINLITHGOW

Private and Personal
D.-O. No. 116-F.L.

Government House, Lahore,
January 27th, 1939

Dear Lord Linlithgow,

The Legislative Assembly session terminated on the 24th of January, the Government having succeeded in passing the Marketing Bill through its second and third readings. The debates on this Bill were prolonged and bitter, but the Government was never in any danger of being defeated. As the result of the disorderly scenes that marked the opening days of the session, when there was deliberate defiance of the Chair, the Premier introduced a Bill for the appointment of [a] Sergeant-at-arms, with deputies if necessary, who will be entrusted with the duty of seeing that the Speaker's orders are obeyed. This Bill too was strongly opposed, but the motion for its reference to a Select Committee was passed.

2. There have been some disquieting secessions in the ranks of the Unionist Party. In paragraph 2 of my letter No. 106-F.L. of December the 8th I mentioned that a member of the Unionist Party, during the course of a discussion on a non-official resolution urging that the charges for canal water should be reduced by 50 per cent., moved an amendment suggesting a 25 per cent. reduction and admitted in the course of his speech that in doing so he was acting contrary to the instructions of his leader, but under pressure from his constituents. The member in question was Mian Nurullah who represents the Lyallpur Constituency. He has now announced that he has resigned from the Unionist Party and will in future sit as an independent Kisan representative. Sikander, on the other hand, states that in reality he has been expelled from the party. So far as I have been able to ascertain the truth is that Sikander had decided to expel him and had issued verbal instructions to the Party Secretariat for a letter to be issued in this sense.

Mian Nurullah came to hear of this and immediately put in his written resignation.

It was also announced that two other members of the same tribe (Arain) as Nurullah, one from Jullundur and one from Sheikhupura, had also resigned from the party, but after this announcement these two members continued to occupy their seats on the Unionist benches and in two divisions on the final day of the session voted with the Government. Sikander does not consider that they have really left his party.

Yet a fourth secession of Chaudhri Ranpat Singh, a member of Sir Chhotu Ram's group, was also announced in the papers. I enclose the announcement[17] that appeared in the *Daily Herald* of the 25th of January and the contradiction[18] that appeared in the *Civil & Military Gazette* of the same date. I understand that this member has had a private quarrel of some kind with Sir Chhotu Ram, but Sikander assures me that he has not really left the Unionist Party at all and that the statement published in the *Daily Herald* was drawn up for him by some member of the Congress party.

3. It is obviously a very troublesome and harassing position to be the leader of a party whose members behave in this irresponsible way. Sikander told me that after the final sitting of the Assembly, which lasted from noon till 10 p.m., he had to preside at a party meeting which did not break up till 1 a.m. Practically the whole of the three hours' discussion was occupied by members of the party who had private grievances to exploit. It must be remembered that most of the members of the Assembly have spent very considerable sums in securing their election and most of them expect some material advantage for themselves in return for this expenditure, e.g. an appointment as Sub-Registrar or Honorary Magistrate or a post in Government service for a relation. It is quite impossible to fulfil all these expectations, but those who consider themselves slighted are inclined to give the leader a lot of trouble. I am afraid the strain is beginning to tell somewhat on Sikander himself. In conversation with me the other day he complained that throughout the session he had been working for 14 hours daily and even so cannot keep abreast with current administrative work and has practically no time at all to think. One of his principal vexations is the continual complaints and grievances brought to him by members of his own party, and he represented that he very much needed the services of a competent Private Secretary, who should in his opinion be a British member of the Indian Civil Service of comparatively senior standing, partly to interview members of his party, but mainly, I gather, to help him in conducting demi-official and personal correspondence. The Parliamentary

Secretaries are not qualified to draft important letters of this type, nor does an interview with a Parliamentary Secretary satisfy a member who wishes to represent a grievance to the Premier. I should like very much to meet Sikander's wishes in this matter, though it will be extremely difficult to find an officer of the right type and standing: but before I agree to such an arrangement, I should be grateful for Your Excellency's advice whether it would be proper to employ an Indian Civil Service officer on duties of this kind.[19] My own view is that on the analogy of the permanent civil servants employed as Cabinet Ministers' Private Secretaries at Home there would be no impropriety.

4. Another point which Sikander made in the course of conversation was that many of his difficulties were caused by failure on the part of permanent officials to realize fully the implications of the recent constitutional changes. Indeed, he spoke with a bitterness quite unusual for him on this subject. He said that though he had done everything he could to maintain the prestige of Government officers, he still felt that many of them, and particularly the more senior, resent what they regard as undue interference by the Ministers and do not make allowances for the obligations arising out of the system of party Government. Over and over again he found that difficulties had been created by local officers either being rude to his supporters or even refusing to see them, or by indiscretions such as speaking slightingly of Ministers in the course of casual conversation, or by curtly turning down requests made to them by the Ministry's supporters and referring them to the Ministers themselves. He gave me several actual instances of the kind of thing of which he complained, of which I will give one illustration. In one of the districts of the Rawalpindi Division some local notables approached the Commissioner[20] and represented that their district was suffering severely from scarcity owing to the failure of the rains, but that no relief measures had been taken commensurate with those taken in the south-eastern Punjab. The Commissioner's reply was something to the following effect:

> 'Well, you see the south-eastern Punjab has a very strong Minister to champion its cause in the Cabinet (i.e. Sir Chhotu Ram). Why don't you bring pressure to bear on your own Minister to take similar action for your relief?'

The result of this was that about 40 of these people came by train to Lahore and waited in deputation on Khizar Hayat Khan, who comes from that part of the world. This was naturally an embarrassing incident during the course of a heavy Assembly session and obviously calculated to cause some discredit to the Ministry. Sikander also quoted several actual instances of rudeness on the part of local officers or refusal to accord an interview to a local M.L.A. Most of these instances referred to British officers, but he also said that he was conscious that there was a certain type of Hindu Government officer who was secretly in sympathy with the Congress and who did everything possible to embarrass or discredit the Ministry.

I am afraid there is a good deal of substance in these complaints. The introduction of the Reforms has in fact made so little outward change in the Punjab, especially as regards the position of local officers, that I think they are apt to forget the implications of the introduction of a democratic form of government, and I have myself heard of behaviour by certain officers which supports this view. I told Sikander that I realised his difficulties and was anxious to do anything I could to remove them. I doubt if a confidential circular from the Chief Secretary would meet the case. It would probably be better for me to call a conference of Commissioners to discuss these matters with a view to devising means by which officers can be induced to use more discretion in their dealings with the local supporters of the Ministry. As regards the alleged manoeuvres of Hindu officers with the deliberate intention of discrediting the Ministry, Sikander admitted that he could suggest no remedy, the methods employed being so subtle as to defy detection.

5. In paragraph 5 of my letter No. 113-F.L. of January the 15th, I mentioned a report about two prisoners in the New Central Jail at Multan, who had succumbed to their injuries after what appeared to be a 'beating up' by the Jail staff. Both a magisterial inquest and a departmental enquiry into this incident have now been held and the reports leave little doubt that these two prisoners and certain others were deliberately beaten in a most brutal manner by some jail warders and convict officials acting under the orders of a Deputy Superintendent of the Jail. The convicts' offence was that they refused to perform their allotted tasks and were violent and abusive. The persons *prima facie* responsible have been suspended and a police investigation is now proceeding. In all probability the Deputy Superintendent and perhaps one or two Assistant Superintendents as well as certain warders will be tried for manslaughter. The incident has brought to light a lamentable state of discipline in this particular Jail.

6. I have recently agreed to the premature release of certain 'political' prisoners of the terrorist type, in most cases on grounds of health. I enclose a note[21] which gives details of the 8 prisoners in question. In all cases they had served a very substantial portion of their sentences and in all cases the C.I.D., who were consulted, agreed to the releases.

7. The state of communal feeling as reflected in the Press and in certain minor incidents that have recently occurred in different places has, I fear, somewhat deteriorated of late, though I am glad to say we had no trouble on 'Hyderabad Day', which was the cause of serious communal rioting in Delhi and Bareilly. One or two small meetings to celebrate this 'Day' were held in the Punjab including one at Lahore, but I do not think that any processions were taken out. In this connection I think I should mention that Sikander expressed the view in conversation with me yesterday that communal tension will go on increasing till the issue of Federation is settled.

8. Sikander unfolded to me the other day and asked me to consult Your Excellency about a plan he has in mind for the formation of a corps of social service volunteers; but this letter is already, I fear, unduly long and I think it would be better to refer this matter in a separate letter, especially as Sikander promised to let me have a written note on the subject, which I am still awaiting.

9. I enclose the provincial fortnightly report for the first half of January.

Yours sincerely,
H.D. CRAIK

79

CRAIK TO LINLITHGOW

Private and Personal
D.-O. No. 123-F.L.

Government House, Lahore,
February 9th, 1939

Dear Lord Linlithgow,

I have just returned from a short visit to two of our colony districts, Montgomery and Lyallpur. At both places I had a crowded programme and received a very warm welcome. At Montgomery I was particularly struck by the cheerful demeanour and keenness of the horse-breeding peasant grantees, some hundreds of whom I met in an informal way at the local race meeting. These races are all for 3 year old fillies, which will be covered next month. They are most admirably managed by the District Remount Officer and the professional element is entirely excluded. Nor are there any facilities for betting except a Re. 1 totalizator. They are evidently very popular, as enormous crowds attended and the keenness of competition between the different breeders was most striking. The system of bound horse-breeding in this colony is most successful, and it will be a great pity if the process of mechanization means its abandonment or reduction.

The Deputy Commissioners of both these districts[22] are comparatively junior Indian officers of the Indian Civil Service, both men of character and capacity, and I was very favourably impressed with the way in which they are running their districts and the respect and admiration which they seem to command among the leading men. Both originally come from the Bombay Presidency, and I believe that a considerable measure of their success is due to the fact that they have no local connections in the Punjab and are therefore immune from the illicit influence which relations are apt to exercise.

2. We were fortunate in that the Bakr-Id festival on February the 1st, passed off without communal disturbance. I rather anticipated that there might be some trouble on this occasion. There was a communal riot of an unusual type on one of the famine relief works in the Hissar district on the 28th of January, in the course of which three Muhammadans and one Hindu were killed. The origin of the fight is somewhat obscure, but it appears to have arisen out of old standing enmity between labourers from a Muhammadan and those from a Sikh village. There was apparently no grievance on the part of the workers against those in charge of the relief works, though in the scuffle a small sum of money intended for the payment of wages was stolen. A magisterial enquiry is proceeding. Meanwhile the Deputy Commissioner has wisely closed down this particular relief work.

3. I have nothing new to report about the famine-stricken areas except that Congress organizations in Hissar are causing some embarrassment to the local officers by urging the people to demand more widely extended relief measures (which are not in fact necessary or practicable) and for enhancement of the daily wages paid to labourers on the relief works, which would not be justified with grain at its present prices.

4. In paragraph 3 of my letter to you No. 113-F.L. of January the 15th I mentioned that the Maharaja of Kapurthala had shown himself in conversation with me somewhat nervous about a meeting of the All-India States Peoples' Conference that is to be held at Ludhiana under the presidency of Pandit Jawaharlal Nehru in February. The date of this meeting is now announced as the 15th to the 17th of February. Wilberforce-Bell recently wrote to the Chief Secretary to the Punjab Government, asking whether the local Government would agree to proscribe this meeting on the ground that it is likely to cause disaffection and disturbance of the public tranquillity or rioting in one or more of the Punjab States. He suggested that Section 5 of the Indian States (Protection) Act of 1934

could be used for this purpose. As the result of a discussion between the Premier and myself the reply, a copy[23] of which I enclose, was sent by the Chief Secretary to the Resident. I have no doubt whatever in my mind that the line taken in this reply is the right one and that it would have been a serious tactical error to proscribe the Conference, much as I regret that it is to be held in the Punjab. It is possible that one result of the Conference may be to start an agitation against the authorities in one or more of our Punjab States, but the Congress in the Punjab is so weak and so rent by internal dissensions that I doubt whether it would be able to put any real drive into such an agitation.

5. While on the subject of the States I may mention that the young Maharaja of Patiala paid a visit to Lahore the other day during my absence on tour. The principal function he attended was one organised by the Managing Committee of the Sikh National College, an institution recently started in Lahore, which has secured affiliation to the Punjab University. The Maharaja announced a donation to the funds of this institution of Rs. 2 lakhs. I rather regret that he should have done this, as the institution is entirely controlled by Akali Sikhs of extremist views, who founded it with the express intention of making it a rival of the Khalsa College at Amritsar. Appointments have been found on the staff for some of the Khalsa College professors, who had been recently dismissed for grave acts of insubordination. The Khalsa College is an institution of old standing and the leading Sikh College in the Province. It is the particular 'child' of my Revenue Minister, Sir Sunder Singh Majithia, who has for more than 30 years been its leading spirit and is the Chairman of the Managing Body. I am afraid the Minister will be deeply pained at the Maharaja's donation to the rival college.

Sikander also told me that the Maharaja after leaving Lahore paid a visit to Ludhiana, where apparently the local Sikhs had invited him. The Premier first heard of the Maharaja's visit to Ludhiana from the Deputy Commissioner,[24] who telephoned to Lahore, saying that there was some talk of the Maharaja having a hostile reception from extremist elements among the Sikhs. The Deputy Commissioner was instructed to do his best to prevent any such demonstration and as nothing has appeared in the Press about it, I gather he was successful in doing so.

The incident might, however, have been embarrassing and Sikander asked me to suggest to the Resident that Ruling Princes should, whenever they propose to attend any kind of public function in the Province, be asked as a matter of courtesy to inform the local Government in advance. I think this is a reasonable request, and I am passing it on to the Resident.

As you know, Sikander's elder brother, Sir Liaqat Hyat Khan, is Premier of Patiala, and Sikander in conversation with me hinted that his brother is finding his position one of growing difficulty whenever a Sikh-Muslim question is raised. A Sikh called Raghbir Singh, who holds some post in the Maharaja's entourage, is said to be exercising a bad influence over him.

6. In the course of this conversation Sikander told me that he was greatly distressed and puzzled at Jinnah's recent attitude in the Central Assembly, more particularly over the Naval Discipline Bill. He described Jinnah as 'absolutely rudderless' and as 'drifting aimlessly without a policy and making enemies everywhere'.

You may be interested to know that Sikander is visiting Delhi on the 12th and 13th of February on the invitation of Zafrulla, who wants him to speak to the Punjab Members of the Central Assembly about the Indo-British Trade Agreement. He will be staying at Western Court.

7. I passed on to Sikander in a general way the gist of your views on his wish to have a Service Private Secretary, as explained in paragraph 2 of your private and personal letter to me of the 6th of February. He again emphasized how greatly he needed relief, more particularly in his administrative work, and how little time he had for reflection. He added that he did not contemplate that his Private Secretary should be necessarily a British Indian Civil Service Officer (as he realises the difficulty of providing a suitable member of this Service), and he now has in mind a young Indian Officer of the Indian Police Service, whose tenure of an appointment in the Provincial C.I.D. is drawing to a close. The officer in question is a young Muslim named Ahmed,[25] by whose work I have been well impressed. He has written some excellent notes and should be capable of drafting important letters.

8. With reference to paragraph 6 of your letter to me of the 6th of February, Sikander has not yet let me have his note on the proposal to raise a corps of social service volunteers and he is so obviously overworked at present that I do not like to press him about it. I think, however, that I know fairly well what he has at the back of his mind, and I shall look forward to having a discussion on this matter with you when I come to stay with you next week.

9. A somewhat disturbing attempt at train wrecking was detected the other day at a station on the main North-Western Railway line between Jhelum and Rawalpindi. I have not the report at hand and cannot at the moment get hold of it, but, so far as I remember the details, the driver of a slow passenger or goods train felt a bump or series of bumps and pulled

up as quickly as he could. On examination it was found that fish plates had been removed from some rails, but the actual rails had not been taken away. Fortunately neither the engine nor any carriages were derailed. A police investigation is in progress, and I understand that our Police are in touch with the Bihar Police in order to verify whether there is any resemblance in the *modus operandi* of this attempt and that of the recent derailments in Bihar.

10. I enclose the Provincial Fortnightly Report for the second half of January.

Yours sincerely,
H.D. CRAIK

80

CRAIK TO LINLITHGOW

Private and Personal
D.-O. No. 124-F.L.

Government House, Lahore,
February 26th, 1939

Dear Lord Linlithgow,

I have seen you so recently that I have not very much to report this fortnight.

2. Since February the 16th there have been a series of good showers over the greater part of the Province, which will be of incalculable benefit. The amounts have of course varied very much from place to place, but the famine areas have received their share. In Hissar the total rainfall within the last ten days has amounted to somewhere about 2 inches and this should do much good to what little *rabi* crops have been sown (these are practically all on irrigated lands). It must also, I fancy, provide a certain amount of natural grazing for cattle and should thus enable us to reduce to some extent our heavy expenditure on the importation of fodder. Whether it will lead to a falling off in the attendance at the relief works remains to be seen, but in any case this long-delayed rainfall should put heart into the people.

3. I have just seen the first forecast of the present wheat crop and the figures are interesting as showing how greatly sowings were restricted owing to the early failure of last year's monsoon. The estimated acreage of the present crop in round figures is only 8,300,000 as compared with 9,940,000 acres last year, and a quinquennial average of roughly 9¼ million acres. The condition of the standing crops is estimated at 85 per cent of the normal.

4. The Budget session of the Legislative Assembly opens tomorrow and is expected to last till at least the middle of April. The budget will be

presented on the 28th of February and will, I fear, show a deficit both on this year's working and in the forecast for next year. But the deficit will be covered partly by the quite legitimate device of taking our 'Extraordinary Receipts' into the Revenue Account as a temporary measure, partly by strict economy and to a small extent by the imposition of taxation on the sales of petrol and lubricating oil. A Bill for the latter proposal will be submitted to the Assembly early in the session. I have not yet seen the Finance Minister's Budget speech, but I have seen the Budget Memorandum, which will be circulated with it. The Memorandum makes it clear that Provincial finances are but for the famine in a sound condition. I understand that the Finance Minister will emphasise this point in his speech.

My Ministers are committed by a public announcement, made shortly after their assumption of office, to introducing prohibition as an experimental measure in certain areas, and I think their intention was to try the experiment in one selected district in each Commissioner's Division. No actual steps have, however, hitherto been taken to implement this undertaking, and the Ministers have now decided that owing to the set-back to Provincial finances caused by the famine, the experiment will have to be postponed indefinitely. The Ministers made it quite clear to me during the discussion which resulted in this decision that none of them are in the least enamoured of prohibition in theory. In fact, I think they all regard it as nothing but a 'stunt'.

5. In addition to the Budget and the Bill for taxing sales of petrol and lubricating oil, the principal Government measure to be laid before the Assembly is the Bill to provide for the appointment of a Sergeant-at-Arms. The Select Committee has already reported on this Bill, which will, I am afraid, give rise to bitter and protracted opposition, and I understand that notice has already been received of hundreds of amendments.

6. I have recently received for my assent the Marketing Bill, which was passed at the last session, and on a careful examination of this measure I see no reason why I should not give my assent to it. I am, however, not conveying my formal assent at the moment, as the Premier thinks it would be better that this should not be announced till a comparatively late stage in the approaching session.

7. The All-India States Peoples' Conference was held at Ludhiana from the 15th to 17th February and you have doubtless seen reports of the proceedings. I had informed you in paragraph 4 of my letter of the 9th February that as a result of discussion between Sikander and myself it had been decided not to proscribe this Conference, although the Resident had requested us to do so. I think events have justified our decision. As was

anticipated, nothing new was said or done at the Conference, and no definite line of action was decided upon. The resolutions passed were, for the most part, vague and couched in general terms. One or two obscure speakers endeavoured to give prominence to alleged grievances of the subjects of the Punjab States, but Jawaharlal Nehru cut them short and emphasised that the Conference was not concerned with the Punjab States in particular but with the problems of the Indian States in general. His own speech was long, academic and somewhat dull. Altogether the Conference seems to have fallen rather flat. Jawaharlal's presence no doubt acted as a draw, and perhaps as many as twelve thousand people attended the first sitting, but the numbers tended to dwindle both owing to the inclemency of the weather and to the fact that the proceedings were in English and most of the speakers from outside the Punjab could not speak Urdu well. Several prominent Punjab extremist politicians, most of them Sikhs, were present. It does not seem that the Conference has been or is likely to be the cause of any particular embarrassment to the Punjab States.

8. In paragraph 9 of my letter No. 123-F.L. of the 9th of February I mentioned a recent attempt at train wrecking on the main line of the N.-W. Railway between Jhelum and Rawalpindi. I have heard no more about this incident, but another somewhat disturbing incident has been reported to me. On the 5th of February a box containing 44 live Nobel High Explosive detonators was found by a watchman in a cavity of a girder about the centre of the railway bridge over the Attock at Kalabagh (which is, of course, strategically of great importance). There is a public foot-path across this bridge alongside the railway line and the box could have been deposited at the place where it was found by anyone walking along this foot-path. There was no fuse in the box and the C.I.D. are not satisfied that it was placed there as an attempt to damage the bridge. It seems more probable that the detonators had been stolen and that the thief had placed them where they were found for purposes of concealment.

9. I think you may be interested to hear of a conversation which I had with Sir Jawala Prasad Srivastava a few weeks ago, which I did not mention at the time. He called on me at Lahore and told me that he was in a position to invest a large amount of capital in starting a textile mill and had come to the conclusion that in view of the greater prospects of stability in the Punjab as compared to most other Provinces he had better locate his mill in the Punjab; and he asked my advice as to a suitable site and also as to the names of Punjabis who would command confidence if appointed to the board of his new company. This is interesting as indicating a tendency on the part of capital to seek an outlet in the Punjab in preference to other

Provinces. As you are doubtless aware, Lala Sri Ram of Delhi started a few years ago a very large textile factory in Lyallpur. I inspected this the other day and thought it a most prosperous concern. It employs between three and four thousand workmen, is running night and day and buys all its raw cotton from the Lyallpur district. Dalmia is building a cement factory at Khewra in the Jhelum district and Imperial Chemical Industries are also constructing a factory in the same neighbourhood. Yesterday Sikander told me that he had been approached by a Mr. Wilkinson of the Elgin Mills at Cawnpore, who had been a brother-officer in Sikander's regiment during the War and who has an idea of starting a branch of his firm somewhere in the Punjab. This tendency of capital to seek an outlet in the Punjab is not altogether surprising in view of the somewhat wild financial schemes of the Congress Governments, e.g. in the recent Bombay and the United Provinces budgets. It may mean in time a considerable industrial expansion in the Punjab and a decrease of unemployment. My Ministers are naturally anxious to do all they can to encourage this tendency.

10. At the same conversation, Sikander told me of his talks with Jinnah at Delhi. I gather he made it clear that he thought Jinnah had made a great mistake in opposing the Naval Discipline Bill and generally in joining with the Congress party in the Central Assembly in its opposition to Government. Sikander pointed out that the Muslim League party in the Assembly is now in a particularly strong position as on practically all questions it holds the balance; but under Jinnah's leadership (or lack of leadership) it had failed to make full use of its opportunities. Sikander, I gather, hoped that Jinnah in his conversations with you would give some kind of undertaking regarding Muslim co-operation with Government, which might eventually lead to a public announcement regarding a more friendly orientation of Muslim policy towards the British. I am afraid, however, that this is expecting rather too much from a man of Jinnah's temperament.

11. Sikander also told me that in conversation with members of the Muslim League party in the Central Assembly (and I think also at a meeting of the party) he had impressed on them the desirability of supporting the Indo-British Trade Agreement provided they received assurances from Zafrullah to the effect that the Agreement would include:

(*a*) a definite undertaking by Manchester to increase its purchases of Indian cotton, and
(*b*) an undertaking that the price of British piecegoods to the Indian consumer would not be increased.

In the latter connection he assured me that something like 60 per cent of the total imports of British piecegoods are absorbed in the Punjab. Sikander has, as you probably know, offered to go down to Delhi again, if necessary, in connection with the Agreement.

12. I enclose two copies of the Provincial Fortnightly Report for the first half of February.

Yours sincerely,
H.D. CRAIK

81

CRAIK TO LINLITHGOW

Secret and Personal
D.-O. No. 127

Government House, Lahore,
March 7th, 1939

Dear Lord Linlithgow,

In the last sentence of your secret and personal telegram No. 340 of the 6th of March you asked me in keep you in touch with reactions in the Punjab to the Rajkot affair.[26]

2. On the whole, I do not think that the Punjab is as yet very deeply stirred. Rajkot is, of course, front-page news in every newspaper and the nationalist papers make it the subject of daily leading articles, in which the line taken is almost invariably that the Mahatma's fast is an act of noble self-sacrifice inspired by divine guidance and that it is the plain duty of the Ruler to give way. But 'Rajkot Day' on March the 5th seems to have been observed only in a comparatively few places by small meetings, and I have not heard of any processions or troublesome demonstrations.

3. As I told Laithwaite on the telephone last night, Sikander has received telegrams from various people urging him to 'bring the utmost pressure to bear on the Viceroy' to interfere. Yesterday he showed me telegrams in this sense from Gopi Chand Bhargava, the leader of the Congress party in our Assembly (this has been published in the Press) and also from Dalmia. I asked Sikander whether he meant to send you any message and he said 'No, certainly not. I should very much resent the Viceroy bringing pressure to bear on me in regard to a matter which was my concern, and I am not going to add to his difficulties by sending any such message to him.' I did not gather that he had discussed the matter with the other Ministers.

4. In regard to Gandhi's fast, I should say that educated and intelligent

Muhammadans are inclined to regard it with somewhat cynical amusement, as a very astute move on the part of one whom they consider a consummate master of political tactics, designed to restore his own prestige which has suffered from Bose's election to the Congress presidency. Muslims do not take Gandhi's claim to be in direct communication with Providence very seriously, but they have undoubtedly a great admiration for him as an astute politician. I have always observed that they are inclined to regard him with somewhat reluctant admiration on every occasion on which he puts Government into a difficulty. They would certainly look on Gandhi's death as a national loss, but I do not think that in the present state of communal feeling it would be the occasion of anything like the general mourning that is usually observed by the Muslim community in the event of the death of a Muslim leader, e.g. Maulana Shaukat Ali.

5. As regards Hindu feeling, it is almost axiomatic with all Hindus, even those who are not adherents of the Congress, that 'Gandhi can do no wrong'. Even among the more conservative Hindus, I should say that the thought uppermost in their minds is not whether Gandhi's recent actions are right or wrong, but what solution can be found of the situation those actions have created.

6. I was present yesterday at a large garden party attended by practically all the leading people in Lahore. I found general agreement among those with whom I conversed that you have been placed in a position of very great difficulty through no fault of your own, and I am inclined to think that in moderate circles there is a good deal of sympathy with you, coupled with relief at the news that you have not allowed things to drift and that you are now in direct contact with Gandhi.

The above are the impressions I have formed from conversations with the comparatively few people I met yesterday, and it must be remembered that all these were men of moderate and friendly views. There can, I fear, be no doubt that, although at present the issue is regarded as one between Gandhi and the Rajkot Ruler, if Gandhi were to die, a large share of the blame would somehow or other be put on Government.

7. In conclusion, may I be permitted to put forward with great diffidence a suggestion in case your present negotiations with Gandhi do not result in any settlement? Would it be possible to put the matter to him somewhat on the following lines?[27]

'The question whether the Thakur has, deliberately or otherwise, misinterpreted his agreement with Patel is after all a comparatively minor issue. It is merely a question of the correct interpretation to be put on what is on the face of it a somewhat ambiguously worded document. Indeed, the question of the composition of the committee is itself not the primary issue. Gandhi's object is presumably to secure for the people of the State some form of representation in its future administration and to protect them from acts of repression by the Ruler. The Thakur, on his side, is pledged to introduce some measure of reform. Surely it should be possible to secure this object without the elaborate machinery of a committee of enquiry instructed to submit recommendations. The Crown Representative is prepared to give every possible assistance in devising a suitable scheme of reforms, e.g. by deputing an officer (not necessarily an officer of the Political Department) for the purpose. And the Crown Representative would further be prepared, provided a scheme can be devised which meets with his approval, to do everything possible to expedite its introduction.'[28]

Yours sincerely,
H.D. CRAIK

82

CRAIK TO LINLITHGOW

Secret and Personal
D.-O. No. 128

Government House, Lahore,
March 9th, 1939

Dear Lord Linlithgow,

In your personal telegram No. 640 of yesterday you asked for a report of immediate reactions either among the general public or in Service or European circles to the Rajkot settlement. I am replying by letter in order to save your staff the labour of deciphering a lengthy code telegram.

All the newspapers I have seen have received the settlement with intense relief and satisfaction. All are agreed that the credit for bringing about the settlement goes principally to yourself and have paid a tribute to the high qualities of statesmanship which led you to take a hand in the matter, and particularly to the rapidity with which you brought about the settlement.

The tone taken by the newspapers probably reflects correctly the view of the general public. I believe every thinking man recognises that it was not possible for you to sit back and take the line that the question at issue was purely one between Gandhi and the Rajkot Ruler, in which you were not concerned. I have only seen one of my Ministers, Malik Khizar Hyat Khan, since the announcement was made. He expressed some misapprehension of the effect which the settlement might have on other States. But he agreed after some discussion that the point at issue in Rajkot was so intricate and peculiar that an exactly similar set of circumstances can hardly be expected to arise elsewhere.

As regards reactions in Service and European circles, I was a guest last night at an Indian Police dinner held in connection with a conference of Police officers now in progress at Lahore. There were about 120 people, of both sexes, at this dinner, and as usual on such occasions I had to spend most of my time talking to ladies. I did, however, have some conversation with our District Commander,[29] the Inspector-General of Police and two or three senior Police officers, and I asked Moon, who was also a guest at the dinner, to make a point of discussing the question with some of the younger officers, both European and Indian. The General was inclined to take the line that 'it was a pity to have given in to Gandhi', but I found that he really had a very confused impression of the whole matter and had not grasped the implications either of the points at issue or of the settlement actually reached. Orde, on the other hand, being much better informed, entirely agreed that you could not possibly have let things slide and expressed his gratification and astonishment that you had been able to arrive at a settlement so quickly without giving way on any material issue. This seemed to be the general view of the two or three other officers with whom I spoke personally; and Moon tells me that he gathered the same impression from his own conversations with a somewhat larger number of more junior officers, both of the I.C.S. and Police. Some of them did, however, express to him their feeling that similar difficulties arising out of the maladministration prevalent in so many States are bound to arise elsewhere, and the view was freely expressed that the extent of control which officers of the Political Department are able to exercise over the internal administration of States is far too limited and in existing conditions inadequate.

Yours sincerely,
H.D. CRAIK

83

CRAIK TO LINLITHGOW

Private and Personal
D.-O. No. 129-F.L.

Government House, Lahore,
March 14th, 1939

Dear Lord Linlithgow,

I enclose the Fortnightly Report for the second half of February.

2. After one day's sitting on the 27th of February for the presentation of the Budget the Assembly was adjourned till March the 13th. This long adjournment was due in part to the Muharram and the Holi holidays but was extended by arrangement between the Ministry and the Opposition to suit the convenience of those Congress members who wished to go to Tripuri. At present the general discussion of the Budget is proceeding and this and the voting on demands for grants will occupy the House till the end of March. Here the custom is for the Governor to allot three days for the general discussion and ten days for voting on demands. Personally I think both periods are too long, but the Premier did not advise their curtailment.

The Budget had on the whole a very favourable reception in the Press. Manohar Lal in presenting it made a lucid and able, but slightly self-satisfied, speech.

The Bill providing for the appointment of a Sergeant-at-Arms will not come up for discussion till April. It is certain to be opposed by the Congress and Socialist groups.

3. Muharram unfortunately did not pass without a communal clash. On the 2nd of March there was a somewhat serious riot in Amritsar, originating in some followers of a Muharram procession knocking over a tray of sweetmeats displayed outside a Hindu confectioner's shop. The confectioner lost his temper and threw boiling *ghee* on members of the procession. This was followed by a general scrap in which one Muhammadan received a fatal blow on the head from a *lathi* and another was stabbed. The Police accompanying the procession appear to have dealt with the matter most efficiently and the assailants of both men were arrested on the spot, a considerable number of other Hindus being arrested later. The city was naturally in a ferment, but two platoons of British infantry were promptly called out and a number of extra police sent to Amritsar from neighbouring districts. A curfew order was immediately proclaimed and altogether the situation seems to have been excellently handled by the local officers. The Hindus in protest against what they claim to be unfair and excessive arrests have been holding a *hartal* for the last few days, but I do not anticipate that this will be extended much longer.

On the same day there was some trouble at Kasur in connection with the Muharram, but in this case the contesting parties were Sunnis and Shias. There was, however, no serious rioting, though a few Police officers and other officials were injured by brickbats.

4. The rainy weather continued till well on into March. The rain has done immense good all over the Province. Unfortunately it was in some

places accompanied by local hailstorms, which did a good deal of damage. I am sorry to say that the attendance at the relief works in Hissar, Rohtak and Gurgaon has not yet begun to decline, as I had rather hoped it would. The Financial Commissioner is, however, now going to visit these areas and will see whether any curtailment of relief operations is possible. It certainly should be possible to restrict to some extent the free distribution of fodder, as there must now be a good deal of natural grazing.

5. A curious incident occurred on the branch railway line from Ludhiana to Jakhal. On the early morning of March the 2nd it was found that near station Qila Raipur one pair of rails, 30 feet in length, with all the sleepers and fastenings had been removed from the track and thrown on the slope of the embankment. It was obviously the work of large gang; the two rails with all the sleepers attached had been removed in one piece, and it must have taken at least 30 men to lift them. At either end of the breach and some 400 yards distant from it red flags and Congress flags had been set up on the line, and these served as a kind of warning. It would seem that it was a case of mischief rather than a deliberate attempt at derailment. Two or three miles away some posters were found pasted to the sleepers calling on the young men of the Punjab to wake up and put an end 'to Bureaucracy and its toadies'.

Qila Raipur is the next station to Ahmedgarh, which was the scene of the notorious train dacoity a few years ago. The surrounding villages are imbued with Congress ideas, and when on discovery of the crime the Police searched the houses of the leading agitators among them, people collected and raised revolutionary cries. The Police consider that there is a good chance of discovering the culprits.

6. The newspapers of March the 8th contained a news item regarding what was described as an unsuccessful attempt to wreck the Sind Express near Raiwind Junction. I have, however, ascertained that what actually happened was that a country-made cracker was placed on the line, but it was not of a type that could have caused any serious damage either to the train or to the railway line. Similar incidents have occurred three or four times previously in this vicinity and are thought merely to have been the work of children.

7. On page 2 of the Provincial report you will see a reference to disorderly intimidation by Congress candidates at the District Board elections in Hoshiarpur district. Subsequent incidents of the same kind have been reported, including a mock funeral procession intended to intimidate a loyalist candidate. This particular form of intimidation is an offence under the Punjab Criminal Law Amendment Act of 1935 and criminal

proceedings are being taken. Hoshiarpur is a district which has in recent years given a good deal of trouble owing to the communist elements, especially among the Sikh population, and I am afraid that lately the Deputy Commissioner[30] has not shown sufficient firmness in dealing with local agitators or prosecuting those who offended against the law. The Commissioner[31] is now proceeding to pay a prolonged visit to this district with the object of administering the necessary dose of 'ginger'.

8. I do not think I can add anything to what I have already told you about Provincial reactions to the Rajkot affair. Nor am I at present in a position to give you any information about the effect in the Punjab of the resolutions passed at Tripuri. As you know, in the Punjab the Congress is split up into two bitterly opposed groups, one led by Dr. Gopi Chand Bhargava and the other by Satyapal. The former represents the right wing of the Congress, but Satyapal's group strongly supported Bose in the presidential election.

9. Many thanks for letting me know in your letter of the 2nd of March of your interesting conversation with Jinnah about Federation.

Yours sincerely,
H.D. CRAIK

84

CRAIK TO LINLITHGOW

Secret and Personal
D.-O. No. 130

Government House, Lahore,
March 20th, 1939

Dear Lord Linlithgow,

I had a talk with Sikander today about the suggestion made in your secret and personal letter to me of the 18th of March that the time has now come when Sikander's Federation scheme should be ventilated.

He asked me to thank you for your message and he explained to me that his scheme has not yet been reduced to black and white in a form for publication. It would take Sikander at least a week to compile a complete statement of the scheme, and he does not anticipate that he will find leisure to do this till the conclusion of our Assembly session about the middle of April. He promised that he would in any case supply a copy of the scheme for your use and one for mine before it is published and will give careful consideration to the question of the manner and occasion to be selected for its release.

Sikander is going to Meerut on the 26th of March to attend a meeting of the Working Committee of the Muslim League. The principal item of the business is the discussion of Sir Abdullah Haroon's scheme of Federation and Sikander hopes to be able to persuade the Muslim League not to adopt this scheme, which he described as 'rabidly communal and likely to arouse bitter criticism from Hindus and also possibly to frighten away the Princes'. I pointed out that if at the Meerut meeting Sikander strongly opposes the Haroon scheme, he might find himself obliged to announce that he has a scheme of his own and possibly would be questioned about its details. He said that if he were so pressed, he would certainly let it be known that he has an alternative scheme of his own, but he did not intend to reveal its details at Meerut.

I seem to recollect having heard or read of Haroon's scheme but I do not remember its details. In the course of our conversation Sikander also mentioned another scheme drawn up, I think, by some Muslim subject of Hyderabad State. I have seen some mention of this in the papers and my impression is that it involves the transfer of large blocks of population from one part of India to another and is on this account alone quite impracticable.[32]

Yours sincerely,
H.D. CRAIK

85

CRAIK TO LINLITHGOW

Private and Personal
D.-O. No. 133-F.L.

Government House, Lahore,
April 2nd, 1939

Dear Lord Linlithgow,

I am afraid my letter this fortnight is a few days later than the due date owing to my having been on tour during the past eight days at Jhelum and Rawalpindi and at the formal opening of the Haveli Project, which has just been completed. This was a most successful function and was attended by all the Ministers and many thousands of people from the countryside, who gave the Ministers and myself a very warm welcome.

2. At Jhelum I presented new Colours to the 1/16th Punjab Regiment, as you had requested me to do, and spent the day with the Battalion. The formal presentation was admirably carried out at a very impressive parade. It was attended by nearly 600 veterans of the Battalion – Punjabi Muslims, Sikhs and Dogras from the Kangra and Hoshiarpur districts. I spent some time at a tea party given for these veterans and was greatly struck by their

evident enjoyment of the re-union. All those to whom I spoke expressed their fervent loyalty and attachment to their old Regiment, and I am convinced by their demeanour and the words they used that if these men are fair specimens of their class, the spirit of loyalty and devotion to the Army among the martial classes is now as firm as ever.

3. From Jhelum I went on to Rawalpindi, where I spent four days, but unfortunately my visit was spoilt by exceedingly heavy rain. There has been a good deal of communal unrest in Rawalpindi city, which has been deliberately fomented by two or three acts of desecration of mosques and temples. The culprits, who were suspected to be communists, have not been detected, but the local officers have handled the situation efficiently and promptly and no actual outbreak has occurred, though for a time there was considerable excitement.

4. From Rawalpindi I visited Dhulian in the Attock district, where the Attock Oil Company has recently struck oil in considerable quantity. Seventeen wells have been bored of which two are discharging, I think, 2,000 barrels a day, while the others have been sealed down. This is as much as the refinery and storage reservoirs at Rawalpindi can deal with. The potential output of the new wells is considerably more than this. The refinery is being greatly expanded and by the end of this year it is hoped that the amount of oil extracted daily will be many times what it is at present. This will, of course, lead to a welcome increase in employment.

5. The Budget Session of the Legislative Assembly is still in progress. The whole of the demands for grants were passed without any reduction. There was a full-dress attack on the general policy of the Ministry on the demand for General Administration and this was defeated by 101 to 36 votes on the 20th of March. The Premier tells me that actually the number of those voting for the Ministry was 106, but five votes were by some mistake not counted. This, I think, is a satisfactory majority for a Ministry that has been two years in office.

The Bill for the imposition of a small tax on the sales of petrol, which I mentioned in paragraph 7 of my letter No. 109-F.L. of December the 23rd, has been passed, but has not yet come to me for assent. The rate of tax is to be 1¼ annas per gallon, which I believe is lower than that imposed in other Provinces. The tax on lubricants has been dropped, as it would have been unpopular and would only have brought in about Rs. 40,000 a year. The Bill providing for the appointment of a Sergeant-at-Arms has not yet come up for discussion.

6. In paragraph 7 of my letter No. 129 of the 14th of March 1939 I mentioned that there had been a good deal of disorderly intimidation by

or on behalf of Congress candidates at the District Board elections in the Hoshiarpur district. The elections are now over, and I am informed that the Congress only secured 13 out of 37 elected seats in spite of the fact that many Congress workers from other districts helped in canvassing. The district is reported to have settled down again after the excitement caused by this election.

7. The Punjabi is essentially a provincially minded person and on the whole there has been very little sign of public interest either in the Congress session at Tripuri or in Gandhi's fast. 'Rajkot Day' was celebrated on the 5th of March but the meetings were few in number and poorly attended.

On the other hand, interest in the agitation against Hyderabad State has recently been stimulated by the visit of certain Hindu emissaries from the State. 43 meetings on this subject are reported to have been held between the 10th and 21st of March and at least 100 volunteers have left for Hyderabad.

8. A meeting was held at Lahore a few days ago to welcome the notorious Maulvi Obaidullah of the 1916 'Jihad' Conspiracy case, who has recently been granted permission to return to India. The meeting was attended by 800 people. The Maulvi is reported to have affirmed his belief in the Congress creed and to have announced his intention of devoting the remainder of his life to training young men in politics and Islamic doctrines. So far as I recollect from the papers I saw about his case in the Home Department, he is now about 70 years' old and will probably reside in Sind, but I am afraid he may give trouble.

9. In paragraph 3 of my demi-official letter to Brabourne, No. 93-F.L. of September the 23rd, I mentioned the conviction of the Pir of Makhad (in the Attock district) and certain of his associates for conspiring to murder the Malik of Kalabagh. The Pir himself was sentenced to a term of 6 years' imprisonment. He appealed to the High Court and the appeal has just been decided with the result that he and three others were acquitted, while the convictions of three men were upheld. On the day the High Court's decision was pronounced the Pir, who is a member of the Provincial Assembly, came to the Assembly and was given a rousing reception by the Opposition benches, although I believe he was actually elected on the Unionist ticket I am afraid that he is likely to prove a thorn in the side of the Ministry, as I understand that he harbours considerable resentment against the Premier, who comes from the same district, on account of his prosecution. The spiritual influence of the Makhad shrine is considerable, as the Pir has a large number of disciples in the north-western districts of the Punjab and in the Frontier Province, many of whom enlist in the Army.

The whole business is unfortunate and I fancy that the general belief is that the Pir is lucky to have been acquitted.

10. I am sorry to have to report that the recent rains have brought little relief to the famine areas in the south-east Punjab. The number of workers and dependents on the relief works continues to rise, and the Finance Minister noted on a file the other day that 'the drain on Provincial finances was becoming intolerable'. I hope to attend a conference within the next few days, at which the Ministers and the Revenue officers concerned will be present, when we shall have to consider seriously whether some curtailment of our relief measures is not now possible. But, as practically no crops were sown in the areas most affected, I fear that the only possible direction in which curtailment will be possible will be in the distribution of fodder.

11. The Maharaja of Kapurthala and one of his sons stayed with me for a couple of days on the 20th and 21st of March, when His Highness visited Lahore to preside at a conference of the Punjab Ruling Chiefs. I imagine he was selected as President, as he is the oldest of the reigning Princes. In conversation with me he expressed the hope that the Local Government would do something to restrict the entry of individual agitators into States, as he asserts that all the trouble in the States is due to the activities of such visitors. We have, however, no legal power to restrict the movements of individual agitators unless they are disturbing the tranquillity in British India.

12. On the 23rd of March there were attempts on the part of peasants of the Lahore district to demonstrate outside the Legislative Assembly Chamber against the reassessment of land revenue recently announced in the district. The demonstrators were not allowed to approach the Assembly Chamber, but a good many arrests had to be made. Similar demonstrations have been made on each successive day on which the Assembly sat and have imposed a considerable strain on the Police. I do not think this is a genuine agitation, but believe that it has been deliberately manufactured by the Congress and Communist parties in order to discredit the Ministry. It is expected to fizzle out in a few days from now.

13. I had a talk with Sikander today about the Indo-British Trade Agreement. He is furious with Jinnah for insisting on the Muslim League party remaining neutral, for he says that Jinnah has gone back on his word. At the meeting of the Muslim League Executive at Meerut on the 26th of March Jinnah promised Sikander that the Muslim League party would support the new Agreement, provided Zafrullah gave Jinnah an undertaking that steps would be taken to terminate the Agreement should Lancashire

not fulfil its guarantee regarding the off-take of Indian cotton. According to Sikander, Zafrullah gave Jinnah this undertaking and the five Punjab members of the Muslim League party as well as one or two others were very anxious to vote for the Agreement, and indeed would have done so had Sikander so advised them, if their votes would have carried the day. But if these six or seven Muslim members had voted for the Agreement, the other eight or nine would have voted against it.

Sikander took the opportunity of declaring his own views on the new Agreement during the course of the debate on one of the cut motions in our Assembly. He made it clear that he considered the Agreement to be greatly in the interests of the cotton-grower and he made a strong attack on the Congress as the puppets of the textile millionaires. In conversation with me he expressed the conviction that Jinnah's attitude was determined by the fact that his daughter has recently married one of the Wadias who have large textile interests!

14. I enclose the Provincial Fortnightly Report for the first half of March.

Yours sincerely,
H.D. CRAIK

86

CRAIK TO LINLITHGOW

Secret — Government House, Lahore,
D.-O. No. 138 — *April 17th, 1939*

Dear Lord Linlithgow,

Will you please refer to the correspondence ending with your secret letter to me of the 10th of April about Gandhi's request for the release of Prithvi Singh.

As regards this convict's present attitude and demeanour, thc Superintendent of the Rawalpindi Jail[33] reports that since his arrival there Prithvi Singh has been a model prisoner. The Superintendent and his staff are of opinion that he has changed his former views. I do not, however, attach very much importance to this opinion, as the Superintendent is a comparatively young British officer, who has recently been transferred from the Indian Army to our Jail Department, and I doubt whether he is a very good judge.

I have recently seen a review of an autobiography written by Prithvi Singh while he was in jail in Bombay, apparently shortly after surrendering himself to Gandhi. According to the review, throughout this work the author repeatedly refers in boastful terms to his own extraordinary personal courage, his super-human ingenuity and his tenacity of purpose. He depicts the horrors of jail life in lurid colours and accuses the Police of vindictiveness, trickery and misrepresentation. He is particularly boastful in regard to his ingenuity in escaping twice from custody. The review which is the work of a very able Punjab Police officer, Robinson (who has just succeeded Jenkin as Central Intelligence Officer), concludes with the following summary:

'The autobiography – some 60,000 words – is written for publication. The author has shown himself to be the pious and stupid humbug that he is. All persons having the slightest knowledge of Prithvi Singh's history cannot for one moment anticipate that on his release from jail he will sincerely devote his life to walking the path of truth and non-violence. His life has been one long sequence of brutal and violent episodes. He has resorted to individual terrorist outrages. His cunning and courage cannot but be admired; but to attribute his surrender and the writing of this autobiography to other motives than those of self-aggrandisement and opportunism is to be misled.

'Ignoring the contents of this misleading autobiography, its value as party and pro-revolutionary propaganda, its abominable attacks on Indian administration, there is no gainsaying the fact that Prithvi Singh is primarily a criminal justly sentenced to death and reprieved from execution by an act of pure clemency who has a life sentence to serve. No similar criminal convict to my knowledge has been permitted to publish his story whilst in jail and I can see no reason why Prithvi Singh should set a precedent.'

Since his incarceration in the Rawalpindi jail, Prithvi Singh has been in communication with Gandhi, and I have seen a copy of a letter which he wrote to Gandhi on the 15th of July last, in which he begs Gandhi to work for his release and professes himself as converted to non-violence and as willing to give an undertaking not to reside in the Punjab after release. He also adds that he intends to devote himself to strengthening the 'spiritual army' which Gandhi proposes to organise for the preservation of communal peace. This letter does not strike me as a very convincing document.

I have today consulted Sikander about the suggestion that Prithvi Singh should be released. Sikander pointed out that our recent experience of releasing prisoners who have given assurances of good behaviour has not been very encouraging and further that the release of Prithvi Singh might lead to embarrassing demands for the release of Gurmukh Singh, whom

Sikander regards as a most dangerous man. The Premier also agrees with me that should there be an outbreak of war, Prithvi Singh, who has resided for many years in various foreign countries, might be a potentially dangerous enemy agent. Both the Premier and I would therefore much prefer, for the present at any rate, to adhere to our previous view that Prithvi Singh should not be released: but the Premier is prepared at a later stage to reconsider the matter.

My own objections to Prithvi Singh's release are based on somewhat more general grounds of principle. It is notorious that it is the accepted Communist practice to employ fraud as well as force in the prosecution of their objects. The Communist Party in India is working for a mass revolution and Prithvi Singh's professed conversion to non-violence may well be part of the general scheme to secure the release of as many revolutionaries as possible. Although Gandhi professes to be personally responsible for Prithvi Singh's good behaviour, it would be impossible for him to prevent Prithvi Singh from engaging surreptitiously in underground revolutionary activities. Moreover, the guarantee would obviously only hold good so long as Gandhi is alive.

Further, Prithvi Singh is a criminal who has been convicted of [a] very grave offence and who has twice succeeded in escaping from lawful custody. It seems to me that to release such an individual merely on the recommendation of an influential person would tend to bring the law into contempt.[34]

Yours sincerely,
H.D. CRAIK

87

CRAIK TO LINLITHGOW

Confidential
D.-O. No. 140

Government House, Lahore,
April 17th, 1939

Dear Lord Linlithgow,

I should have written before to acknowledge your letter to me of the 22nd of March about Sikander's project for the formation of a Volunteer Corps, but I was hoping to have an opportunity of discussing the question at length with Sikander and of informing you of his reactions. Unfortunately he is during the Assembly session so terribly overworked that I have had no opportunity of a full discussion with him: but I have told him in general terms that both you and the Secretary of State view his scheme with grave misgiving, and though he seemed to be a little taken aback by this, I am confident that he will take no actual steps to put the scheme into execution without taking me fully into his confidence. As soon as he is free from preoccupations connected with the Assembly session I will have a full discussion with him.

Meanwhile, I have seen a report from our Central Intelligence Officer regarding the intention of the Akalis and the Congress Socialist Party to raise Volunteer Corps of their own. I enclose a copy of this report in case it has not reached you through Ewart.

Yours sincerely,
H.D. CRAIK

ENCLOSURE TO NO. 87

REPORT BY ROBINSON

April 12th, 1939

It was decided to build up an Akali volunteer organisation, to be known as the 'Akali Fauj' or 'Akali Sena' at a joint meeting of the Shiromani Akali Dal and City Akali Jatha of Amritsar on the 4th of April 1939. Master Tara Singh presided over this meeting and about 40 prominent Akalis were present. It was agreed that this Akali Fauj should be raised in order that it might perform social services to the Sikh community at religious fairs and festivals, that a school should be opened at Tarn Taran where military training would be imparted, that retired military officers should be employed as instructors and that the volunteers should be clad in khaki uniforms with red *pugrees*. Professor Ranga at a public meeting on the 9th instant explained that such a volunteer organisation was essential, for those of the Indian National Congress, the Muslim League and the Khaksars menaced Hindu communal interests. Tara Singh at this meeting declared that the Muslims were getting too powerful owing to the facilities granted to them and therefore an opposition 'Akali Fauj' must be raised. Further, a poster issued by Darshan Singh Pheruman declares that the Akali Fauj will give Sikhs an opportunity to serve and improve their physique. Sikhs must therefore enlist and subscribe to this Army, which is to be led by Tara Singh and Jathedars Udham Singh Nagoki and Mohan Singh.

Sardar Partap Singh M.L.A., in a statement to the Press on the 5th of April 1939, has given the immediate programme of a similar organisation, which he calls the 'Punjab Kisan Fauj', to be:

(1) To secure reduction in the land revenue and canal water rates;

(2) To abolish indirect irrigation tax which totals one crore and eighty-five lakhs of rupees;
(3) To abolish Chahi rates which come to about rupees forty-two lakhs;
(4) To abolish *Panchotra*, a sum of rupees twenty-one lakhs given as commission to the headmen of the villages in lieu of their services of collecting the land revenue for the Government.

As far as is known, there is little difference between the Akali Fauj and the Kisan Fauj. Both organisations will be run for the benefit of the Akali Party and will be supported from Akali Party (Gurdwara?) funds. The formation of these volunteer organisations is the outcome of enmity and jealousy between the Akali Party and the group of rural agitators controlled by the Ghadr Conspiracy Case convicts (the Babas). These Babas have from a long time past been gaining increasing influence in the Amritsar district through the propaganda effected by their Bandobast Committee. To combat their growing influence, the Akali party under the lead of Udham Singh Nagoki launched the Amritsar Kisan Morcha in which Udham Singh Nagoki was imprisoned. The present Kisan Morcha in Lahore is further detracting from Akali influence and Akalis have therefore started, under the generalship of the recently released Udham Singh Nagoki, the formation of their Kisan Fauj.

The efforts so far made by the Akali leaders to enlist volunteers have been remarkably unsuccessful. The poor are unable to pay for their uniforms, and the rich are sceptical of joining another of Master Tara Singh's doubtful organisations. The services of one retired military officer, Balwant Singh, have however been obtained and the Tarn Taran School will shortly be started. Master Tara Singh has stated that he will give the whole of his time to this movement, and he hopes that his appeals at Panja Sahib on 'Baisakhi Day' will result in the enlistment of a large force. So far the Lahore District Kisan Fauj has alone been active, and this on paper. The President and Secretary are Tara Singh Thethar and Gopal Singh Qaumi, and it is said that they have received Rs. 1,000 from the Akali Party funds to start a 'morcha'.

The Punjab Congress Socialist Party, it appears, will not lag behind in the formation of their own army which is to be called the National Militia. This National Militia is intended, so it is said, to prevent Unionist 'Goondas' from disturbing socialist meetings. Gurcharan Singh Sainsera, of the 'Kirti', and Ghulam Jilani have been put in charge of enlistments. Their early efforts were not very successful.

W.D. ROBINSON
Central Intelligence Officer, Lahore

88

CRAIK TO LINLITHGOW

Private and Personal
D.-O. No. 141-F.L.

Government House, Lahore,
April 18th, 1939

Dear Lord Linlithgow,

I have not very much to report this fortnight. The Budget session of the Assembly is still in progress, but it is hoped that it will terminate about the end of this week. The Bill for the appointment of a Sergeant-at-Arms passed its third reading yesterday. During the course of the discussion on clauses Government accepted an amendment that made a material modification in the operative clause. As originally introduced this read:

> 'The Punjab Government shall appoint a Sergeant-at-Arms and may appoint one or more deputy sergeants-at-arms.'

As amended the clause now reads:

> 'The Governor or such person as he may direct may appoint a Sergeant-at-Arms and one or more deputy sergeants-at-arms.'

The Assembly has now to deal with a Bill for the regulation of primary education, but I understand this is likely to be re-committed to the Select Committee. I do not think there is any further important legislative business.

2. There have recently been three somewhat important secessions from the Unionist Party. The first and most important of the seceders is the Pir of Makhad, about whom I wrote in paragraph 9 of my letter of April the 2nd. It is generally believed that the Pir is likely to join with the Congress party and I noticed the other day a report that he attended a private meeting of the Congress and Ahrar leaders in Lahore on the 12th of April, when the newly elected President of the Punjab Provincial Congress, Dr. Kitchlew, described him as having joined the Congress. The Pir himself has, however, made no public announcement that he has joined the Congress. Should he decide to do so, he might be a useful tool in the 'Muslim Mass Contact movement'.

The second seceder is K.L. Gauba, a comparatively recent convert to Islam and son of the late Lala Harkishan Lal of Peoples' Bank notoriety. Your Excellency will remember the case of Gauba's brother, who is still undergoing imprisonment for contempt of court. K.L. Gauba was himself prosecuted for various acts of embezzlement connected with the Peoples'

Bank, but to the general surprise was acquitted. I am told that he contemplates bringing a suit against the Secretary of State for malicious prosecution and claiming heavy damages. He had the effrontery to suggest to the Ministry that should he institute such a suit, it should not be contested by the Crown. The reason for his defection from the Unionist Party is alleged to be the Ministry's refusal to agree to this preposterous suggestion.

The third seceder is a retired Tahsildar, Jalal-ud-Din Amber, who represents one of the Christian constituencies. I believe he has left the Party because he is jealous of another representative of the Christian community who has been made a Parliamentary Under Secretary. When he was in Government service Jalal-ud-Din had a bad reputation for corruption.

3. Counting these three deserters from the Unionist Party, the Opposition now claim to have a total strength of 61 in a house of 175, but this claim is not really justified by the facts. It is true that there are now 61 members who do not belong to the Unionist Party, but many of these describe themselves as 'Independents', and it is by no means certain that they would in any particular division support the Congress opposition. Indeed, some of the so-called 'Independents' often vote with the Ministry.

4. There are, however, other members of the Unionist Party who are very shaky in their allegiance, and I am told that 10 of these have secretly given written undertakings to the Congress leader to secede from their party and to support a vote of no-confidence in the Ministry, should one be moved. Seven other members are reliably reported to have given oral assurances to the same effect, but in Punjab politics little or no reliance can be placed on oral assurances.

It is thus just possible that should a vote of no-confidence be moved, the Opposition might secure the support of 61 *plus* 17 = 78 members. I received information that during the last few days the Congress leaders have been carefully considering whether they should move such a motion, and it was thought possible that notice of a motion would be given yesterday. The Premier told me he would rather welcome a no-confidence motion, as it would mean a public 'show-down' of some of his wobbling supporters, but he was doubtful whether the Opposition would have the courage to make the motion, and they did not in fact do so yesterday. This morning I have heard rumours of a possible motion of no-confidence in (*a*) the Deputy Speaker, a Sikh; and (*b*) Sir Chhotu Ram, the Minister for Development.

5. The Kisan demonstrations, to which I referred in paragraph 12 of my letter of the 2nd of April, continued up till the 15th of April, by which date

670 arrests in all had been made. The number of arrests made daily was steadily dwindling as the result of heavier sentences being awarded to the demonstrators. On the 16th of April the Premier received a deputation representing the demonstrators, and I enclose a press report[35] of the proceedings. I do not think any further arrests have been necessary since then. Public interest in these demonstrations had practically entirely evaporated before the Premier received the deputation.

6. Muslim opinion has been deeply stirred by the 'rape of Albania'. Speaking to me on this subject a few days ago the Premier said that if we are going to have a war, it was a pity we could not have it on this issue, as the British Empire would have Muslim opinion all over the world solidly behind it. In this connection he expressed the hope that there would be an early settlement of the Palestine problem and one satisfactory to Muslim opinion.

7. I enclose the fortnightly report for the second half of March.

8. I am leaving Lahore on the morning of the 19th for a brief holiday in Kulu, returning on the morning of the 23rd of April. I am making the journey both ways by air, which should only be a matter of about two hours. The aeroplane which takes me there will remain at Kulu so that in case of a crisis I could return to Lahore immediately.

Yours sincerely,
H.D. CRAIK

89

CRAIK TO LINLITHGOW

Private and Personal
D.-O. No. 146-F.L.

Government House, Lahore,
May 1st, 1939

Dear Lord Linlithgow,

The Budget Session of the Legislative Assembly concluded on Monday, the 24th of April, in a somewhat sensational manner. In paragraph 4 of my letter to you of the 18th of April I mentioned that there were rumours of a possible motion of no-confidence against either the Deputy Speaker or the Minister for Development. A day or two later the Opposition gave notice of a motion of no-confidence against the Deputy Speaker, being of course well aware that under Section 65 (2) of the Government of India Act 14 days had to elapse between the giving of the notice and moving the resolution. The effect of this section was, as the Premier pointed out in the

House, that the motion could not be moved at this session. At the same time, the Premier taunted the Opposition with their failure to move a motion of no-confidence in the Ministry. To this their reply was that they would do so in their own good time.

The Premier, who, as I told you in my last letter, had informed me that he would welcome a motion of no-confidence, thereupon got one of his own supporters to put down a motion of confidence in the Ministry. This successfully forced the hands of the Opposition and they then tabled motions of no-confidence against the Ministers for Education and Development and against the Premier personally.

2. When these motions came up for discussion on Saturday, April the 22nd, the Speaker ruled that the motion of confidence in the Ministry having been received first must be discussed before the motions of no-confidence. There was a long wrangle on the point of procedure, but the Speaker adhered to his ruling and thereupon the Opposition walked out. The motion of confidence was then briefly discussed, only a few speeches being made by back-bench supporters of the Ministry, and was passed by 107 votes to nil.

Thereafter the House commenced the discussion of the motion of no-confidence in the Education Minister (Mian Abdul Haye) and the discussion was not concluded when the House adjourned till Monday, the 24th of April. On that date the motion was rejected by 112 votes to 55. The similar motion directed against the Minister for Development (Sir Chhotu Ram) was also rejected by 112 votes to 54 and that against the Premier by 112 votes to 53.

The maximum number voting on any division was thus 167 out of a total House (including the Speaker) of 175. The seven absentees included two faithful supporters of the Unionist Party, who were unable for domestic reasons to attend, three members of the Opposition, one Independent whose vote was uncertain and one Communist (Teja Singh Satintra) who is a State prisoner.

3. On the whole, the result must be regarded as a distinct triumph for the Ministry, which is admitted to have scored a tactical victory even by newspapers which usually oppose the Ministry. The 17 members of the Unionist Party whom I mentioned in paragraph 4 of my letter of April the 18th as being rumoured to be shaky in their allegiance all voted for the Ministry.

4. There was one rather interesting episode in connection with these motions of no-confidence. On the afternoon of the 24th of April I gave an interview to the Pir of Makhad (vide paragraph 2 of my letter to you of the

18th of April). He spoke to me at considerable length regarding his recent misfortunes and stressed the point that he had had to undergo 13 months' imprisonment on a charge of which the High Court ultimately held him to be completely innocent and alleged that he had to expend on his defence Rs. 1¼ lakhs. He further asserted that he was in grave apprehension in regard to his personal safety, as he felt that his enemies might attempt to get him murdered. He assured me that he had no intention of joining the Congress and protested that he would maintain the traditional loyalty of his family to the British connection and was willing to co-operate with the Unionist Party. I strongly advised him that if this was his real intention, he had better seek an early opportunity of seeing the Premier and of re-establishing his former friendly relations with him. This he promised to do.

The Pir must have gone straight from my House to the Assembly and it is perhaps significant that although he voted for the motions of no-confidence against the Ministers of Education and Development, he abstained from voting on the motion directed against the Premier.

5. On the day after the conclusion of the session (April the 25th) I presided at a Cabinet meeting and found all the Ministers very pleased with the proceedings of the previous day, which they feel have pulled the party together. Most of the Ministers have now left Lahore with the object of getting a short holiday after the labours of this prolonged session. Sikander has gone to Palampur in the Kangra district, where he has a house, but he told me that he would have to spend most of his holiday composing an address for the approaching meeting of the Muslim League at Sholapur, at which I think he is to preside. Mian Abdul Haye and Khizar Hayat Khan are also attending the meeting.

6. I fear, however, that in spite of this apparent success for the Ministry there is still a good deal of discontent in the ranks of the supporters. While I was away in Kulu, Moon had a long talk with Khan Bahadur Mian Mushtaq Ahmad Gurmani, one of the more intelligent of the younger supporters of the Ministry, and recorded a note of this gentleman's views, which I enclose herewith and on which I have made a few comments. Mushtaq Ahmad's views are certainly of interest, but I think in certain respects unduly pessimistic. For example, it is not true to say that the Unionist Party has no well-established policy. The main plank of their policy is to relieve the peasantry from the burden of debt and to do everything possible to improve their economic position, and I believe that this policy is generally well recognised.

7. I am sorry to say that I was wrong in expressing the opinion in

paragraph 5 of my last letter that the Kisan demonstrations in Lahore would fizzle out as the result of the reception by the Premier of a deputation representing the demonstrators on the 16th of April. A few demonstrators continue to offer themselves for arrest every day; their ostensible object being still to reach the Assembly Chamber, although the session has concluded! Up to the 24th of April the total arrests made were 868. There is, however, practically no public interest in these demonstrations.

8. There is one matter connected with the services which I think I ought to mention. One of the measures of economy approved by the Ministry in consequence of the heavy expenditure on famine was the curtailment of leave to cases in which it is genuinely necessary. I found that in one or two cases leave had been refused to officers of the I.M.S. without my knowledge, and I have had to call the attention of the Minister and the Secretary concerned to the provisions of Section 247 (2) of the Government of India Act, under which any order relating to leave of not less than three months of any officer of the Secretary of State's services must be made by the Governor in the exercise of his individual judgement. There has, however, been no case in which I have felt it necessary to differ from the advice given by the Minister.

9. I am leaving Lahore in a day or two and making a short tour on my way up to Simla, where I am due to arrive on May the 9th.

10. I enclose the fortnightly report for the first half of April.

Yours sincerely,
H.D. CRAIK

ENCLOSURE TO NO. 89

NOTE BY MOON[36]

April 22nd, 1939

I had a long conversation the other day with K.B. Mushtaq Ahmad Gurmani, M.L.A., about the Unionist Party, which may perhaps be of some interest to His Excellency.

2. He was very pessimistic. He pointed out that the party has no programme, no organisation and no cohesion, and that no steps are being taken to remedy this state of affairs.

3. As regards a programme, he said that the party leaders had no well-considered schemes in regard to any branch whatever of the administration, [This is much too sweeping an assertion. H.D.C.] nor were any serious or systematic efforts being made to devise any. The Premier is wholly

engrossed with the details of day-to-day administration, and has no time to sit back and think out broad lines of policy. [This is true, but if the Premier can be provided with an official Private Secretary, he should have more leisure. H.D.C.] The other Ministers will do nothing without consulting the Premier. He drew a contrast with the Congress Provinces, where, he said, the Ministers leave the routine of administration to the permanent officials, [I doubt if this is correct. H.D.C.] and concentrate their own energies on working out plans for giving effect to their general ideas of policy. The Unionist leaders are purely opportunist and without any settled ideas of policy. They have no plans whatever for the future and are living from hand to mouth. [Too sweeping. H.D.C.]

4. As regards organisation, he pointed out that at the last election Unionist members got in on the strength of their own personal influence in the constituencies. [Broadly speaking, this is true. H.D.C.] There was no party machine from which they could obtain any effective assistance. [Not altogether correct. The party machine has functioned successfully in one or two recent bye-elections. H.D.C.] The same is still true. Other political parties, e.g. the Congress and the Ahrars have strong local organisations and put up candidates for local bodies. For instance, the Ahrars have recently captured the Ludhiana Municipal Committee [I had not heard this, but will enquire. H.D.C.] and are now making a bid for the capture of Jullundur as well. All this greatly helps when it comes to a general election for the Assembly. But neither the Unionist Party nor the Muslim League have any live organisation in the districts, and are not establishing themselves in the local bodies.

5. The Premier has endeavoured to hold the party together by distributing loaves and fishes. This was a fatal policy and has largely contributed to the present discontent in the party. [I am afraid there is a good deal of truth in this. H.D.C.] It has meant in effect that the loaves and fishes have been given to the worst self-seekers, who resort to the threats if their demands are not granted. He cited several examples:

(*i*) Nawab Sir Mehr Shah, who, in contravention of Government's declared policy has been granted a lease of 22 squares [*sic*] in Lyallpur. [This was done before my time. The Nawab is a notorious and dangerous intriguer. H.D.C.] His brother's roll for E[xtra] A[ssistant] C[ommissioner] was also called for by the Premier, though it had not been sent up by local officers. [The brother will not, I think, be accepted as an E.A.C. candidate. H.D.C.]

(*ii*) K.B. Muhammad Akram. He belongs to Sir Mehr Shah's clique. His nephew [This appointment was made before my time, I think.

H.D.C.] has been appointed Inspector, Local Bodies, Lahore – a post for which he was quite unqualified.

(*iii*) The Nawab of Mamdot. He was granted a Knighthood in January at the Premier's instance. [Correct. But his wealth and position as one of the largest landowners in the Province made him a suitable recipient. H.D.C.]

The effect of this policy is:

(*a*) to bring the Government and the Unionist Party into contempt among the general public;

(*b*) to cause uneasiness and dissatisfaction amongst officials;

(*c*) to accelerate the disintegration of the party, as members have come to believe that the best way of satisfying their personal ambitions is to threaten secession. [There is a good deal of truth in this. H.D.C.]

6. According to Mushtaq Ahmad Gurmani, he has himself always urged the Premier to adopt Sir Fazl-i-Husain's policy and resolutely refuse to listen to personal requests from party members. [I doubt if Sir Fazl-i-Husain was as impervious to such requests as represented. He was never a Minister under the new Constitution and had not as much patronage as Ministers now exercise. H.D.C.] To facilitate this policy he had advocated:

(*i*) that as much 'patronage' as possible should be handed over to the Public Service Commission;

(*ii*) that in regard to other appointments and in regard to postings, the recommendations of local officers and Heads of Departments should be accepted.

7. In recent weeks he has again been urging this on the Premier; he considers it even now not too late to go back on the policy hitherto adopted. So far he has not definitely won the Premier over to his views. But he intends to press them on him again even more insistently during the leisure days when Government is moving up to Simla. He hinted that, if he was not successful in persuading [the] Premier, he would have to consider forming what he called a 'left-wing group' in the Unionist Party, which would act independently. He boasted that he had a number of supporters, but I don't think this is the case.

8. Another matter to which he alluded in connection with the discontent in the party is the old one of the unpopularity of the Premier's immediate entourage. [I have heard the same complaints of these three gentlemen from others, and I fancy Premier is well aware of their defects. H.D.C.]

The three persons he mentioned were, of course:

(*a*) Mir Maqbool Mahmood;
(*b*) Afzaal Ali Hasnie;
(*c*) Ahmad Yar Khan Daultana.

About the first two he said nothing particular except that they were in fact corrupt and were generally reported to be so.

Ahmad Yar, he said, is disliked, because he is ungracious and unbusinesslike, because he is a liar (he says he will do things and then does not do them) and because he is believed to have a preter-natural influence over the Premier, which he uses for his own personal ends. He exploits to the full this belief in his influence over the Premier, and many officials have started paying court to him and approaching him with requests. By way of illustration of the general belief in Ahmad Yar's influence he mentioned that it was popularly supposed that Qurban Ali's appointment as Anti-Corruption Officer was Ahmad Yar's work, for Qurban Ali is a great friend of Daultana [I was not aware of this. Qurban Ali is, however, quite one of the best of our Indian Superintendents of Police, and is I think very well qualified for the appointment in question. I believe he was very reluctant to accept it, as it will be an unpleasant kind of job. H.D.C.] and habitually stays with him in Lahore.

E.P. MOON

90

CRAIK TO LINLITHGOW

Private and Personal — Barnes Court, Simla,
D.-O. No. 147-F.L. — *May 17th, 1939*

Dear Lord Linlithgow,

I have not very much to report since I wrote to you last on May the 2nd. I was myself on tour from that date till my arrival here on the 9th and only one of my Ministers has yet reached Simla. Three are expected to arrive today. Khizar Hayat is due on the 19th, but Sikander is not expected until the 22nd. He is paying a short visit to his home in the Attock district, and I hope very much he is having a holiday.

2. In your letter to me of May the 5th you expressed your uneasiness about Sikander's visit to Sholapur, accompanied by two of his Muslim colleagues and several Parliamentary and Party Secretaries, to preside over the Muslim League meeting, and you mentioned the possibility of

the Bombay Government raising the question of the constitutional propriety of an official team making such a visit with such an object. Sikander had no discussion with me as to this aspect of the visit before he left and he was already at Sholapur when your letter reached me. You have, I think, read the speech he delivered there. Although it made a very strong attack on the general policy of the Congress High Command, it did not include any criticism of the Bombay Government, and although I have seen numerous articles in the Congress Press condemning his speech on various grounds, I have not noticed any which raised the question of the propriety of his visit.

3. When Sikander told me towards the end of April of his intention to preside at the Sholapur session, he mentioned that he rather hoped that Jinnah would not be present, as he thought that parts of his address would not be palatable to Jinnah. I notice that towards the end of his address there is a passage in which Sikander stated that Jinnah had 'given the fullest possible freedom of action, subject to the creed of the Muslim League, to the Provincial Leagues and the representatives of Mussalmans in Provincial Legislatures'. From this I infer that Sikander has induced Jinnah to accept the principle that there is to be no interference on the part of the Central Muslim League in Punjab local matters. Sikander has often expressed in conversation with me the view that the All-India League would amount to nothing without the presence in it of the Muslims of the Punjab and Bengal, and that both he and the Bengal Premier[37] were agreed in using this fact as a lever for insisting that there should be no interference by the Central League in local affairs. Jinnah was, I understand, present at Sholapur.

4. I have just received from the Political Department a note on the agitation in Hyderabad State with a covering letter from Herbert, in which it is stated that Your Excellency would be grateful if suitable action could be taken to discourage this movement, and to deter the despatch of *jathas* to Hyderabad from the Punjab. I will discuss this question with Sikander as soon as he arrives in Simla. The agitation is certainly increasing in strength in the Punjab and the only effective way of stopping it is by the use of the Indian States (Protection) Act, 1934. I will ask Sikander to consider whether it is advisable to make use of this weapon on the ground not only of the embarrassment caused to the Hyderabad authorities by the agitation, but also of the communal tension caused in the Punjab by the despatch of these *jathas*. An instance of this tension that may have very embarrassing results to the Ministry occurred on Saturday last at Rohtak. I have not yet seen any official report of this incident, but I understand that a procession of Arya Samajists, who were about to start for Hyderabad,

marched past the principal local mosque singing and shouting slogans. Muslims from the mosque threw brick-bats at the procession and a scuffle ensued, in which between 20 and 30 Hindus and about 8 Muslims received injuries. There were no fatal casualties, but, according to the *Hindustan Times* of May the 16th, one of the Hindus injured was Chaudhri Phul Singh, who is a prominent local supporter of Sir Chhotu Ram (whose home is in the Rohtak district) and a leader of the local Arya Samaj. The same paper reports that after the riot a Hindu meeting was held at Rohtak, at which a Jat speaker said that this deplorable incident was the direct result of Sikander's Sholapur speech, in which, you will remember, he very strongly condemned the Hyderabad agitation. The same speaker called on Sir Chhotu Ram to resign from the Ministry, as some of the victims belonged to his own caste and were his ardent supporters. You will appreciate the possibility that this incident may cause a rift within the Cabinet, and even if it does not have this result, it may hamper Sikander in taking effective local action to discourage the despatch of *jathas* from the Punjab.

5. In paragraph 6 of my letter to you, No. 124-F.L., of February the 26th last I mentioned that the Marketing Bill passed in the January session of the Assembly had come to me for my assent, but that at the Premier's suggestion I was not going to announce my assent till a comparatively late stage of the Budget session. As soon as that session was over I conveyed my assent. The Non-Agriculturists' Association thereupon announced that a *hartal* would be held on May the 9th to protest against my assent to this measure, but I have seen no announcement that any *hartal* actually took place, and I gather that the movement was a failure.

On a careful examination of the Bill for the appointment of a Sergeant-at-Arms I have found it necessary to reserve this measure for your assent on the ground of a technical 'repugnancy'. Moon is writing to Thorne officially on this subject.

6. I am sorry to say that the tiresome Kisan demonstrations at Lahore still continue. The total number of arrests made up to the 10th of May were 1,127, including 157 women. About 7 arrests a day are still being made, but I understand that funds to finance the movement are now running low.

7. There has recently been a welcome falling-off in attendance at the famine relief works in the south-eastern districts, probably due to the demand for labour in connection with the harvesting of the *rabi* crop. In Hissar the daily average of workers, including dependents, fell in the first three weeks of April from 223,000 to 140,000. My Ministers are

considering various devices for reducing famine expenditure, including a suggestion to reduce slightly the daily wage of 2 annas paid to all full-time workers on these relief works in the case of people whose villages are within a 4-mile radius of the work. I think they will probably decide to reduce the daily rate from 2 annas to 1½ annas. The Financial Commissioner (Dobson) visited the famine areas about the end of April and reported of Hissar that the organisation of relief continued to be admirable.

8. You will notice in the Provincial report for the second half of April (two copies of which are enclosed) a statement that it is at present too early to judge the reaction in Congress circles to the resignation of Subhas Chandra Bose.[38] Judging by the tone of the Congress Press there is a good deal of public sympathy with Bose and a general feeling that he has been badly treated by Gandhi and the 'old guard'. But there is little sign that the Left Wing is gaining strength in the Punjab. Dr. Kitchlew's election as President of the Punjab Provincial Congress is, of course, a proof of Right Wing predominance and his Working Committee of 21 includes only two or three Congressmen who can be described as supporters of Bose's 'Forward Bloc'.

9. The deputation of prominent All-India Muslim League personalities, formed to show up the oppression perpetrated by the Congress Governments on the Muslim minorities in certain Provinces, is at present touring in the Punjab. The meetings organised by this deputation are attracting large audiences and some astounding allegations of Hindu excesses are being made. I am afraid that these meetings are likely to increase communal tension and also to intensify Hindu opposition to Sikander's Ministry.

Yours sincerely,
H.D. CRAIK

91

CRAIK TO LINLITHGOW

Private and Personal — Barnes Court, Simla,
D.-O. No. 151-F.L. — *June 5th, 1939*

Dear Lord Linlithgow,

My Ministers have now all arrived in Simla and I presided at a Cabinet meeting on May the 31st. The principal item for discussion was the possibility of reducing expenditure for famine relief in Hissar, Rohtak and Gurgaon districts. As explained in paragraph 7 of my letter to Your Excellency, No. 147-F.L. of May the 17th, one of the suggestions was that the daily rate of wage paid to workers on the relief works should be reduced from 2 annas to 1½ annas. It was calculated that assuming the arrival of the monsoon at about the normal date, this reduction would only mean a saving of about ¾ lakh of rupees, and the decision of the Cabinet was that this saving would not be sufficient to justify the odium which the reduction would cause. The following decisions were, however, taken:

(1) that every effort should be made to reduce attendance at relief works by weeding out undeserving cases, especially those coming from villages within a 4-mile radius of the work;
(2) that in villages where the excavation of tanks has been commenced, those desiring relief should be instructed that only work on the tanks was open to them and that they would not be admitted to other forms of relief work;
(3) that local officers should be given discretion to withhold the 'rest day' allowances hitherto paid;
(4) that relief works at which the daily attendance falls below 1,000 should be closed at once.

It is hoped that these measures will result in a considerable financial saving.

2. The Deputy Commissioner of Hissar[39] reported on the 22nd of May that the total attendance at relief works on the 20th of May, including dependants, was a little under 104,000. This is a reduction of about 36,000 in the last month. Four out of 26 relief works have been closed down, and it is expected that more will shortly be closed. One hundred and thirty-five village tanks have been selected for excavation work and work has actually been started on about 100. This type of labour is placed as piece-work and not by a daily wage.

3. I have written to Your Excellency separately, in my letter No. 148 of the 26th of May,[40] about the agitation against Hyderabad State. The warning which Sikander gave to a meeting of leading journalists in Lahore regarding the desirability of toning down their articles on this agitation has received somewhat unfavourable comment in the Press. The *Tribune*, for example, criticised the Premier's warning as an unwarranted interference with the liberty of the Press, and called attention to the fact that he did nothing to restrain the speeches of the delegation from the All-India Muslim League which recently toured the Punjab (see, paragraph 9 of my letter No. 147-F.L. of May the 17th).

I have also seen an intercepted letter from Deshbandhu Gupta, a Punjab M.L.A., who is, I think, editor of the Delhi *Tej*, to a journalist friend in Lahore, proposing some form of public protest against Sikander's warning. Nevertheless, I think that the warning has had some effect, as I have noticed no particularly bad articles lately and there have been no further disturbances in the Punjab arising out of the Hyderabad agitation. This, however, is possibly due to the fact that Mahasha Krishan, a Lahore journalist who has been very prominent in collecting volunteers and funds on behalf of the Arya Samaj, has recently completed a tour in the Punjab and left the Province presumably for Hyderabad.

4. The Lahore Kisan demonstrations still drag on, though considerable difficulty is being experienced in finding people willing to come forward for arrest and on two or three days towards the end of May none were forthcoming. Among those recently arrested were a Bengali and an ex-terrorist convict. No more women have been arrested, but two unfortunate incidents have arisen out of the earlier arrests of women. One woman arrested had an infant in arms, whom she took with her into the jail. The baby fell ill and both the mother and child were transferred to one of the Lahore hospitals, where the baby died. Another female satyagrahi died about the end of May in the female jail. The agitators have naturally been trying to make capital out of these two deaths.

My Ministers recently issued a long statement to the Press, exposing the artificial origin of this agitation, the hollowness of the alleged grievances and the economic loss which it is causing to the peasantry. I think this exposure has had good results.

5. In paragraph 1 of my letter to you, No. 72-F.L. of May 26th, 1938, I mentioned the somewhat striking success of the Unionist Party in a bye-election to the Assembly from Amritsar. As almost invariably happens after a hotly contested election, an election petition was brought against the successful Unionist candidate, Shaikh Muhammad Sadiq, and this has recently been decided against him. I have not yet seen the report of the Elections Tribunal, but I understand that the main ground for unseating Shaikh Muhammad Sadiq is that he did not disclose his election expenses in sufficient detail. The Premier is much upset by this decision and in conversation with me expressed the view that the President of the Tribunal, a retired Hindu District and Sessions Judge, had been bribed. This is the second election for this particular seat which has proved abortive, and in view of the expense that is bound to fall on any candidate who may stand, the Unionist Party will have considerable difficulty in finding a strong local candidate to contest the seat.

6. Lahore municipal affairs have recently attracted a great deal of publicity. The Municipal Committee was suspended towards the end of 1936 for inefficiency and corruption and since then the municipal administration has been run by a senior Indian Civil Service Officer, Macnabb, whom I think Your Excellency knows. I mentioned to you in conversation a short time ago the very serious situation created in Lahore by the recent strike of municipal sweepers, in sympathy with whom the majority of sweepers in private employ also struck. I have not yet been able to ascertain whether there was any genuine grievance at the bottom of this strike, but however that may be, the Administrator, though he gave the sweepers a hearing, refused to give way and the attempts made to import sweepers from outside failed, as those so imported were afraid to work in face of hostile demonstrations. After the strike had lasted three days it was settled by the intervention of the Minister for Public Works (Major Khizar Hayat Khan), who was passing through Lahore on his way to Simla. Had the strike lasted longer, I am certain that there would have been the risk of a very serious epidemic. Khizar promised the sweepers that their grievances would be sympathetically investigated and that those who returned to work at once would not be victimized.

Macnabb, however, incurred much odium and a great deal of Press criticism on account of this strike. Even the *Civil & Military Gazette*, usually a consistent supporter of the Ministry, published a somewhat embarrassing leading article on the subject, a cutting[41] of which I enclose. I am afraid there is a certain amount of truth in its criticism of Macnabb. Although he is extremely industrious and inspired by a genuine desire to reform the municipal administration, he is a man of somewhat rigid mentality and, I fancy, rather inclined to stick to his desk and does not go about enough in the city. I have talked the matter over with the Premier and Khizar Hayat Khan and I find that neither of them is in the least inclined to let Macnabb down. The agitation against him is largely inspired by interested persons, who were members of the old Municipality and who have managed to secure the support of the local 'Rate-payers Association', an organisation which is mainly directed by Congressmen. There is, moreover, a communal aspect of the matter. Macnabb is alleged – quite falsely so far as I am aware – to have a pro-Muslim bias and it is believed by Hindus that in enforcing economies in the administration he has got rid of an unduly high proportion of Hindu employees. The communal aspect of the question is likely to have the effect of stiffening the Ministers in their determination to support Macnabb, but there is much talk in the Press and elsewhere of a monster petition praying for his removal, and I fear that we are likely to have a good deal more trouble over this question. It is possible, for example, that we have not heard the last of the sweepers' strike.

7. I enclose two copies of the fortnightly report for the first half of May.

Yours sincerely,
H.D. CRAIK

92

CRAIK TO LINLITHGOW

Secret and Personal
D.-O. No. 153

Barnes Court, Simla,
June 8th, 1939

Dear Lord Linlithgow,

Many thanks for your secret and personal letter of the 5th of June, in which you told me of the interesting news of Rajendra Prasad's[42] approach to Sikander.[43] Sikander had not previously mentioned this to me, but I had a talk with him on the subject yesterday. The intermediary was a certain Professor Shah of Bombay, who is, I understand, a Professor of Economics and whose acquaintance Sikander had formed when he was Deputy Governor of the Reserve Bank. I gather Shah first approached Sikander while the latter was stopping in Bombay on his way back from the Sholapur session of the Muslim League and subsequently Shah came to see Sikander the other day, either in Lahore or Simla.

Sikander did not tell me anything very definite about Rajendra Prasad's terms and I did not like to press him on this subject. But he did say that he had impressed on Shah that there was no prospect of his (Sikander's) accepting any arrangement based on the withdrawal of opposition to the introduction of Federation. I also gather that the next step will be for Shah to bring or send to Sikander something in writing from Rajendra Prasad and that on receipt of this Sikander will consider whether he should lay the proposals before the Executive of the Central Muslim League. He told me that he had impressed on Shah the need for extreme secrecy in the matter, as premature publicity will for obvious reasons completely wreck any chances of coming to an understanding.

As regards the latter part of your letter, I entirely agree that it would be a good thing for you to have a talk with Sikander as soon as an opportunity presents itself.

Yours sincerely,
H.D. CRAIK

93

CRAIK TO LINLITHGOW

Secret
D.-O. No. 153 [?154]

Barnes Court, Simla,
June 12th, 1939

Dear Lord Linlithgow,

Many thanks for your private and personal letter of the 10th of June,[44] which I received last night. I am very glad to hear you are to have a talk with Sikander on Wednesday next. He mentioned your invitation when I saw him this morning and also showed me the enclosed copy of the letter[45] which he wrote to Shah, Rajendra Prasad's intermediary, after their interview in Simla about the end of last month. I told Sikander that I thought you would be very interested in this letter and he himself suggested that I should send it to you, so that you can read it and hand it back to him on Wednesday.

I have not kept back the letter for careful study and indeed it is a little difficult to follow it without Shah's statement of conditions (which I have not seen, as Sikander did not offer to show it to me), but it seems to me that Sikander's conditions contain some which the Congress will have difficulty in swallowing, more particularly the stipulation about the composition of the Army[46] (see the bottom of page 7 of the letter).

I understand that Shah has written again to Sikander, suggesting that these negotiations should now be put on a more formal basis, by which expression I understand he implies that an approach should now be made to the Executive of the All India Muslim League. Shah and those whom he represents fully appreciate that this necessarily implies bringing in Jinnah, but there is no way of avoiding this. Sikander told me that he thought it possible that there might be a meeting in Bombay towards the end of this month, as he thinks that the Congress Working Committee is in any case meeting then.

2. As regards the general question raised in paragraph 2 of your letter to me of the 10th of June,[47] I would like to think over this for a day or two and sound a few people, on whose judgment I rely, before sending you a reply.

Yours sincerely,
H.D. CRAIK

94

CRAIK TO LINLITHGOW

Secret Barnes Court, Simla,
D.-O. No. 156 *June 19th, 1939*

Dear Lord Linlithgow,

In paragraph 2 of your private and personal letter to me of the 10th of June[48] you asked for a more formal indication of my views on the subject of Muslim opposition to Federation. I dealt with the Punjab aspect of this question in paragraphs 6 to 13 of my letter to you, No. 74 of the 5th of June 1938. But a good deal has happened since that letter was written, more particularly the recent decision of the Princes, and a review of the position may be useful. But I should like to preface what follows with a caution that I put forward my estimate with the greatest diffidence and not in any dogmatic spirit. Such as it is, it has been formed partly on the reports that reach me from the Central and Provincial Intelligence agencies, partly on conversations with leading Muslims of moderate views (Sikander and other Punjabis as well as a few from other Provinces), and partly on material supplied to me by Moon as the result of contacts with his Muslim friends.

2. To begin with, I agree with your view that we need not take too seriously the various forms of the Pakistan project. To the best of my recollection, the original Pakistan project was conceived, or at any rate sponsored, by the late Sir Muhammad Iqbal, the famous Lahore poet. It visualised an Islamic state stretching from the Ravi to the Bosphorus and uniting the Punjab, Sind, the North-West Frontier Province, possibly also the Kashmir and Bahawalpur States with Afghanistan, Iraq, Iran and Turkey. This visionary scheme was at one time given a certain amount of publicity, so far as I remember, by a small group of Muslim students in England, but I do not think it has ever been taken seriously by any thoughtful section of Muslims in India.

A modified form of the Pakistan idea contemplates, I believe, the splitting up of India into two separate entities, both of which would remain within the British Empire. Muslim India would include the Punjab, Sind, the North-West Frontier Province and perhaps also Kashmir and Bahawalpur. I have never seen any reasoned attempt to define the relations of this Muslim group with the rest of India. But this scheme too is not, to the best of my belief, taken seriously by thoughtful Muslims. Sikander, for example, appreciates that the financial objections alone are overwhelming. As he put it to me, the Punjab already provides nearly 60 per cent. of the Indian Army, but only a comparatively small portion of the cost of Defence falls on this Province. Under this scheme a more or less independent Muslim India would have to provide the finance as well as the personnel required for its defence, a burden which it could not possibly sustain.

Then there is the scheme for dividing India into the Hindu and Muhammadan 'cultural zones', which has received a good deal of publicity within the last few months. This scheme seems to be gaining a certain amount of favour with the unthinking masses of Muslims, but it is obviously quite impracticable, as it entails the shifting of vast masses of population from one area to another.

Though all these schemes are visionary and ill-defined, it would, I think, be a mistake to assume that the Pakistan idea is dead in the sense that we shall hear no more about it. I feel that it will continue to figure prominently in the columns of the more irresponsible Muslim newspapers and to be ventilated on the platform, but as a possible solution of our present difficulties I do not think it merits serious consideration.

3. I need not say anything about Sikander's own scheme,[49] as I believe he will very shortly send it to you in writing. He has asked me to let him have the services of Moon one day this week to help him to put it into shape. I gave a description of the scheme, as explained to me orally by Sikander a year ago, in my letter to you of the 5th of June 1938.

4. Muslim opposition to the scheme of Federation contained in the Act of 1935 is of course founded on the apprehension that the Central Government under that scheme will be predominantly a Congress Government, rigidly controlled by the Congress High Command; that the safeguards provided in the Act by the Governor-General's responsibility for the protection of minorities and by his control of the reserved subjects will not in practice be effective; and that the Central Executive will be disposed to meddle unduly in purely provincial matters, particularly in those Provinces where Muslims are in a majority. These apprehensions are, I believe, genuinely felt by the majority of politically minded Muslims. They were not voiced when the Act of 1935 was under consideration, because before the end of 1936 few foresaw that Congress would obtain overwhelming majorities in 8 [7] Provinces or that the Ministers of these Provinces would contain practically no genuine representation of Muslim interests. In the case of the Punjab there is an additional and special reason for anxiety. It is felt here that a Congress Central Ministry would bring

continually increasing pressure on the Governor-General to relax his control in respect of 'Defence' and that in course of time this pressure would become irresistible. Sikander and his party believe that a Congress Ministry at the Centre would insist on giving each Province a share in the Defence forces roughly equivalent to its population and that the existing Punjab predominance in the Army, which is of course of enormous economic importance to the Province, would gradually disappear.

5. This hostility towards Federation has been considerably intensified since the Patna session of the All-India Muslim League last December, at which, you will remember, great prominence was given to allegations of oppression of Muslims in the Congress Provinces, allegations which were repeated at length and in detail in the pamphlet recently circulated by Jinnah. A strong deputation of the All-India Muslim League has recently been touring in the Punjab and North-West Frontier Province, repeating these stories at crowded meetings, and this tour has in my judgment had considerable effect in intensifying communal feeling generally and Muslim determination not to tolerate Hindu domination in particular.

6. As regards the question of the form which Muslim opposition would take if Federation were imminent, as it seemed to be till a few days ago, my own view has always been that if the two other main parties, i.e. the Princes and the Congress, were ready to accept Federation without haggling or making difficulties, the Muslim opposition would not in that case take an extreme form such as civil disobedience. One of my Muslim friends, Sir Abdur Rahim, surprised me the other day by saying that if Federation were imminent, he would advise Muslims to boycott it, and when I asked what he meant by 'boycott', he said he meant a refusal to return Muslim representatives to the Federal Assembly. But Sikander, when I mentioned this view to him, pooh-poohed it as fantastic. Disunity among Muslims reduces the chance of wide-spread unconstitutional resistance on their part. Jinnah is of course an uncertain quantity and I would not care to gamble on the line he might take. But he is nearly 70 and I am told losing influence and grip. The Ahrars, who represent, speaking generally, the more uneducated Muslims of the urban lower classes, are in strong opposition to the Muslim League and might quite possibly in the near future join forces with the Congress. They would not, I think, support Muslim opposition to the Federation on a communal basis. Moreover, the Muslim leaders in the North-West Frontier Province and to some extent in Sind would probably be precluded by their close association with the Congress from resisting Federation on such a basis. The Punjab Unionists, who represent in the main the large landholders and other stable elements,

would not be disposed to lend their support to any form of opposition likely to endanger public order.

7. But apparently Federation is not at the moment imminent,[50] as the other interested parties – more particularly the Princes – are making difficulties, and in view of recent developments the Muslim dislike of Federation assumes very much greater significance than it did before. I imagine that the shrewder Muslim leaders are well aware that their attitude of opposition is likely in existing circumstances to be of decisive importance, and the probability is that they will maintain this attitude, if for no other reason than simply to gain time. It must be remembered that:

(*a*) the existing form of Government at the Centre with an irremovable Executive, anomalous as it is, suits the Muslims at the moment very well. They are in power in four Provinces and can never hope to have power in more than these, and their interests at the Centre are adequately protected by the present form of Government. Sikander, for example, has expressed quite recently his opinion that the existing state of affairs could be carried on for some years without bringing about an absolute deadlock;

(*b*) compared to the Congress, the Muslim political organisation is extremely ill-developed and they require time to improve this;

(*c*) they are by no means united, as pointed out above, and there is a good deal of general uncertainty as to what they really want. Time is required to promote unity among their own ranks and for their objections to take definite shape.

Yours sincerely,
H.D. CRAIK

95

CRAIK TO LINLITHGOW

Private and Personal — Barnes Court, Simla,
D.-O. No. 157-F.L. — *June 21st, 1939*

Dear Lord Linlithgow,

I enclose the provincial fortnightly report for the second half of May; that for the first half of June has not yet reached me.

2. The most important event since my last report on June the 5th has been the advent of the monsoon at least three weeks before the usual date. There has been abundant rainfall in Hissar and the other two districts,

Rohtak and Gurgaon, where famine has been severe. No less than 3 inches of rain fell at Hissar in a single day and the relief works have perforce been closed down, at any rate temporarily, as all the bullocks required to bring water to the works are now wanted for ploughing. The distribution of 'taccavi' for the purchase of seed and bullocks is now in full swing and ploughing for the *kharif* crop will commence at once. I do not think it likely that many workers will return to the relief works (which in Hissar had been reduced to 16 in number before the rain came) unless we have a long break in the monsoon. The premature advent of the monsoon will bring considerable relief to provincial finances, and I hope that the full amount provided in the provincial budget for famine relief will not now be required. On the other hand, this early arrival of the monsoon makes one apprehensive of its premature cessation.

3. Following the example of their Lahore brethren, the sweepers employed by the Amritsar Municipality presented a number of demands to the Municipal Committee under the threat of a strike. Although most of their demands were accepted, the strike was started on the morning of June the 12th. I understand that the main grievance of the sweepers was that the Municipality have introduced at a considerable cost an improved type of conservancy carts. The strike commanded little or no popular sympathy and the sweepers were foolish enough to play into the hands of the authorities by disorderly and riotous conduct. This was very promptly and effectively dealt with by the police and a large number of arrests, which included several of the strike leaders, were made. The strike collapsed on the evening of June the 13th, and I think the sweepers have had a good lesson.

Nevertheless, these two recent strikes in Lahore and Amritsar are matters for grave concern and had either been prolonged beyond two or three days, there would have been the gravest danger of a serious epidemic. Had the Amritsar strike lasted any longer, it would, in my judgment and in that of my Ministers, have been necessary to promulgate an Ordinance under Section 88 of the Government of India Act to deal with the emergency. Under a section of our Provincial Municipal Act a sweeper employed by a Municipal Committee, who refuses to work or absents himself from work without due notice or sufficient cause, commits an offence for which he can be sent to prison. But this section might be useless in case of a general strike because the offence is non-cognizable, i.e., the police cannot arrest without a Magistrate's warrant, and is also bailable. The contemplated Ordinance would have empowered the police to arrest without warrant and the Magistrate to refuse bail. The Ordinance has actually been drafted and will remain as a weapon in reserve in case there should be similar strikes in other places. But I am advised that under Section 88 (1) (*b*) it could only be issued on your instructions, as it conflicts with an existing law. This point is being further examined.

4. The Lahore Kisan *morcha* continues intermittently. For some days early in this month no demonstrators came forward to offer themselves for arrest, but the Provincial Kisan Committee continued its efforts to provide Satyagrahis. On June the 12th a *jatha* of about 50 from the Jullundur and Amritsar districts was arrested. My Ministers' patience with this tiresome and artificial agitation has now been exhausted and on the 15th of June it was decided to adopt a more vigorous policy and to prosecute about a dozen organisers. At the same time it was decided to issue the press communiqué of which I enclose a copy.[51]

A somewhat amusing incident has come to my notice in connection with this agitation. We have reason to believe that urgent invitations were issued to Swami Sahajanand, the well-known Kisan agitator of Bihar, and to Professor N. G. Ranga of the Central Assembly to visit Lahore in order to give the agitation a fillip, and my Ministers decided to serve both these gentlemen on arrival with orders externing them from the Punjab. However, we saw an intercepted letter dated the 12th of June from the Swami to Ranga, announcing that the Swami did not intend to visit the Punjab and advising Ranga not to go either. The letter concluded somewhat to the following effect:

> 'Sir Sikander will certainly arrest us, as he knows his business well. We will only gain some cheap publicity and praise, but we will not be able to render any effective aid to our comrades in the Punjab.'

This was very sensible advice and I imagine Ranga, who has been previously externed from the Punjab, will accept it.

5. Subhas Chandra Bose paid a short visit to Lahore on the 16th of June at the invitation of a newly-formed organisation which calls itself 'The All-India Radical Youth League'. This organisation is run by an entirely unknown young man, who probably in one way or another made a good deal of money out of Bose's visit. Bose was welcomed at the Lahore railway station by a crowd of about four thousand, the great majority of whom were students.

6. I saw a somewhat disquieting report the other day from the Superintendent of Police[52] at Ferozepore. A special train containing explosives, said to be destined for certain stations in the Mediterranean, left the Ferozepore Arsenal for Bombay or Karachi on the 11th of June,

after its departure had been postponed several times. The train developed *two* hot axle boxes at Kot Kapura and Bhatinda stations and according to the report the risk of explosion was considerable. The Superintendent of Police expressed the view that this was either a deliberate attempt at sabotage or else criminal carelessness on the part of the Railway authorities. The Railway police are investigating the matter.

7. I think Your Excellency is aware of the bitter campaign which the Ahrars have for some years now been carrying on against the Ahmadis, whom they regard as apostates. A big Ahrar conference was announced to be held on the 17th-19th of June at Qadian in the Gurdaspur district, the headquarters of the Ahmadis. The holding of the conference at this place was intended as a deliberate provocation to the Ahmadis and the District Magistrate[53] was authorised by Government to prohibit it under Section 144 of the Code of Criminal Procedure. When his order banning the conference was published, the Ahrars announced their intention of defying it on a large scale, but my latest information is that they will not do so, as prominent members of the party do not wish to be in jail during the approaching bye-election in Amritsar city.

8. A somewhat serious riot took place a few days ago at Thatta, a village in the Attock district, where the landowners are Khattars (the tribe to which Sikander himself belongs). I am told that a considerable number of Hindu moneylenders and shopkeepers live in this village and the local Congressmen organised a procession in which a number of Red Shirts from the Frontier Province took part. The procession insisted, in spite of a prohibition by the police officers on the spot, on marching through the Muslim quarters of the village. They were attacked by the local Muslims and in the course of the scuffle one of the Frontier Red Shirts received injuries, from which he subsequently died. The Congressites appear on this occasion to have been deliberately provocative.

9. I had a conference with my Ministers the day before yesterday about the Hyderabad agitation. Sikander's appeal to the Press to exercise moderation in discussing this agitation (vide my letter to you, No. 148 of May the 26th) has had little or no effect. In fact the tone of the Hindu Press in the Punjab has recently been distinctly worse, while on the other hand Muslim resentment against the agitation is intensifying. Maulana Zafar Ali Khan, a Member of the Central Assembly, made a somewhat violent speech on the subject in Lahore the other day and has announced that the 23rd of June is to be observed by Muslims as 'Hyderabad Day'. This is intended to be a sort of reprisal to the provocative action taken in certain places by *jathas* of Arya Samajists *en route*, who have indulged in

such slogans as 'Death to Islam', 'Death to the Nizam', &c. There have been no further actual clashes, but these have been narrowly averted in one or two places, notably in Panipat in the Karnal district, a place with a very bad record for communal rioting.

During the conference on the 19th Sikander stated that he was in personal touch with the Hyderabad authorities and was hopeful that an announcement would be made shortly meeting the Arya Samaj demands regarding the right to preach and the right to construct temples. Sir Chhotu Ram, who is himself an Arya Samajist, thought there was some chance of the Central Arya Samaj organisation issuing instructions that the agitation was to be damped down. Hyderabad is not, of course, the only State against which agitation is proceeding in the Punjab at the moment, though the anti-Hyderabad agitation is far more prominent and dangerous than that against any other State. There have, however, been a good many meetings lately and some attempt to form *jathas* in connection with Patiala, Chamba, Bikaner and Bahawalpur. It was eventually decided to issue at once a notification bringing into force Sections 4, 5, 6 and 7 of the Indian States (Protection) Act of 1934 throughout the Province. This will enable District Magistrates to prohibit meetings of five or more persons in furtherance of any design to send *jathas* into State territory and will also enable them to issue orders to any individual or to the public generally to abstain from any act calculated to obstruct the administration of a State or to cause a disturbance of the public tranquillity or a riot in a State.

The intention is to issue a communiqué explaining the reasons for this decision and referring to the agitation against the various States named above without giving special prominence to Hyderabad. The communiqué will call attention both to the embarrassment caused by this form of agitation to the State authorities and also to the effect which it has in intensifying communal hatred within the Punjab. Instructions will also be sent to all District Magistrates explaining the provisions of the States (Protection) Act and their powers thereunder and authorising them to use these powers whenever they think local circumstances justify such use. I will send you a copy of the communiqué as soon as it is published.

Yours sincerely,
H.D. CRAIK

96

CRAIK TO LINLITHGOW

Private and Personal Barnes Court, Simla,
D.-O. No. 161-F.L. *July 7th, 1939*

Dear Lord Linlithgow,

The announcement of my Ministry's decision to bring into force the Indian States (Protection) Act of 1934 (see paragraph 9 of my letter to you of June the 21st last) gave rise to much comment in the Press. Hindu papers were unanimous in condemning the enforcement of this Act as an act of 'repression', but the Muslim Press was equally emphatic in commending the Government's decision. Although there is a [*sic*] little sign of any slackening of the Arya Samaj movement against Hyderabad, while on the other hand there is no doubt that Muslim resentment against it is increasing, the decision of my Ministers to enforce the Act has, I think, had some effect in restraining the more offensive and provocative aspects of the agitation. Our C.I.D. recently intercepted a secret circular issued by the Punjab Hyderabad Satyagraha Committee warning branch Sabhas against the employment of irresponsible speakers and instructing them to stop all public demonstrations connected with the despatch of volunteers to Hyderabad.

That this warning was required was illustrated by an incident that took place at Kaithal, a town in Karnal district, on the 25th of June. A *jatha* of Hindus and Sikhs, who were on the point of starting for Hyderabad, marched in procession through the town and their conduct caused resentment among the local Muslims. The police were just able to prevent a serious clash by hustling the Hindu processionists into the grain market and closing the gates at both entrances to the market. The Muslims failed in their attempts to break down these gates, but nevertheless there were some sporadic assaults on the Hindus in other parts of the town, in which 17 Hindus or Sikhs received injuries. The armed police reserve had to be fetched from the district headquarters.

2 I have some hope that the Lahore Kisan *morcha* will now shortly collapse, as a considerable number of the more prominent organisers have been arrested and are being prosecuted, and the local authorities have been instructed to deal with *jathas* trying to enlist recruits in the districts adjoining Lahore as unlawful assemblies. During the second half of June

only 124 arrests were made in Lahore on four days. On most days no people offered themselves for arrest.

3. Another so-called 'Kisan *morcha*' was started a few days ago in a village called Chuhar Chak in the Moga tahsil of Ferozepore district. This village is the home of a notorious communist M.L.A. named Baba Rur Singh, who incited the villagers to refuse to pay the cess on the land revenue from which the village Chaukidars are paid. Some 15 villagers were committed to the civil lock-up at Moga for refusing to pay this cess and their arrest led to demonstrations by other men from the same village, necessitating further arrests. The movement, however, excited no sympathy among the neighbouring villages and was well-handled by the local officers, with the result that it collapsed after a few days and should discredit those who organised it.

4. I recently received a letter from Haig,[54] asking me if my Ministers could do anything to discourage Punjabis from participating in the Sunni-Shia trouble at Lucknow. I understand that something like 800 volunteers from the Punjab have proceeded to Lucknow during the last fortnight and that the agitation is to a great extent being kept alive by these Punjabis. I have told Haig that I am confident that my Ministers will do what they can, and I will talk the matter over with Sikander on his return to Simla in a day or two. He went down to Bombay at the end of June to attend the meeting of the central executive of the Muslim League.

5. In paragraph 5 of my letter of the 21st of June I mentioned Subhas Chandra Bose's brief visit to Lahore on the 16th and 17th of June. I have now seen further reports and an estimate of the effect of this visit. It is significant that Dr. Gopi Chand Bhargava, M.L.A., the leader in the Punjab of the right wing of the Congress, and Dr. Kitchlew, the newly elected President of the Provincial Congress Committee, were conspicuous by their absence from any of the functions in Bose's honour. It is doubtful if Bose's visit had any permanent effect in securing support for his 'Forward Bloc', but it has certainly accentuated the split between the two wings of the Congress in the Punjab.

6. The hundredth anniversary of Maharaja Ranjit Singh's death was celebrated with considerable enthusiasm at many places in the Punjab on the 23rd of June. Processions were taken out and eulogies pronounced on the Maharaja, while most of the principal newspapers had special supplements for the occasion. The proceedings seem to have been everywhere orderly and I have not heard of any undesirable speeches.

7. In some of my earlier letters I have mentioned the Non-Agriculturists' Association formed to resist the enforcement of the agrarian legislation

passed by my Ministry last year. The President of this Association was Sir Gokal Chand Narang, a leading barrister of Lahore, who before 1937 was for some years a Minister. I have recently been informed that he has resigned from the leadership of this Association which, beyond holding a few meetings, never accomplished anything effective, and I doubt whether anything more will be heard of this Association.

8. In paragraph 6 of my letter of the 21st of June I mentioned a disquieting incident regarding a train containing explosives despatched from the Ferozepore Arsenal to Bombay or Karachi. A later report makes it clear that there was no attempt at sabotage and that the hot axle troubles were entirely due to mechanical defects, for which the railway authorities are solely responsible. Nevertheless, the development of two hot axles on one train in a comparatively short run seems to argue an extremely high degree of inefficiency.

9. I enclose the Provincial fortnightly report for the first half of June.

Yours sincerely,
H.D. CRAIK

97

CRAIK TO LINLITHGOW

Secret
D.-O. No. 162

Barnes Court, Simla,
July 10th, 1939

Dear Lord Linlithgow,

Sikander has just returned to Simla from his visit to Bombay for the meeting of the Muslim League Executive and during the course of a conversation today he told me something of his doings there, which will I think be of interest to you.

2. He informed the other members of the Executive Committee of the approach that had been made to him by Professor Shah on behalf of Rajendra Prasad. Jinnah professed to be as ready as any one else for an understanding with the Congress on the communal issue, and asserted that he was quite prepared to meet Rajendra Prasad on the subject, but Sikander's impression is that Jinnah is not really anxious for a rapprochement, and this impression is, I gather, shared by most of the other members of the League Executive. The majority of them, according to Sikander, suggested to him that it would be much better if the preliminary negotiations were to be conducted on behalf of the League by Sikander himself and

that if these preliminary negotiations seem likely to lead to any really useful result, then and not till then should Jinnah (and presumably the Muslim League Executive generally) be brought into the picture.

I understand that this view was generally accepted and that the question has accordingly been left there, i.e. that Sikander is to continue preliminary negotiations with the Congress leaders.[55]

3. Presumably as the result of this conclusion, Sikander had two long private conversations with Gandhi at Bombay. I did not like to press him as to the subjects discussed, but he did tell me that Gandhi is to give him at leisure his (Gandhi's) reactions to the proposals put forward in Sikander's last letter to Professor Shah, a copy of which I sent you under cover of my letter No. 153 of the 12th of June last.[56]

4. Sikander told me that Gandhi seemed to be in excellent physical health and mentally as alert as ever. Jinnah, on the other hand, is in Sikander's opinion distinctly losing grip. Possibly as the result of advancing years he is apt to get peevish more quickly than he used to, and according to Sikander he is more than ever inclined to be critical of any proposals put forward, but never in a constructive way. Sikander thinks that the confidence which Jinnah commands among the Muslim League leaders is weakening.

5. As regards Sikander's scheme for Federation,[57] he has given copies of this in confidence both to Jinnah and to Gandhi and is awaiting their reactions. He apparently explained the scheme in general terms to his colleagues on the League Executive, probably in somewhat greater detail than in his speech at the Taj Mahal hotel luncheon, which was reported in the Press. He told me that on the whole the reception of the scheme by his colleagues was favourable.

6. Sikander told me that the most interesting discussion at the meeting of the League Executive dealt with the attitude to be adopted by the League should there be an outbreak of war. This was an entirely secret discussion and nothing appeared in the Press about it. I gather that Sikander himself initiated it with a definite suggestion that should war be declared, the League should at once make an announcement in terms of its Sholapur resolution (I am not delaying this letter to look up the terms of that resolution, but so far as I recollect it was to the effect that in its own interests Muslim India should support Great Britain in the event of a world conflict). Sikander in support of his proposal said that it was essential from his point of view that the position of the League in the event of war should be clarified. He and his Government were in any event pledged to support Great Britain and so, he added, is Bengal. In case the League did

not take the same view, Sikander and his colleagues (and I gather also the Bengal Muslim Ministers) would have no option but to resign from the League, and their resignation would be a very severe blow to the prestige and influence of the League, and to Muslim solidarity generally.

The majority of the League Executive expressed agreement with Sikander's proposal. Jinnah was at first inclined to be obstructive, but eventually modified his attitude in deference to the wishes of the majority. He pointed out, shrewdly enough, that any immediate announcement by the League of its intention to assist the Empire in case of war would be certain to provoke controversy with such Muslim bodies as the Ahrars, &c., which are opposed to the League. Eventually I gather the general view was that while the League was not prepared to make a definite announcement *now* regarding its own attitude in case of war, Sikander was quite at liberty to make his own position clear immediately war should break out, and apparently he was given to understand that his position would be endorsed by the League The general feeling seems to have been that an announcement by Sikander would by itself make it clear to the British Government that they could rely on the support of Muslim India and that the League would not use the outbreak of war in a bargaining spirit.

7. I cannot vouch that the foregoing paragraphs are an absolutely accurate account of my conversation with Sikander. It was a fairly long one, lasting for the better part of an hour, and I have of course to rely on my memory for what he said. But I think it is substantially correct.

Yours sincerely,
H.D. CRAIK

98

CRAIK TO LINLITHGOW

Private and Personal

Barnes Court, Simla,
July 13th, 1939

Dear Lord Linlithgow,

With reference to the first paragraph of your letter of the 11th of July, I enclose for your information a copy of my letter of that date to Haig about the participation of Punjabis in the Shia-Sunni agitation at Lucknow.

Yours sincerely,
H.D. CRAIK

ENCLOSURE TO NO. 98

CRAIK TO HAIG

Private and Personal

Barnes Court, Simla,
July 11th, 1939

My dear Haig,

I am writing in continuation of my private and personal letter of the 3rd of July[58] about the Shia-Sunni trouble at Lucknow.

Sikander has just returned to Simla from a visit to Bombay, having spent a couple of days in Lahore on his way back, and I had a talk with him yesterday on this subject. He is much distressed about the part taken by Punjabis in this agitation and tells me that he has for some time been doing his best to dissuade Shias from this Province from going to Lucknow. According to his information there are now as many as 1,200 Punjabis in jail in the United Provinces. When he was at Lahore the other day he saw Maulana Zafar Mehdi, who is a very influential Shia divine. The Maulana is doing his best to dissuade his fellow Shias from taking part in this agitation and other prominent Shias in Lahore, more particularly the Qizilbash family, are doing the same.

2. Sikander does not, however, think that it is practicable to take any legal action to restrain Punjabis from participating in the movement. So far as I am aware, the only possible action would be by means of orders under Section 144 of the Code of Criminal Procedure, and I am in agreement with Sikander that (*a*) it would not in practice be possible to enforce such orders, and (*b*) their issue might only intensify the agitation. Sikander will, however, continue to do what is possible by way of persuasion and the exercise of his own and his friends' personal influence.

3. It may perhaps interest you to hear Sikander's views about this movement. He considers that the initial mistake was that your Ministry departed from what was found to be the *status quo* by a committee that sat in 1932 in allowing the Sunnis to recite the Madhe Sahaba in public, which had never previously been done. He tells me that, according to his information, your two Muslim Ministers, Kidwai and Hafiz Ibrahim both of whom are, I understand, Sunnis, were mainly responsible for this change. But Sikander understands that the Shias would now be prepared to drop the agitation if the Sunnis could be induced to say that, their right to recite the Madhe Sahaba having been asserted, they will not exercise this right in future. He also told me that his information is that the two men primarily

responsible for keeping the agitation alive are two Lucknow Sunnis, Zafrul Mulk and Maulvi Abdul Shakoor. The former of these in particular did all he could to discount the statement signed by a number of Muslim leaders (including Sikander himself) which was issued from Simla in May last.

Yours sincerely,
H.D. CRAIK

99

CRAIK TO LINLITHGOW

Private and Personal
D.O. No. 163-F.L.

Barnes Court, Simla,
July 23rd, 1939

Dear Lord Linlithgow,

The past fortnight has been a quiet one and I have little to add to the provincial reports for the second half of June and the first half of July, which I enclose herewith. I only returned to Simla on the 21st from a brief holiday in Dehra Dun and Saharanpur and have not seen any of my Ministers since my return.

2. There has been some increase recently in the number of anti-recruitment speeches and references to this subject are generally to be found in the speeches of Dr. Kitchlew, President of the Provincial Congress Committee. I do not think these speeches are having any adverse effect on recruitment, but the Premier is keeping a careful watch on them and is quite prepared to prosecute on a suitable occasion.

3. The more vigorous policy adopted by the Ministry in dealing with the Lahore Kisan *morcha* has, as pointed out in the provincial report, brought the *morcha* practically to a stand-still. A number of the organisers have been arrested and are being prosecuted, and I doubt very much if we shall hear more of this troublesome agitation.

4. I am not at the moment in a position to say whether Sikander's efforts to discourage Punjabis from participation in the Shia-Sunni agitation at Lucknow have had any effect. C.I.D. reports are to the effect that about 150 Shia volunteers left for Lucknow in the first fortnight of July.

5. I am glad to say that in the last day or two there has been good rainfall over the greater part of the famine area, with the exception of the Sirsa tehsil of Hissar district and one part of Rohtak district. This timely rainfall should ensure the maturing of the crops sown with the earlier rain in June, and I hope that it will very soon be possible to practically close

down famine operations, except in Sirsa and one tehsil of the Rohtak district. So much money has been poured out in these areas within the last 7 or 8 months that the people should be able to manage on their own resources till the crops now in the ground mature. Preparations are being made for Your Excellency's visit to Hissar early in August.

6. There have been two more defections from the Unionist Party. The two seceders are members of the Assembly belonging to the well-known Jilani family of Pirs in the Multan district. The Jilanis have always been on bad terms with the other leading Pir family, the Qureshis, and the defection is due to the fact that one or two Jilanis have recently been defeated in the local District Board elections. As the Jilanis have considerable spiritual influence in the south-west Punjab, I am afraid these two defections may be somewhat embarrassing to the Ministry.

7. We had another threat of a sweepers' strike in Multan city the other day, but no strike actually occurred. In paragraph 3 of my letter to you of June the 21st I informed you that an Ordinance had been drafted to deal with the very serious emergency that might be caused by a strike of sweepers in a large city, but that I was advised that under Section 88 (1) (*b*) of the Government of India Act such an Ordinance could only be promulgated on your instructions, as it conflicts with an existing law. This point has been further examined and I am satisfied that the advice tendered to me was correct. Moon has now addressed your Secretary (Public) officially on the subject.

Yours sincerely,
H.D. CRAIK

100

CRAIK TO LINLITHGOW

Private and Personal — Barnes Court, Simla,
D.O. No. 165-F.L. — *August 11th, 1939*

Dear Lord Linlithgow,

The past fortnight has again been a fairly quiet one, though there have been some disturbing communal incidents, to which reference is made on page 2 of the enclosed provincial report for the second half of July. These were of a comparatively minor character, but the general atmosphere is distinctly tense.

2. Nearly all my Ministers have been on tour for most of the fortnight.

Sikander went to Bombay, in connection with the provincial loan which we are about to float, to see prominent people with influence in the money market. A few weeks ago we were advised by the Reserve Bank that they had sounded the money market in regard to our loan and that though our requirements were about 2½ crores only, the banks were only prepared to underwrite 141 lakhs and some of the tenders for this amount were as low as 96 per cent. This was a most disturbing report and Sikander suspected that it was not entirely due to the disturbed condition of Europe and the reluctance of investors to lock up capital in low interest investments with the possibility of war in the near future. He felt that the Indian money market had been frightened by the Bombay prohibition scheme and was inclined to be distrustful of all provincial loans in consequence, and he also had an idea that Congress influence was working prejudicially to the success of our loan. I mentioned this latter idea to Raisman in conversation the other day, but he did not think Sikander's suspicion was well-founded. Sikander, however, decided, with my entire concurrence, that it would be a good thing for him to go to Bombay and see some of the leading people in the money market with whom he had had connections when he was Deputy Governor of the Reserve Bank. The visit was entirely successful and we are now advised by the Reserve Bank that the whole amount we require this year (2½ crores) has been underwritten, and we are announcing our loan in a day or two, the rate of interest being 3 per cent. and the price at flotation 98.

3. We had an interesting discussion in Council on the 24th of July regarding a Bill to limit the hours of work for shop assistants and commercial employees and to make certain provisions regarding their holidays, wages and terms of service. The Bill *inter alia* prohibits the employment of children under 14 years of age in shops and commercial concerns, fixes a maximum of 61 working hours per week and 11 hours per day, and directs that all shops, &c., shall be closed on Sundays. The Bill is modelled on one which has been introduced in the Bombay Presidency and is to apply at first only to six of our largest towns. It is intended to introduce this Bill at the October session and to move for its circulation. Although the provisions of the Bill are generally moderate, and I think on the whole desirable, the difficulty will be that it will require a very large staff to enforce them.

4. I am considerably disturbed about the growth of volunteer organisations in some of our larger towns, regarding which you will see a paragraph on page 2 of the provincial report. This movement is particularly prominent in Rawalpindi, Lahore and Amritsar, and I am afraid that unless

something is done to check it, we must expect clashes between these rival communal bodies. I have sent the Premier a note on the subject and urged him to consider whether legislation, possibly on the lines of the English Act of 1936, is not practicable.

5. Although the Press originally gave a very unfavourable reception to the announcement of reforms in Hyderabad State, the despatch of *jathas* has now been suspended, and I think the agitation against the State authorities will now rapidly subside so far as the Punjab is concerned. Only 8 volunteers left for Hyderabad in the week ending the 29th of July and none in the following week.

6. Interest in the Sunni-Shia agitation in Lucknow is also declining. Thirty-two volunteers are reported to have proceeded to Lucknow from the Lahore, Jhelum and Multan districts during the week ending the 29th of July, but only 3 left in the following week. A good many of the volunteers from the Punjab have now returned considerably disillusioned.

You may have noticed in the newspapers that when Gandhi was passing through Lahore on the 26th of July on his way from Abbottabad to Wardha a small band of Shias made a hostile demonstration against him at the railway station. I understand that Sikander wrote to Gandhi apologizing for this unseemly incident.

7. Another sweepers' strike started in Multan city on the 23rd of July and the Deputy Commissioner[59] telegraphed asking for the promulgation of the Ordinance to which I referred in paragraph 7 of my letter to you of July the 23rd. I had not at that time received your sanction to its promulgation, but fortunately owing to vigorous action by the local officers and the importation of sweepers from outside the Multan strike collapsed on the 26th, and by the time your sanction to the Ordinance was received it was no longer required at Multan. It will, however, be a useful weapon in case we have further strikes of this nature. There is some reason to think that the strike at Multan was promoted, or at any rate encouraged, by the Jilanis, to whom I referred in paragraph 6 of my letter to you of the 23rd of July.

8. I am afraid Sikander must be disappointed at the reception which his Federation scheme[60] has had in the press. Practically all the comments which I have read, even in Muslim papers, have been unfavourable. I understand that the method he selected for revealing the scheme to the Press was somewhat unfortunate. He gave a luncheon party here, to which he invited only the European press correspondents, and he also invited the Indian press correspondents to a tea party, I think, on the same day. The Indian correspondents took offence at this discrimination and I am

told that none of them accepted his invitation to the tea party. This procedure was hardly calculated to give the scheme a favourable start.

9. I had a long talk with Sikander yesterday, at which he expressed his very great appreciation of the success of your visit to Hissar. He also told me that he proposed to take at least a fortnight's holiday some time in September, as he is feeling very stale and tired and wants a rest before the next session of the Assembly, which promises to be a protracted and trying one, starts about the 25th of October. He contemplates going either to Kashmir or possibly to Mysore, where I understand he has been invited by Sir Mirza M. Ismail. I told him I thought this was a very wise decision, but it will, of course, mean that during a considerable part of September both he and Manohar Lal will be on leave.

Yours sincerely,
H.D. CRAIK

101

CRAIK TO LINLITHGOW

Barnes Court, Simla,
D.-O. No. 166 *August 25th, 1939*

Dear Lord Linlithgow,

Will you please refer to the correspondence ending with your letter to me of the 6th of June last about Gandhi's request for the release of the terrorist convict Prithvi Singh.

2. You are, I think, aware that when Gandhi's Secretary, Mahadev Desai, was in Simla the other day, he renewed in a conversation with Sikander, Gandhi's request for the release of this man. I understand he brought a letter from Gandhi to Sikander on the subject, though Sikander did not show it to me. According to Mahadev Desai, Gandhi is completely convinced that Prithvi Singh has genuinely abandoned all ideas of violence. Gandhi undertakes to keep Prithvi Singh in his Ashram at Wardha under his own eye for a period of six months. Thereafter, provided there is no indication that Prithvi Singh has had any kind of 'moral relapse', Gandhi proposes to employ him on propaganda work among communities, over whom Gandhi considers he would have considerable influence.

I understand that Sikander stipulated that if Prithvi Singh is to be released on the above understanding, he should give a written undertaking to remain outside the Punjab. Mahadev Desai intimated to Sikander that Prithvi Singh would be prepared to give such an undertaking.

3. Sikander has now made a definite recommendation for Prithvi Singh's release on the conditions specified above, viz., (*a*) a written undertaking that he will not re-enter the Punjab without the permission of the Provincial Government, and (*b*) Gandhi's promise that Prithvi Singh will remain in the Wardha Ashram for a period of at least six months after release.

I pointed out to Sikander that in view of my previous correspondence with Your Excellency it would be necessary to consult you before arriving at a decision, and he asked me to convey his views to you, provided I approve of them.

4 I stated my own views at length in my secret letter to you, No. 138 of April the 17th last, to which I would ask you to refer. One point I took (in which Sikander then agreed with me) was that the release of Prithvi Singh might lead to embarrassing demands for the release of Gurmukh Singh, who was convicted in the same case as Prithvi Singh in 1915 and is at present serving a sentence of transportation for life in the New Central Jail at Multan. Together with Prithvi Singh he twice escaped from custody, on the first occasion in 1922 when he was being transferred from one jail to another in Madras. On that occasion he was arrested after a few days, but again escaped in 1923 during transfer and was arrested under a false name at Lahore in 1936. In the interval he had travelled all over the world, including Russia, and I think for a large part of the time was in Prithvi Singh's company. As regards the possibility of embarrassing demands for Gurmukh Singh's release, Sikander now takes the view that we could justify the release of Prithvi Singh on the grounds that he has now become a reformed character and that his conduct since his confinement in the Rawalpindi Jail has been excellent (this last point is quite correct). Gurmukh Singh, on the other hand, has shown no signs of reformation; he took a prominent part in organising a hunger-strike among the Punjab terrorist convicts repatriated from the Andamans in the winter of 1938 and has made no pretence of abandoning the ideas he has always entertained.

5. As regards the more general grounds of principle on which I objected to Prithvi Singh's release, these were explained in the penultimate paragraph of my demi-official letter to you of the 17th of April. I still hold that these objections have great force and, indeed, that the release of Prithvi Singh at the present moment, when we are menaced with a world war, would be attended with even greater risks than in normal times. On the other hand, in view of the contemplated condition that the convict should

remain outside the Punjab, I cannot hold that the proposal for his release would attract my special responsibility for the prevention of a grave menace to the peace or tranquillity of the Province. I take it, therefore, that the constitutional position is that I should accept the advice tendered to me by the responsible Minister. Orders will not, however, issue until I have your approval, and I am confident that, should you decide that it is wiser to keep Prithvi Singh in jail for some time longer, Sikander would be quite prepared to accept this view.

6. In his conversation with Sikander, Mahadev Desai also mentioned two other prisoners in whose release Gandhi is particularly interested. These are (1) Gaya Parshad, who is, I believe, at present confined to the Lucknow Jail. The grounds on which Gandhi asks that this man should be released are that he has been recently operated on for appendicitis and is said to be suffering from diabetes; (2) Sucha Singh, now confined to the Hazaribagh Jail in Bihar. This man is said to be 75 years old. Sikander is looking into these cases, in regard to which I am not at present in possession of details.

Yours sincerely,
H.D. CRAIK

102

CRAIK TO LINLITHGOW

Private and Personal
D.-O. No. 167-F.L.

Barnes Court, Simla,
August 25th, 1939

Dear Lord Linlithgow,

The imminent menace of war overshadows everything else, and it is difficult to divert one's thoughts from what is happening in Europe to our daily administrative problems and difficulties.

I had satisfactory (and separate) talks yesterday with the two leading personalities in my Ministry, Sikander and Chhotu Ram. Both fully appreciate the extreme gravity of the situation and neither has any illusions on the subject. I was impressed with the courage and equanimity with which they seem ready to face the tremendous strain that almost certainly lies ahead of all of us. Neither made any attempt to minimize the gravity of the difficulties with which we are likely to be confronted, but both assured me that I could rely to the full on their loyalty and assistance. Both are entirely confident that the martial classes in the Punjab will make as magnificent a response to the call that will surely be made on them as they did in the Great War.

Chhotu Ram made the observation that though he anticipates the ultimate resignation of the Ministries in the Congress Provinces, we in the Punjab are not likely to find the Congress opposition to war measures a very formidable difficulty. I am inclined to agree in this view, but I am afraid we shall have a lot of trouble with visits from agitators from other Provinces. I feel confident that such visits will be firmly checked by the Ministers.

2. As regards special war precautions, I reminded our Inspector-General of Police[61] yesterday of the urgent necessity of perfecting our arrangements for the recruitment of additional police. He tells me that our obligation to protect vulnerable points (such as railway bridges, &c.) will require about a thousand additional men. Plenty of good material will be forthcoming, but we shall probably have to provide the actual recruiting staff ourselves, as the Army Recruiting Officers will presumably be fully occupied. There should be no difficulty in doing this.

I also gave instructions, with the full concurrence of the Premier, for the immediate arrest of one or two highly suspect Germans employed in public utility concerns, such as electric power-houses. One of these is actually employed in the Simla Power-House. These men can be detained under one of the sections of the existing Foreigners Act pending promulgation of the War Ordinance. I understand that our arrangements for the rounding up of enemy aliens immediately on the outbreak of war are quite complete.

3. In our conversation yesterday Sikander himself brought up the subject of volunteer organisations, to which I referred in paragraph 4 of my letter to you No. 165-F.L. of August the 11th. He agreed that in the event of war these organisations would have to be suppressed, but the first step he proposes to take is to warn the organisers that these bodies are becoming a grave menace to public peace and severe restrictive action may be necessary. He hopes that this will possibly have the effect, at any rate in some cases, of inducing the leaders to disband these bodies. I doubt very much if this method will be effective, but I see no objection to giving it a trial.

4. The full figures regarding our recent provincial loan are now available. We actually received applications for 279 lakhs 'real money', though the amount of the loan was limited to 250 lakhs. The under-writers will thus not have to take up any part of the loan. We were extraordinarily lucky in the moment chosen to float the loan, as I imagine no provincial loan would have much chance of success in existing conditions.

5. Owing to the failure of the monsoon the conditions in the three famine districts remain exceedingly grave. A few areas have received fairly ample rainfall but in the greater part the crops sown on the arrival of the rains in June have now all withered, and it now seems practically certain that famine conditions will prevail at least throughout the winter. The time for sowing *kharif* crops has passed and unless there is a fairly good rainfall in October (I fear a very unlikely contingency) no *rabi* crops can be sown on unirrigated areas. The prospect of having to continue famine relief measures for a further indefinite period is exceedingly disturbing. We budgeted for a deficit of about 30 lakhs on our Revenue account for the current year, but land revenue and irrigation receipts having come in badly the deficit would in any case, even if we had been able to close down relief measures this month, have been at least double that anticipated. It now seems possible that we may have to spend another 50 or 60 lakhs on relief measures before the end of this financial year and this sum of money can only be found by ruthless measures of economy in other departments.

We had a big conference two days ago up here, attended by the Ministers,[62] the Financial Commissioners,[63] the Commissioner of Ambala[64] and the Deputy Commissioners of the three famine districts.[65] I presided and gave the conference the gist of a note prepared by the Finance Secretary[66] on the position of provincial finances and pointed out the great gravity of the situation. It was generally agreed that in any case relief measures could not be continued on the present scale. It was eventually decided *inter alia*:

(*a*) that the rate of daily wage for workers on relief works should be immediately reduced from 2 annas to 1¼ anna, the rate laid down in the Famine Code. It is now evident that the enhancement to 2 annas, which was decided upon by the Ministry when famine operations first started, was a grave mistake, and it is to be hoped that the reduction will mean a curtailment in the numbers attending these works The rate is now so low that it will attract only those who are really destitute;

(*b*) the distribution of fodder for milch cattle will have to be stopped and the amount to be provided for the maintenance of stud bulls will have to be reduced;

(*c*) a few relief works in certain areas are now to be closed down, but others will have to be opened, and there will be no reduction in the total number of relief works;

(*d*) the question of promulgating an Ordinance to prohibit the export of fodder from certain areas was discussed, and the Fodder Adviser[67] is to look into this matter and ascertain whether such an Ordinance is really required. It is doubtful whether there is an appreciable amount of fodder available for export. If there is, the Fodder Adviser will probably buy it up at once.

6. Manohar Lal flew from Karachi on the 22nd by K.L.M. to London. He was considerably perturbed before starting at the prospect of an early outbreak of war in Europe. He sent me a somewhat pathetic telegram from Karachi, which read as follows:

> 'Flying immediately with some anxiety. Pray [*sic*] your very particular and vigilant attention to our finances.'

I take it the odds are that the League of Nations Conference, which he has gone to attend, will now be cancelled. I only hope he will be able to make his way back to India as soon as possible.

Major Khizar Hayat Khan, the Minister for Public Works and Local Self-Government, has just left Simla with the object of taking a short holiday in Kashmir, but Sikander is trying to catch him in Lahore and stop him from leaving the Punjab. I am afraid the prospects of Sikander's own holiday are now very remote.

7. There was a nasty little riot in Lahore on August the 20th arising out of the agitation against the proposed house-tax. There was a general *hartal* throughout the city and a procession was taken out and led to the Town Hall, ostensibly to register objections against the new assessments. What happened is described in the official communiqué that appeared in today's papers, of which I enclose a copy.[68] On the whole, I am inclined to think that the disorderly conduct of the mob is likely somewhat to discredit the leaders of the agitation, who were quite unable to control their followers, but I fear the opposition to the tax is very general and will give us considerable trouble in the near future. The Ministers are, however, firm in their resolve that the tax must be imposed and in this, I think, they are quite right. The person primarily responsible for the disorder in Lahore was Begam Rashida Latif Baji who represents the Lahore Women's Constituency in the Legislative Assembly. She has hitherto been a nominal supporter of the Unionist Party and has now announced her resignation from the party. She is evidently a fire-brand of a very unbalanced temperament and it may be necessary to take action against her in the criminal courts.

8. In paragraph 5 of my letter No. 151-F.L. of June the 5th I mentioned that Shaikh Muhammad Sadiq, the Unionist candidate who had succeeded

in winning a recent bye-election for the Amritsar City Muhammadan seat, had been unseated on petition. It seemed probable until the other day that the resulting bye-election would be a straight fight between the Unionist and Muslim League candidate Shaikh Sadiq Hassan (Muhammad Sadiq's brother) and the Ahrar candidate, Chaudhri Afzal Haq, but on the eve of nomination the Congress decided that their provincial President, Dr. Kitchlew (who is a resident of Amritsar), shall also stand. The Ahrars are furious at this decision, which of course means that there will be a three-cornered fight, and showed their resentment by breaking up a Congress meeting held at Lahore to protest against the proposed house-tax. The incident is described on page 1 of the fortnightly report for the first half of August, which I enclose. I am afraid that polling days at Amritsar, fixed for the latter half of September, may be the occasion for considerable disorder. Full police precautions will, of course, be taken.

Yours sincerely,
H.D. CRAIK

103

CRAIK TO LINLITHGOW[69]

Secret and Personal
D.-O. No. 171

Barnes Court, Simla,
August 28th, 1939

Dear Lord Linlithgow,

I think you will be interested to hear of a talk I had with Sikander this morning. He is very pleased with the unanimously cordial reception given by the Muslim Press of the Punjab to his recent statement[70] on the attitude of India in the event of war.[71] But he realises that this statement must have been extremely unpalatable to Jinnah and the central executive of the All-India Muslim League. Indeed, he thinks it quite possible that the ultimate result may be the withdrawal of all Punjab support from the Muslim League and that this may be followed by a similar withdrawal on the part of Bengal Muslims. The League would then cease to be representative of Muslim opinion, as I believe that the Punjab and Bengal Muslims form 80 per cent of the total population of [?Muslims in] India.

Sikander is afraid that Jinnah may be so upset by his statement that he may attempt to stampede the Punjab Muslim Press away from its present satisfactory attitude. Jinnah has funds which he might employ in influencing the Press. A cheque from Hyderabad for Rs. 30,000 actually passed through

Sikander's hands to Jinnah. As you know, the Press is very easily bribed and Sikander thinks that in case of war it would be well worth while for us to spend a considerable amount of money to keep it straight, should that be necessary.

He also thinks that a number of more or less professional agitators could be pretty easily persuaded by a suitable financial inducement either to refrain from agitation or even to promote such objects as a 'recruitment campaign'.

I am of opinion that expenditure on a fairly generous scale on these objects would be fully justified in war time and would be money well spent. Our own provision for secret service expenditure is very limited and I do not think that it would be possible to find the funds ourselves. Do you think that Ewart could let Sikander have a sum of (say) Rs. 2,000/- p[er] m[onth] for the next few months for this purpose, should war break out? Every possible precaution would, of course, be taken to ensure secrecy in all dealings of the kind suggested.

Yours sincerely,
H.D. CRAIK

104

CRAIK TO LINLITHGOW

Private and Personal
D.-O. No. 174-F.L.

Barnes Court, Simla,
September 13th, 1939

Dear Lord Linlithgow,

I am afraid this fortnightly appreciation is a little late, but the provincial report for the second half of August only reached me yesterday. I enclose two copies of this.

2. The news of the declaration of war on Germany has been the occasion of a remarkable wave of enthusiastic loyalty in the Punjab. As you are aware, immediately this news became public, Sikander issued a second brief statement explaining the justice of our cause and calling on the Punjab to demonstrate its sympathy for Britain in practical fashion and to maintain the splendid traditions of the Province as 'the sword arm of India'. This was received with a chorus of approval by the Press. The statements of Britain's case issued by Mr Chamberlain excited practically no hostile comment in any section of the Press, and almost all newspapers which I have seen (and I see cuttings from a very large number, both English and vernacular) have expressed their appreciation of our reasons for declaring

war. The statement in the first paragraph of the provincial report that the Congress Press 'is maintaining its intransigent attitude' may have been true at the time it was written, but since the actual declaration of war even the Congress papers have admitted the justice of our cause and have for the most part called on India to give practical co-operation. The only points on which I have seen critical comment have been as regards the extreme reticence of official news regarding the actual progress of the war and the delay in putting a check on profiteering. This latter criticism has now, of course, been met, but the unjustifiable advance in nearly all necessities of life caused much uneasiness, especially in the large towns, and if prompt steps had not been taken, I think we might have had some cases of looting of shops and even of food riots.

3. Gandhi's statement since his interview with you has been hailed with universal approval, and I think the general feeling is that Congress will now probably 'come in' unconditionally. They are, however, taking a long time to make up their minds! Jinnah's distinctly hesitating and equivocal statement has not elicited any expression of approval from Punjab Muslims. The Muslim League is to decide on its attitude at its meeting in Delhi on September 17th, which Sikander and a large contingent of his supporters are to attend. It is generally expected that the League will endorse Sikander's attitude.

4. I have myself been inundated with loyal offers. They are coming in at the rate of about 100 a day and generally take the form of placing the writer's 'personal services and all his resources' at the disposal of Government. Most of these are from individuals, but many are also from District and Municipal Boards, from District Soldiers' Boards, from spiritual leaders on behalf of their followers and from various tribal and communal associations. All are being acknowledged as fast as my Secretariat can cope with them and the names of the writers are being published. But I think it may also be desirable for me in a few days to broadcast on the Radio an acknowledgment of these offers.[72] Should I decide to do so, I would probably make the following points:

(*a*) the undeniable justice of our cause, which has been acknowledged by practically every political party and every community in India, even by circles which are generally inclined to be critical or hostile to the British connection;

(*b*) the remarkable enthusiasm of the Punjab and its clearly expressed determination to live up to its great traditions;

(*c*) an appreciation of the fact that those who have offered their services wish to be told what to do and an appeal to them to wait patiently till it is clear in what form India can make the most helpful contribution to winning the war. I would emphasize that it is certain that the war will be a grim and prolonged struggle and equally certain that before it ends India will be called upon to make the maximum effort possible.

5. As regards this last point, it is somewhat unfortunate, as I pointed out in conversation with you a few days ago, that we cannot take immediate advantage of the present general enthusiasm by initiating a great recruiting drive or something of the kind. Sikander has assured me that if we were asked to do so, we could supply half a million recruits of the best class within a few weeks.[73] I had a brief conversation on this subject with the [Commander-in-] Chief on the 11th September and quite recognise the difficulties, but from the Punjab point of view the sooner the call comes, the better.

6. Sikander is now away on a short tour to Lahore and Amritsar and will then go to Delhi for the Muslim League meeting. At Lahore he saw a representative gathering of journalists and conveyed to them his appreciation of the attitude which the newspaper Press as a whole had taken up regarding the war. He also explained to them the main provisions of the Defence of India Ordinance and Rules and made it clear that while Government would be very reluctant to apply these drastic powers, it would not hesitate to do so should there be unreasonable opposition to its policy of whole-hearted co-operation with the Empire in the war. He also intended to have a talk with some of the more prominent agitators who have been making anti-recruitment speeches and to repeat to them the warning contained in a recent Press communiqué (a copy of which I enclose) that 'prejudicial' acts and statements will not in future be tolerated. He may also have an opportunity of warning the organisers of the volunteer bodies which have been such a nuisance lately that the Defence of India Rules give the Local Government drastic powers of stopping their activities and advising them to close down. The most troublesome of these bodies, the Khaksars, has been greatly discredited by the manner in which the leader and his followers 'caved in' when firmly handled by the Lucknow authorities recently.

7. Before he left Simla, Sikander put to me in conversation a somewhat surprising proposition that in case the Congress decides to give unconditional support and co-operation in the prosecution of the war, he should take into his Cabinet two prominent Congressmen with a view to securing a Ministry representative of all shades of opinion. The two persons whom he has in mind are Pandit Gopi Chand Bhargava, the leader of the

Congress opposition in the Punjab Assembly, who represents the Congress 'right wing' and is a supporter of the High Command; and Mian Muhammad Iftikhar-ud-Din, a Muslim Congressite. The latter comes from the well-known Baghbanpura family of Lahore and is closely related to the late Sir Muhammad Shafi and his daughter, Begum Shah Nawaz, who is one of our Parliamentary Secretaries. He is a man of considerable wealth, but of distinctly 'leftist' ideas. I am not sure whether he belongs to the right or left wing of the Congress, but I fancy the former.

Sikander's expectation is that if these two men are asked to join the Ministry, they will accept only the orthodox Congress salary of Rs. 500 a month, and he proposes that this amount should be found by making corresponding reduction in the aggregate salaries of the present six Ministers.

I am not personally very enthusiastic about this proposal,[74] as I am afraid that the presence of these two individuals in the Cabinet may disturb our existing harmony and may on occasions be decidedly embarrassing. But if Sikander presses it, I think I should accept it. I would, however, be grateful for your advice. I should repeat that the contingency will only arise should the Congress decide to give unconditional co-operation in the prosecution of the war.

8. A deputation of the Kisan leaders saw the Premier on the 28th of August and, after hearing what he had to say about the Lahore Kisan agitation, decided to call this movement off unconditionally. Sikander made no promise that he would release those who are serving sentences for participation in this agitation, but he does in fact intend to order the release of the rank and file. I do not think he will be in any hurry about releasing the leaders and organisers now in jail, but he will probably consider the case of each of them individually on its merits.

9. There has been a certain amount of rain recently in parts of the three famine districts, but I am afraid that it has been scattered and on the whole the situation does not show much improvement. The attendance at relief works has, however, declined owing to the curtailment of the daily wage in all three districts.

10. We are up against an extremely difficult financial problem in regard to the Thal irrigation project. This is a project for putting a barrage across the Indus in the neighbourhood of Kalabagh and irrigating large areas in the Mianwali, Muzaffargarh and Shahpur districts. We have placed large contracts for steel and cement for the construction of the headworks, the steel contracts being principally with Tatas, and establishment and a certain amount of labour have been collected at Kalabagh. The headworks alone

will cost something in the neighbourhood of 1½ crores during this and the next financial year. It might be possible to finance the construction of the headworks alone, partly out of our recent loan and partly by sales of land, but this is doubtful. The completion of the project, i.e. the construction of the main and branch canals, will require further large loans and these will almost certainly be impossible to raise during the next two or three years except at rates of interest which would make the project unproductive. My Finance Minister's view, in which I am personally inclined to agree, is that the whole project, including the construction of the headworks should be postponed indefinitely, but some of my Ministers argue that after the war we are certain to find the prices of steel and other raw materials far higher than those agreed upon in our contracts, and that in view of this consideration we should construct the headworks, but defer the construction of the main line and its branches till after the war.[75] We have already discussed this problem, which is one of vital importance to provincial finances, in one Cabinet meeting, but no final decision has been reached and a further discussion will take place as soon as Sikander returns to Simla. The Ministers are in a difficult position, as they announced publicly last spring that it was their intention to proceed immediately with this project. I am afraid that the people who are likely to benefit by the project will not easily appreciate the almost insuperable difficulties of finding the necessary finance in war conditions.

Yours sincerely,
H.D. CRAIK

105

CRAIK TO LINLITHGOW

Secret — Barnes Court, Simla,
D.-O. No. 178 — *September 25th, 1939*

Dear Lord Linlithgow,

Sikander asked me today to convey to you the following message in view of the interview which you are going to grant to Jinnah on Wednesday, the 27th of September.

The first point is as regards that part of the recent Muslim League resolution which deals with Federation.[76] The actual wording of the resolution is that 'no declaration regarding the question of constitutional advance for India should be made without the consent and approval' of the League. Sikander tells me that there was a very long discussion as to the exact wording of this part of the resolution at Delhi, but he is convinced that Jinnah would be prepared to accept 'consultation' only, instead of 'approval and consent', if the League could also be given an assurance that in any future scheme of Federation Muslim interests would be amply protected.

Secondly, Sikander asked me to suggest for your consideration the advisability of giving Jinnah an assurance that if the Muslim League co-operates fully in the prosecution of the war, you are convinced that their attitude will not be overlooked by His Majesty's Government.

Thirdly, Sikander feels convinced that if in the course of your interview you put to Jinnah the same question as you put to Sikander the other night, viz., whether, if Congress adopts an obstructive attitude, the Muslims would in that event co-operate with Government, then you would receive from Jinnah the same reply as you received from Sikander.

Yours sincerely,
H.D. CRAIK

106

CRAIK TO LINLITHGOW

Private and Personal
D.-O. No. 179-F.L.

Barnes Court, Simla,
September 26th, 1939

Dear Lord Linlithgow,

Declarations of loyalty, offers of help and gifts of money continue to be received in large numbers by my Ministers, by District Officers and by myself. But I am not sure that the feeling of loyal enthusiasm is at the moment quite as intense as it was a fortnight ago. I have an impression that some disappointment is felt by those who have offered their services and resources, because they have so far received no indication of the way in which they can make themselves useful. The sooner we can be given a lead in this matter, the better.[77]

2. The Commissioner of the Rawalpindi Division[78] wrote the other day:

> 'I had expected that by now Government would have started a war fund and that meetings would be necessary for encouraging subscriptions. So far, however, there has been no indication of this; and I also understand from the Recruiting Officer that for the present

there is no need of special recruiting measures. The people generally are enthusiastic about the war, offers of assistance being constantly received, and I am sure that if subscriptions to a war fund were invited now, the response would be striking.'

The Commissioner of Ambala[79] reports that 'there is no doubt that the great mass of the people are behind Government in this war and that thousands of recruits could easily be obtained, if required mainly, it must be admitted, for economic reasons, but loyalty to the Crown is very deep-seated among the martial classes.'

I have also seen an interesting report from the (Indian) Officer in charge of the Kasur Sub-Division of the Lahore District,[80] which I enclose as an appendix to this letter.[81] This is encouraging, as the tract in question is one of the most criminal in the whole Province and its population is for the most part distinctly turbulent and lawless.

3. The declarations of the All-India Congress Working Committee[82] and the Muslim League[83] have not, so far as I can judge, had any very marked effect in the Punjab, though since the Congress statement was issued, the attitude of the Punjab Congress press has not been as satisfactory as it was before. On the other hand, a good many supporters of the Congress have publicly denounced the bargaining spirit underlying the Working Committee's statement. For example, I received a letter from the Secretary of the Congress Committee of the Mianwali district, declaring that he and his friends on the Committee considered that Congress should have promised unconditional support in the prosecution of the war and that they had all in consequence resigned their membership, with the result that there is no longer a Congress Committee in that district. The Working Committee's resolution is, moreover, so lacking in any guidance as to the line Congress is to take in the immediate future that even the most devoted Congressmen are puzzled and do not understand what they are expected to do.

As regards the Muslim League statement, it is generally deplored by loyal Muslims, and I do not think it will have any real effect in diminishing the general approbation which Sikander's published statements on the war elicited.

4. In spite of the warning issued in our Press communiqué of September the 12th (a copy of which I enclosed with my letter to you, No. 174-F.L. of September the 13th) to the effect that speeches calculated to prejudice the efficient prosecution of the war and particularly to prejudice recruitment would no longer be tolerated, opposition to recruitment and other war

measures by members of the 'Forward Bloc' and the Ahrars has recently intensified. It is reported that the Ahrars have promised the 'Forward Bloc' full support in their opposition to all war measures. A considerable number of arrests and prosecutions under the Defence of India Rules have been made, but the defiance of these rules is clearly deliberate and it will, I fear, continue. As you are aware, in my view the best possible answer to this dangerous type of opposition would be a successful recruiting drive.

5. Polling for the three-cornered contest in the Amritsar city bye-election (see paragraph 8 of my letter to you, No. 167 of August the 25th) began on September the 23rd and will conclude today. This bye-election has been the cause of much local excitement, but full precautions against any disturbances were taken, and I understand that the first day's polling passed off peacefully. Some very bad anti-recruitment speeches have been made by supporters of the Ahrar candidate, and some of the speakers will be prosecuted as soon as polling is completed. Sikander anticipates that the Unionist candidate will have a majority of somewhere between 1,500 and 2,000 votes over both the Congress and the Ahrar candidates.

6. Sikander has not again referred to the proposal, which I mentioned in paragraph 7 of my letter to you of September the 13th, to add two Congress representatives to his Ministry. I take it that he has abandoned this idea in view of the attitude taken up by the All-India Congress Committee.

7. Moon has sent Laithwaite a separate note[84] explaining the decision taken by my Ministry in regard to the Thal Irrigation Project.

8. I am leaving Simla tomorrow, the 27th, and reach Lahore on the morning of Saturday, the 30th. I enclose two copies of the provincial report for the first half of September.

Yours sincerely,
H.D. CRAIK

107

CRAIK TO LINLITHGOW

Secret and Personal — Government House, Lahore,
D.-O. No. 183 — *October 7th, 1939*

Dear Lord Linlithgow,

I expect Your Excellency has been shown by Ewart a report,[85] dated the 30th of September 1939 from the Central Intelligence Officer, Lahore, giving an account, on information supplied by an agent, of what happened at the meeting of the Muslim League Executive held in Delhi from the 16th to the 19th of September. This report contains the startling statement that both Fazl-ul-Haq and Sikander placed in Jinnah's hands their signed resignations from the office of Premier on Jinnah's affirming that 'he would only use them in case of extreme necessity and delicacy, whence he might possibly find no other way out'.

This report reached me a day or two ago, and as I found great difficulty in reconciling the statement about Sikander with what he had told me, both before and after these meetings, I sent for Robinson, the Central Intelligence Officer, and discussed the question with him last night.

Robinson had little to add to what he had already written in the covering note which he attached to the report and which you have doubtless seen. He did not tell me, nor did I ask, the name of the 'source', but obviously this must have been one of Jinnah's close adherents. Robinson admitted that he was not himself altogether convinced of the truth of the source's statement and, as he has explained in a later report dated the 6th of October, there has been no opportunity to interrogate the 'source' further.

Personally, I find it almost impossible to believe that Sikander should have acted in the way alleged. Not only would such conduct have been entirely incompatible with what he told me of his intentions before the Delhi meeting, but it does not in any way fit into what he told me (and what I understand he repeated to Your Excellency at your dinner party on the 21st of September) of what had happened at the meetings. Moreover, it seems to me inconceivable (*a*) that Sikander, who is extremely shrewd in these matters, should have given Jinnah, whom he profoundly distrusts, a document of which Jinnah could make such damaging use; (*b*) that, considering the number of people present when the alleged written resignation was handed over, no hint of this transaction should have appeared either in the Press, which would be only too ready to pay for and publish an item of news so damaging to Sikander's reputation; (*c*) that Sikander could have been intimidated into taking, without any adequate or obvious motive, an action which might, if it became public, involve his own and his Party's political extinction.

I think it only fair to Sikander that I should let you know the grave doubts which I feel about the accuracy of these reports.[86]

Yours sincerely,
H.D. CRAIK

108

CRAIK TO LINLITHGOW

Personal
D.-O. No. 185

Government House, Lahore,
October 10th, 1939

Dear Lord Linlithgow,

Many thanks for your personal letter of the 6th of October, enclosing a copy of a private and personal telegram[87] from the Secretary of State about the Shahidganj appeal.

As you are probably aware, the present position is as follows: Our High Court held that the building which the Sikhs demolished had not been used as a mosque for something over 150 years (if indeed it ever had been a mosque) and that the site of the building was the absolute property of the Sikhs. When the appeal to the Privy Council was lodged by the Muslims, the High Court granted an injunction prohibiting the Sikhs from erecting any other structure on the site pending the decision of the appeal. I imagine it is 'any odds against' the Muslim appeal being successful.

The site is in the possession of the local Akali Committee and I do not think that there is any possibility of inducing that body to agree, in the event of the Privy Council deciding in their favour, to refrain from erecting some building on the site. The Akali leaders are at the moment in a somewhat truculent mood and bitter in their opposition to Muslims generally and to the Unionist Ministry in particular. I believe they would commence building on the site the moment they secure legal power to do so, knowing that their action would provoke Muslim resentment and create a situation embarrassing to the Ministry.

It might perhaps be possible to persuade some moderate Sikhs to put forward quietly a suggestion that their community should, by way of a generous gesture to Muslims, agree to leave the site unbuilt on, but railed off and open to access by the public. This was broadly the line on which Sikander endeavoured unsuccessfully to reach a compromise in the spring of 1938, and I am very doubtful if a similar endeavour now would have any better results. The more moderate Sikhs, such as Sir Sunder Singh's followers, would probably admit that this was a suitable solution, but might be afraid to put it forward publicly and would in any case probably not be able to induce the Akalis to accept it.

I would suggest that your reply to the Secretary of State's telegram should be that after consulting me you fear there is little prospect of inducing the parties concerned to sink their differences. The announcement of the Privy Council's decision, whatever that may be, is almost certain to revive bitter tension on a question that has excited little interest during the last 18 months; and I fear the only way of avoiding this result is to secure a postponement of the hearing of the appeal. Is there any way in which this could be done?

To change the subject, Sikander returned from Delhi this morning in good spirits and told me some interesting news. I gathered that Jinnah was much more accommodating than at one time seemed probable. If this is correct, I offer you my hearty congratulations.

Yours sincerely,
H.D. CRAIK

109

CRAIK TO LINLITHGOW

Personal — Government House, Lahore,
D.-O. No. 186 — *October 11th, 1939*

Dear Lord Linlithgow,

There was a small inaccuracy in my letter to you, No. 185 of yesterday, about the Shahidganj case. The High Court, by an order of the 28th of April 1938, granted an *ad interim* injunction directing the respondents (i.e. the Sikhs) 'to abstain from interfering with the *status quo* or raising any kind of structure or building beyond what is on the spot'. This injunction was granted on an *ex parte* application by the Muslims pending the hearing of the application for leave to appeal to His Majesty's Council.

Then, on the 20th of May 1938, the appeal to His Majesty's Council having by then been presented, the Court ordered, with the agreement of counsel for both parties, that the *ad interim* injunction already issued should be continued till the 31st of December 1939.

I have little doubt that if the hearing of the appeal were to be postponed, the High Court would direct that this injunction should remain in force pending the decision of the appeal.

2. As regards my suggestion that it might be possible to secure a postponement of the hearing of the appeal, it has occurred to me that this might be facilitated if a representation were made on behalf of one of the parties that owing to war conditions it is extremely difficult for counsel to travel from India to England at present. I will consult Sikander as to the

possibility of the Muslims being advised quietly to put in an application to this effect.

Yours sincerely,
H.D. CRAIK

110

CRAIK TO LINLITHGOW

Confidential
D.-O. No. 187

Government House, Lahore,
October 12th, 1939

Dear Lord Linlithgow,

Very many thanks for your confidential letter of the 10th of October. I was very glad to see in this morning's papers the announcement regarding the system of registration for recruits and also that there is to be an increase in the Territorial Branch of the Army. These measures, limited as they are in their scope, will do something towards meeting the general wish of the Punjab to be allowed to participate in some active contribution towards winning the war.

2. As regards Zetland's enquiry regarding the probable attitude of the Akali Sikhs towards recruitment, I would refer you to Moon's Demi-Official letter to Laithwaite, No. 4907 of the 4th of October,[88] with which he forwarded copies of the resolutions passed by the Shiromani Akali Dal (the Chief Akali organization) at Amritsar on October the 1st. The resolution followed very closely the lead of the Congress resolution, but did not specifically mention recruitment, and Moon's letter gave expression to my opinion that it was not likely to have much effect on recruitment. But the Akali resolution did conclude with a repudiation of what it described as 'the audacious claim' of Sikander to represent the martial classes of the Punjab and declared that the Sikhs have no faith in him.

You will be seeing 'Master' Tara Singh, the Akali leader, on the 15th of October and will perhaps have an opportunity of forming your opinion as to his probable attitude towards a call for recruitment. I am inclined to think that for economic reasons he will not take any active steps to discourage Sikhs from enlistment. If he did so, he would stultify the position taken up in the resolution of October 1st that the Sikh representation in the Army is inadequate.

3. I have today given an interview to an old friend of mine, who is zaildar (a village official) in the Tarn Taran tahsil of Amritsar district,

one of the tracts that has in the past been a particularly good recruiting ground, but which enjoys an unenviable reputation for turbulence and violent crime. He told me that in his opinion plenty of recruits would be forthcoming owing to economic conditions, but at the same time he thought that subtle anti-recruitment propaganda by Congress and Communist agents had lately had some bad effect in this tract. I have seen recent reports of similar bad effects from such propaganda in other areas, notably Jullundur District.

4. By the way, I think I ought to mention that Sikander was rather disturbed when he heard on the radio last night the announcement of your forthcoming interview with Tara Singh. Only yesterday in a speech at Lahore (reported in the *Civil and Military Gazette* of today: I enclose a cutting[89] in case you should have missed it) Sikander expressed his displeasure at the present leadership of the Sikh community, the reference being of course to the Akalis. He has suggested that, in order to counter-balance your interview with Tara Singh, you should also see Rai Bahadur Sardar Baisakha Singh of Jantar Mantar Road, New Delhi, who is President of the Chief Khalsa Diwan, which represents the more loyal and conservative section of the Sikhs and supports Sir Sunder Singh Majithia. I agree in this suggestion.

5. Tara Singh recently sent me a copy of the correspondence between himself and Sikander in September, in which he very truculently refused an invitation from Sikander to come and see him in connection with the war situation and wrote bitterly of the 'repression and oppression of the Sikhs' by Muslims during the Unionist Party's régime.

Yours sincerely,
H.D. CRAIK

111

CRAIK TO LINLITHGOW

Private and Personal
D.-O. No. 188-F.L.

Government House, Lahore,
October 13th, 1939

Dear Lord Linlithgow,

During the last few days the chief topic of discussion in the Press and elsewhere has been your meetings with Gandhi, Jinnah and other leaders in Delhi and these leaders' discussions among themselves. The result of these talks is eagerly awaited. The Press comments have for the most part displayed the usual communal jealousies. The Muslim papers, for example, argue that you should not have accepted Congress as the premier political organisation in the country. The Hindu papers on the other hand, urge that you have created difficulties for yourself by bringing the Muslim League into the picture. During the last few days criticism, especially on the part of the Hindu Press, has tended to concentrate on the point that it was a mistake on Your Excellency's part to have called into consultation so many leaders of minor groups or organisations, but this line of criticism may be discounted as merely a consequence of the conventional attitude that Congress is the only political organisation that represents the views of India as a whole. There is a general scepticism as regards the prospects of any communal agreement emerging from the recent conversations between Jinnah and Nehru.

2. As regards the war situation generally, I found on my arrival at Lahore that the profiteering which followed the immediate outbreak of war had everywhere been successfully stopped. There are no further complaints on this score, except as regards the unavoidable rise in the cost of imported medicines. There was a short run on the savings banks in certain districts, but this ceased after a few days.

There has been a considerable spate of anti-recruitment speeches, particularly during the course of the Amritsar bye-election campaign, polling for which took place in the last week of September. The result of this election was that the Muslim League Unionist candidate was elected by a majority of nearly 900 votes over the Ahrar candidate, the Congress candidate, Dr. Kitchlew, being a bad third. As soon as polling was over, the Ahrar candidate, Chaudhri Afzal Haq, was arrested under the Defence of India Rules for a bad anti-recruitment speech, and a large number of his prominent supporters were similarly arrested. One of them, Shaikh Hissam-ud-Din, the so-called Ahrar dictator, was sentenced to two years' imprisonment, which has had a good deterrent effect. Numerous arrests had also to be made on the same ground in the Multan Division.

The Unionist Party has just won another bye-election in the Multan Division Towns (Muslim) Constituency.

3. There is considerable apprehension as regards the possibility of an attack by Russia on India and there is a good deal of wild talk of air bombardment, etc. A successful practice 'black-out' took place in Rawalpindi city and cantonments on the 12th of September.

4. Most of my Ministers have been touring in various districts since they left Simla, and they tell me they have addressed large and successful meetings. Everywhere the enthusiasm for service in the war of some kind was most marked. There was a particularly large meeting at Niaz Beg, a village only a few miles from Lahore, yesterday, which was addressed by

the Premier and other Ministers, and I am told that great enthusiasm prevailed and that the recitation of poems in praise of Great Britain's attitude in the war was loudly applauded.

5. On the other hand, I find that many of the reports from District Officers refer to the general disappointment caused by the fact that offers of service have not been accepted and by the delay in starting recruitment on a large scale. I enclose a series of extracts from such reports,[90] which I think you should see. As I observed in my letter to you of yesterday, something will be done to mitigate this disappointment by the announcement made yesterday of the starting of a system of registering recruits. I hope it may be possible to give all recruits who volunteer and are accepted a recruiting badge, made of some indestructible material, which they can wear prominently. I feel sure that this would be a popular move.

6. Considerable excitement has been caused in the Punjab by the unfortunate incidents connected with the Khaksar campaign against the United Provinces Government, culminating in the shooting by the police at Bulandshahr on the 8th of October. Our District Officers were, under the instructions of Government, doing their best to restrain Khaksar volunteers from joining in the 'invasion' of the United Provinces, and a day or two before the Bulandshahr incident the Premier had a satisfactory interview with the Khaksar second-in-command, who seemed prepared to accept the Premier's advice to call off this agitation. But the killing of five Khaksars at Bulandshahr has entirely changed the situation and has aroused intense indignation among Muslims in the Punjab. All the Muslim newspapers in Lahore have taken up an attitude of strong support for the Khaksars and condemn the United Provinces Government for its alleged oppressive attitude towards Muslims generally. Since the 8th of October the daily figures of volunteers proceeding to the United Provinces has increased to about 150, most of them being newly enlisted recruits to the Khaksar movement. The bodies of the five men killed at Bulandshahr were brought to Lahore in lorries by a party of their companions on the 9th of October. The Bulandshahr police sent us no information as to this, but fortunately the Delhi police were more alert and warned us of the imminent arrival of this party. It was at one time expected that there would be a public funeral of these five victims at Lahore, which would have aroused intense communal excitement. Fortunately it was decided to take them straight through Lahore to their homes in the western Punjab and North-West Frontier Province. The police did everything they could to expedite the passage of the party through Lahore and even provided funds for payment to the lorry drivers, with the result that their passage through Lahore was hardly noticed.

I fear, however, that this Khaksar affair is likely to increase communal bitterness generally throughout northern India for some time to come.

7. As regards the Sikh attitude towards the war, Moon sent to Laithwaite with his demi-official letter No. 4907 of the 4th of October 1939,[91] copies of the resolutions passed by (*a*) the Chief Khalsa Dewan, and (*b*) the Akali leaders headed by the Shiromani Akali Dal organisation at Amritsar on the 1st of October. Moon's letter added some comments of my own on these resolutions. A report subsequently received regarding the discussions that took place during the conferences revealed that there were considerable differences of opinion in the Akali meeting, though in the end the published resolution was carried unanimously. Much time was devoted to discussing the alleged grievances of the Sikhs under the Communal Award and the reduction in their representation in the Army. Several speakers expressed apprehensions regarding the possibility of a Russian attack on India. The Akali resolution was not allowed to pass without comment. A day or two later a number of retired Sikh Army officers published a statement repudiating the claim of the Akali conference to speak in the name of the entire community, particularly the Sikh martial classes 'which have full confidence in the leadership of the soldier Premier of the Punjab'. This statement went on to say that the Sikh martial classes were 'ready to respond to the Premier's call to arms in defence of the King and country and that they do not believe in bargaining with the British Government when their own country is in danger'. I dealt with the subject of the probable effect on Sikh recruitment of the Akali attitude in my letter to you of yesterday.

8. We have recently had two long Cabinet meetings, considering the possibility of retrenching expenditure during the current year. We went through practically the whole budget item by item. The decisions eventually taken amount to a retrenchment of roughly Rs. 33⅔ lakhs in the Revenue Account, Rs. 62⅔ lakhs in the Capital Account and Rs. 7¾ lakhs under Loans and Advances. These economies were necessitated by our heavy famine expenditure.

9. One of the three famine districts, Gurgaon, had excellent rainfall during the first three weeks of September and may now be considered as out of the wood. Rohtak had a little rain during the same period, which will be of some help for *rabi* sowings, but the supply was far from being sufficient. In most parts of Hissar unfortunately there was hardly any rain at all, and I am afraid there is no doubt that that district is still in an extremely bad way and that famine conditions are now almost certain to prevail till the advent of the next monsoon, unless there are exceptionally good winter rains. It is a most melancholy outlook.

10. I enclose the provincial fortnightly report for the second half of September.

Yours sincerely,
H.D. CRAIK

112

CRAIK TO LINLITHGOW

Government House, Lahore,
D.-O. No. 190 *October 24th, 1939*

Dear Lord Linlithgow,

Will you please refer to the correspondence about the Shahidganj appeal in the Privy Council ending with your personal letter to me of the 13th of October. I have just heard through Sikander that a letter has been sent by a Muslim Advocate in Lahore, who is in charge of the appellants' case, to their Solicitors in London asking the Solicitors to apply to their Lordships for a postponement of the hearing of the appeal on the ground that owing to the situation created by the war it has become impossible for local Counsel to secure a passage to England. The letter to the Solicitors in London further states that it is understood that the Sikhs had also made arrangements for their representation by local Counsel before the Privy Council, but that their Counsel also are prevented by the war from proceeding to England.

You may care to pass this information on to the Secretary of State. In my opinion, as you are aware, a postponement of the hearing of the appeal is much to be desired.

Yours sincerely,
H.D. CRAIK

113

MOON TO LAITHWAITE

Government House, Lahore,
D.-O. No. G.S.-920 *October 26th, 1939*

My dear Laithwaite,

I am desired to forward the enclosed copy of a note recorded by Mr.

Bennett, D.I.G., C.I.D., on the reactions in this Province to the present political situation.

I also enclose a copy of a resolution that will be moved by three supporters of the Unionist Ministry in the Legislative Assembly.

Yours sincerely,
E.P. MOON

ENCLOSURE 1 TO NO. 113

NOTE BY BENNETT

October 23rd, 1939

The first reactions to the Viceroy's announcement[92] have been expressed very temperately. No one seems to have expressed any doubt that Congress would not be satisfied, and it is interesting to note that Bhai Parmanand took merely the communal view that the Muslims would take advantage of any conflict between the Congress and Government. It is also interesting to find that the *Vir Bharat* declares that no one wishes Congress to start an unconstitutional war at this juncture. I think Hindu opinion in the Province, while it may be disappointed that Government did not go further to meet the Congress demands, realises that the Right Wing of Congress would have been satisfied to leave things as they were and to co-operate with Government in this emergency but for the very active opposition of the Left Wing. Punjab Hindus were in the beginning mostly for unconditional co-operation with Government. In their loyalty to Congress they modified their attitude somewhat, but they will be extremely disappointed if Congress goes as far as to non-co-operate.

2. The Sikhs, as usual, are sitting on the fence and waiting for Congress to make its announcement before they say anything about the situation.

3. The Muslim press has not changed its decision. It still offers unconditional support to Government and rather pertinently points out that Congress has only itself to blame; if it had treated Muslim minorities with more consideration it might have been considered more representative of the whole country and not merely a political party.

J.T.M. BENNETT
D.I.G., C.I.D., Punjab

ENCLOSURE 2 TO NO. 113

PUNJAB LEGISLATIVE ASSEMBLY

Notice

Sardar Bahadur Sardar Gurbachan Singh, M.L.A.
Major Sardar Sir Muhammad Nawaz Khan, M.L.A.
Rao Pohop Singh, M.L.A.

This Assembly approves of the policy of the Punjab Government towards the present international crisis in condemning Fascist and Nazi aggression and declares its determination to resist this aggression and to protect the security and honour of the Punjab and India with all available resources of the Province. It further desires that it should forthwith be made absolutely clear that the Constitution of India shall be examined *de novo* at the end of the war with a view to the immediate attainment of the objective of Dominion Status with effective protection of the due rights of the minorities and other sections and in consultation with and agreement of all the parties concerned.

114

CRAIK TO LINLITHGOW

Private and Personal
D.-O. No. 191-F.L.

Government House, Lahore,
October 29th, 1939

Dear Lord Linlithgow,

I have already reported the early reactions in the Punjab to your statement of the 18th of October, and I do not think I have any reason to modify what was contained in that report. Since then events have, of course, moved rapidly and the first Congress Ministry has now tendered its resignation. My impression is that most Hindus in the Punjab deplore this and other imminent resignations and regard with genuine dismay the prospect of a period of serious political unrest and possible disorder. As you know, in the Punjab Congress does not carry very much influence and the devotion to Congress ideals on the part of most Hindus of the professional and trading classes is not sufficiently strong to enable them to face with equanimity a state of affairs that must inevitably mean serious material loss to themselves.

It seems to be generally held in Congress circles that the resignation of the Congress Ministries will almost certainly be followed, though perhaps not immediately, by a campaign of civil disobedience, and I have received information that preparations for such a campaign are already being made by the more extreme organisations.

2. We have had separate correspondence on the possibility of Sikh recruitment to the Army being prejudiced by the Akali support of the Congress attitude. In this connection I noticed the other day a comment in one Sikh paper, which is of interest. The article while describing your statement as 'niggardly' nevertheless advised Sikhs to help Government in the present war and particularly to enlist freely in the Army.

On the other hand, I had a report from one of my officers a day or two ago that a Recruiting Officer, who was endeavouring to recruit 80 Jat Sikhs in the Amritsar district, was actually able to recruit only about 12. This poor response was probably due to the effects of secret anti-recruitment propaganda conducted by the local communists, etc., and I have little doubt that if a serious recruiting drive were made with the assistance of the local civil officers, plenty of recruits would be forthcoming.

But the atmosphere of unrest and possible political disturbance that is almost sure to follow the resignation of the Congress Ministries may have a distinctly prejudicial effect on recruitment and any other kind of war effort in some parts of the Province. The north-western districts, which are almost entirely Muslim, are not likely to be affected, but I fear that the response in the eastern and possibly also in the central Punjab to any appeal for co-operation in the war may be less enthusiastic than would have been the case a month ago.

3. As regards the reactions to the debate in the House of Commons, I gather from such comments as I have seen in the local Press (which of course represents mainly the Hindu nationalist point of view) that the general feeling is that the debate has not materially modified the situation. Wedgwood Benn's speech has been criticised as being negative and weak in tone and inaccurate as regards facts, and though the conciliatory tone of Hoare's speech is appreciated, it is held that in essentials it indicates no change in the attitude of His Majesty's Government. At the same time, there is an undercurrent of hope that some agreement may be reached that will enable the Congress Ministries to remain in office.

4. As regards Muslim views, I think there is general satisfaction at the refutation of the claim of Congress to represent the whole of India. Here in the Punjab, where Muslims are in a majority, we have no illusions as to

the depth and reality of the communal issue, and personally I am fully convinced that the impression left on you by your conversations with the various minority representatives (*vide* paragraph 2 of your letter to me of the 17th of October[93]) is correct, and that you are completely right in thinking that communal differences have been greatly aggravated since April 1937 by the practical working of Provincial Autonomy. Even a man so sane and moderate in his outlook as Sikander has repeatedly expressed to me in private conversation his conviction that the Congress Governments have gravely oppressed the Muslim minorities in their charge.

5. It has always seemed to me that Muslim administrators and men of affairs have a more realistic outlook than Hindus, and my view is confirmed by the present crisis, in which I have been struck by the extent to which Congress spokesmen are the slaves of such rhetorical expressions as 'independence' and 'self-determination' and by their inability to grasp the realities of the present world situation. If there is one thing which the present war has proved, it surely is that no nation can be 'independent' of its neighbours, and you may remember that in a speech of 15 years ago Baldwin described the phrase 'self-determination' as 'a rhetorical term that may some day lead the nations into a bloody war' – a striking prophecy.

6. The Ahrar campaign against recruitment continues, though on a somewhat reduced scale. There have been a few more arrests of Ahrar speakers under the Defence of India Rules. There is some talk of the formation of *jathas* of Ahrars from other Provinces, particularly the North-West Frontier Province, to court arrest in the Punjab, but there is apparently not much enthusiasm for this project. It is, however, pretty clear that if a non-co-operation campaign of any kind is started, the Ahrars will take a prominent part.

7. Meetings to express sympathy with the Khaksar victims of the shooting incident at Bulandshahr on the 8th of October have been held in several districts, but the audiences were small and on the whole less interest was displayed than I had expected. The Muslim Press still continues to make much of the 'cruelties' perpetrated on the Khaksars by the United Provinces Government, in spite of warnings to moderate their tone. I have noticed that even one or two Hindu papers have published articles bitterly criticising that Government's general administrative record and particularly its weakness and failure to maintain law and order.

8. The Turkish pact with Great Britain and France has caused great satisfaction in Muslim circles and has been welcomed by many Hindu newspapers. This has come at a particularly opportune moment.

9. The session of the Legislative Assembly started on the 24th of October

and is expected to be a very long one. Hitherto the proceedings have been fairly quiet. The Congress opposition tabled an adjournment motion in regard to your statement, but the Ministry forestalled them by making certain of its supporters table a resolution approving the policy of the Punjab Government in offering co-operation in the prosecution of the war. The precise terms of this resolution were published in the *Statesman* of October the 26th. I understand it will come up for discussion on Monday or Tuesday.

10. The enclosed cutting regarding an offer made by a sweeper of Ludhiana may perhaps interest you. To the best of my belief this is a perfectly genuine offer.

11. I enclose the fortnightly report for the first half of October, which owing to the rapid movement of events is now somewhat out of date.

Yours sincerely,
H.D. CRAIK

ENCLOSURE TO NO. 114

The Civil and Military Gazette dated 29th October 1939

'TOKEN OF EVERLASTING GRATITUDE'
SWEEPER'S WAR CONTRIBUTION

An offer of Rs. 5 per mensem as a contribution towards the expenses of the present war has been made by a sweeper of Ludhiana district.

The donor, who is in the employ of a municipal committee, in the course of a letter to His Excellency the Governor of the Punjab, says:

> 'As a humble token of the everlasting gratitude of our unfortunate community to the British Government, I offer to the Government, (1) a contribution from my personal income of a sum of Rs. 5 per mensem towards the expenses of the present war from now till its final conclusion, and (2) the personal services in any part, whether of India or of the world, of my elder son.'

He has followed up his letter with the remittance of his first monthly contribution.

115

CRAIK TO LINLITHGOW

Government House, Lahore,
D.-O. No. 192 *October 29th, 1939*

Dear Lord Linlithgow,

In your letter of the 25th of October, you sent me certain extracts from Woodhead's private and personal letter to you of the 21st of October[94] and asked for my views on the points raised therein.

I find some little difficulty in appreciating what exactly is the issue discussed in paragraph 8 of Woodhead's letter. I certainly have never contemplated that should a Section 93 situation come about in other Provinces, we should on that account make any kind of change of a general nature in our system of administration in the Punjab. In other words, we will carry on exactly as hitherto, the Ministers remaining responsible for all administrative measures including such Law and Order measures as may be necessitated by developments in the Punjab arising out of the situation in other Provinces.

2. I do not anticipate any hesitation on the part of our officers in taking action against unlawful Congress activities, but naturally their actions in this direction will be under the general direction and control of the Ministers. Hitherto there has been no tendency on the part of Ministers to hamper District Magistrates in the application of the Defence of India Act or Rules.

Yours sincerely,
H.D. CRAIK

116

CRAIK TO LINLITHGOW

Secret — Government House, Lahore,
D.-O. No. 193 — *November 15th, 1939*

Dear Lord Linlithgow,

Many thanks for your secret letter of November the 11th[95] on the subject of the recent desertion of 35 Sikhs from the 3rd/1st Punjab Regiment in September last. The day before I received your letter I had one from the

Commander-in-Chief and I do not think I can do better than send you a copy of my reply[96] to him, which deals at length with all aspects of this matter.

I do not think it would be fair to deduce from this most regrettable incident, or from other incidents of the same kind among Sikh soldiers in the Army, that the Sikh community as a whole is infected with disloyalty. There is undoubtedly a subtle and pernicious underground agitation in progress, but the community as a whole is still, I believe, perfectly sound. Sikander tells me that in the voting on the war co-operation resolution, passed in our Assembly while I was at Delhi, only about half a dozen of the communist Sikhs voted against the Government resolution, while some of the Akalis, a party which on all subjects consistently and strongly opposes the Ministry, remained neutral.

You may be interested to know that Master Tara Singh, the Akali leader to whom you recently gave an interview, approached me just before I went to Delhi through Sir Jogendra Singh. The latter handed me a copy of the note which Tara Singh left with you and told me that Tara Singh was very perturbed about the rumours regarding the possible curtailment of Sikh recruitment, but was afraid to come into the open as an advocate of recruitment, because his influence among the Akalis depends on his consistently opposing Government. Tara Singh had heard some rumours about the possibility of closing down recruitment in the Doaba and had asked Sir Jogendra Singh to ascertain my views on a suggestion that he should make the closure of recruitment in this area the occasion for starting an agitation against the Army authorities. The point of this suggestion apparently was that Tara Singh would be able to pose simultaneously as an opponent of Government and a strong advocate of Sikh enlistment in the Army. I told Sir Jogendra Singh that I could not of course countenance any such suggestion. Tara Singh has also recently told the Deputy Commissioner of Amritsar,[97] with whom he apparently maintains contact *sub rosa*, that he would like to see me, though I understand that he is afraid of 'losing face' among his own people if it becomes known that he has seen me.

I have told the Deputy Commissioner to let Tara Singh know that I am quite prepared to see him. If he does come to see me, I will try to convince him that the communists, whom he detests, are doing infinite damage to Sikh interests and that it is his duty to oppose them openly.

Yours sincerely,
H.D. CRAIK

117

CRAIK TO LINLITHGOW

Private and Personal
D.-O. No. 195-F.L.

Government House, Lahore,
November 16th, 1939

Dear Lord Linlithgow,

I am afraid this letter is a day or two behind the proper date, but we have met so recently that I have not very much to report.

2. When I left Delhi I travelled by train to Hissar. A number of Khaksars were travelling in the same train, presumably men who had been released from various jails in the United Provinces and were returning to their homes. Before I arrived at the railway station these people wanted to make what they called 'a loyal demonstration' outside my saloon, but they were persuaded to refrain from doing so. The Khaksars have practically disappeared from the news altogether since the resignation of the United Provinces Ministry and they do not at the moment seem inclined to give any more trouble.

3. I spent two days at Hissar and inspected three of the relief camps. I was agreeably surprised to find that the workers were for the most part in pretty good heart in spite of the fact that famine conditions have now prevailed for more than a year. At one of the camps I visited a considerable number of the workers have built themselves shelters and stay at night on the camp to save themselves long journeys to and from their villages. The Assistant Commissioner in charge told me that he frequently heard the women singing in chorus at night, which I take to be an indication that their morale has not fallen. I paid particular attention to the appearance of the women and children at all these works. I noticed some signs of malnutrition among the small infants, but the children who are old enough to work all looked bright and alert. Among the adults I saw no signs of malnutrition, except among a very few of the older people.

I am satisfied that the people generally, though naturally depressed at the long duration of famine conditions, are by no means in despair and are still grateful for all that Government has done for them.

4. From Hissar I went to Ferozepore, where I spent two days. I was greatly struck by the cordiality of my reception, both from the townspeople and from the very large number of rural notables who had assembled for my visit. The addresses which I received from the District Board, the District Soldiers' Board and a newly-formed War Co-operation Board,

were all couched in fervent terms of loyalty, and all my visitors emphasized their readiness to do anything possible to assist in the prosecution of the war. The tone of this district, which is the headquarters of the Malwa Sikhs and which has a great martial tradition, is everything that could be desired and my Ministers assure me that the same tone prevails in the great majority of the districts throughout the Province.

5. Sikander is very pleased with the result and the general tone of the debate that took place in the Legislative Assembly on the resolution about co-operation in the war. The Ministry's majority was larger than was expected and was obtained without any special effort on the part of the whips. The speeches delivered by the Opposition were for the most part moderate in tone and only two of them were at all objectionable.

6. There have been a few more arrests of Ahrars, mostly quite unimportant people, for anti-recruitment speeches. I have seen a report that on the 14th of October five Ahrar volunteers from Peshawar arrived in Rawalpindi. They wandered round the town, shouting anti-Government and anti-recruitment slogans, but were disappointed to find that they were ignored by every one, including the Police. They returned to Peshawar after a completely unprofitable stay of three days in a depressed mood. I think the sting has now been taken out of the Ahrar agitation and I doubt if we shall hear much more of this.

7. Here, as in other Provinces, some of the District Congress Committees are reported to be making preparations for the 'impending struggle'. For example, they have entrusted their documents to a selected individual who is not openly connected with the Congress; they have set up war councils and prepared lists of 'dictators' and of volunteers willing to court arrest. All these preparations are of course being made in secrecy and there is no open sign of unrest anywhere in the Province, so far as I am aware.

8. As regards reactions to the Delhi conversations and the subsequent published statements, I do not think I can usefully add anything to what I told you in Delhi. One result of these conversations has certainly been to send up Jinnah's stock considerably, not only among Muslims but also I think among other communities.

9. I enclose an extract from a report[98] by the Deputy Commissioner of Sialkot,[99] which I think you should see. I am afraid there is still a good deal of impatience on the part of Government officers about what they consider the failure of Government to give the country a lead. I alluded to this in my speech at Ferozepore and endeavoured to point out in a general way the practical difficulties with which Government is confronted in regard to this matter.

10. I enclose two copies of the provincial report for the second half of October.

Yours sincerely,
H.D. CRAIK

118

CRAIK TO LINLITHGOW

Private and Personal
D.-O. No. 197

Camp, Gurdaspur,
November 28th, 1939

Dear Lord Linlithgow,

I am writing in reply to your private and personal letter of November the 18th,[100] under cover of which you sent me translations of certain correspondence that had passed between Sir Abdullah Haroon and one Shaikh Abdul Rahman, an Indian in Damascus, as well as a letter from His Majesty's Counsel [Consul] in Damascus.[101]

I took Sikander into my confidence about this matter and have just heard from him that he had had a talk with Sir Abdullah Haroon, who was passing through Lahore on the 26th of November. Sikander suggested to him that he should not appoint any correspondent on behalf of the Muslim League in the Islamic countries without consulting the Home Department of the Government of India. Sir Abdullah Haroon accepted this suggestion and has agreed to consult the Home Department before finally selecting correspondents of the League in the Near East. Perhaps you will be good enough to instruct the Home Department to assist Sir Abdullah Haroon with advice regarding the suitability of such correspondents.

Yours sincerely,
H.D. CRAIK

119

CRAIK TO LINLITHGOW

Private and Personal
D.-O. No. 198-F.L.

Government House, Lahore,
December 1st, 1939

Dear Lord Linlithgow,

The fortnight that has elapsed since I last wrote to you has been politically a quiet one. The considerable number of prosecutions that have taken place under the Defence of India Rules for anti-recruitment speeches have had the desired effect and hardly any such speeches are now being made. In several districts anti-Congress meetings have been held, at which the attitude of the Punjab Government towards the war was eulogised.

2. Congress supporters are inactive and, I fancy, impatient at the lack of a clear and unambiguous lead from the High Command. Meanwhile, the Left Wing is continuing its secret preparations for 'the impending struggle' and endeavouring to recruit volunteers. I feel, however, that the saner elements that generally support the Congress, as well as moderate Hindu opinion generally, consider that the Ministerial resignations have been precipitate and foolish. The Congress attitude towards the war has commanded by no means general approval, even in those sections of the press which are usually pro-Congress. There is undoubtedly a general hope that civil disobedience may be avoided.

It is perhaps significant of the waning influence of Congress that in the recent elections for the District Board in the Montgomery district 18 of the 27 elected seats were uncontested and not a single candidate stood on the Congress ticket.

3. Among Muslim organisations, the Ahrars are now keeping pretty quiet, as most of their leaders are in jail. The Khaksars have also been comparatively inactive, but seem to be endeavouring to establish better relations with the Provincial Government. I notice that a prominent Khaksar of the Jhelum district announced the other day that the Khaksars were prepared to resist civil disobedience if it was started; and the Premier has just received an offer from a well-to-do landowner, who is a Khaksar and who has already given or promised Rs. 3,000 to the war fund, an offer to give a further sum of Rs. 2,000 'in his capacity as a Khaksar in order to prove that the Khaksars are a loyalist organisation'. This may be a somewhat embarrassing offer and the Premier has asked for my advice whether it should be accepted. I will take an early opportunity of discussing the matter with him.

4. Prices of wheat and cotton have risen sharply of late, and in Amritsar city, which is one of the principal wheat markets of the Province, there have been violent fluctuations in the price of wheat, due, according to the Deputy Commissioner, to wild speculation in 'futures'. There is no shortage of supplies, but *ata* is already selling at about 9½ seers a rupee and the poorer classes of the city are seriously discontented, as wages show no tendency to rise. The situation is being carefully watched, as it may be necessary for Government to step in and control prices.

5. The press, and more particularly the Muslim press, exhibits a quite definite hardening of opinion against Germany, both in regard to the recent numerous sinking of Allied and Neutral vessels by mines with its callous disregard for human life and also in regard to the aggressive attack of the Soviet Union on Finland. Our arrangements for war publicity and propaganda are now in the discreet and experienced hands of J.D. Anderson, whom you will remember as Secretary in the Legislative Department. The Assembly has voted Rs. 75,000 for war publicity and Anderson is getting excellent stuff into the local vernacular dailies, including reproductions of some of the most striking cartoons of Hitler, etc., published in English newspapers.

6. I have just returned from a short tour to the Hoshiarpur and Gurdaspur districts. You will remember that we have had recent correspondence about disquieting incidents among Sikhs recruited to the Army from the Doaba tract, of which Hoshiarpur is a part. I mentioned in paragraph 7 of my letter to you No. 129-F.L. of March the 14th last that Hoshiarpur was a district which had in recent years given a good deal of trouble owing to the communist elements, especially among the Sikh population, and that I was afraid that this type of agitator had not been dealt with sufficiently firmly. I am glad to say that since then there has been a very marked improvement in the state of this district. A large number of political prosecutions have been instituted, practically all of which hitherto decided have ended in conviction and substantial sentences. Seventeen or eighteen cases are still pending. The impression I received from the numerous visitors to whom I gave interviews and from those with whom I conversed at a re-union of old soldiers, was that the agitators have received a sharp lesson and that the loyalists have now definitely got 'their tails up'. My reception at Hoshiarpur was in all respects cordial and satisfactory and the addresses which I received from the District Board and the District Soldiers' Board were ardently loyal in their tone. In my reply I gave a stern warning as to the damage that had been caused in this district by the dissemination of communist doctrines and drew particular attention to the danger that if such dissemination persisted, it might be difficult for the district to maintain its regular flow of loyal and trustworthy recruits. I have sent the Commander-in-Chief a copy of the speech.

7. At Gurdaspur, a district which had an excellent record for recruitment and general assistance in the Great War, my reception was almost embarrassingly cordial. There is a strong Sikh element in Gurdaspur, but Dogras and Punjabi Mussalmans are also recruited there. The countless people to whom I spoke offered their services and resources in connection

with the war and the one question that I was constantly asked was what could they do to help. The district gave practical proof of its enthusiasm for the cause by giving me a purse of Rs. 17,000 (all in currency notes!) subscribed by the leading men of the district. As there are a very few wealthy landowners in this district and the largest individual subscription was Rs. 500, this was a most creditable and encouraging effort. In Ferozepore, which I had visited a week or two earlier, I was told that a sum of Rs. 26,500 had been given or promised for the war fund, but in that district there are many more wealthy landowners.

In replying to the addresses of welcome presented at Gurdaspur I endeavoured to explain to those who felt disappointed that their offers had not been accepted the difficulty felt by Government in deciding how advantage can best be taken of the generous impulses that had prompted them. As this is a question in which I know you take a deep interest, I am enclosing a newspaper report[102] of this speech, in which I have marked the relevant passage.

8. In this connection may I venture to express the hope that your appeal on behalf of the War Purposes Fund will not be long delayed? Moon wrote to Laithwaite on the 27th of November, making certain enquiries as to the organisation of this Fund and particularly whether there are to be Provincial appeals or only one appeal from you; but he has not so far received a reply. I am afraid that if the appeal is further postponed, it may miss the psychological moment, as I fear the appeal issued by the Central Red Cross has done. The day after the latter appeal was published we followed it up by a special appeal directed to the people of the Punjab, signed by Sikander and myself and reproduced in the newspapers of the 23rd of November; but I am sorry to say that neither the appeal issued on behalf of the Central Committee nor our Provincial appeal has received any mention in editorial articles, and although I sent a personal subscription to the Provincial Branch on the same day as our appeal was published, the Secretary of that Branch informed me yesterday (a week later) that only three other small subscriptions have been received. This is very disappointing, and though when we really get going money will doubtless be forthcoming, I fear that the delay in issuing the appeal has been unfortunate.

9. I think I ought to report to you an incident that occurred during the fortnight. On the 25th of November my Government received a telegram from the Sind Government, which I quote in full:

'All armed police of this Province occupied in suppressing disorder

> Sukkur district. Military reinforcement applied for, but in the event of their not being available, could you lend five hundred armed police to report to Rohri. This is preliminary enquiry and if affirmative reply received, would send requisition in case of need.'

Our Inspector-General of Police pointed out that it would be dangerous to let as many as 500 of our additional police go, especially as we could not arm so large a number, but he suggested that we could promise 200 armed men at once and offer to recruit 300 more if Sind would find the arms. When this note was submitted to the Premier for orders, he sent the papers to me with the following note:

> 'I am afraid it would be inexpedient to send Punjab Police at the present juncture. Our action is likely to be misconstrued and would be strongly criticised by the Legislature. Apparently the additional police is required to suppress communal riots and the Muslim public in the Punjab will resent our action in view of the strong feelings voiced by the public and press over "Manzilgah" affair. In the circumstances we should politely express our regret and say that our additional police is fully occupied in war and other work. We might, however, add that we would be prepared to assist in recruiting additional police for Sind if it is desired.'

My own preference would of course have been to come to the assistance of a neighbouring province in its difficulties, but I recognised the force of the Premier's objections as regards the embarrassing reactions which might arise in the Punjab, and I felt that the matter was one in which no special responsibility of mine was attracted and in which I was bound therefore to be guided by the Premier's advice. A telegram was accordingly sent to the Sind Government, expressing the regret of the Punjab Government that it was unable to lend armed police, as its force was fully occupied in war work and other pressing duties, but expressing its willingness to recruit additional police for Sind, if required, on the understanding that the Sind Government would provide the necessary arms. It was added that the Punjab Government estimated that it could recruit 250 men within one month and a further 250 in the following month.

I mention this incident, as it raises a somewhat interesting constitutional point. So far as I can see, one Provincial Government is under no obligation to supply police to help in quelling disorder in a neighbouring province, though the Governor-General could apparently issue an order to the Governor under Section 126 (5) of the Government of India Act.

10. I enclose the Provincial fortnightly report for the first half of November.

Yours sincerely,
H.D. CRAIK

120

CRAIK TO LINLITHGOW

Private and Personal
D.-O. No. 201-F.L.

Government House, Lahore,
December 15th, 1939

Dear Lord Linlithgow,

Many thanks for your private and personal letter from Rewa of the 10th of December, which was in reply to my last fortnightly appreciation.

2. I have little to report for the first fortnight of December, as the Province has continued to be quiet. I was at one time somewhat apprehensive lest Sir Abdullah Haroon and Ali Muhammad Rashdi (one of the Secretaries of the Muslim League) who have been spending some time in Lahore, might succeed in working up excitement in the Punjab about the Manzilgah dispute in Sind and the disorder in Sukkur. I received information that Abdullah Haroon was throwing money about freely to Muslim newspapers and Rashdi, who I gather is a jackal of Haroon's, made a very bad and intemperate speech to Muslim students in a Lahore mosque. I warned Sikander about these activities, the news of which had reached me through the Central Intelligence Officer, and told him that I thought he would be well-advised to try and induce Haroon and Rashdi to leave the Punjab as soon as possible, as any serious agitation about Manzilgah was bound to have embarrassing reactions for his Ministry, as the facts of Manzilgah appear to be very similar to those of the Shahidganj affair. I fancy Sikander gave the necessary warning to Haroon and Rashdi, as I understand they have now both left Lahore. Fortunately, although there have been some bad articles in our local Muslim newspapers, no real excitement seems to have been aroused.

3. Moon has written to Laithwaite,[103] giving the provincial reactions to Jinnah's 'Deliverance Day' message.[104] I had a talk with Sikander on this subject the other day and he told me that Jinnah had issued this message entirely on his own. The only person he took into his confidence was Nawabzada Liaqat Ali Khan, the Secretary of the Central League. Sikander

thought Jinnah's statement a very grave tactical mistake, and I should say this is probably the view taken by most moderate Muslims.

4. The Assembly has now adjourned for about a month for the X'mas holidays: the sittings are to be resumed on January the 8th. The Village Panchayats Bill has passed its third reading and will shortly be submitted for my assent. The Lahore Corporation Bill has been referred to a Select Committee. The main business when sittings are resumed will be a Primary Education Bill. I gather the session has so far gone well for the Unionist Party; their majority has been maintained and there have been no further defections from their ranks. All adjournment motions have either been easily defeated or talked out.

5. Stafford Cripps arrived here from Delhi on the morning of the 12th of December and returned to Delhi the same evening. He put up with Mian Iftikhar-ud-Din, an extremely Left-Wing Congress member of our Assembly. He had a long talk with Sikander and also met the other Ministers. He rang up Government House in the course of the forenoon and asked if I could see him, and I sent a message that I would be glad to see him any time after 5 p.m. I was at that time (and still to some extent am) somewhat incapacitated by my riding accident a week earlier. Cripps replied that he had so many engagements in the evening that he would be unable to come and see me. I gather that Sikander found Cripps extremely ignorant about India. Their conversation seems to have turned mainly on the idea of a Constituent Assembly and Sikander explained at length the Muslim objections to this project. A deputation of orthodox non-Congress Hindus, consisting of Rai Bahadur Lala Ram Saran Das of the Council of State, Raja Narendra Nath, and Bhai Parma Nand of the Central Assembly, also saw Cripps and expressed the strongest objection to a Constituent Assembly.

6. I have now sufficiently recovered to see my Ministers and attend to urgent business, &c. I hope to be 'in full working order' in less than a week.

7. I enclose the provincial report for the second half of November.

Yours sincerely,
H.D. CRAIK

121

CRAIK TO LINLITHGOW
Telegram

Private and Personal
No. 16-G. *December 21st, 1939*

Statements in today's newspapers regarding Sikander's alleged secret mission are to the best of my belief entirely imaginary.[105] He told me he was merely going to Bombay for a rest and holiday which he badly needs and would probably not see Jinnah till the eve of his departure. He is I believe staying at Bombay in a house lent him by Bikaner.

122

CRAIK TO LINLITHGOW

Personal and Secret Government House, Lahore,
D.-O. No. 203 *December 22nd, 1939*

Dear Lord Linlithgow,

I must apologise for not having answered earlier your personal and secret letter of the 2nd of December about the possibility of forming a Ministry in the North-West Frontier Province. The letter arrived just about the time of my accident and it was not till some ten days later that I had an opportunity of having a talk with Sikander on the matter. He told me that he was interesting himself in it, but I understand the difficulty is that there are two candidates for the Premiership, Saadullah Khan and Aurangzeb, who cannot come to an understanding between themselves. Even if this question could be settled, their party still wants two more votes to give it a clear majority in the Assembly. Sikander told me that he was endeavouring to do what he could to secure these two votes, and I understand he has addressed personal letters to one or two of the waverers, one of whom is the son of the Nawab of Dera Ismail Khan. Sikander is, however, not very hopeful of success.

I was of course careful to keep your name out of the discussion altogether.

Yours sincerely,
H.D. CRAIK

123

CRAIK TO LINLITHGOW

Private and Personal
D.-O. No. 204-F.L.

Government House, Lahore,
December 28th, 1939

Dear Lord Linlithgow,

I am glad to be able to report that the Province has remained entirely quiet during the last fortnight. My Ministers have all, with the exception of Manohar Lal, left Lahore for the Christmas holidays, Sikander to Bombay, Khizar Hayat, Mian Abdul Haye and Sir Chhotu Ram for Hyderabad and (I think) Calcutta, and Sir Sunder Singh, so far as I know, is at his home in Amritsar. As usual when he leaves Lahore, Sikander asked me to dispose of really urgent matters in his absence on the assumption that he would agree to my decisions. This is, of course, an entirely private arrangement between him and myself, which I am careful to keep absolutely secret. Though not quite constitutional, it is convenient as it enables him to get an entire holiday, which he badly wants, from official work. You will be glad to know that he told me the other day that Abbott, his I.C.S. Private Secretary, was of immense help and had substantially lightened the burden of work that falls on his shoulders.

2. 'Deliverance Day' on December the 22nd passed off without any disturbance. Sikander very wisely gave the Lahore branch of the Muslim League a very strong hint that in his opinion the proceedings should be confined to passing resolutions in the mosques, that there should be no speeches and particularly there should be no meetings outside the mosques; and a circular letter was issued to all District Officers instructing them to do their best to get the local Muslims to make similar arrangements. These instructions had the desired effect.

3. There has been no further excitement about the Manzilgah trouble in Sind, which now seems to have dropped out of the news here. A man named Mahbub Ali, who is Secretary of the Manzilgah Mosque Restoration Committee, came to Lahore about the middle of December and made strong efforts to induce the Ahrars to take up this agitation, but he found himself handicapped by the fact that Sikander had warned the Muslim press at Lahore not to publish any news or editorial comment likely to cause disturbance in the Punjab. I gather that the Ahrars rebuffed Mahbub Ali's advances, partly on the ground that their leading people were now all in jail and partly on the ground that the Sind leaders who had promoted this agitation, such as Abdullah Haroon and Rashdi, had deserted their co-

religionists in Sind when the agitation boiled up into violence. So Mahbub Ali's mission ended in disappointment.

The Sind Government have, however, asked us to recruit 200 armed police for their Province and this is being done. We have also been asked to recruit a small body of armed police for Orissa.

4. Our main anxiety at the moment is caused by the increasing unrest at the rapid rise in the prices of necessities. There have been a good many meetings on this subject in the bigger towns and the Ahrars, socialists and 'left-wingers' generally are doing their best to make capital out of the hardships caused by the rise, which is aggravated by the continued lack of rain. We have now had no rain at all since the middle of September and every district is suffering. So there is a probability that the next wheat crop will be a short one.

Gregory paid me a short visit just before Christmas to deliver the annual address at the Convocation of the University, and I had considerable discussion with him on this difficult problem. He also had lengthy interviews with J.D. Anderson and Garbett, the Financial Commissioner concerned, on the subject and I gather reached general agreement with them. Gregory takes the view, in which I entirely agree, that although the Government of India cannot do more than lay down general principles as regards the control of prices, it is essential that the policy of the different Provinces should be co-ordinated. The recent embargo on the export of wheat from the North-West Frontier Province, for example, is not likely to be helpful. Gregory put forward a suggestion, which I hope very much will materialize, that a conference of the authorities of the wheat-producing Provinces (the N.-W.F.P., Sind, the Punjab, the U.P. and perhaps the Central Provinces) should be held at Lahore in January, if possible with your Commerce Member, Mudaliar, in the Chair. I hope the latter's engagements will enable him to preside at this conference, and I should be most grateful if you would be kind enough to advise him to do so, if he can possibly manage it. I need hardly say that I shall be delighted to put Mudaliar up, if he can come.

5. Very many thanks for your personal letter of the 21st of December. I shall be interested to know how Cripps' visit to you passed off.

I am glad to say that I am making excellent progress, but I assure you that I am faithfully observing the doctor's directions and am taking things easily for the present.

6. I enclose the provincial report for the first half of December.

Yours sincerely,
H.D. CRAIK

NOTES

1. Mr J.B. Kripalani.
2. On 6 July 1939, Mr Moon wrote to Mr Laithwaite to say that Sir Henry Craik had at that date nothing further to add to this report on his Ministers. R/3/1/61.
3. Sir Maurice Hallett was the Governor of Bihar at this date.
   The text of this letter is taken from L/P&J/5/240 as it is not included in R/3/1/61. The letter was forwarded to Lord Linlithgow on 12 January 1939 (see No. 73) and for that reason it is printed in the present volume. Hallett's reply to the present letter (Enclosure to No. 75 below) is included in R/3/1/61.
4. This letter has not been traced. However in paragraph 7 of his fortnightly report of 6 January 1939 to the Viceroy, Sir Maurice Hallett wrote of the League's Patna meeting:
   'Next came the Prime Minister of the Punjab, Sir Sikander Hayat Khan, and he, much to my astonishment and regret, seems to have accepted the view that the grievances and complaints of the Muslims in these Congress Provinces were fully justified. He apparently considered that the exercise by Governors of this [?their] special power was improbable and concluded by saying that "if worst came to the worst, the Muslims would have to be prepared for civil war."'
   R/3/1/19.
5. See No. 69, note 40.
6. See No. 72, note 4.
7. See No. 72.
8. Not printed.
9. This letter was sent by Lord Linlithgow to Lord Zetland. However the copy on the India Office file omits the last three sentences of the first paragraph and the whole of paragraph 3. L/E/9/567.
10. Not printed. This letter (D.-O. 115) is on R/3/1/61.
11. See No. 58, note 31.
12. In a lengthy letter of 5 February 1939 to Lord Zetland (4/H.E./39), Lord Linlithgow explained why he wished to give his assent to the Punjab Bill as it stood. On 15 February Lord Zetland minuted: 'The good Craik appears to be in a state of some irritation over this matter. I dare say that we could produce answers to his various criticisms of the suggestions which we made but I do not think that any good purpose would be served by prolonging controversy, and my inclination is to telegraph to the Viceroy to assent to the Bill. Any objection?' The Secretary of State instructed the Viceroy to assent to the Bill in telegram No. 340 of 21 February 1939. L/E/9/567.
13. Mr W.S. Read, Superintendent of the Government Cattle Farm Hissar (Civil Veterinary Department).

14. Maulvi Fateh-ud-Din.
15. Mr P.K. Kaul.
16. Lord Linlithgow minuted: 'Interesting and I am so glad the Governor is so well satisfied.'
17. Not printed.
18. Not printed.
19. Lord Linlithgow minuted: 'I see no reason why not. But the point is an important one of principle. S./S. should know.'
20. In the nine months prior to the date of this report, three I.C.S. officers had held the post of Commissioner of the Rawalpindi Division. Mr J.D. Anderson took up office on 21 March 1938; Mr F.C. Bourne took up office on 9 August 1938; and Mr P. Marsden took up office on 4 November 1938. Sir Sikander's remarks could, therefore, have referred to any one of these officers.
21. Not printed.
22. Mr N.M. Buch was Deputy Commissioner of Montgomery and Mr J.M. Shrinagesh was D.C., Lyallpur.
23. Not printed.
24. Mr Nasir Ahmad.
25. Mian Ghulam Ahmed, the author of Enclosure to No. 70.
26. In March 1939, as part of the Congress campaign to bring about responsible government in the Princely States, Mahatma Gandhi undertook a fast in Rajkot, a State in the Kathiawar peninsula. At his request, Lord Linlithgow intervened, and the Chief Justice of India (Sir Maurice Gwyer) was asked to arbitrate between the Thakur Saheb of Rajkot and Mahatma Gandhi, who thereupon broke his fast. He later issued a statement apologising for his action in attempting to put pressure on the Thakur and the Paramount Power by undertaking a fast, which he now realised had been coercive and therefore not in accordance with the principles of non-violence.
27. Lord Linlithgow minuted: 'I had this plan in mind but preferred the alternative course which I took [because] it seems to offer hope of limiting the outcome to Rajkot. Sir H.C.'s plan could be too easily called for from any State in India.'
28. Sir Henry Craik wrote again to Lord Linlithgow on 8 March when he had heard that the Rajkot issue had been resolved. In this later letter Craik wrote: 'Please accept my warmest congratulations on your very successful handling of this difficult business. I am confident that it will have the best results and can only hope that you will not be troubled with a similar situation again.' R/3/1/61.
29. Major-General M. Saunders.
30. Mr E.H. Lincoln.
31. Mr E. Sheepshanks, Commissioner of the Jullundur Division.
32. Lord Linlithgow minuted: 'We must coax these schemes out into the open one by one!'

33. Captain E.M. Hodder.
34. Lord Linlithgow minuted: 'This is final. I think it well, on return to Simla, to tell Gandhi that Prithvi Singh's release is not at present possible.'
In his letter D.-O. 150 of 2 June 1939, Sir Henry Craik reported to Lord Linlithgow that a day or two before, Pandit K.M. Munshi, the Bombay Home Minister, had asked Sir Sikander Hyat Khan whether Mr Prithvi Singh could be transferred to a jail in Bombay. Sir Henry Craik was 'personally very much against it, as I feel certain that if Prithvi Singh were to be transferred to Bombay, Gandhi would very soon bring pressure to bear on the Bombay Government to release him.' R/3/1/61.
35. Not printed.
36. Sir Henry Craik's comments are shown within square brackets in the text of this note.
37. Mr A.K. Fazl-ul-Haq.
38. Mr Subhas Chandra Bose resigned as President of the All-India National Congress at the end of April 1939.
39. Mr G.M Brander.
40. Not printed.
41. Not printed.
42. Dr Rajendra Prasad was President of the All-India National Congress at this date.
43. The significant sentences of Lord Linlithgow's brief letter of 3/5 June 1939 read: 'Sikander mentioned to me when we were talking after dinner on Tuesday here that Rajendra Prasad, through an intermediary, had quite recently made an offer for an arrangement between Congress and the Muslim League which Sikander thought workable and probably worthy of acceptance. I gather that it was based on an agreed programme of moderate nationalism. . . . I cannot help thinking incidentally, reverting to the earlier part of this letter, that it is significant that Rajendra Prasad should have gone to Sikander and not to Jinnah.' R/3/1/61.
44. In his letter of 10 June 1939, Lord Linlithgow told Sir Henry Craik that he had written to Sir Sikander inviting him for dinner and a talk the following Wednesday. Linlithgow continued: 'I will take the opportunity to sound him a little further both on the general Muslim position and on his suggestion for an understanding between Muslims and Hindus about which we have been in correspondence separately.' R/3/1/61. There is no further letter on the outcome of the Viceroy's meeting with Sir Sikander in this source.
45. This letter is not reproduced in R/3/1/61. In view of the significance of the proposals which Sir Sikander submitted to Dr Prasad (through Professor Shah), considerable efforts have been made to trace the letter containing them but without success. A copy of the letter was sent to Lord Zetland by the Viceroy (MSS EUR F. 125/7, Section 2, p. 233) but it has not been traced in the India Office Records. The letter is not printed in the relevant volume of Dr Prasad's correspondence where the only mention of the episode

is a single sentence in a letter from Sardar Vallabhbhai Patel dated 5 July 1939. This sentence reads: 'Shah and his friend saw Bapu [Gandhi] yesterday and has left his scheme with Bapu for his own reaction in the matter.' (See Valmiki Choudhary (ed.), *Dr Rajendra Prasad: correspondence and select documents*. Vol. 3: *January to July 1939*, p. 146, New Delhi: Allied, 1984.) It seems likely that the terms offered by Sir Sikander would have been along the lines of the proposal he published shortly afterwards as a modification of Federation; see Appendix III. Sir Sikander's meetings with Mahatma Gandhi are referred to in No. 97 below.

46. See Nos. 47 and 49, paragraph 9 for Sir Sikander's views on Punjab's role in the Indian Army.
47. In paragraph 2, Lord Linlithgow asked Sir Henry Craik for his views on the suggestion made with increasing frequency by prominent Muslims that the Muslim community remained whole-heartedly opposed to Federation and would not be prepared to acquiesce in its introduction.
48. See previous note.
49. See Appendix III.
50. Lord Linlithgow minuted: 'Don't be too sure.'
51. Not printed.
52. Khan Bahadur Abdul Qaiyum Ahmad Khan.
53. Mr W.G. Kennedy.
54. Sir Harry Haig was Governor of the United Provinces at this date.
55. In paragraph 10 of his letter of 21 July 1939 Lord Linlithgow gave Lord Zetland a rather different account of the reaction of the Muslim League Working Committee to the Sikander-Rajendra Prasad contacts. The Viceroy wrote: 'My earlier anticipation that nothing very much is likely to come of Sikander's contacts with the Congress is confirmed by information received from Ewart [Director of the Intelligence Bureau] to the effect that the general sense of the Muslim League Working Committee, supported by Jinnah's view, is that the League should not reopen talks with Congress except on the basis of admission by the latter that the League was the sole organisation representing the Muslims in India. This is how I should have expected things to develop.' MSS.EUR.F. 125/8.
56. See No. 93 and its note 45.
57. See Appendix III.
58. Not printed. See No. 96, paragraph 4.
59. Mr K.H. Henderson.
60. See Appendix III.
61. Mr P.L. Orde.
62. For the list of Ministers, see the 'Principal holders of office' at the start of the volume.
63. Sir Malcolm Darling and Mr B.H. Dobson. (Both men were on the point of leaving these posts.)
64. Mr J.W. Hearn.

65. Mr P.K. Kaul (Gurgaon), Mr G.M. Brander (Hissar) and Sardar Garewal Balwant Singh (Rohtak).
66. Mr H.D. Bhanot.
67. Maulvi Fateh-ud-Din.
68. Not printed.
69. This letter is not included in R/3/1/61 and the text has been taken from L/P&J/5/242: ff 109-10.
70. In a statement issued on 25 August 1939, Sir Sikander Hyat Khan said with respect to the coming war:
    'There is no room for vacillation or doubt. As a self-respecting and God-fearing people we must unequivocally throw in our lot with the nations which stand for justice, righteousness and self-determination for all, strong and weak alike.... So far as the Punjab is concerned, I need do no more than repeat the assurance which I gave, on behalf of the province, in September last, when I guaranteed that the manpower and resources of the Punjab will be unhesitatingly and ungrudgingly placed at the disposal of Great Britain and her allies.... If unfortunately a war cannot be avoided, then the Punjab will rise as one man to fight the enemies of peace and freedom – their motto – "For my God, my country and my home."'
71. In a letter of 29 August 1939 to Lord Linlithgow, Sir Sikander thanked the Viceroy for his very kind and generous appreciation of his (Sikander's) statement. Later in this letter Sir Sikander wrote:
    'As I anticipated Mr Jinnah has again given proof that he attaches more importance to his personal vanity than to the interests of his country and community. He has deliberately flouted the wishes and views of Bengal and Punjab as also of a large majority of Muslims in other provinces, and in utter disregard of the decision of the Working Committee of the League. The position has now become intolerable and I am afraid there is no course open to those who place the interests of their country and community above all other considerations except to part company with Mr Jinnah and his League.' L/P&J/5/242: ff 111-12.
72. Lord Linlithgow minuted: 'The question arises, if one Governor why not eleven? And if eleven, would not the occasional use of the radio by the G.-G. lose a good deal of power? H.M. Communications, may comment.'
73. Lord Linlithgow minuted: 'If we took their names ("Derby Scheme") I suppose they would expect immediate payment, though they were not as yet called up to serve.'
74. Lord Linlithgow minuted: 'I should but expect it to much good [*sic*] (and there are grave risks involved, in any event) unless the Congress and the Muslim League had a pact of unity for the purpose of supporting the war effort. The Congressmen would look to their Working Committee.'
75. Lord Linlithgow minuted: 'I think a rather important consideration is that the canal is to pass through Sikander's principal political preserves!'

76. See note 83 below.
77. Lord Linlithgow minuted: 'I am a little tired of this theme! But I had better let S/S know (I think I already have) that the G. thinks enthusiasm is falling off – though unless he, S/S, can persuade the Chancellor to buy a couple of Divs. off India, I don't see he can do much to help.'
78. Mr P. Marsden.
79. Mr J.W. Hearn.
80. Sardar Nalwa Balwant Singh.
81. Not printed. Sardar Balwant Singh reported that he had met representatives of 39 villages most of which were situated in the Manjha tract. He said that 'each one of those present assured me unequivocally that he and his fellow villagers were determined to stand by the Empire at all hazards and at all costs in this time of crisis. In fact, some of the enthusiasts declared that if the British Government demanded their aid in men and money, the last pie that they had and the last drop of blood that ran through their veins would be consecrated to the service of their Empire, which was fighting against barbarism.' R/3/1/61.
82. On 14 September 1939, the Congress Working Committee at Wardha issued a lengthy statement in regard to the war crisis in India. In this it announced that the Committee had taken no final decision on the war at that stage. Congress could not 'associate themselves or offer any co-operation in a war which is conducted on imperialist lines and which is meant to consolidate imperialism in India or elsewhere'. The Committee invited the British Government 'to declare in unequivocal terms what their war aims are in regard to democracy and imperialism . . . in particular, how these aims are going to apply to India and to be given effect to in the present'.
83. At its meeting held in New Delhi on 18 September 1939, the Muslim League Working Committee passed a lengthy resolution on the war. This called for the complete abandonment of the Federal Scheme and urged the British Government to 'review and revise the entire problem of India's future constitution *de novo*'. The League sought justice and fair-play for Muslims in Congress-governed provinces. It also asked for an assurance from the British Government that no declaration regarding the question of constitutional advance for India should be made without the League's consent and approval. In conclusion the resolution appealed to all Indian Muslims to stand solidly under the League's flag.
84. This note is not included in R/3/1/61. It and other papers on the Thal Project have not been traced in the India Office Records. According to Ian Talbot the Project was eventually suspended because of war time shortages. However the Khushab branch work went ahead in connection with the Government of India's 'Grow More Food Campaign'. Ian Talbot, *Khizr Tiwana, the Punjab Unionist Party and the partition of India*, 2nd edn., Karachi: Oxford University Press, 2002, p. 105.

85. Neither of the intelligence reports mentioned in this document has been traced.
86. Lord Linlithgow minuted: 'I had *not* seen this, and feel I ought to have been shown it. Perhaps its reliability was or is doubtful to make it worth sending to the Viceroy.'
87. The telegram from Lord Zetland referred to here (No. 696 of 5 October 1939) asked Lord Linlithgow and Sir Henry Craik to consider the possibility of inducing the parties concerned in the Shahidganj appeal to sink their differences at least temporarily in view of the war emergency. R/3/1/61.
88. Not included in R/3/1/61.
89. Not printed.
90. Not printed.
91. This letter is not included in R/3/1/61.
92. In his Statement 'India and the War' issued from New Delhi on 17 October 1939 (Cmd. 6121), Lord Linlithgow announced that he was authorised by the British Government to say that at the end of the war they would be very willing to enter into consultation with representatives of the several communities, parties and interests in India, and with the Indian Princes, with a view to securing their aid and co-operation in the framing of such constitutional modifications as might seem desirable. Lord Linlithgow also announced the immediate establishment of a consultative group, representative of all major political parties in British India, and of the Indian Princes, which would have as its object the association of public opinion in India with the conduct of the war and questions relating to war activities.
93. The conclusion of paragraph 2 of Lord Linlithgow's letter of 17 October 1939 read: 'I am left with a stronger feeling than ever of the depth and reality of the communal issue, and of the extent to which it has been aggravated since 1937 by the practical working of Provincial autonomy.' R/3/1/61.
94. Sir John Woodhead was Acting Governor of Bengal at this time. His letter of 21 October 1939 to Lord Linlithgow has not been traced but it is clear that it dealt with the steps that would be necessary in Bengal in the event of a break with Congress.
95. In this letter Lord Linlithgow reported that 35 Sikhs had deserted from the 3rd/1st Punjab Regiment on 14 September 1939 – the eve of the departure of their battalion for service overseas. It had been decided that no further confidence could be placed in the Company. The 35 deserters would be dealt with under the Army Act. Others suspected of being privy to the desertions would be discharged. The remainder of the Company (approximately 140 men) would be granted mustering out terms. R/3/1/61.
96. Not printed.
97. Mr A.A. Macdonald.
98. Not printed.
99. Mr C. King who had only taken up the post at Sialkot on 9 October 1939.

100. In this letter, sending on the enclosures detailed by Sir Henry Craik, Lord Linlithgow commented: 'it seems most unfortunate that the League should choose as its representatives in Syria and Palestine, and possibly (though we have no confirmation of this) in Egypt and Iraq also, persons who are notorious for their anti-British activities'. Lord Linlithgow wondered if it would be possible to do anything through Sir Sikander 'as to the desirability of choosing more suitable persons as the League's agents in Islamic countries, where it is most important that a false impression of the quality of the loyalty of Indian Muslims generally to Allied war aims should not get abroad'. R/3/1/61.
101. Mr G. MacKereth.
102. Not printed.
103. This letter is not in R/3/1/61.
104. On 6 December 1939, Mr Jinnah asked all Indian Muslims to observe Friday, 22 December as a day of deliverance and thanksgiving that the Congress governments had at last ceased to function.
105. The Indian newspapers of 21 December 1939 carried a statement by Sir Sikander Hyat Khan's secretary that Sir Sikander had left Lahore suddenly on the evening of 19 December for an unknown destination. It was believed in Lahore that Sir Sikander had gone to Bombay on a secret mission to meet Mr Jinnah.

APPENDIX I

Sikander-Jinnah Pact[1]

Lucknow, October 1937

October 15th, 1937

Sir Sikander Hyat-Khan had consultations with Mr. Jinnah today after which he attended the meeting of the Council of the All-India Muslim League by special invitation. At the meeting, the following statement was made:

(*a*) That on his return to the Punjab Sir Sikander Hyat-Khan will convene a special meeting of his party and advise all Muslim members of the party who are not members of the Muslim League already, to sign its creed and join it. As such, they will be subject to the rules and regulations of the Central & Provincial Boards of the All-India Muslim League. This will not affect the continuance of the present coalition and Unionist Party.

(*b*) That in future elections and bye-elections for the Legislature after the adoption of this arrangement, the groups constituting the present Unionist Party will jointly support candidates put up by their respective groups.

(*c*) That the Muslim members of the Legislature, who are elected on or accept the League Ticket, will constitute the Muslim League Party within the Legislature. It shall be open to the Muslim League Party so formed to maintain or enter into coalition or alliance with any other party consistently with the fundamental principles of the policy and programme of the League. Such alliances may be evolved before or after the elections. The existing combination shall maintain its present name, the 'Unionist Party'.

(*d*) In view of the aforesaid arrangement, the Provincial League Parliamentary Board shall be reconstituted.

NOTE

1. This text is taken from file 785: f. 97 in the Quaid-e-Azam Papers at the National Documentation Centre, Pakistan. It would appear to be a press release. The newspapers of the following day (16 October 1937) carried reports with a similar wording.

   There is a further version of the Pact (in three copies) elsewhere in the Quaid-e-Azam Papers. This further-version has only minor textual differences from the version printed here and none of these affects the meaning. One of these further copies carries underlining in Mr Jinnah's hand. File 1049: ff. 1-3.

APPENDIX II

Note by Ewart[1]

Secret

Intelligence Bureau,
Home Department,
Government of India
March 26th, 1939

TOUR NOTES – PUNJAB

Perhaps the most important impression to be derived from a visit to the Punjab at present is that one can see in Lahore the new Constitution working very much as it is intended to work. The activities of the Governor approximate to those of a Governor in a Dominion. He sees, I think, much less of departmental or Secretariat officials than any other Governor. I met no suggestion that this method of working is defective. The Chief Secretary, senior Police Officers, etc., say that in the general routine of administration there is no material change from pre-1937 methods. There is some feeling that there is a tendency for policy regarding approach to and handling of major problems to be insufficiently co-ordinated. As put by the Chief Secretary, 'Under the late Governor one had too many conferences; under the present one not quite enough.' While I was told that a good many District Officers were dissatisfied with the tendency of political patronage to replace official patronage, e.g. in the filling of posts on Local Bodies, etc., a particularly intelligent Indian official expressed the view that the methods of administration had not yet been sufficiently modified to harmonize with the principles of the new Constitution.

2. I had an interview with the Premier, who opened the conversation by asking my opinion of the plans which he had in mind for immediate action should war break out. The chief point was his opinion that he ought immediately to place under restriction all known revolutionary organizers or agitators in the Province, whether or not specific suspicion attached to them of association with enemy nationals. The Premier's view is that action

must be immediate and comprehensive, even if drastic, and that revision and modification can be carried out later at leisure and when the situation is clearer. The reassuring nature of this outlook requires no comment. Sir Sikander Hyat Khan also expressed the view that the response in the Punjab to recruiting or any other war demands would be fully satisfactory, and he thought that Congress would very possibly be more disposed to co-operate than they would have been in September. Sir Sikander said that he felt conscious of a change in the attitude towards his Government of Dr Gopi Chand, the leader of the Congress Opposition, since Tripuri, and was inclined to think that Dr Gopi Chand might have received advice, in view of the break between the right and left wings of the Congress, not to go to extremes which would be to the advantage of the left wing. I promised to follow up this suggestion and try to get definite information. Sir Sikander gave me the impression of being very serene, clear-minded and confident.

J.M. EWART

NOTE

1. Sir John Ewart was Director of the Intelligence Bureau, Home Department, Government of India. This note was sent by Mr Laithwaite (Private Secretary to the Viceroy) to Mr Clauson (Private Secretary to the Secretary of State for India) in his letter no. 2019 of 5 April 1939. The note is included in the India Office file of Punjab Governor's Reports for the first half of 1939. L/P&J/5/241: ff 67-8.

APPENDIX III

Sikander Hyat Khan to Laithwaite[1]

Personal and Confidential

In train,
June 29th, 1939

My dear Laithwaite,

I have after all managed to put on paper my ideas about an alternative Federal scheme. I enclose a draft copy for His Excellency's perusal. I am afraid it might appear to be somewhat patchy and incomplete; but I trust His Excellency would appreciate that it had to be dictated hurriedly during the few rare and odd moments which I was able to snatch from my day's work and other engagements.

The introductory note explains some of the more important features of the scheme. You will notice that the retention of British connection on a firm and permanent footing constitutes the basic foundation of my proposals. This is a consideration which outweighs all others from the British point of view and incidentally from my own personal point of view for reasons which His Excellency is aware. Fortunately, the interests of my country and my personal sentiments are not in conflict over this matter. It is my unshakeable convictions [*sic*] which, I believe, I share with the vast majority of my countrymen that the political salvation and safety of India depends on the British connection. If, God forbid, the link between Great Britain and India is severed or materially weakened, the country will go to bits and revert to the chaotic conditions which it has witnessed in the past and eventually be enslaved by some other power. It is for this reason that, while I have suggested an immediate declaration regarding the grant of Dominion Status, I have at the same time provided in my scheme a 20 years' period of apprenticeship in such vital matters as Defence and External Affairs. This would furnish ample time and opportunity to test the loyalty and *bona fides* of the Indian nation in regard to British connection. Moreover, I consider that a representation on a regional basis both in the Federal Executive and Legislature as proposed by me will constitute an effective check against anti-British propensities which unfortunately are being openly encouraged by certain political organisations and their spokesmen.

The appendix[2] referred to in my note is not ready yet. The distribution of subjects between the Centre, 'Zones' and Units requires some thought. I have prepared tentative lists, but they need further consideration, and will be submitted on my return from Bombay.

I do not propose to release my scheme for publication until my return from Bombay in case His Excellency may care to summon me for the purpose of explaining or further elucidating any of the proposals embodied in my scheme. Meanwhile, I propose to canvass the opinion of some of the prominent Muslim and non-Muslim leaders who happen to be in Bombay in connection with the meetings of the Working Committees of the Congress and the Muslim League on the basic principles of my scheme.

I am writing this in train on my way to Bombay.

With kind regards.

Yours sincerely,
S. HYAT KHAN

Attachment to Appendix III[3]
OUTLINES OF A SCHEME FOR INDIAN FEDERATION (EXTRACT)

THE SCHEME IN GENERAL OUTLINE

For the purpose of establishing an All-India Federation on a Regional basis the country shall be demarcated into seven 'Zones' as under:

Zone 1. Assam + Bengal (minus one or two western districts in order to reduce the size of the 'Zone' with a view to approximate it to other 'Zones') + Bengal States and Sikkim.

Zone 2. Bihar + Orissa (plus the area transferred from Bengal to Orissa). This would benefit Orissa which is at present handicapped to some extent on account of its limited resources and area.

Zone 3. United Provinces and U.P. States.

Zone 4. Madras + Travancore + Madras States and Coorg.

Zone 5. Bombay + Hyderabad + Western India States + Bombay States + Mysore and C.P. States.

Zone 6. Rajputana States (minus Bikaner and Jaisalmer) + Gwalior + Central India States + Bihar and Orissa States + C.P. and Berar.

Zone 7. Punjab + Sind + N.-W.F.P. Province + Kashmir + Punjab States + Baluchistan + Bikaner and Jaisalmer.

NOTE 1: *The proposed composition of these Zones is only tentative and can be altered if necessary in consultation with the various interests concerned.*

(2) There shall be a Regional Legislature for each 'Zone' consisting of representatives of both British Indian and Indian States Units included in that 'Zone'. For the purposes of representation in the Regional Legislature every Unit will be entitled to send representatives in accordance with the share allotted to it in the scheme embodied in the Government of India Act, 1935, for representation in the Federal Assembly.

(3) The representatives of the various regional Legislatures shall collectively constitute the Central Federal Assembly which will consist of 375 members[4] (250 from British India and 125 from the Indian States).

(4) One-third of the total number of representatives in the Federal Assembly shall be Muslims.

(5) The other minorities also shall be allotted the share apportioned to them in the Federal Assembly by the Government of India Act, 1935.

(6) The Regional Legislature shall deal only with subjects which are included in the Regional List under this scheme, but may at the request of two or more Units included in the Zone, legislate with regard to subjects falling in the provincial list in order to secure uniformity and facility of administration within the Zone. Such enactments would for application in any Unit within the region require confirmation by the Government of the Unit concerned and shall thereafter supersede any provincial (or State) legislation on the subject.

(7) In the Regional Legislature no Bill or other measure having the force of law, relating to a subject included in the regional list shall be considered to have been passed unless two-thirds of the representatives vote in favour of the measure. (This limitation is suggested in order to give additional security to the smaller units.)

(8) The Regional Legislatures may by a resolution authorize the Federal

Legislature to undertake legislation with regard to subjects included in the Regional and Provincial lists. But such authorization shall not be effective unless at least 4 out of the 7 Zones ask for such action. And unless such authorization is endorsed by all the 7 Regional Legislatures the enactments so passed shall have force only in those Zones which ask for such legislation.

(9) Any law enacted by the Federal Legislature at the request of the 'Zones' and by the Regional Legislatures at the request of the units shall be repealed if in the case of the Federal Legislature at least 3 'Zones' and in the case of the regional Legislatures at least half the number of units in that Zone ask for its repeal.

(10) The Federal Executive shall consist of His Excellency the Viceroy and Governor-General as representing His Majesty the King and a Council of Ministers, as far as possible, not less than 7 and not more than 11 in number, including the Federal Prime Minister.

(11) The Federal Prime Minister shall be appointed by His Excellency the Viceroy and Governor-General from among the members of the Federal Legislature and the remaining Ministers also from among the members of the Legislature in consultation with the Federal Prime Minister, but subject to the following conditions and exceptions:

(*i*) that each Zone shall have at least one representative in the Cabinet;
(*ii*) that at least one-third of the Ministers so appointed shall be Muslims;
(*iii*) that at least 2, if the number of Ministers does not exceed 9, and at least 3, if the number is in excess of 9, shall be chosen from amongst the representatives of Indian States.

NOTE 2: *There will be no objection to (ii) and (iii) overlapping, i.e. if a Minister representing an India State happened to be a Muslim, he could be counted towards the minimum stipulated under (ii) and vice versa.*
NOTE 3: *Every attempt will be made to provide adequate representation to other important minorities also.*

(*iv*) that during the first 20 (or 15) years from the date of the inauguration of the Federal Scheme His Excellency the Viceroy and Governor-General may nominate 2 of his Ministers either from among the members of the Federal Legislature or from outside and entrust to them the portfolios of 'Defence' and 'External Affairs'. Thereafter all the Ministers shall be selected from among the members of the Legislature.

NOTE 4: *A tentative allocation of portfolios and designation of Ministers is suggested as under:*

1. Federal Prime Minister.
2. Minister for Defence.
3. Minister for External Affairs.
4. Federal Finance Minister.
5. Minister of Interior (Home).
6. Minister of Communications.
7. Minister to look after minority interests.
8. Minister of Co-ordination (Civil).[5]
9. Minister of Commerce and Industries.

NOTE 5: *The Minister of External Affairs could also be entrusted with the work connected with the affairs of Indian States.*

(12)

(*a*) The normal term of office of the Ministers shall be the same as the life of the Federal Legislature (i.e. 5 years).

(*b*) The Ministers will retain office at the pleasure of His Majesty's representative, i.e. the Viceroy and Governor-General.

(*c*) A Minister representing a particular Zone shall be removed if he loses the confidence of the majority of the representatives of his Regional Legislature.

(*d*) The Ministry as a whole except the Ministers referred to in paragraph 11 (*iv*) above shall resign if a vote of no-confidence against the Ministry is carried in the Federal Legislature.

(13) The representatives of the Regional Legislatures shall be chosen in the following manner:

(*i*) In the case of the British Indian Units by the provincial Legislature in accordance with the procedure laid down in the Government of India Act, 1935, for the election of representatives of the Federal Assembly.

(*ii*) In the case of the Indian States, as nearly as may be possible in accordance with the procedure outlined hereunder:

(*a*) during the first 10 years from the date of the inauguration of the Regional and Federal Legislatures three-fourths to be nominated by the Ruler and one-fourth to be selected by the Ruler out of a panel to be elected by the State Assembly or other similar institution which shall be set up for this purpose;

(*b*) during the next 5 years two-thirds to be nominated by the Rulers and one-third to be elected as in (*a*) above;
(*c*) after 15 years one-half to be nominated and one-half to be elected as in (*a*) above.
(*d*) after 20 years and thereafter one-third to be nominated and two-thirds to be elected as in (*a*) above.

NOTE 6: *If the number of seats allotted to a State or group of States is less than 2, then the Ruler shall nominate for the first 15 years and thereafter the State's representatives shall be elected as in (a) above by the State Assembly or such other institution as may be set up for the purpose.*

(14) There shall be a Committee of Defence to advise in matters relating to defence. The Committee shall consist of:

(*i*) H.E. The Viceroy and Governor-General – *President.*
(*ii*) The Federal Prime Minister;
(*iii*) The Minister for Defence;
(*iv*) The Minister for External Affairs;
(*v*) The Federal Finance Minister;
(*vi*) The Minister for Communications;
(*vii*) H.E. the Commander-in-Chief;
(*viii*) The Chief of the Central Staff;
(*ix*) A Senior Naval Officer;
(*x*) A Senior Air Force Officer;
(*xi*) Seven Regional representatives, one from each 'Zone';
(*xii*) 5 official experts to be nominated by the President;
(*xiii*) 2 non-officials to be nominated by H.E. the Viceroy;
(*xiv*) The Secretary to the Defence Department.

(15) A Committee shall also be constituted to advise on matters connected with External Affairs with:

(*i*) H.E. The Viceroy as President; and
(*ii*) The Federal Prime Minister;
(*iii*) The Minister for External Affairs;
(*iv*) 7 Regional representatives (one from each 'Zone') to be selected by the President from among the members of Regional Legislatures;
(*v*) 4 other members (2 officials and 2 non-officials) to be nominated by H.E. the Viceroy; and
(*vi*) The Secretary for External Affairs, as members.

NOTE 7 TO PARAS 14-15: *If in any of these Committees the number of representatives from the States falls short of 3, the difference shall be made up by the appointment by the President of additional members selected from a panel proposed by the Chamber of Princes.*

(16) The Federal Railway Authority shall be so constituted as to include at least one representative from each of the 7 Regional 'Zones'.

(17) Effective safeguards shall be provided in the revised constitution:

(*i*) for the protection of the legitimate interests of the minorities;
(*ii*) to prevent racial discrimination against British-born subjects;
(*iii*) against violation of treaty and other contractual rights of the Indian States;
(*iv*) to preserve the integrity and autonomy of both British Indian and Indian States Units against interference by the Federal Executive or Federal or Regional Legislature;
(*v*) to ensure the safety of India against foreign aggression, and the peace and tranquillity of the Units as also of the country as a whole;
(*vi*) to prevent subversive activities by the citizens of a unit or a Zone against another unit or Zone;
(*vii*) to protect the culture and religious rights of the minorities.

(18) The composition of the Indian Army (as on the 1st day of January, 1937) shall not be altered. In the event of a reduction or an increase in the peace-time strength of the Indian Army the proportion of the various communities as on the 1st of January 1937 shall not be disturbed. This condition may be relaxed in the event of a war or other grave emergency which may arise on account of a threat to the safety of the country.

NOTE 8: *As regards Indianization of the officers' ranks see my evidence before the Indianization Committee.*

(19) Only those subjects, the retention of which is essential in the interests of the country as a whole and for its proper administration, shall be allocated to the Centre, e.g., Defence, External Affairs, Communications, Customs, Coinage and Currency, etc. The remaining subjects, at present included in the Federal List, shall be transferred to the Units or 'Zones'. Residuary powers in regard to subjects which are not specifically included in the Federal List shall vest in the Units, and, in the case of subjects allocated to the 'Zones', in the Regional Legislatures. The concurrent list in the Government of India Act, 1935, shall be revised and limited to legislation only subject to the following conditions:

(*a*) that the federal legislature shall not undertake legislation on any matter within the concurrent list unless at least four Zones have applied for it; and

(*b*) that any legislation so enacted shall apply only to the Zones which have applied for it.

(I have attempted tentative revised lists of Federal, Concurrent, Regional and Provincial subjects which are attached herewith as Appendix 'A'.[6])

(20) In the event of a doubt or difference of opinion as to whether a subject is Federal, Concurrent, Regional or Provincial (or State), the decision of H.E. the Viceroy and Governor-General in his discretion shall be final.

(21) The Federal Legislature shall be unicameral.

NOTE 9: *If it is desired that the 'special interests' for whom representation in the Central Legislature had been specially provided in the Upper House (Council of State) under the Federal scheme embodied in the Government of India Act should also be given representation in the Unicameral Legislature, then the number of seats in the re-constituted Federal Assembly might be increased to secure them adequate representation. If it is decided to provide additional seats for these 'special interests', then I would suggest that such additional seats should be distributed equally among the 7 'Zones', say, 14 for each Unit or 98 in all. Of these 98 additional seats, 60 should be reserved for representation of British Indian Units and 38 for the Indian States subject to the proviso that the distribution shall be so arranged as not to affect the representation of Muslims and other minorities in the Assembly as a whole as stipulated in paragraphs (4) and (5) supra.*

(22) Adequate and effective machinery shall be set up both at the Centre and in the Provinces to look after and protect the interests of the minorities.

NOTE 10: *One way of securing this would be to set up statutory committees consisting of representatives of the minorities.*[7]

NOTES

1. The text of this letter is taken from L/P&J/8/689: ff. 385-6.
2. This appendix is not printed. Sir Sikander's scheme envisaged a limited Centre. Some 45 matters were assigned to it including defence, external affairs, currency, posts and telegraphs, railways, maritime shipping, explosives, opium, banking,

duties on customs, emigration and naturalisation. Some 57 matters were left with the individual Provinces. Many of these were functions assigned to them under the existing Government of India Act, 1935. Sir Sikander envisaged that the regional 'Zones' would be responsible for some 13 matters. These included: broadcasting, historical monuments and archaeological sites, regulation of labour, law of insurance, excise duties, salt, state lotteries and criminal tribes. As indicated in paragraph (6) of his scheme, legislation could, in certain circumstances, be undertaken by the 'Zones' in respect of matters that fell within the Provincial List. Sir Sikander provided a separate Concurrent List to cover this aspect of his scheme. Ibid: ff. 372-7.

3. The text of this Attachment is taken from the published pamphlet of Sir Sikander's scheme rather than the draft he sent Mr Laithwaite. There are only minor differences between the two texts. The pamphlet does not give any details of a place of publication, publisher or date. However it is stated that it was printed by Mufid-i-'Am Press, Lahore. Ibid: ff. 359-77.
4. Footnote in original: See para. 21.
5. Footnote in original: He will keep in touch with Regions and arrange co-ordination and uniformity in matters of common concern.
6. See note 2 above.
7. A member of the India Office staff minuted on Sir Sikander's scheme: 'A three-tier constitution like this would be very cumbrous.' Lord Zetland added: 'And 4 different legislative lists – Federal, Regional, Provincial and Concurrent – a nightmare.' L/P&J/8/689: f. 383.

Index

Certain terms, such as Hindus, Muslims, Sikhs and Punjab, occur in almost every document and have therefore not been indexed. For the same reason there are no index entries for Lord Linlithgow. Lord Brabourne is not indexed for the period when he was Acting Viceroy. Sir Henry Craik and Sir Herbert Emerson are only indexed for those documents which are of a date when they did **not** hold office as Governor of the Punjab.

The index entries refer to document numbers.